Civil War St. Louis

Louis S. Gerteis

Civil War
St. Louis

University Press of Kansas

© 2001 by the University Press of Kansas
All rights reserved

Published by the University Press of Kansas (Lawrence, Kansas 66049),
which was organized by the Kansas Board of Regents and is operated and
funded by Emporia State University, Fort Hays State University, Kansas
State University, Pittsburg State University, the University of Kansas, and
Wichita State University

Library of Congress Cataloging-in-Publication Data

Gerteis, Louis S.
    Civil War St. Louis / Louis S. Gerteis.
        p. cm. — (Modern war studies)
    Includes bibliographical references and index.
    ISBN 0-7006-1124-x (alk. paper)
        1. Saint Louis (Mo.)—History—Civil War, 1861–1865.   2. Saint Louis
    (Mo.)—History—Civil War, 1861–1865—Social aspects.   3. United
    States—History—Civil War, 1861–1865—Social aspects.   I. Title.
    II. Series.
    F474.S257 .G47 2001
    977.8'66044—dc21   2001001126

British Library Cataloguing in Publication Data is available.

Printed in the United States of America

10 9 8 7 6 5 4 3 2 1

The paper used in this publication meets the minimum requirements of the
American National Standard for Permanence of Paper for Printed Library
Materials z39.48-1984.

For the native St. Louisans in my family,
Joseph, Jessie, Emily, and Alexander;
and for Janice, an immigrant from Iowa

Contents

Illustrations

Acknowledgments

I T IS a pleasure to thank those who have been a part of this project. The idea for a book on St. Louis in the era of the Civil War originated with Michael Briggs, editor in chief of the University Press of Kansas. To Professor Mark Neely of Penn State University I owe thanks for suggesting me as a potential author and for subsequently providing a critical reading of the manuscript. I appreciate the support provided by Professor Phillip Paludan of the University of Kansas when this project started. I also owe thanks to Professor Daniel Sutherland of the University of Arkansas for his thoughtful and useful comments and criticisms. Marshall Hier of the St. Louis Civil War Roundtable kindly read and commented on several chapters, as did State Archivist Kenneth Winn. James Neal Primm, professor emeritus of the University of Missouri–St. Louis and the preeminent historian of the city, read and criticized the manuscript with a particularly sharp eye for detail, nuance, and style. I hope that my notes and bibliographic essay accurately and fully recognize the historians whose work has been indispensable to my own. All errors of interpretation and fact in this book are my fault alone.

In this kind of study, where identities and loyalties constitute much of the subject matter, it is, perhaps, not an act of self-indulgence to say who I am and where I come from. My great-grandfather immigrated to the United States from Germany in 1869 and settled in eastern Kansas. There, my grandfather married into a family of New England descent. My mother's family was Scotch-Irish from southwestern Missouri (Neosho, to be precise). My parents met and married in Kansas City, Missouri, where I was born in 1942. War-related work took my family east, and I grew up in Arlington, Virginia, where my parents lived out their lives. College and graduate school brought me to the Midwest in the early 1960s, and employment, as a Civil War historian, led me to St. Louis in 1969. When, in 1996, Michael Briggs approached me about writing this book I realized that in one way or another I had been thinking about the subject for more than twenty years.

Introduction

A s WAR loomed late in 1860, president-elect Abraham Lincoln closely and anxiously watched St. Louis, a flourishing metropolis about ninety miles southwest of his Springfield, Illinois, home. Lincoln knew that St. Louis represented a key strategic asset for the Union in the West. Since the late 1840s, the city had swelled with tens of thousands of German and Irish immigrants, as well as migrants from the Northeast, to become the eighth largest city in the United States. Aside from the city's economic importance, the Federal Arsenal in St. Louis held the largest cache of weapons and ammunition west of the Mississippi. Moreover, Jefferson Barracks, the army's principal staging area for military actions in the West since the Black Hawk War, lay just eight miles south of St. Louis.

Without firm control of St. Louis, it would be difficult for the Union to protect vital river traffic between the upper Mississippi Valley and the Ohio Valley. If rebels could disrupt river traffic, they could deny the North full access to the rich agricultural belt stretching from Illinois to Pennsylvania. With St. Louis firmly in federal control, however, the Union could harness the city's energy and resources to thrust southward into the very heart of the Confederacy.

As Lincoln well knew, the federal government faced serious challenges in St. Louis, and more broadly in Missouri, a slave state poised aggressively on the frontier of southern territorial expansion. In January 1861, President James Buchanan's War Department moved two companies of U.S. troops from eastern Kansas to St. Louis to help protect the Arsenal. But with federal military power in the West stretched dangerously thin, the president-elect understood that holding St. Louis for the Union required significant political investments as well. In the months between his election and subsequent departure for Washington in February 1861, Lincoln eagerly sought out former Kentuckian Edward Bates, a prominent St. Louis attorney of Whig antecedents and one of his rivals for the Republican presidential nomination. Lincoln wanted Bates to be his attorney general and wanted him badly enough that he offered to travel to St. Louis to present his case. In the end, Bates saved Lincoln the trip and traveled to Springfield himself to accept the nomination.[1]

Shortly thereafter, Lincoln turned to Montgomery Blair, a native Virginian and a former St. Louis resident who had retained strong connections in the city, to fill the patronage-rich post of postmaster general. Blair, a Jacksonian Democrat, brought with him the influence of a powerful political family. Francis P. Blair, the family patriarch and close personal friend of Missouri senator Thomas Hart Benton, had led the final Free-Soil exodus from the Democratic Party. He had also presided in 1856 over the Republican Party's first national convention, helping to secure the presidential nomination for Benton's son-in-law, the western explorer John C. Frémont. At the urging of Francis, Montgomery, and Congressman Frank Blair (publisher of the leading Republican newspaper in St. Louis), Lincoln soon appointed Frémont himself to oversee the Union's military operations in the West. By late July 1861, Major General Frémont had set up headquarters in the river city.[2]

These appointments represented Lincoln's concerted attempt to draw from and knit together the nation's "middle borders," the convergence of North and South, East and West. St. Louis lay at the geographical and ideological center of this borderland, and Lincoln understood that neither his determination nor the good intentions of his allies in the city would automatically lead to the strategic outcomes he hoped to achieve.

Indeed, to some merchants and financiers in the Northeast—antislavery men who were eager to invest in a West free of slavery—St. Louis's population and location seemed disadvantageous to the Northern cause.[3] In fact, St. Louisans were divided along lines of regional heritage. In this regard, they displayed in microcosm the forces that divided the nation. And, as events soon revealed, the city did not serve the Union cause without a struggle. Moreover, even among Unionists in St. Louis, Southern family ties and proslavery sentiments complicated the war experience. St. Louis Unionists distinguished themselves easily enough from the men who took up arms against the United States. But when they considered what measures should be taken against disloyal civilians and whether, or how, slavery should be ended, dissension prevailed. As wounded soldiers, federal prisoners, displaced civilians, and runaway slaves filled the city's hospitals, prisons, and makeshift camps, St. Louis exhibited the enormous human cost of the war and struggled with the sweeping social transformations wrought by Union victory and by Confederate defeat. Throughout the war, neither Lincoln nor his military commanders in St. Louis managed to hew a straightforward path through this thicket of discord.

Nevertheless, the presence of a booming city in a slave state lent credence to the prediction of the abolitionist orator Wendell Phillips, made shortly before the war, that "a middle class of trading, manufacturing energy" would soon "undermine the aristocracy of the slaveholding South."[4] Most St. Louisans looked to the future and saw slavery receding and markets widening. Thomas Hart Benton died in 1858, before he could add his voice to the Civil War debate. But no one demonstrated more clearly and dramatically than he that proslavery convictions and the capacity for violence that sustained them could be transformed in the advancing age of industry, even as Southern identities remained strong. Benton's rise to power in St. Louis illustrates how extensive that transformation was.

A native of North Carolina, Benton moved to St. Louis from Tennessee in 1815, following a bitter feud and gunfight with Andrew Jackson. In St. Louis, Benton opened a law practice and found new battles to fight. In 1817 he killed Charles Lucas in a duel, an event that redefined political allegiances in St. Louis and placed Benton at the forefront of the faction that led the Jacksonian Democracy in Missouri. The young man whom Benton killed stood high in the ranks of the Jeffersonian political dynasty. He was the son of John B. C. Lucas, at the time one of the most powerful men in St. Louis.[5] Young Charles Lucas studied law, and in 1814 he was admitted to the bar in St. Louis. In 1817 President James Madison appointed the twenty-five-year-old Lucas U.S. attorney for the Missouri Territory. Benton, then thirty-five, regarded Lucas as a professional and political rival. The fight that led to the duel began in August 1817 when Lucas questioned Benton's right to vote. At the time, and throughout the Civil War era, Missourians practiced viva voce voting; voters gathered at the polling place and cast their votes verbally and publicly. When Benton began to voice his vote, Lucas questioned his eligibility. Had Benton paid his taxes, Lucas asked. Benton replied that he would answer to the proper authority on the matter but not to any "puppy" who crossed his path. That was a fighting word, "puppy," and Benton knew it. Lucas promptly sent a note to Benton demanding "that satisfaction which is due from one gentleman to another for such an indignity." Benton, already known for his fight with Jackson, accepted the challenge with alacrity.[6]

On 12 August 1817, two boats pulled into the Mississippi River and headed toward a location known to St. Louisans as Bloody Island. One boat carried

Lucas, the other Benton, along with each man's second and surgeon. After the two boats landed on the island's sandy shore, the participants in this "private meeting between Benton and Lucas" set about their work. Benton and Lucas had agreed to face each other at thirty feet with pistols drawn. They were to fire on command. The two men steadied themselves, and on the command, fired their weapons. Lucas's ball grazed Benton's knee, leaving little more than a scratch and a bruise. Benton's ball pierced Lucas's neck, missing the windpipe and arteries but causing significant loss of blood all the same. Lucas's second asked his fallen friend if the fight had satisfied his honor. Growing faint, Lucas responded that it had. Benton's second asked Benton the same question, and he answered that it had not. As honor required, Lucas promised to give Benton satisfaction as soon as he had regained sufficient strength. With help from his second and surgeon, Lucas struggled to his boat and fell unconscious. The two men met on Bloody Island again on 27 September.

In the weeks that separated the two fights, Benton's friends appealed to him to free Lucas from his obligation, but he would not give ground. He blamed Lucas's friends for continuing to spread rumors that he, Benton, had fled from Tennessee to avoid punishment for misdeeds. Benton proposed harsh terms for the second encounter. Perhaps compelled by the wishes of his father, Lucas agreed to them. They would stand ten feet apart, a distance all but certain to produce a serious wound. On the count of three, both men fired. Benton was not hit. Lucas fell mortally wounded by a ball that passed through his left arm and lodged in his chest. The dueling code required a dying man to forgive his adversary, and Benton went to Lucas's side. At first Lucas turned his head away. "You have persecuted me and murdered me," he said. "I cannot forgive you." But he understood that honor could not be satisfied with final words of bitterness and rebuke. Minutes before he died, he turned to Benton to say, "I can forgive you—I do forgive you."[7]

In the last years before his own death four decades later, Benton wrote an autobiographical sketch for inclusion in his two-volume memoir, *Thirty Years' View*. Writing in the third person, he said of himself that he had "not been heard to speak" of the encounter with Lucas "except among intimate friends, and to tell of the pang that went through his heart when he saw the young man fall." That affair of honor had become a very bad memory.[8]

There is no reason to doubt that Benton felt genuine remorse for killing Charles Lucas. But his remorse did not reflect hostility toward the tradition of dueling that remained embedded in the Southern and western codes of honor that formed the bedrock of his cultural identity. In fact, Benton always held in high regard one particular duel—an affair of honor between Secretary of State Henry Clay of Kentucky and U.S. Senator John Randolph of Virginia. In his *Thirty Years' View*, Benton nostalgically recalled the 1826 encounter and cited it for its refined and morally uplifting sense of honor. By the time he offered his account of that famous event, however, dueling had been made illegal in all the states, and the practice had ended everywhere except in the South.[9] For his part, Benton acknowledged that "dueling is bad and has to be put down." With these words he reluctantly, perhaps, accepted the idea that a man could obtain "satisfaction" in a court of law.[10] Yet even as he turned against slavery, he never fully abandoned his ideal of Southern honor. Indeed, it became clearer in his mind as the Jacksonian Democracy collapsed and North and South prepared for war.

As the nation prepared for hostilities, a great many St. Louisans like Benton remained true to their Southern and western roots. They did not shy away from a fight. But what they would fight for, and why, had changed dramatically during the antebellum decades. Benton, Blair, and Bates, and thousands of others, came to St. Louis dedicated to slavery and to the Southern agrarian tradition. In an expanding world of commerce and manufacturing, however, St. Louis became the nation's great inland city and a citadel of free labor in a slave state. This transition, and its consequences, is the subject of this book.

1

"A Citizen of the United States"

I N THE MIDDLE DECADES of the nineteenth century, slavery and race became enmeshed in the developing culture of American capitalism. In the process, the spirit of accommodation that had once prevailed between slave states and free states began to fade. In part, the sectional equanimity of the early Republic had rested on the fact that the institutions of the free and slave states evolved largely in isolation from one another. As long as physical mobility remained limited and markets remained local, the cultural frictions that later led to civil war could be contained. But beginning in the 1820s, regional and ethnic cultures intermingled in the United States as never before. In the process, St. Louis emerged from its role as a remote outpost of European Empire to become a thriving city of the American West. A growing network of canals linked the Northeast with a western hinterland, stretching north to the Great Lakes and south to the Ohio Valley. Western waterways in the South, from western Georgia to eastern Texas, carried that region's new staple, cotton, to the major Gulf ports at Mobile and New Orleans. Located at the center of this burgeoning western commerce, St. Louisans justifiably envisioned their city as the nation's great inland emporium. By the 1820s, more than thirty steamboats provided regular packet service linking St. Louis with Keokuk, Galena, and Davenport to the north; Louisville, Cincinnati, and Pittsburgh to the east; and Memphis, Vicksburg, New Orleans, and Mobile to the south.[1]

A new fluidity characterized social relations and commerce, giving rise to new visions of social progress and perfection as well as to new fears of social disorder and decay. St. Louis prospered, but the city existed uneasily on the border of an increasingly distinct and antagonistic North and South. For the South, slaves became a rapidly appreciating commodity as eastern centers of colonial slavery exported surplus labor to the new cotton-growing regions of the Gulf Plains. For the North, territorial and economic expansion widened the horizons of free labor as farmers and artisans migrated west from New England, New York, and Pennsylvania. In St. Louis, the South and the North commingled as never before and did so at a time when events that once had held significance only within a local community could generate far wider interest and impact. Rumors and enthusiasms had always had the potential of engulfing entire communities. Now, however, with communities linked together along waterways of commerce, the passion of a locality could become the passion of a nation.

The disappearance of William Morgan in upstate New York in 1826 offered an early example of the new phenomenon. A disgruntled member of the Masonic Order, Morgan published a book in which he claimed to reveal the society's secrets. News of his disappearance spread quickly and widely over the new Erie Canal. Formally opened in 1824, the canal connected Albany, on the Hudson River, with Buffalo, on Lake Erie. It created a direct water route from New York City, at the mouth of the Hudson River, to the Great Lakes. It also provided a passageway to the West for people in upstate New York and New England. Throughout the Northeast and into the mid-Atlantic region, the rumor spread that Morgan had been murdered in a Masonic conspiracy. Anti-Masonic sentiment led to organized efforts to prevent members of the order from being elected to public office. In 1832 an Anti-Masonic political party nominated former attorney general William Wirt as its presidential candidate. The speed with which the rumored murder of Morgan mushroomed into a quasi-national anti-Masonic crusade offers one measure of the way in which the new intermingling of peoples, in what historians of the period have come to call the Market Revolution, reshaped the social landscape.[2]

St. Louis soon offered other, more lurid examples of the new social volatility: the 1836 lynching of Francis L. McIntosh, a free mulatto boatman, and the related killing of the antislavery newspaper editor Elijah P. Lovejoy, in nearby Alton, Illinois, in 1837, became events of national significance. Both incidents contributed measurably to the antislavery movement across the North. But they also revealed a great deal about St. Louis itself. In the McIntosh lynching, observers experienced and remembered events in significantly different ways. Those sympathetic with the lynchers described McIntosh as a defiant killer cursing his white tormentors as he died. They remembered the heroic actions of the men who apprehended him and the collective action of the community in killing him. On the other hand, those who deplored the actions of the lynchers described McIntosh's excruciating pain and suffering. They remembered an act of mob violence that threatened the foundation of law and civilized society. As a result of these different perspectives, accounts varied concerning the length of time it took for McIntosh to die. Defenders of the lynchers remembered a quick death; critics remembered a lengthy ordeal. Critics also remembered the lynching as the event that led to Lovejoy's death, though the defenders made no such connection. They remembered McIntosh's burning as a moment of great clarity for men who considered their role in the community to be that of guardians of public safety and (with no sense of irony) order.

The day after McIntosh died, the *Missouri Republican,* the city's leading newspaper and Whig in its political sympathies, published an account of the lynching. Most accounts agreed on the accuracy of the *Republican*'s report. On the evening of 28 April 1836, St. Louis's deputy sheriff, George Hammond, joined the city's deputy constable, William Mull, to arrest Francis McIntosh. Later reports identified McIntosh as a Pittsburgh resident who had arrived in St. Louis with the steamboat *Flora,* on which he was employed as a steward. Hammond and Mull took McIntosh into custody because he had interfered with them when they tried to arrest two unruly sailors. With McIntosh's help, the sailors had run off. Hammond and Mull apprehended McIntosh, secured a warrant for his incarceration, and marched him off to the city jail, located directly west of the courthouse. When the group reached the northeast corner of the courthouse square, McIntosh drew a knife. He struck first at Mull, who dodged the blade. Turning, McIntosh struck Hammond on the lower chin and drove the knife into his neck, severing the right carotid artery. Struggling to aid Hammond, Mull received a serious wound in his abdomen. According to later reports, McIntosh then ran south on Fourth Street toward Market. Hammond fell dead in the street while Mull shouted out an alarm and gave chase as best he could before passing out. By later accounts, a crowd of about fifty men pursued McIntosh and cornered him in a private lot near Fourth and Walnut Streets. They disarmed him and took him to jail.[3]

As word of Hammond's murder spread, a crowd gathered at the jail. Soon, "the assembled multitude," as the *Republican* described the mob, pushed its way into the jail, forcibly removed the keys from the sheriff's pocket, took hold of McIntosh, and dragged him into the street. Unnamed persons chained him to a tree, stacked wood around him, and burned him to death.

Accounts varied concerning exactly what happened after the mob took McIntosh from the jail. John F. Darby, the mayor of St. Louis at the time of the lynching, described the event in his memoirs more than four decades later.

A native of North Carolina, Darby had moved to St. Louis in the mid-1820s and practiced law. A Whig and an ardent supporter of public expenditures for internal improvements, Darby served as mayor from 1835 to 1837 and served a second one-year term in 1840. He did not claim to have been an eyewitness to McIntosh's lynching, but he recalled the event with great assurance and in considerable detail. It was "a strong and brave Irishman" who disarmed McIntosh after the death of Hammond, recalled Darby. It was a Connecticut man who first made the suggestion that the captive be burned. In Darby's account, McIntosh died quickly in a "brisk" fire that "ran up far above his head into the tops of the trees." The whole business, from the murder of Hammond to the death of McIntosh, had occurred within an hour, according to Darby.

Darby's account functioned in part as a rebuttal to an antislavery interpretation of the event, which had its origin in Theodore Dwight Weld's *American Slavery As It Is* (1839) and which was reiterated in accounts of Lovejoy's subsequent death. In the antislavery interpretation, McIntosh's death had been a sadistic affair. Moreover, both the lynching and the subsequent killing of Lovejoy represented a lawlessness endemic to a slaveholding society. Weld wrote his account to disprove the proslavery claim that "Public Opinion Is a Protection to the Slave," and he emphasized the public nature of the lynching. McIntosh, he wrote, had been burned "*in the midst of the city . . .* in open day." The St. Louis German editor, Henry Boernstein, who arrived in St. Louis from Europe in 1849, learned about the lynching from his colleagues on the city's first German language newspaper, the *Anzeiger des Westens.* In his 1881 memoirs, Boernstein recorded the antislavery version of the affair. A mob, "roused by the slaveholders" chained McIntosh to a tree on the outskirts of town. They lit a fire around him and watched as "the unfortunate man was slowly roasted to death." In Alton, where Lovejoy continued his attacks on slavery and on St. Louis lynch law, "rowdies and scum" joined "a gang from Missouri" to kill the editor.[4]

Some aspects of these antislavery accounts should be questioned. The *Republican* originally reported that Hammond had arrested McIntosh at about seven o'clock in the evening. If the events leading up to McIntosh's death occurred as quickly as Darby recalled, it is possible that the lynching took place while some light remained in the sky. But Weld's statement that the lynching took place "in open day" was an exaggeration if not an error. So, too, was Weld's claim that McIntosh died "*in the midst of the city.*" By most accounts, the lynching took place on the edge of town. The *Republican* reported that the mob took McIntosh to "the border of town." A visiting salesman from Vermont wrote to his wife that the mob took McIntosh to "the common, west of the city." Darby, writing in 1880, recalled that McIntosh had been burned "about where the [O'Fallon] Polytechnic building is now." That would locate the site of the lynching on the western outskirts of the city, on a block between Seventh and Eighth and Chestnut and Market. Boernstein shared Weld's abolitionist perspective but located the lynching "at the corner of Seventh and Chestnut." Yet by the 1880s, when J. Thomas Scharf wrote his *History of St. Louis City and County,* memories of the event diverged sufficiently to produce a confused account. Scharf wrote that "the negro was . . . dragged to the bank of the river, where he was tied to a tree." In the next sentence, however, he added that "the place where the negro was burned is now Tenth and Market Streets, then a common."[5] In any case, the lynching did not take place, as Weld implied, in full daylight and in the middle of town.

The antislavery conclusion that the barbarism of slavery produced the lawlessness that cost McIntosh and Lovejoy their lives also requires scrutiny. Neither killing was the product of a slaveholders' conspiracy. In the McIntosh lynching, the mob undoubtedly included a number of prominent citizens, although no one publicly admitted participating. In Alton, the leaders of the mob were the town's most prominent physicians.[6]

Concerning the McIntosh lynching, Mayor Darby wrote without remorse or apology, as if he had witnessed the event. There is reason to think that Luke Lawless, who, as judge of the St. Louis Circuit Court, later convened a grand jury to investigate the lynching, also witnessed it. On the other hand, one purported eyewitness account is open to doubt. The diary of an unidentified St. Louis physician claimed that a group of ten to twenty men actively participated in the lynching. He recorded that an alderman, whom he did not name, threatened to shoot anyone who tried to loosen the chains binding McIntosh to the tree. McIntosh died very slowly, the physician recorded; the diary provided gruesome detail. As the fire burned through McIntosh's abdomen and his entrails spilled out, someone in the crowd asked the victim if he still felt pain. McIntosh answered that he felt a great deal of pain. But the diarist also reported that the mob had chained McIntosh to a tree "back of the jail." The writer probably composed his diary entry from the accounts of others.

In the aftermath of the lynching, St. Louisans tried to sort through their emotions and make sense of the affair. It was in this tense environment that Lovejoy became the object of the mob's fury. The *Republican* feared, correctly, that the lynching might "damage the fair name of our town." It reported a "revolting spectacle" but offered no detailed description of the lynching. The editor focused instead on the crowd. It seemed important to note that the killing of McIntosh had taken place without any other violence or disorder. "There was no tumult," reported the *Republican,* "no disturbance of any kind." Instead, "the crowd retired quietly to their several homes." The editor hoped, vainly as it turned out, that the episode would be quickly forgotten: "Let the veil of oblivion be drawn over the fatal affair." The editor of the Whig newspaper, the *St. Louis Bulletin,* went a bit further to condemn "the atrocious violation of law, (and perhaps we may say humanity)" but said no more about the event. William Weber, editor of the *Anzeiger des Westens,* asked pointedly why the city's elite militia, the St. Louis Grays, had not appeared to restore order. When a community ignored the rule of law, the German editor warned, it jeopardized the whole fabric of constitutional government.

The *St. Louis Observer,* a Presbyterian paper edited by Elijah P. Lovejoy, took a very different view. A New Englander of moderate antislavery views, Lovejoy saw in the lynching a level of lawlessness that threatened civilized society. His account drew from the description previously published in the *Republican* to report the arrest of McIntosh and the murder of Hammond. But Lovejoy offered a detailed description of the lynching, not, he wrote, to suggest that its brutality reflected "the moral condition of St. Louis," but to denounce the spirit of "mobism" that it represented. Lovejoy had not witnessed the lynching. He constructed his account, he said, from a number of reports he regarded as reliable. When McIntosh, chained with his back to the tree, realized that the mob intended to burn him, not whip him, he pleaded to be shot. As he felt the flames on his body, he "commenced singing a hymn and trying to pray." When he grew silent and his head dropped, someone in the crowd speculated that he had died. With most of his facial features destroyed by the fire, McIntosh managed to speak. He still felt the pain, he said. He could hear all that was said around him. Again he pleaded to be shot. Lovejoy did not condemn the St. Louis mob alone. He saw a similar spirit of mobism in the August 1834 burning of the Ursuline convent in Charlestown, Massachusetts, and in the July 1835 hanging of five white gamblers in Vicksburg,

Mississippi. Lovejoy described McIntosh as "a hardened wretch certainly, and one that deserved to die—but not *thus* to die."[7]

On 16 May a grand jury, presided over by Luke Lawless, met to investigate the McIntosh lynching. It was Lawless who had served as Benton's second in the 1817 duel that took the life of young Charles Lucas.[8] Lawless understood the tradition of honor that compelled men to fight to the death, and he understood as well a tradition of collective violence that often defied laws and constitutions. He opened the proceedings with a lengthy address. Normally, he said, he would conclude his remarks after offering general comments regarding the jury's duties; under these circumstances, however, he could not do so. His "fellow citizens might well expect from the Judge of the Court, a special notice of the dreadful events that have so recently thrown a gloom over our prosperous and generally peaceful city." The murder of Hammond, the wounding of Mull, and "the destruction of the murderer himself" raised the question of what, if any, "action of the Grand Jury is called for by them." In the killing of McIntosh, the grand jury confronted "a force unauthorized by law" and "a mode of death forbidden by the Constitution," which forbade "cruel and unusual punishment." Clearly, "chaining the prisoner to a tree, and burning him to ashes" was both cruel and unusual. If Lawless had left the grand jury "to their own unassisted deliberations upon this question," he feared that his silence would be construed as timidity. That he considered "unworthy of a Judge." Instead, he offered his frank views about "what your oath and function, as Grand Jurors of the County, require of you to do or abstain from doing, under existing circumstances."

Since McIntosh was dead, there was no need for the grand jury to consider issuing an indictment for the murder of Hammond or the attempted murder of Mull. The only question that remained was what action should be taken regarding "those persons who effected the destruction of the murderer." The question was not a straightforward one, Lawless thought. He regarded it as "novel" and "depending for its solution, on considerations not generally influencing the decisions or proceedings of a Grand Jury." He could find no "parallel case on record." Having looked to the law and having found no answers, he concluded that "rational action" in the matter made it "necessary to take into view principles of even higher import to the community than those which govern the ordinary march and administration of criminal law." There was nothing ambiguous about the killing of McIntosh, Lawless admitted. "The difficult work which presents itself," he explained, "arises as to the possibility and expediency of visiting on the perpetrators of that act the penalties of the law."

The grand jurors may have already suspected the conclusion toward which Lawless was leading them. Perhaps he sensed a degree of irreverence among the jurors. Abruptly, he launched into a denunciation of the lynching. He could not imagine the existence of an American citizen "of sound mind, and not under the influence of passion," who would not admit that McIntosh's death involved "an outrageous violation of the Law and Constitution." Those who justified the act by pointing to McIntosh's undisputed guilt overlooked the possibility that the man might have been "a lunatic—not morally responsible, and therefore, in the view of God and man, innocent." Any country "calling itself civilized" must recoil from the act, the more so in "this chosen land of liberty." If law is not supreme, liberty cannot exist, Lawless lectured. If the people disregarded the law, anarchy would prevail and there would be no safety "for life or property." He could only pray that the fire that consumed McIntosh would become "a beacon light to warn away the citizens of Missouri from the perpetration of similar horrors."

Still, the question remained what the responsibility of the grand jury was. Lawless told the jurors that he had "reflected much on this matter" and that he felt it to be his duty "to state my opinion . . . that, whether the Grand Jury shall act at all depends upon . . . whether the destruction of McIntosh was the act of the 'few' or the act of the 'many.'" If the jurors determined that "a *small* number of individuals separate from the mass" committed the killing, he expressed his opinion "that you ought to indict them all without a single exception." If, on the other hand, McIntosh's killing had been the work "of congregated thousands, seized upon and impelled by that mysterious, metaphysical, and almost electric phrenzy . . . then, I say, act not at all in the matter—the case then transcends your jurisdiction—it is beyond the reach of human law."

Lawless then examined the lynching, as Lovejoy had in the *Observer*, in the context of recent outbreaks of mob violence elsewhere in the country. He noted the attack in Massachusetts on the Ursuline convent. Although there had been no loss of life in that event, he denounced the "horrid spirit of sectarian bigotry" and compared McIntosh's killing favorably with it because it had been a "generous excitement," the natural response of St. Louisans to the inconsolable weeping of Hammond's wife and children, that led to the lynching. "Is not something to be allowed for human sympathies in these appalling circumstances?" he asked. "Is there not some slight palliation of that deplorable disregard of Law and Constitution, which is now the subject of our deliberations?"

Lawless admitted that efforts in Massachusetts to punish the anti-Catholic rioters had met with some success. But there had been "no ground of extenuation" in the Charlestown riot, and in any case, the prosecution of the rioters had done nothing to cure Massachusetts of its anti-Catholic bigotry. By contrast, in the McIntosh killing the persons "most actively engaged in this tragic scene, must ALREADY REGRET WHAT THEY HAVE DONE." They must understand that faithful execution of the laws would have ended in justice and would have offered "no pretense for . . . outcry" by the "unprincipled men engaged in the anti-national scheme of abolitionism." Had the laws been faithfully executed, the public mind would have been able to concentrate entirely on the atrocities committed by McIntosh. Here, Lawless believed he had arrived at the central issue in the whole affair. What had excited the mob was something more than the killing of Hammond. McIntosh's crime took its place among "similar atrocities committed in this and other states BY INDIVIDUALS OF NEGRO BLOOD AGAINST THEIR WHITE BRETHREN."

Lawless then spoke as if he had firsthand knowledge of the lynching. The "passions and intellect" of the "wretched McIntosh," Lawless charged, had been influenced by abolitionists. This "seems to me to be indicated," he continued, "by the peculiar character of his language and demeanor." McIntosh had not died penitent. Lawless noted "his rapid denunciations of the white man—his professions of deadly hostility to the whole race—his hymns and his prayers, so profanely and frightfully mixed up with those horrid imprecations." In his death throes, McIntosh revealed the influence on him of the "incendiary" doctrines of abolitionism.

Lawless, then, lay the moral responsibility for the murder of Hammond and the subsequent lynching of McIntosh at the feet of the abolitionists. And he defined abolitionism broadly enough to include Lovejoy's cautious advocacy of gradual emancipation. Lawless handed the jurors a copy of Lovejoy's *Observer* and noted that although the paper professed to be "exclusively devoted to religious object," the edition published immediately after McIntosh's death offered a graphic description of the burning and two sermons, one stating that "slavery is a sin and ought to be abandoned," the other lamenting the "abandonment of virtue" and the "prostration of principle" among the "Pro-Slavery men of modern times." When such "fanaticism" reached the "fiery, unreasoning instinct of the negro," continued Lawless, the "ruthless, remorseless revenge" of the African race is inevitably unleashed. "The negro then kills and burns for the love of God and in the name of the Divine Redeemer, and rushes on to crime and carnage under the influence of what appears to him a holy impulse and aspiration." Lawless did not mention the Nat Turner rebellion, nearly five years earlier in Southampton County, Virginia. But his description of the Negro as divine avenger must have triggered memories of that bloody uprising in the minds of the grand jury. Lawless had finally reached the conclusion of his instructions. He urged the jurors to focus their attention on methods of silencing the voice of abolitionism in Missouri and promised to send their recommendations on that matter to the state legislature.

To Lawless and the grand jurors, the decision not to issue indictments no doubt seemed a victory for the community. The jurors had selected John O'Fallon as their foreman. A native of Kentucky, he had been raised as the ward of his uncle, Missouri's territorial governor William Clark. By 1830 O'Fallon had established himself as one of the wealthiest merchants in St. Louis, and through the 1840s he led the city's Whig Party. Before his death in 1865, he devoted a portion of his vast wealth, estimated to be $8 million, to the establishment of O'Fallon Polytechnic Institute on a city lot that Mayor Darby remembered to have been the site of the McIntosh lynching.[9]

O'Fallon undoubtedly agreed with a Whig newspaper, the *Bulletin*, when it praised the wisdom of Lawless's remarks. The Catholic weekly, the *Shepherd of the Valley*, similarly endorsed the judge's stance. Lawless's comments contained "much sound wisdom and discretion," wrote the Catholic editor, who then equated abolitionism with Protestantism and with revolt against all authority, spiritual and secular. To Lovejoy, who reacted to Lawless's tirade against abolitionism with a tirade of his own against Catholicism and slavery, it seemed clear that Catholicism condoned slavery and that slavery promoted barbarism. Noting Lawless's Irish birth and Catholic faith, Lovejoy saw "the cloven feet of Jesuitism, peeping out from under the veil of almost every paragraph of the judge's instructions to the jury." He knew that his refusal to let the matter rest exposed him to mob violence, but he pressed on. He did not seek "martyrdom," he wrote. But it would be better that he should be "chained to the same tree as McIntosh and share his fate, than that the doctrines promulgated by Judge Lawless from the bench should become prevalent in this community." Lovejoy's fellow New Englanders doubtless shared his outrage, but they were not prepared to stand with him in this instance. After two attacks on his press in St. Louis, he announced that he would move the *Observer* to Alton, Illinois. More mob attacks followed. Lovejoy would not again flee. "Should I attempt it," he wrote, "I should feel that the angel of the Lord, with his flaming sword, was pursuing me wherever I went. It is because I fear God that I am not afraid of all who oppose me in this city."[10]

After Alton mobs destroyed three presses, Lovejoy resolved to defend the fourth. The newly elected mayor of Alton, John M. Krum (later elected mayor of St. Louis and involved in the Dred Scott case), seemed sympathetic to Lovejoy's requests for protection. Ultimately, however, Krum's efforts to restrain the mob failed. Perhaps he did the best he could. He sought authority from the Alton Common Council to appoint special constables, but the council took no action on the matter. At a public meeting that, in effect, ordered Lovejoy to leave town or face violent consequences, Krum offered a resolution that pleased but did not placate the crowd. The resolution expressed "regret that persons and editors from abroad have seen proper" to agitate against slavery in Alton. Krum managed to station a few constables at the warehouse where Lovejoy's press was stored, but they were too few and too indecisive to deter the mob. Krum stalled for time by acting as the mob's emissary to Lovejoy. It was Krum who delivered the ultimatum: surrender the press or the building would be burned. When Krum left the warehouse with nothing but Lovejoy's defiance to offer the mob, he made his last effort to halt the violence, warning that his police would shoot anyone who attempted to commit arson. In the end, he was ignored by the mob and by the police. As Lovejoy tried to deter an arsonist setting fire to the building's roof, he was shot and killed.[11]

Lovejoy became a martyr to the antislavery cause. As John Quincy Adams observed, Lovejoy's death sent "a shock as of an earthquake throughout the continent." Across the North, the antislavery cause won fresh, dedicated recruits. Adams had already joined the movement. After serving one term as president, he won election to the House of Representatives and, by the time of Lovejoy's death, he had taken the lead in Congress in the fight against the antiabolitionist "gag rule."[12] At Lovejoy's graveside, one of the martyr's younger brothers, Owen (who later won election to Congress from Illinois), dedicated himself to the antislavery cause. In Hudson, Ohio, Laurens P. Hickok, professor of theology at Western Reserve College, presided over a prayer service memorializing Lovejoy. A young John Brown (of Harper's Ferry fame) attended. "The crisis has come," said Hickok. "The question now before the American citizen is no longer alone, 'Can the slaves be made free?' but, are we free, or are we slaves under Southern mob law?" When Hickok finished speaking, Brown stood up, raised his right hand, and swore before God and the witnesses at the meeting that he would devote his life to the destruction of slavery.[13]

In Vermont, two young men also felt the shock of Lovejoy's death. One was Zebina Eastman, already an abolitionist in sentiment and soon to be active in the cause. In 1839, after a failed attempt as a newspaper editor in Vermont, he moved west to Illinois, where he joined the veteran abolitionist, Benjamin Lundy, and John W. E. Lovejoy (another of Elijah P. Lovejoy's younger brothers) to edit the *Genius of Universal Emancipation*.[14] Eastman later recalled discussing the Lovejoy murder in the Newfane, Vermont, law office of his friend Roswell Field. Field, as Eastman remembered, was a "firm believer in the Jacksonian democracy of the hour," and he used "his caustic powers to speak against the abolitionists."[15] But Lovejoy's killing deeply affected Field and turned him against the proslavery wing of the Democratic Party. He could not have forgotten the affair when he moved to St. Louis two years later.

The aftershocks of the McIntosh lynching and the Lovejoy murder continued to unsettle St. Louisans as well. The killings remained vivid memories for a lifetime, and the passions associated with them helped to infuse a greater degree of animosity into the widening debate over slavery. In St. Louis, and soon throughout the nation, that debate focused on the Dred Scott case.

The plight of Dred Scott, his wife Harriet, and their two daughters focused attention on the legal line separating slavery and freedom. By the time Dred Scott and his family came to national attention, the case already defined for St. Louisans a new climate of enmity that sharply divided those who defended slavery from those who considered the institution antiquated and doomed to eventual extinction. For proslavery St. Louisans, the legal line between slavery and freedom seemed fragile, frayed, and dangerously permeable, and they sought firmer constitutional safeguards for their human property. A greater diversity of opinion characterized the antislavery side of the debate. No one in St. Louis openly spoke the language of radical abolitionism. Individuals, like the Unitarian minister William Greenleaf Eliot, who harbored abolitionist sympathies (that is, those who viewed slavery as a sin and favored its immediate, uncompensated abolition), kept their views private. Nevertheless, among the city's political and commercial elite, the opinion prevailed that slavery and progress were incompatible. As the defenders of slavery became outnumbered and embattled, they also became more desperate and dangerous. The Dred Scott case began as a straightforward freedom suit. In the new climate of animosity, however, it became a national test of the legal foundation of slavery.

Dred Scott marked the end of a tradition of equanimity in jurisprudence treating issues of slavery and freedom. The Missouri Supreme Court's decision in *Winny v. Whitesides* (1824) had defined the earlier tradition, and it fell victim to a proslavery onslaught as the Dred Scott case made its way through the Missouri courts. In *Winny,* the Missouri high court upheld a Saint Louis Circuit Court's decision that declared Winny free because she had resided in Illinois in 1799. If she had fled from Missouri to Illinois, her master might have reclaimed her as a fugitive slave, as stipulated by the federal Constitution. If she had been a "sojourning" slave, passing through a free state or territory to another slave state, her status would remain that of a slave. But the Missouri Supreme Court agreed with the St. Louis Circuit Court that Winny had been freed as soon as she became a resident of Illinois. Because the Northwest Ordinance (1787) prohibited slavery in Illinois, the court ruled that the federal Constitution's provisions regarding interstate comity required that Winny's status as a free person in Illinois made her a free person in Missouri. As in other state supreme court rulings of the same era, the *Winny* decision sought to identify a flexible distinction between citizenship and slavery. Article 4, section 2 of the federal Constitution provided, "The Citizens of each State shall be entitled to all Privileges and Immunities of Citizens in the several States." This was the interstate comity provision cited by the Missouri high court in the *Winny* decision. But the same article and section of the Constitution contained the fugitive clause, which guaranteed that "Persons held to Service or Labour" who fled to a free state did not become free and "shall be delivered up on Claim of the party to whom such Service or Labour may be due." Freeing Winny, who had resided as a citizen in Illinois, fulfilled one half of a constitutional bargain that also provided for the return of fugitive slaves.[16]

In the *Winny* decision, the Missouri Supreme Court took much the same position that state supreme courts had assumed in Mississippi (1818) and in Kentucky (1820).[17] Servants who had resided with their masters in a free state or territory became free and did not revert to the status of slavery simply because they returned with their master to a slave state. In accordance with the *Winny* decision, the Missouri Supreme Court ruled in *Rachel v. Walker* (1836) that a slave owned by an army officer who had resided with her in the Wisconsin Territory had been freed. Over the years the *Winny* decision also gave rise to a substantial body of case law involving freedom suits in the St. Louis Circuit Court, where more than sixty slaves found their way to freedom through the application of these precedents.[18]

It was in this jurisprudential context that the lawyer Francis B. Murdoch appeared in the St. Louis Circuit Court to represent two slaves, Diana and Josiah Cephas. Both claimed to be free because they had resided in Illinois. Murdoch had recently moved to St. Louis from Alton and at the time of Lovejoy's death had served as state prosecutor there. He had brought Lovejoy's accused killers to trial, but a jury had acquitted them. In the *Cephas* case, Murdoch became acquainted with Missouri's slave law. He cited *Winny* to argue that the slaves had not simply passed through Illinois on their way to Missouri but that they had resided in Illinois and had been emancipated as a result. As it happened, Josiah died in July 1842, two years after his freedom suit had been filed and a year before his case finally came to trial. But in September 1843, the precedent of *Winny* prevailed, and a jury freed Diana.[19] In fall 1844, John M. Krum, the former mayor of Alton who then served as judge of the St. Louis Circuit Court, appointed Roswell Field to represent a slave named Martha Ann in her freedom suit. Krum undoubtedly felt a degree of kinship with Field. A native of New York State, Krum graduated from Union College before entering the bar. After moving to St. Louis from Alton early in the 1840s, he became a member of William Greenleaf Eliot's Unitarian church and was appointed judge of the circuit court in 1843. Field had graduated from Middlebury College in Vermont and moved to St. Louis in 1839. He, too, became part of the growing community of immigrants from the Northeast.[20] Krum left the bench before Field's *Martha Ann* case could be resolved, but he had provided the New England attorney with an opportunity to acquaint himself with Missouri slave law. The first trial in the *Martha Ann* case resulted in a hung jury. Before the second trial could begin, Judge Alexander Hamilton replaced Krum on the circuit court bench. Hamilton and Field became close personal friends, and both, together with Murdoch, became involved in the Dred Scott case. A second hung jury in the *Martha Ann* case necessitated a third trial in which, finally, Field won the slave's freedom. By that time, December 1849, the Dred Scott case was well under way.[21]

On 6 April 1846 Murdoch drafted for Judge Krum what must have seemed like a routine petition for freedom. Dred Scott placed his mark (an X) on the document, and Murdoch filed it in the circuit court. The petition identified Dred Scott as "a man of color . . . claimed as a slave" by Irene Emerson and explained that she was the widow of Dr. John Emerson, who had purchased Scott in St. Louis from Peter Blow and subsequently had taken him to Rock Island, Illinois, and to Fort Snelling (in present-day Minnesota). Dred Scott, therefore, petitioned the court "to allow him to sue said Irene Emerson . . . in order to establish his right to freedom."[22]

Although the case began as an ordinary freedom suit, it became distinctive over time because it came to represent all the conflicts in law and public policy that were embedded in the developing sectional crisis over slavery. This was not an accidental development. The personalities involved in the case and its timing in the courts combined to make Dred Scott's freedom suit a celebrated one, first in St. Louis and later throughout the nation.

The facts of the case were not disputed. Dred Scott, born a slave in Southampton County, Virginia, about 1800, moved to St. Louis with his owner, Peter Blow, in 1830. In the next year or two (no record of the sale has survived) Blow sold Scott to John Emerson, a Pennsylvania physician then living in St. Louis. Emerson later received an army commission (in December 1833) and took Scott with him to Fort Armstrong in Rock Island, Illinois. In 1836 Emerson moved with Scott to Fort Snelling, west of the Mississippi River in the Wisconsin Territory.[23]

Emerson did not remain long at Fort Snelling. Unhappy with the cold climate, he sought and received (in October 1837) reassignment to Jefferson Barracks, south of St. Louis. Soon he received new orders to proceed to Fort Jessup in western Louisiana. Emerson made the trip, first to St. Louis and, later, to Louisiana without Scott. By the time Emerson left Fort Snelling, Scott in 1836 had met and married Harriet, the black servant of an army officer, and soon after became a father. After their marriage, a civil ceremony that would not have been possible among slaves in slave states, Harriet's master either sold her or gave her to Emerson. The Scotts remained at Fort Snelling, waiting for Emerson to send for them. He made his move to Fort Jessup alone, but once there, he married Irene Sanford of St. Louis. Eventually, at Emerson's direction, the Scotts made the trip down the Mississippi River to Louisiana. With free territory on both sides of the river north of Keokuk, and with the free state of Illinois on the east bank of the river north of its confluence with the Ohio River, the Scotts might have asserted their freedom during this journey. Instead, they voluntarily joined Emerson in Louisiana.

Again, the army reassigned Emerson, sending him back to Fort Snelling. He once more traveled north into free territory with his wife and the Scotts. On this trip, Harriet bore the couple's first child, a daughter. Two more years passed for Emerson and the Scotts at Fort Snelling. Then the army assigned Emerson to Florida, where federal troops continued to battle Seminole Indians in a protracted guerrilla war. In spring 1840, Mrs. Emerson and the Scotts moved from Fort Snelling to St. Louis while Emerson journeyed alone to Florida.

As long as the Scotts remained the property of Emerson, they evidently felt secure as a family. That security abruptly ended when Emerson, after falling ill in Florida, returned to St. Louis and died in 1843. Irene Sanford Emerson became the owner of the Scott family and, with good reason, the Scotts became apprehensive. Irene Emerson's father, Colonel Alexander Sanford (an owner of four slaves on a farm in St. Charles County, northwest of St. Louis), advised his daughter on financial matters. He knew that the Scotts' status as slaves would be open to question if his daughter attempted to sell them. Dred Scott's stay in Illinois and the couple's residence in the Wisconsin Territory meant that Irene Emerson's ability to transfer title in a sale almost certainly would be questioned. Probably following her father's advice, she hired the Scotts out, a common practice in St. Louis. She undoubtedly shared her father's proslavery views, and it is probably for this reason that she also turned a deaf ear to Dred Scott's proposals to purchase his freedom and that of his family.

A combination of factors probably induced the Scotts to sue for their freedom when they did. The decision to sue may have come from Harriet Scott, who had recently joined a congregation of black Baptists in St. Louis. John R. Anderson, a free black man, led the congregation, and like so many others associated with the Dred Scott case he, too, had been a close observer of the Lovejoy affair. Anderson's mother had migrated to St. Louis from Virginia with Edward Bates and his family. After learning the printing trade in the St. Louis office of John and Charles Knapp, Anderson worked for Lovejoy's *Observer* and had relocated in Alton with him. After the mob killed Lovejoy in November 1837, Anderson returned to St. Louis, where he soon led the Baptist congregation that included Harriet Scott. It is entirely possible, as historian Kenneth Kaufman has observed, that Anderson knew that the Scotts had lived in Illinois and in the Wisconsin Territory and that it was he who urged Harriet to join the growing number of slaves who successfully sued for their freedom in the St. Louis Circuit Court.[24]

The proslavery views of the Sanford family probably contributed to the decision as well. In the same week that Irene Emerson filed her pleas in the initial suit by Dred Scott, her father became one of a dozen members of a select committee of the St. Louis Anti-Abolitionist Society. John O'Fallon presided over the society, which promised to meet secretly to fight the "evil designs of abolitionists and others" who threatened the stability of slavery in the city. The members vowed to enforce all laws regulating slavery in St. Louis and to seek restrictive legislation to control free blacks, particularly to ensure that "a regularly ordained or licensed white minister or priest" led the congregations of black churches. These defenders of slavery cited the growing free black population in St. Louis as the occasion for their heightened vigilance.[25]

It is possible that free blacks (like the minister John Anderson) had become more active in freedom suits and that Sanford, O'Fallon, and their supporters responded accordingly. But a sense of vulnerability probably motivated the antiabolitionists as well. Although the number of free blacks in St. Louis increased from 531 in 1840 to 1,398 in 1850, free blacks as a percentage of the total population declined from slightly over 3 percent in 1840 to less than 2 percent in 1850. Perhaps more to the point, from Sanford's and O'Fallon's perspective, was the fact that while the population of slaves rose from about 1,500 in 1840 to about 2,600 in 1850, as a percentage of the total population, slaves fell from 9.3 percent in 1840 to 3.4 percent in 1850. The rapid relative decline of the city's black population—particularly its slave population—may have triggered the proslavery reaction. The total black population in St. Louis had reached almost 25 percent in 1830. It had declined to 12.5 percent in 1840 and to 5.2 percent in 1850.[26] To an observer like Thomas Hart Benton, and to others who shared the view that slavery obscured the path of progress, its declining importance and the declining relative population of blacks signaled the gradual demise of slavery and the expansion of the white republic.[27] As the black population of St. Louis shrank in relative terms, so too did the social and political standing of the old slave-owning elite.

Whatever the cause of the proslavery alarm, Colonel Sanford's Anti-Abolitionist Society acted quickly to enforce regulations restricting free blacks. Within two weeks of the society's formation, city authorities arrested seven people of color, charging them with failing to carry the freedmen's license required by state law. Opponents of the restrictions on free blacks pressed a test case before Judge Krum in the circuit court. At issue in the case (*State v. Charles Lyons*) was the question of Negro citizenship, the very issue that would rise to the fore in the Dred Scott case. Uriel Wright served as attorney for Lyons, a free black man arrested for not carrying a license. At the time, Wright supported the antislavery views of Senator Benton, although he later broke with the antislavery Democrats and joined the Confederacy. In the *Lyons* case, Wright argued that the arrest of Lyons had been illegal because the state statute requiring licenses for free blacks "is inconsistent with the Constitution of the United States." Presumably, Wright found the state law inconsistent with the federal Constitution's Privileges and Immunities clause. Arguing the state's case was, among others, Henry S. Geyer, the proslavery Whig who defeated Benton for the Senate in 1850 and who later argued against Dred Scott before the U.S. Supreme Court. A native of Maryland and a veteran of the War of 1812, Geyer served as a member of the Missouri Territorial Legislature and in the first three state assemblies. Judge Krum, notwithstanding his later expression of antislavery views, found for the state in the matter of regulating free blacks. Responding to Wright's constitutional argument, and echoing the views of many of his fellow Democrats, Krum argued that free blacks and mulattos "were not citizens of the United States in the meaning of the word as expressed in the Constitution." Only free white persons enjoyed "the rights of citizenship," he concluded. On the issue of interstate comity that had been such a prominent part of the state supreme court decision in *Winny*, he argued emphatically that "the State of Missouri has jurisdiction and control over all persons and things within its territorial limits in all respects as a sovereign and independent government."[28]

When Colonel Sanford died in 1848, there was no diminution of the Sanford family's resolve to resist the Scotts' freedom suit. The responsibility for advising Irene Emerson fell to her brother, John Sanford, who had married Emilie Chouteau, the daughter of Pierre Chouteau Jr. The Chouteaus were one of the oldest and wealthiest French families in St. Louis and were also one of the largest slaveholding families in the city. John Sanford inherited his father's small St. Charles estate and sold it, together with the four slaves, to James H. Lucas, another prominent member of St. Louis's slaveholding elite.[29] Awareness of the Sanford family's commitment to slavery probably contributed to the Blow family's determination to assist their former slave in his freedom suit. Murdoch had initiated the Scotts' freedom suit, but he did not stay involved in it for very long; before it came to trial in June 1846, he left St. Louis for California. Another lawyer, Charles D. Drake (later the leader of Radical Republicans in Missouri), assumed responsibility for preparing the case for trial. It is at this point that the Blow family's support became apparent and critically important for the Scotts. Kenneth Kaufman has attributed this support primarily to the oldest of the Blow children, Charlotte.

Peter Blow and his wife Elizabeth arrived in St. Louis from Virginia in 1830. In July 1831 Elizabeth died at the age of forty-six; Peter died less than a year later. In 1831, before her parents died, Charlotte married Joseph Charless Jr., a prominent importer and wholesaler, whose father had established the *Missouri Gazette*.[30] Charless financed the education of his wife's brothers and later brought them into his business as partners. Of the Blow children, only Charlotte could have known Dred Scott at all well. When Murdoch left St. Louis, Scott may have appealed to her for assistance. It was probably Charlotte who persuaded her brothers, for whom she had become a surrogate parent, to provide financial support so that the Scotts could continue their litigation. And it was probably Charlotte who prevailed on her brother-in-law (Drake's wife was Martha Ella Blow, Charlotte's younger sister) to finish the work that Murdoch had begun.

The first circuit court trial took place in June 1847 amid a popular celebration of returning troops from the Mexican War. At this point, St. Louis papers made no mention of the Dred Scott case, reveling instead in the civic festivities that featured a grand parade of firemen, returning Missouri soldiers, and a speech by Senator Thomas Hart Benton. Testimony in the trial did not convince the jurors that Mrs. Emerson held the Scotts as slaves (since they worked for wages), and the jury found in favor of the defendant, leaving the Scotts' status unchanged. In December 1847 Judge Alexander Hamilton granted the plaintiffs' request for a new trial, noting the ironic outcome of the first, which effectively had denied the Scotts their freedom because they had not proved they were slaves. With continued help from the Blow family, the Scotts managed to overcome the legal technicalities and delaying tactics employed by Irene Emerson's attorneys, and in January 1850, more than two years after the first trial, they won their case in the circuit court. In February 1850 Irene Emerson appealed that decision to the Missouri Supreme Court. Soon thereafter, the case became enmeshed in the national debate over slavery. At issue were fundamental questions involving the meaning of citizenship in the United States and the authority of the federal government over slavery in the territories. Dred Scott became emblematic of a struggle between the advocates of Southern Rights and an antislavery opposition that eventually coalesced in the mid-1850s as the Republican Party. National issues and national political figures began to shape the case.

Benton's break with the proslavery Democrats in Missouri and his defeat for reelection to the Senate in 1850 signaled the beginning of an ideological struggle that soon engulfed the Dred Scott case. In Washington, D.C., the leader of the Southern Rights movement, Senator John C. Calhoun of South Carolina, met with his supporters in December 1848 and January 1849 to draft a comprehensive opposition to the "aggression and encroachment" of the North on the slaveholding rights of Southerners. In a document that became known as the Southern Address, the defenders of Southern Rights insisted that "the Federal Government has no right to extend or restrict slavery, no more than to establish or abolish it," and asserted that slaveholders "shall not be prohibited from migrating with our property into the Territories of the United States." Benton viewed the Southern Address as part of an "ominous movement," inspired by his old enemy, Calhoun, and intended to advance slaveholding interests at any cost, even that of the Union.[31]

As Benton expected, Southern Rights activists in Missouri joined Calhoun's crusade. The Jackson Resolutions, taking their name from Claiborne Fox Jackson, later governor of the state and a leader of the anti-Benton opposition in the Missouri Democratic Party, directed Missouri's senators—most pointedly Senator Benton—to support Calhoun's doctrines.[32] The Jackson Resolutions had been drafted (at Claiborne Jackson's behest) by Judge William B. Napton, one of the three justices on the Missouri Supreme Court as it prepared to hear Irene Emerson's appeal of the circuit court decision freeing Dred and Harriet Scott. Judge Napton recorded in his diary that he intended to use the case to bring the principles of Calhoun's Southern Address to bear on Missouri law. To do so, Napton and his colleagues needed to overturn the prevailing precedent of *Winny* and the state supreme court's more recent decision in *Rachel v. Walker*. Moreover, they needed to do so in a manner that did not conflict with the U.S. Supreme Court's decision in *Strader v. Graham* (1851), in which Chief Justice Roger B. Taney, writing for the majority, ruled that the law of the state in which a slave's suit was tried would determine the case's outcome. Without the radical shift in constitutional doctrine that Judge Napton intended to introduce, the *Strader* decision seemed to indicate that the precedent established in the *Winny* and *Rachel* cases prevailed and that the Scotts would be freed. But, as Napton understood, the *Strader* decision had turned on a question of a conflict of law. When the law of one state conflicted with the law of another (as was often the case in issues that related to slavery and freedom), judges needed to decide which law should prevail. For some time, antislavery attorneys in the free states had used the principle adopted in *Strader* to argue that the law of slavery could not intrude into a free state. For a proslavery ideologue like Judge Napton, the *Strader* decision required that the precedent set in *Winny*, a precedent based on interstate comity, be overturned.

Neither Judge Napton nor his fellow proslavery supreme court justice, James B. Birch, attempted to disguise their Southern Rights views. Edward Bates recorded in his diary that the third supreme court justice, John Ferguson Ryland, a Virginia native and a moderate on the slavery issue, confided to him that "the majority of the Court—Judges Napton & Birch—were about soon to give an opinion over-ruling all former decisions of the [Missouri] Supreme Court declaring negro slaves emancipated by a residence northwest of the Ohio, in virtue of the Ordinance of 1787." Ryland also told Bates that his two fellow judges embraced the views expressed in the Southern Address and in the Jackson Resolutions, to the effect that Congress had no authority to legislate concerning slavery in the territories. Judge Ryland intended to draft an opposing minority opinion, he told Bates.[33]

As it happened, Napton and Birch were denied the opportunity to overturn *Winny* and with it *Rachel v. Walker*. Before they had prepared their decision in the Dred Scott case, the voters in Missouri turned them out of office in August 1851. Elected in their stead were William Scott and Hamilton R. Gamble, the latter a Whig moderate and Edward Bates's brother-in-law and legal partner. Gamble had migrated to Missouri from Virginia in 1818 and had quickly gained prominence as Bates's law partner. He retired from his private law practice in 1851 and in August of that year was elected to the court. William Scott was a proslavery Democrat representing the anti-Benton forces. The incumbent, John Ryland, won reelection. In October 1851 the court opened its session in St. Louis and in November accepted new briefs in the Dred Scott case. In March 1852 the justices delivered their verdict in *Scott v. Emerson*. Ryland, shifting to the proslavery side of the argument, joined with Judge Scott to find against Dred Scott. In a two-to-one decision, the court overturned the circuit court decision. Judge Scott, who had joined with Napton to draft the Jackson Resolutions, said that he felt justified in overturning established precedent because "the times now are not as they were when the former decisions on the subject were made." Since then, individuals and entire states embraced the "dark and fell spirit" of abolitionism. "It does not behoove the State of Missouri," he concluded, "to show the least countenance to any measure which might countenance this spirit." Hamilton Gamble filed his moderate dissent, emphasizing the "settled opinion and repeated adjudications of this court."[34]

For whatever reasons, Ryland joined Judge Scott's rigid states' rights opinion to rule that "every State has the right to determine how far, in a spirit of comity, it will respect the laws of other States. Those laws have no intrinsic right to be enforced beyond the limits of the State for which they were enacted."[35] This was a curious reading of Article 4, section 2 of the federal Constitution, and for a defender of slavery, it was extraordinarily shortsighted as well. Judge Scott, evidently without being aware of it, enunciated a central theme of antislavery constitutional thought. Beginning in the 1840s, a number of political abolitionists had begun to argue that slavery's legal existence depended entirely on the positive laws of existing states. Slavery had no extraterritorial effect beyond the borders of those states.[36]

The Scotts' supporters, led by Roswell Field, faced a difficult choice after the 1852 state supreme court decision. Field had entered the Dred Scott case convinced that the issues it involved required adjudication in federal courts. Now he faced the difficult task of entering the federal court system. If he appealed the Missouri decision directly to the Supreme Court it seemed likely that it would follow *Strader* and defer to the state's law of slavery. That course would let the Missouri court's decision stand. The alternative was to attempt to enter the federal courts directly and avoid the issue of state jurisdiction. There were two ways to accomplish this. First, under the terms of the Judiciary Act of 1789, an appellant could seek a remedy in federal court if it could be shown that a right guaranteed by the federal government had been infringed by the state. *Strader* seemed to foreclose this option because in that decision the Supreme Court had made it clear that state law determined Scott's status. The second possibility involved Article 3, section 2 of the federal Constitution, which gave the Supreme Court original jurisdiction over "Controversies . . . between Citizens of different states."

In November 1853, while litigation continued in the Dred Scott case in the circuit court (to which the case had been remanded by the Missouri Supreme Court), Scott, as a citizen of Missouri, sued John Sanford, Irene Emerson's brother, a citizen of New York. Field declared that "Dred Scott, of

St. Louis, in the State of Missouri, and a citizen of the United States, complains of John F. A. Sanford, of the city of New York, and a citizen of New York, in a plea of trespass." Sanford's attorney, Virginia-born and University of Virginia–trained Hugh Garland, responded that "Dred Scott, is not a citizen of the State of Missouri, as alleged in his declaration, because he is a negro of African descent; his ancestors were of pure African blood, and were brought into this country and sold as negro slaves." Field responded that being of African descent did not prevent Scott from being a citizen and from having the right to sue in federal district court.[37] Judge Robert W. Wells, also a native of Virginia, presided over the federal district court in St. Louis. Wells, a slaveholder but a moderate on the slavery issue, had served for a decade (1826 to 1836) in the appointed post of state attorney general. In 1836 President Andrew Jackson appointed him U.S. district judge for the District of Missouri.[38] Wells heard arguments in the Dred Scott case on 24 April 1854 in a temporary courtroom at 38 Main Street. Delivering his decision the next day, he ruled that there existed no hard-and-fast barrier between people of African descent and the status of citizenship. Blacks who were foreign aliens could sue in the federal courts, the judge noted, and he accepted the jurisdiction of the federal court in the Dred Scott case without considering the full meaning of citizenship or Scott's status as a slave. Field then read to the court an "Agreed Upon Statement of Facts" and asked Wells to instruct the jury that based on those facts they should find for Scott. Although he later declared his sympathy for the Scotts, Wells instructed the jury to follow *Strader*. The jury found that Scott remained a slave in accordance with the state supreme court's decision in *Scott v. Emerson*.

The Scotts remained slaves, but the fact that the case had been tried before a federal jury raised an important issue for the Supreme Court. The Fugitive Slave Law of 1850 specified that fugitives did not have a right to habeas corpus proceedings in state courts. But if Scott's suit for freedom could be tried before a jury, in federal court, what would prevent an alleged fugitive slave from securing a federal jury trial in the pursuit of freedom? If Judge Wells's decision on Scott's citizenship stood, the federal courts might become a new battleground for freedom suits. To the St. Louis Circuit Court judge Alexander Hamilton, it had seemed clear from the outset that the Dred Scott case would eventually reach the Supreme Court. When the case came back to Hamilton's court from the state supreme court in January 1854, he noted in the court's record book that the state's case had been "continued by consent, waiting decision of U.S. Supreme Court."[39] Field also understood that Judge Wells's determination raised fundamental issues concerning citizenship that the Supreme Court would engage. If it allowed Wells's ruling to stand, Field noted, "the Fugitive Slave act would undoubtedly become of little value." This, in itself, suggested to him that the Supreme Court would pursue a "strong argument against allowing black men to sue as citizens." He made these remarks to Montgomery Blair, whom he urged to represent Scott and to bring the case before the federal high court. Field advised Blair to emphasize American case law that is "nearly uniform in holding that a removal of a slave by his master into a free state makes him free forever."[40]

Montgomery Blair represented Dred Scott as the case entered its final and most dramatic phase. A graduate of West Point and Transylvania College in Kentucky, he was the son of Francis P. Blair, the leading member of Andrew Jackson's Kitchen Cabinet. At his father's urging Montgomery Blair had established himself as a lawyer in St. Louis, where Thomas Hart Benton served as a powerful ally. Montgomery's younger brother, Frank, joined him in St. Louis, as did their cousin Benjamin Gratz Brown. In 1853 Montgomery Blair moved his law practice to Washington, D.C. In 1856, he argued for Dred Scott's freedom before the U.S. Supreme Court.

For Roswell Field, John Krum, and John Anderson, the lynching of McIntosh, the related killing of Lovejoy, and the emergence of the Dred Scott case were episodes in a historical narrative that led to the Civil War and, eventually, to emancipation. But this was not the only historical narrative to be generated by the McIntosh lynching. For those who had supported it, memory traced a different narrative, one that emphasized a tradition of male valor and sacrifice in contrast to what Luke Lawless referred to as the "fiery unreasoning instinct of the negro." A firemen's historical narrative, represented in a hand-drawn, colored map of St. Louis that was handed down among firemen over the next forty years, took no notice of Lovejoy or Dred Scott. Instead, the map linked McIntosh's lynching to acts of murder and arson by four black men in 1841 and to an act of heroism by a fireman in the great St. Louis fire of 1849.[41]

In the memory of the firemen, the great fire of 17 May 1849 became a central historical event. At 10:00 P.M., a fire broke out on the steamboat *White Cloud,* tied up at the St. Louis levee. An unusually strong wind, uncharacteristically blowing out of the northeast, fanned the flames into crates and barrels stacked along the levee, and from there the fire spread into the city. Soon, twenty-three boats were burning along a mile of the waterfront, and much of the city center was on fire. The efforts of the city's volunteer fire brigades to quench the flames proved ineffective. Thomas B. Targee, captain of Fire Company no. 5, took charge in a desperate effort to contain the fire by using gunpowder from the U.S. Arsenal to blow up buildings in its path.

Targee, of French ancestry, was a native of New York. He had come to St. Louis in 1836 and joined Union Fire Company no. 2; three years later, he founded Missouri Fire Company no. 5. As one of the city's aldermen watched the conflagration from Market Street, he saw Targee rush past. Begrimed with sweat and soot, Targee carried a cask of gunpowder and paused long enough to tell the alderman that he intended to blow up the Phillips Music Store at 42 Market, two doors east of Second Street. No sooner had Targee entered the building than it exploded (evidently because others had already placed explosives in it), and the horrified alderman watched as one of Targee's legs fell from the sky in front of his horse. Fellow firemen gathered what pieces of Targee's body they could find for burial. His remains were taken to Christ Church where the Episcopal priest, Cicero Stephens Hawks, conducted a solemn funeral.[42]

The firemen's map shows the location of the *White Cloud* and indicates the direction of the wind. Colored in vermilion are the sections of the city destroyed by the fire. It also shows the place where Targee died and the location of the city's volunteer fire companies, the principal churches, theaters, and a number of prominent businesses. Moreover, it leads the viewer back in time to link Targee and the great fire to past events. The map locates a counting house on the levee that had been set on fire by four black men after they had killed two white men and robbed the building late on the night of 17 April 1841. Union Fire Company no. 2 fought the fire early the next morning. When the gable of the burning building fell, it killed the fire company's engineer. The black murderers and their victims, Jesse Baker and Jacob Weaver, are also named on the map. Both men were employed at the counting house and shared sleeping quarters there. The murderers where Madison Henderson (called Madison), a footloose slave from New Orleans; Amos Alfred Warrick, a freeman born in Newbern, North Carolina; James W. Seward, a freeman born in Oneida County, New York; and Charles Brown, a freeman born in South Carolina.

The 1841 crime captured the attention of St. Louisans. Confessions secured from each of the prisoners were printed for public sale, and tens of thousands turned out for the executions in July. The confessions told a story of rootless men traveling freely through the land along bustling routes of commerce, robbing and stealing wherever the opportunity presented itself. Although technically a slave, Madison, perhaps with his master's permission, frequently signed on as a cabin boy on steamboats navigating the Mississippi and Ohio Rivers and often joined his master in St. Louis on the way to or from New Orleans. Warrick, although born a freeman, had agreed to be purchased as a slave to move with successive owners to Charleston and, later, to New Orleans. He traveled as a steward to New York and Liverpool before joining forces with Madison and the others in St. Louis. Seward left upstate New York for New Orleans and shipped as a cook to St. Louis. Brown left South Carolina for New Orleans and traveled frequently to St. Louis and other river cities. Seward said that he confessed because his captors warned that he could not otherwise be protected and, in all likelihood, would be burned when he was returned to St. Louis. An enormous crowd gathered for the executions. The *Republican* reported that "every place from which a view could be had was covered in excess." Escorted by a guard drawn from two of the city's volunteer militia companies, the Grays and the Washington Guards, the condemned men passed unharmed through the throng to the gallows.[43]

The firemen's map also commemorates the McIntosh affair. It shows where Hammond died, where McIntosh had been captured, and where he had been "burnt." At the last location, on a block bordered by Pine and Chestnut on the north and south, and by Eighth and Seventh on the west and east, the artist drew a tree, its canopy of leaves and its surrounding grass brightly colored green. Six years after the McIntosh lynching, the firemen of St. Louis counted their former mayor, John Darby, as one of their own. In 1841 he joined with another two-term mayor of the city, John M. Wimer (elected in 1843 and again in 1857), to form St. Louis's sixth volunteer fire company, the Liberty Fire Company. It became the largest in St. Louis and won the reputation for being the most competitive as well. In 1857, when public opinion favored replacing the volunteer companies—with their hand-drawn and pumped engines—with a paid, professional fire department equipped with steam-powered engines, the Liberty Company led the resistance to the use of "hirelings" to replace a "Republic of Volunteers."[44] In all likelihood, one or more of the volunteer fire companies, probably in the presence of Mayor Darby and Judge Lawless, took the initiative in the lynching of McIntosh.

As the firemen's map reveals, the Market Revolution had been a mixed blessing. An expanding economy and increased physical mobility made it possible for the young men who formed the volunteer fire companies to seek new opportunities in St. Louis. But the same social dynamics increased the sense of danger, from what Lawless called Negro "atrocities," and rendered elusive the firemen's ideal community in a "Republic of Volunteers."

St. Louis in 1841

St. Louis Mercantile Library Association at the University of Missouri–St. Louis

Frank Blair
Library of Congress

Dred Scott, 1858 (photograph of a daguerreotype)
Missouri Historical Society, St. Louis

Thomas Hart Benton
Missouri Historical Society, St. Louis

2

"A High Wall and a Deep Ditch"

T HE METROPOLITAN AMBITIONS of St. Louis never meshed smoothly with the political culture of Missouri. The clash between city and state began in earnest in the 1840s when the effects of a transportation revolution produced new markets along waterways of commerce. In the preceding two decades, new canals, improved wagon roads, and short-haul railroads had generated new patterns of trade, linking St. Louis to the developing West and to the growing cities of the Northeast. In the federal census of 1850, it ranked among the ten largest cities in the United States and maintained that status for the next century.

As St. Louis forged ties to the Northeast, its relationship to the state grew increasingly tense. Missouri had entered the Union in a spirit of national compromise. At the time, the Missouri Compromise seemed to settle the issue of slavery expansion. Even so, there were features of the state's constitution (other than its recognition of slavery) that proved to be disadvantageous for St. Louis. Missouri became a state during the midst of an economic depression that followed the panic of 1819. The drafters of the state's constitution shared the Jeffersonian agrarian view that a "paper system" of credit and debt encouraged speculation and the financial instability that produced hard times. Missouri had held tightly to these principles in the Territorial period. The Territory's two banks—the Bank of St. Louis and the Bank of Missouri— had held directors liable for debt, and the new state adhered to the same course. The Alabama Constitution offered the most recent codification of Jeffersonian principles, and the drafters of the Missouri Constitution borrowed its language on matters relating to banks and corporations, holding stockholders personally liable for the debts of the corporations in which they invested. The constitution also forbade the incorporation of more than one bank in the state.[1]

In the decades after the Missouri Compromise, the contrast between city and state grew sharper and more antagonistic. Most Missourians lived in rural areas, and the vast majority of them had migrated to the state from Kentucky and Tennessee. With them came slaves. In the decade of the 1820s and again in the 1830s the state's slave population increased by over 100 percent. However, the free population grew at a faster pace, and slaves as a percentage of the total population fell steadily from 1820 to 1860. The counties of the central region of the state, known as Little Dixie, contained most of the slaves and the largest number of slaveholders. Throughout Missouri, however, only 20 individuals owned more than 50 slaves, and only 365 owned more than 20. These slave owners raised cash crops of tobacco and hemp (for cotton-bale rope) and benefited from St. Louis's growth as a market center. Yet they were not united as a political interest. Issues other than slavery divided Whigs and Democrats. The political leaders of Little Dixie owned slaves, but Sterling Price, a Democrat, resided in predominantly Democratic Chariton County, and James S. Rollins, a Whig, resided in predominantly Whig Boone County.[2] Slavery never dominated the state's economy, and until the late 1840s and early 1850s it did not have a dramatic effect on political alignments. In subtle ways, however, the "peculiar institution" contributed to the growing alienation between city and state. Slaveholders in Missouri were as fearful as their counterparts in the Deep South that the social underpinnings of slavery could not be maintained without the tacit support of the non-slaveholding majority of small farmers. As the Market Revolution advanced in the first half of the nineteenth century, Missouri's small farmers grew increasingly fearful that they would become enmeshed in an expanding marketplace and lose their status as an independent people.[3] In Missouri, as in other Southern states, the Democratic Party, the party of Andrew Jackson, proved to be somewhat more successful than its Whig opposition in connecting a partisan political appeal to the uncertainties and fears of small farmers. For a time, the Jacksonian language of agrarian independence did not contradict economic expansion. The Jacksonian appeal sustained slavery within an embrace of traditional agrarian values, but it also sought to create a political majority that glorified "Young America," and with it the expanding continental empire in which St. Louis aspired to greatness. Until the political crisis of the late 1840s and early 1850s, Missouri's most successful politician, Senator Thomas Hart Benton, managed to maintain a rhetorical bridge over the growing chasm between city and state. Until the late 1840s, Benton and the Democrats generally carried the state by a margin of more than 55 percent.[4]

In the balance that Benton struck between agrarian independence and economic greatness, Missouri maintained a conservative course regarding state-funded projects to promote education or to improve transportation. Compared to the Northeast, Missouri lagged. The St. Louis Whig *Missouri Republican* complained in 1841 of the unwillingness of the state to invest in its economic future. "Missouri has not one single mile of railroad, turnpike or canal," wrote the editor, "not a single bridge, lock or dam, not a single improved road or river, not a single school, academy or college, built or endowed by the State."[5] Missouri was not backward in this regard. Illinois became a state two years before Missouri, and it could boast no more in the way of state-financed development. For many St. Louisans, however, development could not come fast enough. As Benton walked a fine line between endorsing economic development and sustaining the interests of independent farmers, he supported national expenditures for internal improvements at the same time that he led the Jacksonian assault on the Bank of the United States. Benton's antibank rhetoric underscored the difficulties facing St. Louis businessmen in the 1830s and 1840s. Benton described the Bank as a conspiracy to transfer millions of dollars "to the Neptunes who preside over the flux and reflux of paper." The Bank of the United States, he said, made "the rich richer and the poor poorer." "Gold and silver is the best currency for a republic," he concluded, in keeping with his nickname "Old Bullion." Gold and silver specie remained relatively free of the fluctuations in value that characterized bank-issued paper notes. Benton insisted that gold and silver "suits the men of middle property and the working people best." In the language of Young America, however, he spoke grandly of territorial and economic expansion.[6]

Benton's hard-money policy guided the thinking of the directors of the Bank of the State of Missouri, the only bank permitted by the state's constitution. In the second financial crash of the antebellum era (following the panic of 1837), the conservative policies of the new state bank initially sheltered Missourians from a widening depression. The same policies, however, deprived St. Louis of an adequate circulating medium and stifled commercial expansion. To circumvent the state constitution's restriction on banking, St. Louis businessmen began providing the missing services themselves. In 1841, nine insurance companies, together with the St. Louis Gas Light Company, operated as private banks. These establishments could not issue their own notes, but they managed to maintain a circulating currency of out-of-state notes that the *Republican* described as the backbone of the city's economy. "At present and for a long time past," commented the editor, the Bank of the State of Missouri "has not been able to do anything in aid of business." The insurance companies and the Gas Light Company had become "the main stay of the whole commercial business of the city."[7] These efforts by St. Louis merchants to maintain a degree of liquidity created a makeshift money supply largely dependent on Illinois banknotes. When the Bank of Illinois suspended its activities in 1842, the effects of the national depression quickly and brutally caught up with Missouri.[8] The state's small farmers cherished their independence from the marketplace, but the sudden collapse of the St. Louis financial system closed markets and produced painfully hard times for them. Predictably, farmers across the state blamed St. Louis merchants for their plight. As historian Jeffrey Adler has observed, "Although state banking policy had forced St. Louis merchants to look outside of Missouri for currency, rural spokesmen held the city and its businessmen responsible for the depression."[9]

Responding to the new economic crisis, rural Missourians acted politically to increase their hold on the state legislature. In 1841 it added seventeen new counties to the state. Because the state constitution limited the size of the general assembly to one hundred seats, and because the body already had ninety-eight representatives, the new counties added only two new seats to the legislature. However, the constitution also required that each county must have at least one representative. The creation of the new counties forced a reapportionment that gave greater strength to thinly populated rural areas. Facing continued hostility from the state, St. Louis merchants and other advocates of economic development looked elsewhere for sources of capital. Throughout the 1840s St. Louis maintained strong ties to Baltimore and New Orleans, but it increasingly aligned itself economically with the commercial and financial centers of the Northeast.

The sectional orientation of St. Louis shifted dramatically during the 1840s as its population more than doubled, from about 36,000 in 1845 to nearly 80,000 by the end of the decade. "Yankees" from the Northeast dominated the new wave of native immigration and added to the distrust of rural Missourians. Almost half of the native-born immigrants to St. Louis during the 1840s arrived from New England, Pennsylvania, and New York. William Greenleaf Eliot illustrated an early example of the new trend. A graduate of Harvard College, Eliot moved to St. Louis in 1836. As pastor of the Unitarian Church in St. Louis, he presided over the spiritual life of many of his fellow New Englanders who moved to the city in the next decade. Three-quarters of Eliot's congregation were transplanted New Englanders. Prominent examples of this group included the Connecticut-born brothers Oliver D. and Giles Filley and their New York cousin, Chauncey Filley. Oliver, the older of the brothers, arrived in St. Louis in 1829; he was joined by Giles in 1834 and by Chauncey in 1850. Oliver and Giles Filley founded the Excelsior Stove Works and brought molders to St. Louis from the New York City area. Oliver won election as mayor in 1858, serving what was at the time a one-year term, and then won reelection to a newly created two-year term in 1859. Chauncey was elected mayor in 1863.[10] Another leading manufacturer, Hudson E. Bridge, founded the Empire Stove Works. A native of New Hampshire, Bridge arrived in St. Louis in 1837 where he too became a member of Eliot's congregation. Members of this congregation who were not natives of the Northeast were closely allied with those who were. This was true for banker James E. Yeatman, a native of Tennessee, as well as for the Kentucky-born merchant Wayman Crow. Crow moved to St. Louis in 1835 and formed a partnership with a cousin from Philadelphia. He served as president of the St. Louis Chamber of Commerce during the booming 1840s and assisted in securing state charters for the Hannibal and St. Joseph and the Pacific Railroads.[11]

In overwhelming numbers northeasterners entered the commercial life of St. Louis. The 1850 census revealed that 90 percent of the adult males who had emigrated from New England to St. Louis worked in commercial establishments or in allied professional positions. Seventy percent of this group were merchants. In addition, 53 percent of adult male immigrants from Pennsylvania and New York filled similar commercial and professional positions, and over one-third of this group were merchants. New arrivals from the Northeast launched nearly three-quarters of the new businesses in St. Louis in the period 1845 to 1847. Taken together, these new arrivals ran almost 20 percent of all of St. Louis's commercial establishments during the 1840s. Not all of these northeastern natives stayed in St. Louis. Many of them viewed the city not as a new home but as a site of commercial activity beneficial to their eastern backers. After the boom of the 1840s, St. Louis became somewhat less Northern and somewhat more Southern. German and Irish immigration rapidly changed the city's demography in the late 1840s and early 1850s, and the Germans, in particular, ensured St. Louis's loyalty to the Union. Nevertheless, part of the crisis of the 1850s for St. Louisans was the perception in New York and Boston that the city could not grow to its full potential because of its location in a slave state.[12] In the early 1850s the total number of businesses operating in St. Louis increased by 43 percent. But in contrast to the late 1840s, the number of firms with northeastern ties rose at only half that rate (23 percent). The result was that the proportion of businesses run by northeasterners declined by more than 30 percent in the early 1850s.

In the heated political climate of the late 1850s, St. Louis seemed to northeasterners to be a battleground where proslavery ruffians challenged the influence of Northern men and methods. Ely Thayer of Massachusetts, in his efforts to use the economic power of the North to advance antislavery goals, urged those who supported the cause of freedom to pressure the merchants of St. Louis into open support for emancipation in Missouri and for the Free State cause in neighboring Kansas. A founder of the New England Emigrant Aid Company, Thayer believed that three-quarters of St. Louis's merchants were sympathetic to the cause. Persuaded by Thayer, William Cullen Bryant used the pages of the *New York Evening Post* to warn St. Louis merchants that eastern investors would shun the city if it accommodated slavery. "Men who have no regard for the rights of others," observed the New York editor, "cannot be expected to pay their debts."

A vocal partisan in the struggle that engulfed St. Louis was Francis Hunt, who arrived in the city from Boston in 1851 to represent the western interests of a Connecticut dry goods firm. Although he publicly maintained his neutrality in the struggle over Kansas, he secretly worked to ensure that shipments of "machinery" from the New England Emigrant Aid Company made their way to the Free State settlers in Kansas. Proslavery forces in the city and state concluded, with good reason, that these shipments included Sharpe's rifles, deemed by the New York clergyman, Henry Ward Beecher, to be more important to the Free State settlers in Kansas than Bibles. In their zeal to disrupt this flow of Beecher's Bibles to the Free State fighters in Kansas, Missourians regularly disrupted and destroyed shipments from St. Louis. Hunt warned that if these attacks continued, the "citizens of St. Louis, and of Missouri" would see an important "source of their prosperity . . . cut off and driven to a northern route." His threat did nothing to dissuade those who were intent on disrupting the flow of arms and supplies. Discouraged, he left St. Louis.

Though New Englanders started over one-half of the businesses in St. Louis during the late 1840s, they opened less than one-third of the new firms in the early 1850s and less than one-sixth during the struggle over "bleeding Kansas." Still, a number of businessmen from the Northeast had become successful in St. Louis. Thomas Allen and Henry D. Bacon of Massachusetts,

Carlos Greeley of New Hampshire, and Daniel Page of Maine were leading businessmen there as the Civil War approached. The migration from the Northeast shaped lasting ties between St. Louis and eastern cities, ties that were substantially strengthened during the war.

As the president of the city's chamber of commerce reported approvingly in 1857, "St. Louis has long been married to New York and Boston." The construction of the Hannibal and St. Joseph Railroad in the 1850s offered a prominent example of this marriage. Begun in 1853 and completed in 1859, the 207-mile line connected the Mississippi and Missouri Rivers, and a connecting line led to St. Louis. The state provided $3 million in bonds to support the project. Another $6.3 million came from private investors, notable among them John Murray Forbes of Boston. Staunchly antislavery and suspicious of the capacity of Southern states to sustain economic development, Forbes understood that the northern two tiers of counties in Missouri contained few slaves and few supporters of slavery. The Hannibal and St. Joe skirted Little Dixie to the north, and Forbes took pride in the fact that the road provided a direct link to Kansas from the East and that over it flowed money, Sharpe's rifles, and Free State settlers.[13]

The impact of foreign immigration also reshaped St. Louis in the late 1840s and early 1850s. In those years, it became the leading immigrant city in the West. Of particular influence were Germans, who arrived by tens of thousands. More than 20,000 Germans came in 1852, and another 25,000 in 1854. By 1860, one-third of the city's population were natives of Germany, and almost all of them had arrived since the late 1840s. Overwhelmingly, they followed artisan trades and were drawn to St. Louis by the high wages commanded by workingmen in the urban West. The Germans and their leaders joined with northeasterners to shape the character of St. Louis at midcentury. Like the northeasterners, most Germans opposed slavery and moved from the Benton wing of the Democratic Party to form the backbone of the city's Republican Party. Adding to St. Louis's ethnic mix were the Irish, who made up almost 16 percent of the city's population in 1860 and nearly half the city's unskilled labor force. The Irish were notably reluctant to see the condition of African Americans—alongside whom they labored on the St. Louis waterfront—improved by emancipation. Many Irishmen became allies of the proslavery Democracy. These combinations proved to be a volatile mix, exploding in two major riots in the 1850s and in numerous outbreaks of violence early in the secession crisis.

St. Louis entered the midcentury flush with the energy and excitement of a booming economy and an expanding city. But its aspirations continued to be frustrated by the agrarian forces that dominated the state and were somewhat dampened as well by the developing sense that it could not grow as a great city in a slaveholding state. In St. Louis, slaveholding interests declined steadily in the 1840s and 1850s, and slavery itself had little or no economic significance. This decline paralleled the diminished influence of the old Creole elite and the original source of their wealth. The fur trade had once dominated the city's economy, but it had virtually disappeared by 1850. Several scions of old families aggressively invested in railroads in the 1850s, adding their wealth to the drive for economic expansion. Pierre Chouteau Jr. invested in the Illinois Central Railroad. John O'Fallon served as president of two railroads and gave his name to two railroad towns, one in Missouri and one in Illinois. The wealth of old St. Louis families also benefited local charities and educational institutions. But when St. Louisans established the Mercantile Library in 1846 as a new cultural pillar for the city, leading members included clergyman William Greenleaf Eliot and fellow New Englanders Henry D. Bacon and Hudson E. Bridge. James E. Yeatman, a Tennessee native who had arrived in St. Louis in 1842, joined forces with the northeastern-oriented business and professional elite in the founding of the Mercantile and in other civic ventures. As historian James Neal Primm has observed, old families in St. Louis retained wealth and social status, but they could no longer claim a dominant role in the city's livelihood or in its social identity.[14]

Throughout the nation, the rapid pace of territorial and commercial expansion left instability in its wake. The political accommodations that undergirded the early Republic, most important the compromises over slavery, collapsed under the weight of change. At the national level, Benton struggled to maintain the old spirit of accommodation and compromise. Nevertheless, his fears for the future became increasingly open and vivid. The Mexican War and the territorial crisis that followed it proved to be a turning point for him. In the four years of James K. Polk's self-imposed single presidential term (1845–1849), the western boundary of the United States expanded southwest from the Sabine River to the Rio Grande and westward from the Continental Divide to the Pacific Ocean. Benton shared Polk's vision of the United States as a continental empire, and although he initially opposed the president's policy toward Mexico, he supported the war once it had begun. But war and territorial expansion left in their wake a heightened degree of sectional tension that quickly unsettled Benton and the Democratic Party. Already divided between the Free-Soil followers of former president Martin Van Buren and the Southern Rights supporters of Polk, the ranks of the Democratic Party grew more deeply divided as the war progressed. When Polk requested from Congress an appropriation of $2 million to help acquire territory from Mexico and to bring the war to a successful conclusion, the House of Representatives responded by passing the Wilmot Proviso. A measure introduced by the Pennsylvania Democrat David Wilmot, the proviso insisted that it was "an express and fundamental condition to the acquisition of any territory" that "neither slavery nor involuntary servitude shall ever exist in any part of said territory." Benton opposed the extension of slavery into the new West but he also opposed the Wilmot Proviso as unnecessarily divisive within the Democratic Party.[15]

The proviso passed in the House on two occasions. Both times it went down to defeat in the Senate, where slaveholding states (before the admission of Wisconsin in 1848) held a two-vote majority. When the proviso came before the Senate in February 1847, Senator John C. Calhoun of South Carolina denounced the effort to restrict slavery as a direct attack on the "safety" and "self-preservation" of Southern society. The Southern Rights doctrine crafted by Calhoun insisted that slave property could not be distinguished from any other form of property protected under the Fifth Amendment's stipulation that "no person shall be . . . deprived of life, liberty, or property, without due process of law." Here the battle lines were drawn between the antislavery North and the proslavery South. Despite repeated efforts at compromise, the divide could not be bridged. Southern Rights Democrats embraced the Calhoun Resolutions, and Free-Soil Democrats held fast to the Wilmot Proviso. This division in the party alarmed Benton. He blamed Calhoun, who responded to the criticism by denouncing Benton as a senator from "a slaveholding State" who refused to stand in solidarity with the other slaveholding states. Benton replied solemnly that he would always be found "in the right place." "I am," he declared, "on the side of my country and the Union."[16]

Benton continued to seek a middle ground upon which the unity of the Democratic Party could be based. He attempted to steer a course between what he perceived to be the twin evils of the Wilmot Proviso and the Calhoun Resolutions. He returned to St. Louis in May 1847 and began a political struggle that culminated in his irrevocable break with the Southern Rights

Democrats. He found the political landscape in Missouri significantly altered. In St. Louis, the previous year had brought the death of an old enemy, Shadrach Penn, editor of the *Missouri Reporter,* but also the death of an old friend and political ally, Luke E. Lawless. German immigrants provided a new source of strength, and Benton warmly accepted the political support offered by the new German-language newspaper, the *Anzeiger des Westens.* A Democratic victory over a coalition of Whigs and nativists in the city elections seemed to bode well for the future. Addressing a crowd in the rotunda of the courthouse, Benton sounded the alarm that he hoped would produce Democratic unity across the state in the coming presidential election. He charged that Calhoun and his "slavery propagandist resolutions" threatened to subvert the Union. Calhoun and his supporters, continued Benton, wished to abolish "all compromises, past and future, on the slavery question." He compared Calhoun with the Northern abolitionists: both stood as enemies to the spirit of compromise necessary to preserve the Union.[17]

When the retired New York merchant Philip Hone visited St. Louis in late June and early July 1847, Benton served as a gracious host to the prominent Whig. Hone traveled west ostensibly to attend the River and Harbor Convention in Chicago, where he intended to add his voice to the call for federal support for internal improvements. He took the long way to Chicago, however, traveling by steamboat down the Ohio and up the Mississippi to St. Louis. Arriving in St. Louis on the evening of 30 June, he savored the scenes of raw vitality that greeted him. He took his lodging at the Planters' House Hotel and after tea set out alone at dusk to tour the levee. An impressive line of fifty steamboats marked the water's edge, with their bows facing the city. "The whole levee," he observed, "is covered, as far as the eye can see, with merchandise landed or to be shipped." Amid thousands of barrels of flour, bags of corn, and hogsheads of tobacco, he took special note of "immense piles of lead," one of the region's "great staples." At the boatyard he found a large congregation of workers—"white and black, French, Irish and German"—drinking, singing, and lounging. "Few travelers would undertake [such an excursion]," Hone reflected, "especially after dark." Yet he welcomed the excitement: "I like it." The next day, Benton took Hone in hand, and in the senator's carriage the New Yorker toured St. Louis more thoroughly, passing by all its major churches, markets, and grand residences. Continuing his journey to Chicago, at the River and Harbor Convention Hone heard Edward Bates, among others, speak on the importance of economic growth.[18]

Later in summer 1847, Benton returned to Washington to resume his struggle to maintain a united Democratic Party. His task was made immeasurably more difficult by the unexpected death of the fifty-two-year-old Silas Wright of New York. Wright had been the leading Democratic presidential candidate opposed to the Southern Rights agenda. His death added greatly to the burden borne by Benton, who had stood with Martin Van Buren and Francis P. Blair to champion Wright as the Democratic candidate for 1848. Some eyes now turned to Benton himself as an alternative candidate. Complicating matters further were the members of Benton's family and the senator's penchant for blending personality and politics. Benton's son-in-law, John C. Frémont (the husband of the beautiful, vivacious, and ambitious Jessie Benton), returned to Washington in fall 1847 to face charges of insubordination and mutiny in a dispute with General Stephen Kearny. Kearny, a St. Louisan, had worked with Frémont to annex California to the United States during the war with Mexico. Benton angrily took charge of Frémont's defense. Shortly before the court-martial began, Benton's son, Randolph, added to the witches' brew of family and politics by making an appearance before President Polk, seeking a military appointment. When the president remained noncommittal, the seventeen-year-old Benton stamped out of the room, "speaking profanely," as Polk recorded in his diary, that "he would do something." The president thought the young man drunk and dismissed him as "in all respects worthless." As the president feared, Benton's family entanglements helped to make the Missouri senator an enemy of his administration.[19]

Frémont's trial began in November 1847 and ended the following January. Throughout the trial Benton launched bitter attacks against Kearny, which drew the censure of the court's presiding officer. In the end, Benton's bluster could not overcome Frémont's vain and self-serving behavior in California. The court-martial found him guilty of all charges and dismissed him from the service. Furious, Benton appealed to Polk for a reversal. The president and his cabinet met and agreed on a middle course. Frémont would stand guilty of insubordination but innocent of mutiny. In a spirit of compromise, Polk directed that Frémont "be released from arrest" and that he "resume his sword, and report for duty." Frémont rejected the peace offer and resigned from the army. Benton's old friend, Francis P. Blair, lamented that the senator remained "absolutely possessed with the Kearny conspiracy against Frémont."[20]

Once joined, these issues of politics and personality could not be separated, and they soon colored the developing struggle over political power and sectional allegiance in Missouri. In Washington, Benton refused to continue as chairman of the Senate Military Affairs Committee because he believed that Secretary of War William L. Marcy had taken Kearny's side in the Frémont court-martial. When Polk put Kearny forward for promotion, Benton saw the old conspiracy resumed, and he took the Senate floor on thirteen separate days to denounce the "crime" against Frémont. Kearny won his promotion, and Benton added further to the personal bitterness that separated him from the advocates of Southern Rights. Senator Andrew Butler of South Carolina challenged Benton to a duel in response to the harsh words the Missouri senator had directed to the South Carolinian during the Kearny debate. Benton refused because, he said, neither the challenger nor his agent—Mississippi senator Henry S. Foote—carried themselves with the dignity of gentlemen.

As the presidential elections of 1848 approached, Benton found himself positioned uncomfortably between the regular party nominee, Lewis Cass, and his rival, Radical Democrat Martin Van Buren. On policy issues alone, Benton stood closer to the Radicals than he did to the equivocal Cass. The senator agreed with the Radicals on the matter of "keeping free territory clear of negroes." But his political survival in a slave state required circumspection in these matters, and Benton did not break with the regular Democratic Party nominee. When Van Buren and his followers joined with antislavery Whigs to form the independent Free-Soil Party, Benton denounced the third party as "an organization entirely to be regretted." On the other hand, he acknowledged the proslavery tenor of the Democratic Party's convention and declared his sympathy for the "watchwords" of the Free-Soil Party: "'Free speech' 'Free labor' [and] 'Free men.'" In St. Louis, Frank Blair advanced the Free-Soil cause and Van Buren's candidacy without breaking with Benton, launching the *Barnburner* as a Radical Democratic newspaper supporting the New Yorker. Benton allowed business interests in Virginia and Kentucky to keep him occupied during the fall campaign, and left Frank and Montgomery Blair free to rally St. Louisans to the Free-Soil cause.[21]

Divisions in the Democratic Party worsened following the Whig Party's success in electing the war hero Zachary Taylor president. National defeat left a factious Democratic Party free to pursue its internal antagonisms as Congress took up the difficult issue of slavery expansion into the new territories won from Mexico. Eighteen forty-nine was a year of great distress in St. Louis for other reasons as well. A cholera epidemic, reaching its peak in May, June, and July, left more than 10 percent of the city's population dead. Cholera had visited the city before, but never with such devastating effect. The first outbreak occurred in 1832, when the city's population stood at about 6,000 and when Seventh Street marked its western boundary. By 1849 the population of the city exceeded 60,000 and its western border had been extended to Eighteenth Street. By May of that year hundreds of people died each week. The symptoms of the disease were unmistakable: violent vomiting and diarrhea were followed by cyanosis (a bluish discoloration of the skin caused by a deficiency of oxygen in the blood) and, frequently, by death. Neither the cause of the disease nor its mode of transmission was known. In an era that preceded the development of the germ theory of disease, physicians focused their attention on contaminated "humors" (bodily fluids) and "atmospheres" (external gasses). Medical treatments varied widely, but most physicians relied on calomel (mercurous chloride) as a purgative to expel debilitating humors.[22] Authorities also isolated the sick and sought to purify the spaces occupied by the dead with pine tar and other caustic agents. As the number of dead mounted, many citizens viewed the devastating fire that spread through the center of the city on 17 May as a welcome means of ridding St. Louis of disease. The fact that the death rate from cholera dropped in the week after the fire, to fewer than twenty victims per day, offered proof to some that the destructive blaze had produced a cleansing effect. It had not. The epidemic reached its zenith in June and July.

Although existing theories of disease were inadequate to explain the cholera epidemic, most observers believed that its cause and its contagion were linked to filth and squalor. Although the wealthy were not immune from cholera, the poorer sections of town were hardest hit. Since these poor neighborhoods were also the sites of cheap saloons, gambling dens, brothels, and immigrant tenements, it seemed to the city's elite that sickness and death visited those individuals already weakened by moral decay. Dr. William M. McPheeters, who took a leading role in the public health activities in St. Louis during the epidemic, found concentrations of the disease among German and Irish immigrants "who have herded together in large numbers." Near these cramped residences, McPheeters also noted "large ponds of stagnant water, some of which covered twenty to thirty acres of ground."[23] Whatever the cause of cholera, it seemed clear to St. Louis's civic leaders that the epidemic required concerted public intervention. A bigger, grander city needed an improved sanitation infrastructure and new bureaucratic systems to implement and enforce sanitary restrictions.

Well before the cholera outbreak, the tremendous growth of St. Louis in the 1840s made residents aware of the city's need for sewers. In this regard, St. Louis stood at the vanguard of urban environmental planning. The peculiar geological features of the St. Louis region, a karst terrain, heightened the problems of pollution that eventually required sewer construction in all urban areas. The limestone rock that underlay the city gradually dissolved in rainwater to produce a system of channels and caves that carried surface pollution directly to groundwater. Sinkholes from collapsed caves filled with stagnant water. The "vapors" arising from these yellow-green ponds alarmed residents well before the onslaught of cholera. Early in 1849 (before the outbreak of disease in St. Louis) the state legislature authorized the city to levy a tax to pay for the construction of sewers. The cholera epidemic lent greater urgency to the issue, and St. Louis's city engineer, Samuel R. Curtis, constructed the city's first sewer to drain a large sinkhole at Ninth and Biddle Streets. By 1850 Curtis (who later commanded the victorious Union troops at Pea Ridge) had developed a plan to drain the entire city with an integrated sewer system.[24]

In addition to the creation of a sanitation infrastructure, the cholera years also gave birth to a spirit of voluntarism that provided the institutional foundations for a loyal homefront movement during the Civil War. McPheeters noted that fear of disease made it impossible to find hired attendants to care for the sick. He praised the volunteers who came forward to meet the need: the Catholic Sisters of Charity as well as the "associations of young gentlemen."[25] The Civil War opened far broader opportunities for volunteerism in St. Louis, although McPheeters did not participate in this homefront movement. His loyalties lay with the South, and he served as a surgeon in the Confederate army.

As St. Louis rallied from the fire and epidemic of 1849, the division between city and state grew deeper and wider on the issue of slavery's place in national affairs. The growing stridency of Southern Rights advocates, and their mounting attack against Thomas Hart Benton, made it increasingly clear that men of proslavery convictions stood squarely in opposition to St. Louis's aspirations to harness the resources of the state and the West to its developmental goals. Benton and his followers had long viewed slavery as incidental to their vision of progress. Now, as sectional hostilities sharpened, Southern Rights advocates began to embrace slavery as the bedrock of the Republic. Like Benton, Judge William B. Napton of the Missouri Supreme Court traced his political lineage to Thomas Jefferson and to the old Virginia school of political economy. The son of a merchant tailor in Princeton, New Jersey, Napton studied law in Virginia, where he came under the influence of Philip Barbour and other leading defenders of the Southern agrarian tradition. He moved to Missouri in 1832 and settled in Little Dixie; by 1840 he was comfortably established on his Elk Hill estate in Saline County. Like Benton, Napton owned slaves. In sharp contrast to Benton, however, he had come to view slavery as the essential foundation of a stable society. Ignoring St. Louis and similar cities in slave states, he compared the slave and free states: "I can only account for the great diversities between society here and that found in our free states by the fact that we have no free white labouring population in our midst. That class which forms a heavy component of northern society has no existence here, but is supplied by our slaves, whose subordination of course depends upon a total deprivation of all voice and vote upon public questions."

Slavery promoted liberty and equality among free white men, Napton believed, because it discouraged the emergence of a white wage-earning class and prevented the development of class antagonisms among whites. Liberty and equality, in turn, promoted civic virtue. Napton emphasized the "modesty" of Southern women who, in contrast to their dissatisfied Northern counterparts, assumed the "dependence and loftiness of sentiment" that also characterized the "poorer and humbler classes" in the South. Where free labor prevailed, social discord followed:

> It seems to be the tendency of society in the free states to discard modesty from the list of female virtues—to break down all distinctions of sex. . . . This is fully displayed . . . in the thousand associations for fanatical purposes, in which men, women and negroes are indiscriminately blended, for maintaining women's rights, African freedom, Maine Liquor laws, and agrarian distributions. . . . Our country . . . is untouched by such disastrous monomaniacs. To slavery we owe this distinction.[26]

It was Napton who articulated the proslavery ideology of Missouri's Southern Rights Democrats as they prepared Benton's political demise.[27]

Benton and Napton remained loyal to the national Democratic Party, but the shifting political currents of the day carried them in very different directions. Benton viewed slavery as a relic of the past and associated the future of St. Louis and the nation with the triumph of free labor over slavery. But his antislavery course threatened to leave him politically isolated in a slaveholding state. In a bold effort to outflank the sectional juggernaut, Benton tied the language of Young America to the theme of economic development and proposed a federally funded "central national road" to link the Mississippi River at St. Louis with San Francisco Bay, thus locating the city at the commercial crossroads of a continental empire. In fall 1848, as Congress continued its debate over slavery in the territories, Benton absented himself from the Senate floor to draft legislation to implement his national road plan. Nothing came of his grandiose scheme, but in its presentation he demonstrated how far he had moved from his Jacksonian origins. He continued to employ the language of Young America, and other echoes remained of his Jacksonian past, notably in his derogatory references to "stockjobbing" for the profit of the few. However, the substance of his remarks focused on the wealth to be generated by a burgeoning capitalist market. The central national road he envisioned would carry the commerce of the nation over "iron railways, where practicable" and on wagon roads "macadamized" or otherwise improved. The federal government showed no interest in funding Benton's scheme, but in 1849 the Missouri legislature chartered the Pacific Railroad with the stated expectation that the new enterprise would increase the wealth and population of the state and raise the value of its agricultural products and manufactures. Construction began in 1852, but progress remained slow. By 1854 only fifty miles of track had been put in operation. St. Louis seemed poised to become the great city that he envisioned, but fulfillment of the dream remained elusive.

Benton's vision of St. Louis as America's great inland metropolis remained compelling for years to come. But just as the city could not reach its full potential in a slave state, he faced for the first time in his career the prospect of political isolation and defeat. Approaching his sixty-fifth year, "Old Bullion," the defender of slavery in Missouri in 1820 and the Jacksonian champion of independent artisans and small farmers, emerged by 1848 as an advocate of free labor, Free-Soil, and an expanding marketplace. The advocates of Southern Rights stood staunchly opposed to the "corrupting" influence of "Yankee capitalists," and they were determined that he would pay heavily for his "defections" from proslavery ranks.[28]

Benton continued to counsel moderation on the slavery issue, even as antislavery and proslavery partisans severely eroded the ground he stood on. Calhoun's 1848 Southern Address described Southerners as a minority in a

Union dominated by antislavery Northerners. The address warned that Southerners faced "a degradation greater than has ever yet fallen to the lot of a free and enlightened people" if the majority opinion prevailed. Northerners intended to impose emancipation on the South, he insisted, and this would force Southern whites to flee "the homes of ourselves and ancestors" and abandon "our country to our former slaves, to become the permanent abode of disorder, anarchy, poverty, misery and wretchedness." Because the Southern Address echoed the language of the Declaration of Independence, Benton believed that it "intimated" Southern secession. Among the politicians signing it were Calhoun and Andrew Butler of South Carolina, Henry S. Foote and Jefferson Davis of Mississippi, and one of the architects of Benton's coming defeat, David Atchison of Missouri. For Benton the political battleground now shifted to Missouri, where he soon discovered that the middle ground he occupied narrowed as the antagonistic ideologies of Free-Soil and Southern Rights began to define mainstream politics.[29]

Throughout Missouri a group of dedicated opponents shadowed Benton and prevented his campaign from developing the momentum it needed for success. Henry S. Foote contributed a pamphlet to the cause as Claiborne Jackson and David Atchison were joined by Missouri congressman James S. Green and former *St. Louis Union* editor Samuel Treat in an anti-Benton campaign that combined Calhoun's Southern Rights arguments with the contention that Benton, the servant of the people, should follow the instructions given to him by the representatives of the people in the Missouri legislature. The battle in Missouri extended to the floor of the U.S. Senate. There Benton continued his attack on the Southern Address as Foote rose to its defense. As Foote warmed to his subject, he referred to "the father of the Senate," meaning Benton, as a "calumniator." With that, Benton rose from his desk and advanced toward the now silent Foote. Drawing a pistol, Foote retreated toward the vice president's podium. There, Henry Clay calmly called for order as one senator managed to disarm Foote and another restrained Benton. The affair ended with the Senate appointing a committee to investigate this breach in decorum. In July the committee reported that Foote had been "offensive and insulting" in his language and that Benton had risen to "assault" or "intimidate" him. With this effort at evenhandedness (and with no recommendation concerning further Senate action) the crisis subsided, and the Senate returned to the business of crafting the Compromise of 1850.[30]

Shortly after Zachary Taylor's new Whig administration took office in 1849, Benton returned to St. Louis to do battle against the Jackson Resolutions, which, he said, intended to make Calhoun's Southern Address the defining issue of state politics. For six months—from May to November 1849—Benton traveled through the state campaigning against the resolutions. In an "Appeal" to "the people of Missouri—the whole body of the people," he explained that he intended to express his views in great detail. "I think it probable," he conceded, "that there are many citizens—good friends of the harmony and stability of this Union—who do not see the Missouri instructions" as he did. Because he saw the Jackson Resolutions—"and their prototype, the Calhoun address"—as a threat to the Union, he took his case directly to the people. "I shall abide the decision of the whole people," he concluded, "and nothing less."[31]

Repeatedly Benton damned Calhoun as the enemy of the party of Andrew Jackson and as the "prime mover and head contriver" of the divisive debate over slavery extension. The Jackson Resolutions, he said, were the work of men who had become the pawns of the South's leading nullifier. The resolutions asserted that Congress had no authority to prohibit slavery in the territories. To the contrary, roared Benton, "Congress *has* the power to prohibit, or admit slavery." He reminded voters that he had opposed the antislavery Wilmot Proviso during the war with Mexico because it seemed to unnecessarily promote tension between North and South. He continued to oppose extremism on both sides of the slavery debate, but he denounced efforts to extend slavery as a nullificationist plot to destroy the Union. He placed his faith with Thomas Jefferson, and he cited the Northwest Ordinance of 1787, initially drafted by Jefferson in 1784 with stronger antislavery language, as unassailable evidence that Congress possessed the power to prohibit slavery in the territories and that Congress had successfully exerted that power in the past. Benton declared himself to be "against the institution" of slavery. If there were no slaves in Missouri, he would oppose admitting them to the state. If there were no slaves in the United States he would similarly oppose admitting them to the country. Since there were now no slaves in the territory wrested from Mexico, he opposed extending slavery into the West. With these principles he declared himself the uncompromising foe of David Atchison, Claiborne Jackson, and other Southern "Ultras": "Between them and me, henceforth and forever, *a high wall and a deep ditch!* And no communication, no compromise, no caucus with them."

St. Louis provided strong new allies for Benton's struggle. Henry Boernstein's *Anzeiger des Westens* warmly applauded his Free-Soil stance. The newspaperman proudly took his place among the "four bad B's," as the anti-Benton press described Benton, Boernstein, Benjamin Gratz Brown, and Frank P. Blair.[32] The *St. Louis Union,* now in the hands of the pro-Benton editor Richard Phillips, also endorsed the senator's position. Phillips replaced Samuel Treat (soon to be appointed judge of the federal District Court for the Eastern District of Missouri), who returned to his law practice and joined the anti-Benton camp. Particularly strong opposition to Benton came from the slaveholding counties along the Missouri River. Audacious as ever, Benton campaigned vigorously in this enemy stronghold during the summer. On 1 September 1849, he dramatically attacked his opponents in their unofficial capital, Fayette, in Howard County. Addressing a hostile gathering on the grounds of Central College, he offered an imposing presence. Amid jeers and groans, the senator faced the crowd with a stern gaze. He removed his white broad-brimmed beaver hat with studied deliberation and then, slowly, removed his black silk gloves. For the next three hours he attacked the Jackson Resolutions as the product of an "odious, and treasonable doctrine" that would deliver to a minority the power to dictate to the majority. Line by line he dismantled the resolutions and subjected them to a withering assault. The audience listened respectfully but offered no expressions of support. After the Fayette speech he continued to tour the state, reiterating his argument as he went. After an extended visit in Jefferson City, he returned to St. Louis in October to address a convention of railroad promoters on his favorite themes, the material progress of the American Empire. After a tour of the state's Mississippi River counties north to the Iowa border and south to Cape Girardeau, he traveled up the Ohio River by steamboat to make his way back to Washington.

The drama of Benton's campaign attracted attention throughout the nation. The Ohio Free-Soil leader Salmon Portland Chase followed the battle intensely. Recently elected to the Senate as a Free-Soil Democrat, Chase looked to Benton with admiration. "Benton has maintained himself grandly," Chase wrote to fellow Ohio antislavery Democrat Edwin M. Stanton in July 1849. "When I see that old man standing up against slavery in the territories, just as Jefferson did in 1784, though not quite so emphatically . . . I am filled with admiration."[33] As the August 1850 state elections approached, Frank Blair worked hard in the pro-Benton camp and assured his brother Montgomery that Benton's "prospects appear to be brightening very much and our friends are taking heart and courage."[34]

Meanwhile, Benton met a new challenge in his opposition to the developing Compromise of 1850. In June, he took the Senate floor to explain why he opposed any further extension of slavery, rooting his argument in the principles of Jefferson. "In that school—that old Virginia school which I was taught to reverence—I found my principles . . . and adhere to them." He concurred with Jefferson on the necessity of colonization abroad as a condition for emancipation. The prospect of emancipation without colonization raised for Benton "the danger which the wise men of Virginia then saw and dreaded . . . the danger to both races from so large an emancipation." Jefferson "knew that the emancipation of the black slaves was not a mere question between master and slave—not a question of property merely—but a question of white and black—between races." Here Benton inserted in his printed speech a footnote quoting Jefferson to the effect that blacks could not be incorporated into the state. "There," he exclaimed, "the wisdom, not the philanthropy, of Virginia balked fifty years ago; there the wisdom of America balks now." And it was here, on the "question of the races," that he found "the largest objection to the extension of slavery." Slavery expansion threatened to confound the dilemma of race that Jefferson's generation and Benton's had been unable to resolve. "The incurability of the evil," he concluded, "is the greatest objection to the extension of slavery."[35]

As the various parts of the Compromise of 1850 came up for a vote, Benton labored to maintain his moderate course. He supported the admission of California as a free state but defected from the Free-Soilers to support the admission of the Utah and New Mexico Territories under the terms of the popular sovereignty doctrine. On the highly controversial issue of a new fugitive slave law, he did not cast a vote. He had tried to make the fugitive law "efficient and satisfactory," he said, but he had failed in the effort. Therefore, he "would neither vote for it nor against it." He viewed the new fugitive slave law as of little benefit to the South and "annoying to the free States from the manner of its execution." He supported the abolition of the slave trade in the District of Columbia. Shortly before adjourning at the end of September 1850, the Senate admitted two new members from California; one of them was Benton's son-in-law, John C. Frémont.[36]

At this chronological juncture, Benton later closed his political memoir, *Thirty Years' View*, with a lament. "A sectional question now divides the

Union," he wrote, "arraying one-half against the other, becoming more exasperating daily." Sectionalism had already destroyed the "benefits of the Union," he thought. "Unless checked," he concluded, it would "also destroy its form." He feared for the future of the Republic but consoled himself in the knowledge that he had "labored in his day and generation, to preserve and perpetuate the blessings of that Union and self-government which wise and good men gave us."[37]

With the adjournment of the Senate after the passage of the Compromise of 1850, Benton could devote his energies entirely to the fight in Missouri. He had fired a salvo from Washington in March 1850 when he repudiated efforts to reach an accommodation between himself and the proslavery wing of the Democratic Party. His anger at the supporters of the Jackson Resolutions remained white hot. "I would sooner sit in council with the 6,000 dead of cholera in St. Louis," he declared, "than go into convention with such a gang of scamps." In St. Louis, Benton supporters prepared for the 5 August state elections by launching a new campaign newspaper, *Old Bullion*. They also enjoyed the support of the *St. Louis Union,* the *Anzeiger des Westens,* and the *Inquirer.* His opponents found their voice in St. Louis in the *Metropolitan* and in the Whig *Missouri Republican.*

As the battle over Benton's reelection began in earnest, the senator returned to St. Louis in mid-October 1850. To his nervous supporters in the city he offered two addresses early in November. On 9 November he spoke in the rotunda of the courthouse, reasserting the themes that he had developed the previous summer. The second speech, given five days later at the invitation of the directors of the Mercantile Library, celebrated "The Progress of the Age." St. Louis, said Benton, stood at the crossroads of the continent. The railroads that would soon link the Atlantic and the Pacific, Hudson Bay and the Gulf of Mexico, would intersect in St. Louis. He predicted that the city would grow to 1 million inhabitants by the beginning of the twentieth century and that "machine power" would render the productive energy of "every operative" equal to that of "fifty men." In this speech, he blended the traditional themes of Jacksonian Democracy with a celebration of modern technology. The Jacksonian Democracy had championed the yeoman farmer and the independent artisan as the foundation of republican virtue and democratic equality. The language of Young America, which Benton employed in the Mercantile Library address, had been characteristically agrarian in its vision of the American continental empire. In

sharp contrast to the Southern Ultras who reacted against the social transformation of the industrial North, Benton reached out to Whigs on economic issues and included "the manufacturer" and "the merchant" with
the "labouring-man" and "the farmer" in his celebration of democracy in
the machine age.[38]

In the state legislature, Benton Democrats were nearly twice as strong as
the Southern Rights Democrats, but the Whigs held the balance of power. In
the selection of the speaker of the house, Whigs joined with anti-Benton
Democrats to elect the Whig candidate, an ominous development for the pro-
Benton forces. Henry S. Geyer, a proslavery Whig who had publicly accepted
the central proposition of the Jackson Resolutions, became Benton's chief
rival. Still, old party ties proved difficult to break. Finally, on 22 January 1851,
on the fortieth ballot, Whigs and anti-Benton Democrats coalesced around
Geyer. The senatorial career of Thomas Hart Benton had come to an end.

For the other three "Bad Bs," Frank Blair, Gratz Brown, and Henry
Boernstein, Benton's defeat marked the beginning of a new political era.
Benton had remained faithful to the Democratic Party despite the opposition he faced within it. In deference to him, the younger men had trimmed
their sails somewhat, but his defeat left them freer to build new political coa-
litions. The establishment of a new newspaper, the *Missouri Democrat*, marked
a first effort in this direction.

On 1 July 1852, a month before the state elections in August, Frank Blair
and Gratz Brown launched the *Missouri Democrat*. Unceasingly critical of
Calhoun and the Southern Rights wing of the Democratic Party, the *Democrat*
championed the cause of free labor as the bedrock of the Republic. Slavery and
the Slave Power, the *Democrat* (which emerged as the city's Republican newspaper) charged, functioned like the aristocracy of Europe to conspire to make
paupers of workingmen and to impose a despotism upon them. For the Blairs,
certainly, the cause of free labor did not imply emancipation or equal rights
for blacks. But free labor did associate the cause of the true democracy with
a worldwide struggle for liberty. Frank and Montgomery Blair were instrumental in persuading the Hungarian republican patriot, Louis Kossuth, to
visit St. Louis in 1852. In the August elections, Benton won a seat in the U.S.
House of Representatives; and Brown and Frank Blair ran fourth and eighth
among twenty candidates seeking the ten seats allotted to St. Louis in the state
legislature. With Free-Soil Democrats evidently in the ascendancy, Montgomery Blair moved to Washington, D.C., in 1853.[39]

Benton's election to Congress enabled him to maintain his presence in

Washington. There he matched his opposition to the Compromise of 1850 with an equally dramatic opposition to the Kansas-Nebraska Act. Introduced in January 1854, with the principal sponsorship of Illinois senator Stephen A. Douglas, the act extended the principle of popular sovereignty to the last unorganized territory of the continental United States. Douglas's bill proposed the creation of two territories. Kansas lay directly west of Missouri; the much larger Nebraska Territory, created by the Kansas-Nebraska Act, stretched north to the Canadian border. Douglas's Southern supporters assumed that under popular sovereignty, Kansas would be organized as a slave state. Few observers doubted that the Nebraska Territory, lying west of Iowa and Minnesota, would develop into free states. However, the entire Kansas-Nebraska Territory had been set aside for free states by the Missouri Compromise of 1820. Douglas's bill specifically called for the repeal of that measure. Benton had supported the 1820 compromise, and in his opposition to the Compromise of 1850 he had made it plain that he opposed popular sovereignty or any other proposed solution to the territorial issue that permitted any further spread of slavery. With equal fervor, he opposed the Kansas-Nebraska Act. When Douglas's bill passed both houses of Congress in May 1854, Benton stood unequivocally with the antislavery camp, and Missouri voters rejected his bid for reelection in August 1854.[40]

In St. Louis, the Benton Democrats had begun to explore collaboration with Whigs, led by attorneys James O. Broadhead and Edward Bates, who opposed slavery extension. Broadhead had moved from Virginia to St. Charles County, Missouri, in 1837. Bates befriended the younger man, employed him in his household as a tutor, and directed his study of the law. In 1846 Bates moved to St. Louis, taking residence with his wife and nine children in a three-story house at the corner of Sixteenth and Chestnut Streets. In the same year, Broadhead was elected to the state assembly. Although Bates opposed any alliance of Whigs with proslavery Democrats to defeat Benton, Broadhead, in the state senate, supported the proslavery Whig Henry S. Geyer for the Senate seat. Somewhat reluctantly, Bates came to Benton's support. He attended Benton's October 1849 address in the rotunda of the courthouse and collaborated with him to promote a railroad to the Pacific. Soon after Geyer's election to the Senate, Broadhead, too, began to view Benton in a different light. Bates attended a meeting in St. Louis (called by Broadhead) to organize the anti-Geyer Whigs.[41] With this Whig support, Frank Blair and Gratz Brown began to lay the foundations for the Republican Party. In the midst of the debate over the Kansas-Nebraska Act, Brown assumed responsibility for the editorship of the *Missouri Demo-*

crat. In August, as Benton went down to defeat in his congressional district, both Brown and Blair won reelection to the state legislature. Politicians on both sides of the sectional fight next turned their attention to the state and national campaigns of 1856.[42]

An early test of strength for the contending factions came in Missouri in August when the state held its congressional and state elections. In the battle for the governorship, the antislavery forces rallied once more behind Benton. The St. Louis lawyer Trusten Polk led proslavery Democrats and succeeded in defeating Benton and a proslavery nativist running on the American Party ticket. Benton ran a distant third, gaining less than 30 percent of the vote; Polk won, with slightly more than 40 percent. This proved to be Benton's last political contest.[43] In failing health and with his political base badly eroded, he retired from an active life in politics and devoted himself to writing his memoirs. An ebullient proslavery Democracy then elected Polk to the U.S. Senate (thereby replacing the proslavery Whig, Henry S. Geyer, whose term had expired).[44] Antislavery forces scored a significant victory, however, as Frank Blair won election to Congress, defeating two opponents, a nativist and an anti-Benton Democrat. Together, Blair's opponents carried nearly 60 percent of the vote, an indication of the difficulties that lay ahead. Gratz Brown also won another term in the state legislature. In the fall presidential contest of 1856, however, Benton supported James Buchanan over his son-in-law John C. Frémont, the first presidential standard bearer of the Republican Party. A disappointed Frank Blair looked on as Frémont went down to defeat in St. Louis and in Missouri. The antislavery coalition that Blair struggled to build had yet to take shape. Too many Benton men refused to support Frémont and too many Whigs voted for the nativist candidate, Millard Fillmore. Blair predicted, correctly, that many of the Fillmore men would be won over to the Republican Party. As for the Benton men, continued defeat in state elections hastened their transition into the Republican Party.[45]

As Benton faded from the political scene, two other St. Louisans, Dred and Harriet Scott, rose to national prominence. At Roswell Field's urging, Montgomery Blair agreed to present the *Dred Scott* case to the Supreme Court. John Sanford attracted equally talented and prominent legal counsel. Hugh Garland, who had previously defended Sanford in Missouri, fell ill and retired from the case. Henry S. Geyer, then finishing his Senate term, joined the prominent constitutional lawyer, Senator Reverdy Johnson of Maryland, as Sanford's attorney.[46]

Blair filed his brief on 7 February 1856. In it he argued that Missouri law, by requiring "free negroes or mulattoes" to "produce a certificate of citizenship from some one of the United States," implied a recognition of Negro citizenship and with it the right to sue in federal court. In the original site of the Supreme Court, in a chamber below the Senate, oral arguments began on Monday 11 February. Blair spoke first and was followed on Tuesday by Henry Geyer and on Wednesday by Reverdy Johnson. On Friday the Court allowed Blair to conclude the remarks he had been unable to complete on Monday. The Court met twice to discuss the case and on 28 February adjourned for a month. When it resumed its deliberations in December it announced that it again wanted to hear arguments from both sides.

Before the Court heard arguments for the second time, Blair obtained the services of George Ticknor Curtis, a prominent Massachusetts attorney. Curtis was a familiar figure before the Court. His first wife (who died in 1848) was the daughter of the late Supreme Court justice Joseph Story. His brother, Benjamin R. Curtis, also sat on the Court and drafted the principal dissent in the Dred Scott case.[47] When arguments resumed in December 1856, the Court allotted twelve hours for the four attorneys. In a heated political environment and in the face of Chief Justice Taney's determination to use the Dred Scott case to resolve fundamental constitutional issues concerning slavery, efforts to maintain judicial restraint collapsed. Justice Samuel Nelson of New York attempted to draft a narrow opinion that relied on *Strader* to uphold the Missouri Supreme Court's decision in *Scott v. Emerson*. In this approach, Dred Scott would remain a slave but the Court would avoid the highly controversial issues of citizenship and the question of federal authority over slavery in the territories. Taney opposed this effort and gained support from Justice James M. Wayne of Georgia. Together, Taney and Wayne drafted a decision that straightforwardly sustained the Southern Rights view that African Americans (free and slave) could not be citizens of the United States and that the federal government had no authority to bar slave property from the territories. Taney and Wayne carried the other three Southern members of the Court and successfully appealed to President-elect James Buchanan to use his influence with his fellow Pennsylvanian, Justice Robert Grier, to join the Southern majority and avoid a strictly sectional decision.

When the Supreme Court handed down its decision in *Dred Scott v. Sanford* (1857), Taney offered the "Opinion of the Court."[48] As far as the Missouri litigation was concerned, Taney ruled that Dred Scott was not a citizen of

Missouri and, therefore, was not entitled to sue in federal court. Consequently, the lower federal court had had no jurisdiction in the matter. According to *Strader,* argued Taney, Scott's status in Missouri could be determined only by Missouri law. The Missouri Supreme Court's decision "that Scott and his family upon their return were not free" stood. Of broader national concern were the central issues of citizenship and the status of slaves in the territories. The chief justice insisted that citizenship existed at two levels: one determined by the states, the other by the federal government. Citizenship granted by a state did not extend beyond the borders of the state. State citizenship alone did not permit an individual to bring suit in federal court. The federal Constitution, Taney insisted, recognized a "perpetual and impassible barrier" between whites and blacks. This barrier defined blacks as a "subordinate and inferior class of being," with no natural rights. Slaves, by definition, were not citizens and had no standing before the federal courts. Taney insisted that free blacks possessed only those rights granted to them by the states. The impassible racial barrier that Taney found in the Constitution forever prevented them from being citizens of the United States and bringing suit in federal court.

This ended Scott's freedom suit. At this juncture, Taney might well have declared the case closed. Instead, intent on bringing judicial resolution to a deepening political debate, he pressed forward to define the federal government's authority over slavery in the territories. Part of Scott's claim to freedom rested on his residence at Fort Snelling in a territory reserved for free states by the Missouri Compromise. Taney ruled that Congress had acted unconstitutionally when it prohibited slavery north of thirty-six degrees, thirty minutes north latitude. He acknowledged that the federal government might acquire new territories and govern them, but in doing so it acted for the common benefit of the people of the United States. The Fifth Amendment, he insisted, obliged Congress to respect the property rights of all citizens, and this protection extended to slave property recognized by law in the Southern states.

Taney's sweeping decision immediately became part of an angry political debate over slavery that swelled the ranks of the new Republican Party. The decision briefly brought Benton back into the political fray. He drew on all his years of struggle against the influence of Calhoun to draft a detailed and scathing denunciation of the Taney decision.[49]

Scholarly analysis of the Taney decision has been almost entirely negative. Many scholars insist that his decision, beyond the issue of Scott's status as a slave and his inability to sue in federal court, did not carry the weight of law because a majority of the justices did not explicitly agree on any other issues. Taney's argument is also judged to be weakest on the issue of citizenship. The chief justice's effort to locate a racial barrier in the Constitution, when the drafters of the document carefully avoided using the words "race," "slave," or "slavery," rested on little more than his own convictions regarding race. The idea that citizenship existed at two levels, state and national, required a loose reading of Article 4, section 2 of the federal Constitution. There it refers specifically to "The Citizens of each State" and declares that they "shall be entitled to all Privileges and Immunities of Citizens in the several States." As Justice Benjamin Curtis observed in his dissent, national citizenship followed state citizenship: if blacks were citizens of a state they were, in the meaning of the Constitution, citizens of the United States. Damning as well was the overtly political tone and purpose of Taney's decision. Blurring any distinction between politics and jurisprudence, Taney embraced the Southern Rights claim that the national government could only enforce and never limit state-recognized property rights in slaves. If Taney's decision were law, Southern Rights doctrine had triumphed and the Free-Soil planks of the Republican Party platform became unconstitutional. Far from settling the issues brought before the Court, Taney's decision inflamed sectional passions and helped to ensure that a constitutional debate over slavery rose to the level of a crisis in constitutional government.

The *Dred Scott* decision ended eleven years of litigation, but it did not, finally, determine Scott's and his family's status. John Sanford probably never learned of his victory: he had been committed to a mental institution in New York City and died within weeks of the decision. In St. Louis, on 17 March 1857, the parties in the still-pending circuit court case of *Dred Scott v. Irene Emerson* waived a jury, and Judge Alexander Hamilton, following the recent Supreme Court decision, found that Irene Emerson "is not guilty" of trespass as "the plaintiff's declaration alleged." But Irene Emerson made no effort to reclaim her slaves from the St. Louis sheriff in whose custody they had been held for the past seven years. In November 1850, having moved to Springfield, Massachusetts, she had married another physician, Dr. Calvin Clifford Chaffee. When Irene Emerson won the legal right to regain her slave property, her husband had just taken his seat as a Republican member of the House of Representatives (Chaffee's term began on 4 March 1857, two days before Taney delivered his decision). Not surprisingly, Chaffee became the object of withering scorn. He had first won election to Congress on the American Party ticket in 1854 and had been reelected as a Republican in 1856. As a Republican, he had made public expressions of antislavery, even abolitionist sentiments, while he kept secret his wife's involvement in the *Dred Scott* case. Now eager to be clear of the embarrassment, Chaffee faced a dilemma. Because he was not a citizen of Missouri, he could not manumit Dred Scott and his family. As the congressman faced his tormentors with the implausible claim that he had no knowledge of or part in the *Dred Scott* case, his wife insisted upon and received the wages earned by the Scotts that had been held by the sheriff during the lengthy period of litigation. Finally, lawyers representing the Blow family in Missouri and the Chaffees in Massachusetts drafted a quit claim deed that transferred the Scott family to Taylor Blow of St. Louis.[50] At Blow's direction, Roswell Field's law partner drew up emancipation papers, and on 26 May 1857, Judge Alexander Hamilton declared Scott and his family free. Dred Scott died 17 September 1858 and was buried in the Wesleyan Cemetery, then on the western edge of the city.[51]

As the Supreme Court delivered its opinion in the *Dred Scott* case, Frank Blair and Gratz Brown continued the difficult work of building an antislavery coalition in St. Louis. But they soon found themselves without the venerable presence of Thomas Hart Benton. After his political defeats, Benton engaged in a series of successful publishing projects in which he maintained a steady drumbeat against what he saw as the treachery of Calhoun and the calumny of those who supported Stephen A. Douglas in the repeal of the Missouri Compromise. He completed his memoirs, *Thirty Years' View*, in May 1856. In November of that year his publisher brought out the first volume of another Benton work, his *Abridgement of the Debates of Congress*. Future volumes brought this digest up to 1850. In winter and spring 1856–1857, Benton completed a strenuous lecture tour in the Northeast. By summer 1857, he had resumed work on the *Abridgement* and ambitiously planned a third volume of *Thirty Years' View*. His publisher urged him to write a popular biography of Andrew Jackson as well.

Sickness first struck Benton in September 1857 as a partial blockage of the bowels. By October his pain had eased somewhat, and he resumed his writing, concentrating on the "unpleasant . . . but unavoidable" task of denouncing Taney's *Dred Scott* decision.[52] Shortly after his seventy-sixth birthday, in March 1858, severe pain struck him again, making "lying down . . . my only practical easy posture." He could eat only food of "the simplest kind, as milk and rice, and it cold with ice." On 4 April Secretary of State Lewis Cass paid his respects to the old Democratic Party faithful. Two days later, Francis P. Blair visited his old friend and found him "in extremis." Blair deeply admired Benton's "stoicism" although it seemed "almost superhuman." As Benton lay dying, Blair thought that his "patience and tenderness . . . and love for his friends increases as vitality decreases." On 9 April President Buchanan visited and heard Benton whisper that they were friends despite their many differences. On the morning of 10 April 1858, Benton died.[53]

Gradually, antislavery politics took hold in St. Louis. Early in 1857, John Wimer, known at the time as an emancipation Democrat, won election as mayor. Wimer's victory seemed to bode well for future antislavery victories.[54] Nevertheless, the road ahead remained rough. In the August state elections of 1858, Frank Blair lost his congressional seat in a second three-way race. Blair charged that his principal opponent, the proslavery Democrat John R. Barrett, employed an "army of Irish Bullies" to keep antislavery voters from the polls. With help from Montgomery Blair in Washington, Frank contested the results. The challenge proceeded slowly in Congress. Early in 1860, the House Committee on Elections took up the case and on 8 June 1860, the full House voted ninety-three to ninety-one to seat Blair over Barrett. Blair served briefly in the Thirty-sixth Congress, from 8 June to 25 June, but then resigned to take his case to the voters in the August 1860 elections. Again Blair ran against Barrett, this time on two separate ballots. One ballot determined who would fill the vacancy in the Thirty-sixth Congress created by Blair's resignation. The second ballot selected a representative to the Thirty-seventh Congress, beginning March 1861.[55]

During Blair's fight to regain his House seat, he and Gratz Brown began to part company politically and personally. In 1859 Blair revived in a particularly strident way the Jeffersonian ideal of a white republic. In an aggressive public campaign, he linked emancipation with empire and called for the colonization of African Americans in zones of U.S. control in Central and South America. Gratz Brown, who had failed to win reelection to the state legislature in 1856, began to speak cautiously, but without preconditions and without Blair's racial imagery, about emancipation. In the same year, the Blair loyalist, Peter Foy, replaced Brown as editor of the *Democrat* amid some criticism of Brown's financial management of the paper. This break marked the beginning of an increasingly bitter estrangement between Blair and Brown that lasted for fifteen years. The issue of race lay at the core of their disagreement. Blair's racial views became increasingly bitter as the Civil War brought emancipation without colonization. Early in the 1850s, Edward L. Pierce, a confidant of Massachusetts's senator Charles Sumner, met Blair during a visit to St. Louis. He described Blair as a Southern man, "one of your generous, liberal, chivalric fellows." But no one should confuse Blair's antislavery sentiments with those of Sumner's. Pierce concluded that Blair did not belong "to that class of stern natures who are destined to be reformers of society." By contrast, the New York abolitionist Joshua Leavitt described Gratz Brown, who shared Blair's Kentucky origins, as "one of the first minds of the country." Brown embraced gradual emancipation in Missouri in a speech delivered in the general assembly in February 1857. He later supported immediate abolition, together with Negro suffrage. Blair only grudgingly accepted emancipation in Missouri, and he fiercely opposed the Fourteenth and Fifteenth Amendments because they prohibited the states from discriminating against persons on the basis of race. Blair insisted on a geographical separation of the races. The only solution to the sectional problem, he wrote Senator Sumner in 1863, lay in the removal of emancipated blacks to "vacant territories . . . protected by our flag."[56] By the mid-1870s, when Blair and Brown found themselves together in the Liberal Republican fight against Radical rule in Missouri, the old disputes receded and their personal friendship resumed.

On 10 March 1860, the Missouri Republican Party held its convention at the Mercantile Library in St. Louis. Frank Blair, Gratz Brown, and Peter Foy led a delegation of eighteen Missouri Republicans to the Chicago national convention.[57] The new party faced vociferous and violent opposition, and Blair began organizing the Wide Awakes as a paramilitary counterforce to the hecklers and thugs who repeatedly tried to break up Republican meetings. Outside the city, he faced violence wherever he attempted to speak. At a speech in Ironton, a railhead south of St. Louis, 300 Wide Awakes accompanied Blair by train to provide protection. The St. Louis lawyer William V. N. Bay was in the party and reported that with the uniformed Wide Awakes at his side, Blair spoke for nearly two hours without interruption. When the Marion County Republican Samuel T. Glover invited Blair to speak at Hannibal, however, the congressman arrived at that railroad junction north of St. Louis without a Wide Awake guard. Hecklers repeatedly interrupted and threatened him, and Blair made no more forays outside of St. Louis until after the Civil War.[58]

3

"The Union, Without an *If*"

THOMAS HART BENTON DIED a loyal Democrat in 1858. But even by the mid-1850s, many old Benton Democrats in St. Louis regarded the national Democratic Party as hopelessly dominated by Southern Rights zealots. Led by Frank Blair and Gratz Brown, these Benton men sought out political alliances with antislavery Whigs and entered a new political coalition, the Republican Party. In 1856 the national Republican Party slogan—Free-Soil, Free Labor, Free Men—very nearly united the free states in opposition to the spread of slavery into the western territories. In 1860 the Republicans succeeded in this regard, and without winning a single electoral vote from a slave state (Missouri included), they elected Abraham Lincoln president of the United States.

During these years, as Republicans gained strength in St. Louis, most Missourians remained loyal to the Democratic Party. Like Benton, however, most of them opposed its Southern Rights wing. Missourians voted for James Buchanan in 1856, hoping, as did Benton, that this staid Pennsylvania Democrat and former diplomat would rise above sectional divisions and maintain a united party and a united nation. In 1860, as St. Louis voted for Lincoln, the state supported the Unionist Democrat Stephen A. Douglas over his Southern Rights Democratic rival John C. Breckinridge. For the new leaders of the Missouri Democratic Party—the men who had defeated Benton—the moderate temperament of the state raised difficulties. Claiborne Jackson and his St. Louis ally, attorney Thomas Reynolds, a native of South Carolina, had made their Southern Rights sympathies plain in the campaign against Benton. As they prepared to run for state office in 1860, Jackson and Reynolds faced strong pressure from Nathaniel Paschall, editor of the *Republican,* to declare for Stephen Douglas. In the campaign, Jackson and Reynolds voiced public support for the Unionist Democrat, and they won election as moderate Democrats. However, as soon as the opportunity arose to forge a link between Southern Rights and secession in Missouri, they eagerly took up the task.

Jackson and Reynolds were not alone in their eagerness to abandon the political center. Although Missouri held to a moderate course, much of the nation did not. Throughout the country the once-hallowed principle of accommodation and compromise between free states and slave states lost its dominant political appeal. Douglas, the last of the great compromisers and chairman of the Senate Committee on the Territories, successfully applied his popular sovereignty remedy to the slavery issue when Congress passed the Kansas-Nebraska Act in 1854. He expected popular sovereignty to cool political passions by allowing new states, as they entered the Union, to decide whether they wanted to permit slavery or not. To his dismay Kansas-Nebraska ignited a firestorm that destroyed the political order he had worked to preserve. After Kansas-Nebraska, the sectional divide in the Democratic Party grew deeper and wider, and the free states began to unite around the antislavery doctrine of the new Republican Party. For Missourians, popular sovereignty failed in an alarming manner. The Missouri-Kansas border became a battlefield, as proslavery western Missourians and Free State settlers took up arms to settle the issue of slavery in the new territory.

On the Missouri-Kansas border latent sectional hostilities erupted into guerrilla war. Elsewhere wars of words became angrier and prompted acts of violence. In the Senate, Charles Sumner of Massachusetts discerned and decried a proslavery "Crime Against Kansas." In a lengthy and bitterly angry speech, delivered over two days (19 and 20 May 1856), he condemned the Missourians and their proslavery allies as barbarians. In a previous debate, Senator Andrew Butler of South Carolina, his speech slurred by a recent stroke, had interjected critical comments on more than thirty occasions as Sumner spoke. Sumner now turned his scorn on his proslavery rival, who had left Washington for his South Carolina home. "The Senator from South Carolina had read many books on chivalry," he said, "and believes himself a chivalrous knight, with sentiments of honor and courage." What Butler took to be virtue, he continued, the rest of the world scorned as vice. "Of course," said Sumner, "he has chosen a mistress to whom he has made his vows and who, though ugly to others, is always lovely to him,—though polluted in the sight of the world, is chaste in his sight: I mean the harlot Slavery." Sumner again turned on Butler: "With regret I come again upon the Senator from South Carolina who, omnipresent in this debate, overflows with rage . . . and, with incoherent phrase, discharges the loose expectoration of his speech."[1] On 21 May, the day after Sumner concluded his Senate speech, Missouri guerrillas (as if to rebuke Sumner's cruel invective) raided the Free State settlement of Lawrence, Kansas, looting and burning as they rampaged through town. The day after the Lawrence raid, Senator Butler's nephew, Congressman Preston Brooks of South Carolina, approached Sumner from behind and caned him into unconsciousness at his desk on the Senate floor. The guerrilla attack on Lawrence and Preston Brooks's attack on Charles Sumner eroded an already weakened political center. For growing numbers on both sides of the sectional divide, the time for debate and compromise had ended.

In St. Louis the political struggle over slavery in the territories produced the city's last formal duel. The principals were two long-standing political adversaries, U.S. Attorney Thomas Reynolds and Gratz Brown, editor of the *Missouri Democrat*. For Republicans in St. Louis, Reynolds posed particularly difficult problems. A graduate of the University of Virginia in 1838, he received a doctorate in law from the University of Heidelberg in 1842. Fluent in German and well-read in German literature, he socialized easily with the German intelligentsia in St. Louis. In politics, he drew substantial support from German voters. In their community, as Henry Boernstein recalled, the rumor circulated that Reynolds was a German-Bohemian, born in Prague, with Jewish ancestry. However, Boernstein discerned in Reynolds's spoken German an "Anglo-Saxon accent" and doubted the rumor. Nevertheless, Boernstein found Reynolds to be a congenial companion although, over time, "the slavery question gradually alienated us . . . and in the end we stood against one another as armed enemies."[2]

Gratz Brown, a Kentuckian by birth, had joined his cousin Frank Blair in St. Louis to support Benton and the antislavery opposition to Southern Rights. By 1856 Brown had allied the *Democrat* with the new Republican Party and, in the fall elections, supported the presidential candidacy of John C. Frémont. Biting attacks in the *Democrat* had nearly resulted in a challenge from Reynolds in April 1854, but friends intervened and persuaded both men not to make their political differences personal. When the attacks resumed in March 1855, Reynolds challenged the *Democrat*'s editor to a duel. Brown immediately accepted but soon announced, through his second, his very unusual terms: "The common American Rifle with open sights, round ball not over one ounce, at eighty yards." Brown may have taken the idea of dueling with hunting rifles from James Hackett's popular comedic stage character, Nimrod Wildfire, a western "roarer" who challenged aristocratic rivals to similar modes of personal combat. In any case, as Brown undoubtedly

expected, Reynolds refused to accept these terms, rejecting the rifle as a bar-
barous weapon for a duel. And at a distance of eighty feet, Reynolds's short-
sightedness would deny him any chance of hitting his target. Reynolds found
a degree of satisfaction in making the terms of the duel public. Nevertheless,
with Brown unwilling to modify his conditions and with Reynolds unwilling
to accept them, a fight had been avoided.

By summer 1856, amid growing sectional violence, a fight became inevitable. With what Reynolds described as "unblushing effrontery" the *Democrat* charged that he and the Southern Rights Democrats "placed Germans
and Irish on a level with the negroes." What Reynolds found offensive was
an argument that turned the powerful issue of race against the defenders of
slavery. The proposition had been adapted from the Jacksonian Democracy
and turned to antislavery purposes by Frank Blair. Jacksonians had appealed
to Northern workingmen with the reasoning that their aristocratic Whig
opponents embraced abolitionism and intended to place white workingmen
on an equal footing with the Negro. Frank Blair's father, Francis P. Blair (living in Silver Spring, Maryland), had argued bluntly in 1841 as editor of the
Washington, D.C., *Globe* that Whigs were an "unfeeling aristocracy" who
sought the "poor white man's degradation" by seeking equality for blacks:
they intended "to put the poor white man on a level with the negro."[3]

In the late 1850s, Frank Blair adapted his father's racial argument to the
Free-Soil critique of the slave South. Slavery degraded free labor, because
wherever slaveholders took their human property, free white men were forced
to compete with them for a livelihood. But the vigor of free labor would prevail over the torpor of slave labor. It was the "Destiny of the Races" in the
United States that the Negro, like the Indian, would disappear from the "tem-
perate zone." Blair envisioned a tropical black republic on the isthmus of
Central America, settled by emancipated American slaves and emigrating free
blacks. Protected by and loyal to the United States, the new black republic
would secure American interests in the region at the same time that the removal of Negroes would end slavery and leave the United States the exclu-
sive domain of the Anglo-Saxon race.[4]

In the pages of the *Democrat,* Brown developed this argument to depict
the proslavery Democrats as the enemy of free white labor and to drive a wedge
between Reynolds and his German supporters. As a defender of slavery in
Missouri, wrote Brown, Reynolds placed immigrant Germans and Irish on
the same level as blacks because he forced the immigrant to compete with

the slave for work. It was, Reynolds thought, an outrageous argument, and he responded to it with a series of insults intended to force Brown to issue a challenge for a duel. Reynolds began by reminding St. Louisans of the dispute a year earlier. At that time Brown had "*refused to fight* the moment he was called on to come within *visible* distance." That act of cowardice, he continued, had made Brown "a public butt" of blackface humor in the St. Louis theater (the comic spectacle of a duel with hunting rifles had been incorporated into "the songs of the Campbell Minstrels").[5] Insults from Reynolds continued, and on 18 August Brown offered the challenge for which Reynolds had been waiting. He accepted eagerly and selected dueling pistols at twelve paces (thirty-six feet). Because state law made dueling a crime, the principals selected as the site for their private meeting an island in the Mississippi River near Selma, Missouri, about forty miles below St. Louis. On 26 August they faced each other with pistols in their right hands. On the command "fire," they discharged their weapons. Reynolds's ball struck Brown in the leg, just below the knee. Brown's shot missed its mark. With Brown incapacitated, the seconds quickly ended the affair. Brown's second wrote a note describing both men as "brave and honorable Gentlemen," along with the suggestion that the principals agree to "withdraw . . . all communications between the parties of an offensive character, and that they shall hereafter meet and recognize each other as Gentlemen." Reynolds's second endorsed it ("I concur in the above suggestion"), and the affair of honor ended. An era had ended as well.[6]

Brown returned to St. Louis wounded but politically undaunted. Indeed, for the fledgling St. Louis Republican Party, 1856 proved to be a banner year: Frank Blair won election to Congress as a Republican, and John How, a Republican and one of the city's wealthiest citizens (until he went bankrupt during the war in the wake of a speculative venture), won election as mayor.[7] Moreover, Gratz Brown won election to the Missouri legislature and offered to a wider audience the racial argument that had incensed Reynolds. In February 1857 Brown rose on the floor of the Missouri House to oppose a proslavery resolution that declared emancipation in Missouri to be "inexpedient, impolitic, unwise, and unjust": "I believe that the African race, and its concomitant slavery, will go down and vanish in these United States as the Indian race has gone down and vanished beneath the tread and march of the Anglo-Saxon. . . . I believe that the demand of the white man for labor, and a field for his enterprise and exertion, will drive away slavery. . . . The labor question will swallow up the slavery question." Slavery would die because free white men would abide neither a system of bound labor nor the proximity of an inferior race. Brown acknowledged that Missourians would never "undertake to abolish the system of slavery . . . as a mere act of humanity to the slaves." Instead, slavery would be abolished "out of regard for the white man and not the negro." Free labor proved superior to slave labor wherever the two came into direct competition. In Missouri, and throughout the nation, "slavery has receded before the advance of the white race." Brown imagined himself standing on the steps of the state capitol in Jefferson City watching the "gangs of slaves driven along on their route to Texas." The imagined sight represented the inevitable decline of slavery in Missouri. To the national Republican emphasis on the dignity of free labor, Brown echoed Blair and stressed also the destiny of the white race. "When white labor shall have gained the ascendancy, the respect, the development that it needs, slavery will linger, only as the Indian races now linger, in the Territories. . . . If you would know the true foundations of the riches and greatness of St. Louis, you must . . . witness . . . the laboring classes struggling on in the daily avocations of life." Slavery denied the white workingman his dignity and the white race its destiny.[8]

When Benton died in 1858, much of his ambition for St. Louis and Missouri remained unfulfilled. The grand highway to the Pacific was still a dream. The Mississippi River at St. Louis had not yet been bridged. Benton's body arrived at the railroad terminus on the east bank of the Mississippi on 14 April and was carried to St. Louis by ferryboat. On 15 April an honor guard escorted the casket to the Mercantile Library. There the former senator lay in state, "lofty, tranquil, and gentle" in Gratz Brown's description. On 16 April, after a funeral service at the Second Presbyterian Church, Benton was interred at Bellefontaine Cemetery on the northern edge of the city.[9]

By 1858 the political reorganization in St. Louis that Benton had resisted was well under way. The new Republican coalition proved to be particularly attractive to a newer class of merchants and manufacturers. Prominent among this group was Barton Able, who had arrived in St. Louis from southern Illinois in 1840. As a lad of seventeen he first found work as a clerk on riverboats plying the Illinois River. Within a few years, he had risen in rank to captain and navigated the Missouri River. With experience in the river trade, he opened a successful commission house in St. Louis (at the corner of Pine and Commercial Streets). Success in business opened the door to an active public life. Able won election as a Benton Democrat to the state legislature in 1856. In the same year he served as a delegate to the Democratic Party's national convention in Cincinnati and supported Benton for the presidential nomination. Following Benton's death, Able moved into the Republican coalition and served as a delegate to the Chicago convention in 1860. There he initially supported the presidential nomination of Edward Bates before joining the emerging majority for Abraham Lincoln. During the early years of the Civil War, Able's knowledge of river transportation served the federal cause well. In spring 1861, General Nathaniel Lyon placed him in charge of transportation as federal forces moved up the Missouri River to take control of Jefferson City and to confront and defeat Claiborne Jackson's state militia forces at Boonville. In August Able organized transportation on the Mississippi River as General John C. Frémont moved men and supplies south to reinforce the federal garrison at Cairo, Illinois, at the confluence of the Ohio and Mississippi Rivers.[10]

The older St. Louis elite, whose wealth had been tied to the fur trade and land speculation, largely remained outside the Republican fold. It was not simply coincidental that the former city residence of Bartholomew Berthold served as the headquarters of Southern Rights Democrats and their Minute Men militia during the secession crisis. Berthold had married the sister of his business partner, Pierre Chouteau Jr., and he exemplified the Southern ties of the older St. Louis elite.[11] Few of its members became outright secessionists, but many, like Robert Campbell, whose wealth had also been established in the fur trade, took their stand as conditional Unionists during the secession crisis. Campbell embraced the proslavery compromise course outlined by Kentucky senator John J. Crittenden. In the conditional Unionist camp as well were scions of old St. Louis families, including the banker James H. Lucas and his business partner Charles P. Chouteau (owners of Chouteau, Harrison, and Valle Foundry and Rolling Mills). Sharing the conditional Unionist perspective were other leading men of Southern birth, including George R. Taylor, a Virginian and president of the Pacific Railroad, and the Kentucky-born wholesale grocer Derrick A. January.[12]

The fact that the "Dutch" (as nativist St. Louisans called the German immigrants) were overwhelmingly antislavery and Republican lent an ethnic dimension to sectional politics in St. Louis. To those sympathetic to the Southern cause, and to many of the conditional Unionists as well, the Germans seemed to be an alien and dangerous class. In St. Louis, as in other

Northern cities, nativist fears generated outbreaks of mob violence in the 1850s. In 1858 German and Yankee voters elected Oliver Filley mayor; he won reelection to a newly created two-year term in 1859. In the fall 1860 elections, Southern sympathizers and conditional Unionists watched, often with sullen anger, as Germans paraded through the streets in the paramilitary garb of the Republican Wide Awakes and as German and Yankee voters delivered the city to the national Republican Party.

Nativist prejudice tainted the unconditional Unionist camp as well. Henry Boernstein, editor of the *Anzeiger des Westens,* sensed in Union commander Nathaniel Lyon the disdain and distrust of a native-born New Englander. Lyon arrived in St. Louis from the Missouri-Kansas border with strong antislavery views that tied him to the Republicans. As a New England Protestant, he probably disapproved of the lager-drinking, "Sabbath-breaking" habits of the Germans, and he probably recoiled from the Germans' tenacious pride in their language and culture. But he could not help but recognize that the Germans constituted the core of Union support in St. Louis. And, like most Republicans, Lyon found that his antislavery and anti-Southern views subsumed his nativist bias. He thus worked with the Germans to hold St. Louis for the Union.

For their part, German leaders viewed the secession crisis as an opportunity to exercise openly and fully their rights and responsibilities as citizens in the Republic. The Republican Party provided the means by which Germans could act publicly and politically in collaboration with native-born Americans. Editors of the German-language newspapers urged their readers to act boldly and bravely. Equivocation in a time of crisis would only weaken the German community and encourage a nativist reaction against them. These editors reminded readers that the Republican Party shunned the nativist (or Know-Nothing) taint of its Whig antecedents and embraced the Free-Soil doctrine of the Benton Democrats. Approvingly, the editor of the *Anzeiger des Westens* noted that "the slightest suspicion of inclination to Know-nothingism has been cleared away from the Republican party."[13] German political leader Friedrich Muench reported with pride from the Republican convention in June 1860 that "the Germans were the only immigrant group represented at the Chicago Convention." He told the readers of the *Anzeiger des Westens* that "German participation in the party of progress is assured for all time to come if we determine to proceed with tact and moderation." Muench added that "ethnic separatist organizations will not work." The

Republicans would not deny Germans access to political influence "if we act as American citizens, but they will oppose us if we try to act as if we were something alien." Participation in the Republican Party promised to make Americans of German immigrants, a prospect that Muench welcomed:

> It is more necessary with the passage of time for more of us to participate routinely in English debate, since they will not care what we argue among ourselves in German. It is not necessary for us to lose our German character, but it is extremely important that we keep it pure without making ourselves continuously obvious in an improper manner. Our mission is difficult, but the goal that stands before us is doubly worth the effort.[14]

The first Republican ticket in Missouri included three men of German birth. One was Arnold Krekel, the editor of the *St. Charles Demokrat*, who had immigrated to farm country just north and west of St. Louis in the 1830s. A slave owner, he was also an ardent Republican and led a Home Guard unit known as Krekel's Dutch. He was the Republican Party's candidate for state attorney general in 1860. Henry Boernstein joined on the ticket as a candidate for the office of superintendent of the St. Louis public schools. Also on the ticket was Friedrich Muench, who ran for a place on the St. Louis Board of Public Works. The *Anzeiger des Westens* urged its readers to seize the day. "It is obvious that there has never been a more propitious occasion for our party to organize across the entire state than right now," the editor opined. "Everywhere the fragments of the old parties are feuding." Most of the native-born Americans who had opposed German political participation in the past were now devoted Republicans and eager to win the support of German voters in the fight against the Slave Power. The nativists of the old parties were "secure in the notion that the votes which go to the Republican ticket will weaken their opponents." This outcome had the happy consequence that when Germans went to the polls to voice their vote, "all the personal danger for Republicans when voting had disappeared."[15]

Krekel's prominence on the Missouri Republican ballot undoubtedly contributed to the party's electoral success in St. Louis County.[16] But he also served as a reminder to Germans that the Republican Party was not a party of abolitionism. Carl L. Bernays, the editor of the *Anzeiger des Westens*, took care to explain to his readers the subtle distinction between abolitionism and Republican Free-Soil politics. In Missouri especially, the editor argued, the ranks of the Republicans could and should include slaveholders. It was an "irresponsible error" to "doubt the motives" of slave owners who joined the Republican Party, he insisted. It was not slavery itself that the Republicans fought but "the politics of proslavery": "It is the system of free labor that is fighting with the system of slave labor; it is true democracy that opposes the oligarchy of the South and the rule of a destructive system . . . and those who want the territories given to the free white man and not to the slave-owning baron of the South; but it is not the nonslave-owners who are struggling with the slave-owners for the freeing of slaves."[17]

At the center of the struggle, he explained, lay the determination of the free states not to be dominated by the slave states. Republicans intended to hem in the slaveholding interest according to a "strict interpretation of the law." Republicans in Missouri could accomplish this task more easily if they welcomed slave owners to their party and remembered that with the participation and leadership of "antislavery" slave owners the victory over "proslavery slave owners" would be hastened. The editor noted that Frank Blair had held slaves until about a year before the 1860 election. The mayor of St. Louis, Oliver Filley, was a slave owner, as was Arnold Krekel. "The great majority of slave owners are proslavery people," the editor conceded, "but that is no reason why a slave owner cannot be the best possible Republican!"[18]

As the Republican Party gathered in Chicago to select its presidential candidate, a potential rift appeared between the Germans and their native-born Republican colleagues. The Blair family gave their wholehearted support to Edward Bates. They were joined in this endeavor by Horace Greeley, the influential editor of the *New York Tribune.* German delegates to the convention followed the lead of Carl Schurz[19] in support of William H. Seward of New York, who had vigorously denounced the Know-Nothings in the 1850s. Bates, by contrast, had expressed his sympathy for the nativist cause. As Schurz made plain, Germans would not forgive or forget. Indeed, a Bates candidacy would have severely tested the loyalty of Germans—particularly the St. Louis Germans—to the Republican Party. Two prominent German leaders in the St. Louis region—Krekel and Gustav Koerner of Belleville, Illinois—stood with the Blairs to support Bates's nomination, although (as the *Anzeiger des Westens* reported) Koerner acknowledged that Bates could not win the nomination "because of the prejudices the Germans held against him."[20]

When Abraham Lincoln emerged as the Republicans' compromise candidate, the St. Louis delegates quickly united in his support, and they did well in placing their men in the new president's cabinet. The City of St. Louis claimed two cabinet posts. As postmaster general, Montgomery Blair remained closely involved in the city's affairs through his brother Frank, and as attorney general, Edward Bates worked closely with his brother-in-law, Missouri's Unionist provisional governor Hamilton Gamble, and with the postmaster general to keep St. Louis on a conservative Republican course throughout the war.

With the dispute over Bates's candidacy resolved, Frank Blair emerged as a powerful figure in St. Louis. He enjoyed close personal and family ties with influential figures in the Lincoln administration, and he had the full confidence of the St. Louis Germans. He campaigned successfully for reelection to Congress in 1860, and he aggressively organized the uniformed German Wide-Awakes' clubs and urged them to march conspicuously in the streets. Waiting for his congressional term to begin in December 1861, he entered into a law partnership ("from necessity," as his sister observed from Silver Spring, Maryland) with the St. Louis attorney William V. N. Bay. Blair needed the income, and Bay, an old schoolmate during Blair's boyhood in Washington, D.C. (during the Jackson administration), willingly provided the assistance. "Frank," as his sister observed, "has his ship fixed to ride out this storm & has at his command too many neighbors" to permit the secessionists to succeed.[21]

St. Louis Germans watched with mounting apprehension as the election of Abraham Lincoln launched the Deep South on its course of secession and as pro-Southern St. Louisans, like Basil Duke and his Ninth Ward Washington Minute Men, prepared their paramilitary organizations. For their part, the Wide Awakes and other German Republican clubs maintained their armed readiness and augmented their numbers by organizing Home Guard militia units. The *Westliche Post* cautioned its readers to remain vigilant and steadfast in the midst of the crisis. "Only a person who lets himself be cowed into silence can be terrorized," wrote the editor. Germans must carry themselves bravely through the time of troubles. "The only way we adoptive citizens can get through this political crisis," he continued, "is to fulfill all legal duties faithfully, to hold with the Union and the Constitution, and to work together with our American fellow citizens to preserve peace, order, and law." Temporizing would shame the German people: "The gaze of the entire Union is directed at the German citizens of Missouri, so let us show ourselves worthy of the expectations that rest on us."[22]

For the moment St. Louis stood safely in the Republican camp. Even men of Southern sympathies, such as Abel R. Corbin (former editor of the *Missouri Argus*), conceded the point. In the 1860 elections Lincoln carried the city with nearly 9,500 votes, compared with 8,500 votes for the Unionist Democrat Stephen Douglas; 4,500 votes for the conditional Unionist John Bell; and 500 votes for the secessionist Democrat John Breckinridge. As James Neal Primm has observed, "98 percent of the city's voters . . . rejected the ultra-Southern position" of Breckenridge.[23] But it was also true that the supporters of Douglas and Bell controlled the largest number of voters in St. Louis, and Republicans soon recognized the importance of accommodating themselves with this political center.

Outside St. Louis, Republicans fared badly. Nevertheless, Union men seemed securely in control. Stephen A. Douglas easily carried the state. Representing themselves as Douglas men, Claiborne Jackson won election as governor and Thomas Reynolds as lieutenant governor. Although South Carolina seceded from the Union on 20 December 1860, and the rest of the Gulf Coast states soon followed, the New Year began in St. Louis with Republican confidence running high. On New Year's Day, in a routine settlement of an estate, the city sheriff offered seven slaves for sale; following tradition, they were auctioned on the courthouse steps. A sizable crowd, dominated by Republican Wide Awakes, gathered for the event, and in high spirits they made a mockery of the proceedings. The crowd held the bidding at three dollars and only gradually allowed it to rise. When the auctioneer failed to reach a price above eight dollars he acknowledged defeat and returned the slaves to jail. Missouri slave owners continued to sell slaves in Kentucky throughout the war, but the St. Louis sheriff no longer attempted a public sale in the city.[24]

News of the crisis in Charleston, South Carolina, soon produced a more somber mood. Having seceded from the Union, South Carolina demanded the surrender of federal forts in and around Charleston Harbor. As state militia forces mustered in the city, President Buchanan replaced the Northern-born commander of federal forces there with a man of Southern birth and sensibility, Kentuckian Major Robert Anderson. Buchanan hoped to forestall an open act of rebellion, but neither he nor Anderson was willing to acquiesce in South Carolina's demand of surrender. To defend his command, Anderson consolidated his small force at Fort Sumter, an unfinished island fortress in Charleston Harbor. On 4 January 1861, President Buchanan proclaimed a

Day of National Humiliation, Fasting, and Prayer and dispatched the un-armed merchant ship *Star of the West* to resupply Anderson's force. When the South Carolina militia fired on the ship and forced it to turn back, the attention of the nation focused on the fate of Major Anderson and the federal garrison at Fort Sumter.

As Buchanan called for national prayer, Claiborne Jackson was inaugurated governor of Missouri. In his inaugural address, he praised South Carolina's action and warned the federal government against coercion. In any crisis, he said, Missouri's "honor, her interests, and her sympathies point alike in one direction, and determine her *to stand by the South.*"[25]

In St. Louis, friends and foes of secession began to mobilize. On 7 January, secessionists, and those leaning in that direction, formed the Minute Men militia at a meeting in Washington Hall chaired by Charles McLaren. Leading this activity were two of Thomas Reynolds's political allies, Basil Duke and Colton Greene. A young man of twenty-five and a Douglas supporter in the election of 1860, Duke was a native of Kentucky who joined the Minute Men as a conditional Unionist. The arrival of federal troops in St. Louis (to guard the Arsenal and the Subtreasury) convinced him that Lincoln's administration intended to use coercion against the seceded states, and his loyalty shifted decisively to the Confederacy (he later fought with John Hunt Morgan). Greene, a native of South Carolina, supported secession from the start. A number of ardent secessionists worked with Duke and Greene. James R. Shaler, Overton W. Barrett, and James Quinlan later fought with the Confederacy; so, too, did J. R. "Rock" Champion, Samuel Farrington, and Arthur McCoy, all of whom died, in Duke's words, "under the Southern flag."[26]

St. Louis secessionists soon recognized influential allies in Reynolds and in Governor Jackson. Once Jackson had secured the passage of a bill that removed the St. Louis police from the control of the Republican mayor and placed them under the direction of a governor-appointed Police Board, he promptly appointed Duke to the commission, along with other secessionists. Duke understood the Police Bill as a war measure and acted accordingly, using the police to keep track of Unionist activities.[27] Drawing on reports from her brother Frank, Elizabeth Blair Lee, in Silver Spring, Maryland, informed family members that St. Louis secessionists "have begun the game of minute men & terrorism." But she shared her brother's conviction that with "freedom of press & speech" the Unionists in the city would prevail.[28]

Blair and the St. Louis Republicans did not simply rely on free speech and a free press to meet the secessionist threat. At a meeting in Oliver Filley's counting room on Main Street they formed the St. Louis Committee of Safety. From nearby Woodward's Hardware Store (also on Main Street) the Republicans purchased all the Sharpe's rifles they could get their hands on. Giles Filley used the weapons to arm about fifty men in his stove factory, and he held this force in readiness to help defend the U.S. Arsenal if that became necessary. Republican governor Richard Yates of Illinois also recognized the danger of a secessionist uprising in St. Louis; and in crates addressed to Giles Filley via Woodward's Hardware Store, he shipped 200 muskets to Unionists in the city. Filley hid these weapons in empty beer barrels and moved them by wagon (with several barrels of beer) to Turner Hall at Tenth and Walnut for distribution to Germans organizing as Home Guards. James Broadhead, who had attended the meeting in Filley's office, recalled that he drilled with a company of German Home Guard in Winkelmaier's Brewery on Market Street. During these exciting days, Samuel Glover kept a rifle visible in his law office at Fifth and Olive as a reminder to clients whose loyalties might waiver that the stalwart Union men intended to fight to hold St. Louis for the United States. From early January into mid-February, the Republicans organized, drilled, and eventually armed sixteen militia companies, totaling about 14,000 men. Most were German.[29]

Secessionists remained active as well. On 8 January, Lieutenant Governor Reynolds addressed a public meeting in the city that adopted a resolution declaring that "we pledge Missouri to a hearty co-operation with our sister Southern States . . . for our mutual protection, against the encroachments of Northern fanaticism, and the co-ercion [sic] of the Federal Government."[30] As news arrived that secessionists had taken control of federal arsenals at Mount Vernon, Alabama (4 January), Apalachicola, Florida (7 January), and Baton Rouge, Louisiana (10 January), the attention of secessionists and Unionists in St. Louis focused on the Arsenal on the city's south side.[31] Between 9 and 26 January, Mississippi, Florida, Alabama, Georgia, and Louisiana withdrew from the Union. Texas followed the exodus, and by early February delegates to a constitutional convention in Montgomery, Alabama, gathered to form the Confederate States of America. Reynolds and Governor Jackson eagerly sought to add Missouri to this slaveholding confederation.

St. Louis Republican leaders met on 10 January at Franklin A. Dick's law office (on Fifth Street near the Presbyterian Church) to prepare for a public meeting the next day that would formally establish the St. Louis Committee of Safety. This group included Mayor Filley, Broadhead, Samuel T. Glover, Henry T. Blow, Peter L. Foy, and Samuel Simmons. Through Blow (whose father-in-law, Thornton Grimsley, was a dedicated secessionist), the men learned that secessionists planned to break up any public meetings of Republicans. Forewarned, Mayor Filley provided a large police force, and the Republican public meeting on 11 January established the Committee of Safety without disruption. Broadhead served on it as did Mayor Filley, Glover, Blair, John Horn, and Julius J. Witzig. Witzig, a prominent engineer, provided an essential link to the German community. Initially, the committee met every evening at Turner Hall; and with the paid services of a detective force (headed by former Chief of Police J. E. D. Couzins), it monitored the activities of secessionists.[32]

Between Basil Duke's secessionists and Frank Blair's Unionists lay a large but as yet ill-defined group of conditional Unionists who supported slavery but were reluctant to urge secession. With varying degrees of commitment they supported the Union, although often with the condition that Lincoln's administration should not use force to compel seceded states to return to it. In the deepening mood of crisis these men met on 12 January at the East Front of the courthouse. Nathaniel Paschall, editor of the *Missouri Republican,* called the meeting. He had been largely responsible for securing Claiborne Jackson's and Thomas Reynolds's earlier endorsement of Douglas. Paschall was joined by the respected jurist Hamilton R. Gamble, the banker James E. Yeatman, and the fur trader turned businessman Robert Campbell. Largely Democratic in composition, the group favored the Crittenden compromise effort.

Frank Blair, joined by Foy, Dick, Glover, and others, urged Republicans not to attend. A handbill posted throughout town exhorted Republicans to hold to the principles they had adopted the day before and to reject the "narrower grounds" to be assumed by these uncertain Unionists. Most Republicans did stay away, but Broadhead attended and recalled that the crowd included "nearly all the leading men of the City." The gathering selected Campbell as president and heard addresses from Hamilton Gamble and the lawyer Uriel Wright (within a few months Gamble was elected provisional governor of Missouri and Wright joined the Confederacy). The men endorsed a resolution expressing the proslavery sentiments of a majority at the meeting: "The possession of slave property is a constitutional right, and as such ought to be ever recognized by the Federal Government." A second resolution expressed the conditional Unionist view that if the federal government "shall fail and refuse to secure this right . . . Missouri will share the common duties and common danger of the South."[33] Urging public calm, the group denounced the seizure of federal property and endorsed the convening of a state convention to determine Missouri's course in the secession crisis. Finally, the group urged the federal government to refrain from coercion against the seceded states.[34]

Blair, Broadhead, Filley, and other members of the Committee of Safety recognized that the principles they had expressed at the Republican meeting of 11 January needed to be accommodated in some fashion to the sentiments expressed at the Democratic meeting of 12 January if Unionists in St. Louis were to avoid being divided and defeated. The need for unity was soon underscored when the state legislature (on 18 January) passed a bill providing for the election of delegates (three from each state senatorial district) to a state convention "to consider the then existing relations between the government of the United States, the people and governments of the different States, and the government and people of the State of Missouri." The legislature set the election of delegates for 18 February and provided for the convening of the convention on 28 February.[35]

To ensure strong Unionist participation in the convention, Republicans reached out to Democrats and called for a broadly inclusive Union meeting at the Mercantile Library on 31 January to identify candidates for the February election of delegates. The coalition effort worked: four of the fifteen men nominated were Republicans; the remaining eleven were either Douglas or Bell supporters. Prominent in the group nominated were John How, the retired theater manager Sol Smith, Hamilton Gamble, and Uriel Wright.[36]

As St. Louis Unionists and secessionists prepared for the state convention, both sides paid increasingly close attention to the federal Arsenal in St. Louis and also to the federal Subtreasury, located in the Post Office at Third and Olive. Major William H. Bell commanded the Arsenal and controlled the largest cache of military supplies west of the Mississippi River: 60,000 muskets, 90,000 pounds of gunpowder, more than 1 million cartridges, 40 cannon, and machinery for the manufacture of weapons. As Unionists and secessionists maneuvered for advantage during January, the matter of Bell's loyalty assumed great importance. Bell, a native of North Carolina and an 1820 graduate of West Point, deferred to the authority of Claiborne Jackson's state government and resisted the efforts of the Unionists to post armed Home

Guards on the Arsenal grounds. Fellow West Pointer Daniel M. Frost, who held the rank of brigadier general in the Missouri State Militia and who commanded the St. Louis Military District, regarded Bell as a collaborator in the governor's effort to control the Arsenal. Frost, a native of New York and a veteran of the Mexican War, had resigned his regular army commission after marrying into the St. Louis elite in 1851. Although he was a personal friend of Gratz Brown (he served as Brown's second when Reynolds challenged him to a duel in 1855), Frost nevertheless stood with Governor Jackson in the secession crisis. On 24 January Frost reported to Jackson that Bell agreed with the proposition that the munitions in the Arsenal should be used to arm the state militia. "The Major is with us," wrote Frost. "The arsenal, if properly looked after, will be everything to our State, and I intend to look after it; very quietly, however." Frost informed Jackson that Bell had agreed to let Frost station guards from the state militia on the Arsenal grounds for its protection. Bell, said Frost, was "everything that you and I could desire."[37]

Isaac H. Sturgeon, the assistant U.S. treasurer in St. Louis, managed the Subtreasury's assets of $400,000. A Kentucky native, he had identified himself politically with the Southern Rights wing of the Democratic Party during the 1850s and had joined with Claiborne Jackson to secure the defeat of Senator Thomas Hart Benton in 1850. In the 1856 election, Sturgeon supported James Buchanan, to whom he owed his appointment as assistant treasurer. In the 1860 election, he supported Breckinridge. For this reason, the secessionist editor of the *St. Louis Bulletin,* Thomas Snead, regarded Sturgeon (as well as Bell) as reliable on Southern Rights. Major Bell kept the Arsenal's accounts at the Subtreasury, and he and Sturgeon met often. At one meeting early in January, Sturgeon asked Bell what protection the major had for the Arsenal. Bell replied that he had none whatever. A single guard patrolled the grounds at night as a precaution against ordinary theft. This reply prompted Sturgeon to write to President Buchanan, an act that Snead later dubbed "Sturgeon's folly" because it brought federal troops to St. Louis to protect both the Subtreasury and the Arsenal. Snead believed that Sturgeon wanted Governor Jackson to gain control of the Subtreasury and the Arsenal and that Sturgeon's letter to Buchanan was intended to bring about this result. James Broadhead took a very different view of Sturgeon, however, concluding that the assistant treasurer had acted out of loyalty to the United States. As Broadhead recalled, Sturgeon's letter to Buchanan stated that "if it was the purpose of the Government to protect the public funds in his hands, and the munitions of war in the Arsenal, action could not be taken too soon." If, as Snead believed, Sturgeon expected Buchanan to support the secession cause, he was disappointed. Buchanan immediately referred Sturgeon's letter to General in Chief Winfield Scott, who promptly dispatched forty soldiers to St. Louis "to be placed by the department commander at the disposal of the Assistant Treasurer." Provost Marshal Major Justus McKinstry initially placed the troops in the upper rooms of the post office. But General Scott also had placed the troops at Sturgeon's disposal, and after Sturgeon consulted with Nathaniel Paschall and with the soldiers' commander, Lieutenant W. J. Robinson, a St. Louisan, he concluded that the presence of the troops at the post office created unnecessary public alarm.

There is no doubt that the arrival of U.S. soldiers attracted the attention of the St. Louis citizenry. The troops arrived at 8:30 A.M. on 11 January, and the *Anzeiger des Westens* reported that a large crowd soon gathered at the post office. People were "drawn more by curiosity than anything else," but the presence of a crowd provided "secessionist leaders" with an opportunity to denounce "the arrival of the United States military as an attempt to place the city under a military despotism." Snead contributed to the uproar by publishing an extra edition of the *Bulletin* to denounce the coercive policy of federal authorities. The *Anzeiger* editor believed that the secessionist agitation failed because of the "good sense of the people" and observed dryly that "those who keep their hands off the Arsenal and the Subtreasury are in no danger of being bothered by the troops stationed there." Nevertheless, to quiet the agitators, Sturgeon directed that the troops be moved to the Arsenal. There, Frank Blair put Lieutenant Robinson in communication with two armed German clubs organized during the 1860 election. One took the common name, the Wide Awakes; the other, somewhat more ominously, employed the German label for military riflemen, Schwarzer Jaegercorp, or the Black Rifles.[38]

In this early crisis, Broadhead commended Sturgeon for his "services to the cause of the Union" and noted that the unconditionally Unionist *Missouri Democrat* of 2 February 1861 had publicly praised him for his loyalty. Snead may have been correct to believe that Sturgeon would have welcomed the success of Governor Jackson and his supporters if Buchanan had met their expectations. But in the face of a concerted federal effort to protect the Subtreasury and the Arsenal from secessionists, Sturgeon (who soon became president of the Neosho Railroad in southwest Missouri) stood with the Union men of St. Louis.[39]

Although the federal government had signaled its intention to hold the Subtreasury and the Arsenal, the forty men in Lieutenant Robinson's command were hardly sufficient for the task if a substantial threat presented itself. The Committee of Safety therefore sought a commander for the Arsenal who would work willingly with them in an emergency. After Bell's 24 January meeting with the Eastern Missouri Militia commander, Daniel Frost, Frank Blair wrote to his brother Montgomery, insisting that Bell be removed. General Scott then replaced him with Brevet Major Peter V. Hagner.[40]

At the time of Hagner's appointment, Lieutenant Robinson and his force of forty men were the only military presence at the Arsenal. Before the end of January, however, Captain Thomas Sweeny reported to Jefferson Barracks with a company of regular troops and soon reinforced Robinson.[41] On 6 February 1861 Captain Nathaniel Lyon arrived at the Arsenal from Fort Riley, Kansas, with another company of regulars. He took command of the troops while Hagner, as an officer in the Ordnance Department, remained in command of the Arsenal and its supplies.[42] Hagner had come to the Arsenal as a seasoned soldier. A native of Maryland and about forty-five-years-old at the beginning of the Civil War, he had graduated from West Point and served with distinction during the Mexican War. He had the confidence of General William S. Harney, commander of the Department of the West. But neither Hagner nor Harney had Frank Blair's confidence. Blair found an avid and effective ally in Nathaniel Lyon, who shared his Unionist views. As Lincoln's inauguration approached, Blair visited the president-elect in Springfield, Illinois, to explain why Lyon should be placed in command. The reasons were political, although Blair noted that Hagner's rank as major was brevet and that Lyon's commission as captain preceded Hagner's, making Lyon, technically, the senior of the two officers. In Washington, however, President Buchanan and General Scott turned a deaf ear to Blair and continued to rely on Harney and Hagner.[43]

By mid-February, St. Louis resembled an armed camp. On 13 February General Frost formally mustered the five companies of Basil Duke's Minute Men into the State Guard; they formed a battalion in Frost's brigade. Three days later, Scott reinforced the Arsenal with an additional 203 men, brought into the city from Jefferson Barracks, the largest federal military base west of the Mississippi. Captain Albert Tracy recorded in his diary that the order arrived at about eleven o'clock the night of 15 February. Tracy had first arrived in St. Louis on 2 February and had traveled by rail south to Jefferson

Barracks. Now he retraced this journey on foot with a force of 200 men "with ten rounds of ball-cartridge." Expecting that they might find it necessary to fight their way into the Arsenal, Tracy's force proceeded as quietly as possible. "We went up with as little noise as practicable," he wrote, "and came to a halt, by the riverfront of the Arsenal. Here, if at all, we were to look for a scrimmage."[44] No enemy appeared, and Tracy quietly entered the Arsenal grounds, where he reported to Major Hagner. Within a few days, General Scott added another 102 men to the garrison, which now numbered 484 men under Lyon's command. Lyon worked closely with his fellow officers to circumvent what he regarded as Hagner's suspiciously weak leadership.[45]

Several of the officers assembled at the Arsenal had known one another from the Mexican War. Tracy had known both Hagner and Lyon during that conflict; he also greeted Captain Thomas W. Sweeny, an old acquaintance, who had lost an arm in the war. John W. Todd, an army officer recently arrived in St. Louis after evacuating the federal Arsenal at Baton Rouge, knew several of his fellow officers at the St. Louis Arsenal. Captain James Totten of the Second U.S. Artillery, now at the Arsenal, had moved north to St. Louis after evacuating the U.S. Arsenal at Little Rock, Arkansas. Tracy also recognized Moses H. Wright, a Tennessean, who resigned his commission in May to join the Confederate army. Increasingly, the question of loyalty strained normal social intercourse. A week before moving up to the Arsenal, Tracy and his fellow officers at Jefferson Barracks had been invited to a ball in St. Louis given by the Volunteers, that is, General Frost's State Guard. There was nothing remarkable about the invitation; it was common for the volunteer militia to socialize with the officers stationed at Jefferson Barracks. Indeed, militia balls ranked high in the city's social life. Tracy, like General Frost a native of New York, sensed that the general used the occasion to probe the sectional loyalties of the army officers. When Frost raised his glass to invite toasts, Tracy led with a declaration of his own unconditional Unionist sentiments: "The Union, without an *if.*" His words seemed "to dampen the general ardor and elicit but a feeble response." Tracy and his companions soon left and spent the rest of the evening at the theater. Recalling his toast a week later as he prepared to defend the Arsenal from rebels, he concluded that the reason for the sullen response at the ball now seemed obvious: "Secessionists, all."[46]

As the federal forces in the Arsenal prepared their defensive position, Tracy noted in Hagner a distinct lack of enthusiasm. "Hagner has not much heart in the matter," the captain recorded in his diary. A stone wall surrounded the courtyard of the Arsenal, and the defenders constructed scaffolding behind it to provide a platform for sentries and for riflemen if the building came under attack. Howitzers protected the structure's two gates, and artillery guarded the railway causeway to prevent an attack from that point. On 18 February Jefferson Davis was inaugurated president of the Confederate States of America. On the same day, Missouri voters selected delegates to the state convention. The next day, as Tracy had his men dig in the howitzers in the Arsenal yard, Hagner warned him sourly "not to spoil his lawn." "*His* lawn!" exclaimed Tracy in disgust.[47]

As preparations for war advanced in St. Louis, the Missouri State Convention met as scheduled in the state capital at Jefferson City on 28 February 1861. The body elected a conditional Unionist, former governor Sterling Price, as its presiding officer. With Price as president, the convention adjourned to reassemble amid more comfortable accommodations and among the Unionist majority in St. Louis. On the night of 3 March, the night before the convention was scheduled to reconvene at the Mercantile Library, the Minute Men raised a flag representing the Confederacy over the dome of the St. Louis Courthouse. At their headquarters in the Berthold mansion, at Fifth and Pine, they flew another. The Minute Men numbered no more than 400, but they were concerted in their action and vociferous in their secessionist sentiments. Duke and his men intended for the flag to defy what they called the "submissionist" state convention. At sunrise on 4 March, before the convention delegates gathered, a custodian quietly removed it from the courthouse. But the Minute Men flew their flag all day from the Berthold mansion as the delegates deliberated the state's course in the secession crisis and while in Washington, D.C., Abraham Lincoln was inaugurated as the fourteenth president of the United States.

At the beginning of the convention, Sterling Price supported the Crittenden compromise, which proposed, among other things, an extension of the Missouri Compromise line west to the Pacific. In a short speech that he gave in his home county of Chariton before being elected a delegate, Price had said that the compromise offered Missouri its best hope to preserve slavery. If the compromise failed, Price implied that the Union would fail with it. At the convention, a wealthy slaveholder, George Gast, proposed an amendment to a resolution that favored the compromise. It insisted that if the North did not accept the compromise, Missouri would "not hesitate to take a firm and decided stand in favor of her sister slave states of the South." Price cast his vote in favor of the Gast amendment, joining a minority of twenty-three delegates as he did so.[48]

On 5 March secessionists in the Missouri legislature introduced a military bill that would put the state on an active military footing. In the senate, Daniel Frost gave the measure his fervent support and helped to secure its passage in the upper house. But the lower house defeated it and forestalled for the time being the effort to deliver Missouri to the Confederacy.[49] On 9 March the state convention issued its final report, delivering another blow to secessionist hopes. Former Missouri Supreme Court justice Hamilton Gamble, who chaired the key committee on Federal Relations, effectively guided the convention to its declaration against secession. "In a military aspect," he observed, "secession and connection with a Southern Confederacy is annihilation for Missouri." Republican delegate James Broadhead echoed that sentiment. Under the circumstances, he said, "Missouri cannot get out of the Union if she would." Adding emphasis to the point, he concluded: "I think I know what I say when I speak it, *Missouri has not the power to go out of the Union if she would.*" Thomas Tasker Gantt, Montgomery Blair's former law partner, worked closely with Gamble at the convention (Gantt later served on General George B. McClellan's staff in 1861 and 1862 before being appointed provost marshal general for Missouri in 1862). The Unionist coalition prevailed, and a secessionist proposal (declaring Missouri's opposition to the Crittenden compromise and promising that the state would stand with her Southern comrades) went down to defeat before the full convention by a vote of seventy to twenty-three. Sterling Price, for the first time, cast his ballot with the secessionists.[50]

The care with which Gamble and Broadhead rooted their Unionism in considerations of practicality underscored the fact that even the most reliable Unionists in St. Louis remained conservative by the standards of the Republican Party throughout the North. Gamble and Broadhead were both natives of Virginia and, although Unionists, both remained firmly committed to protecting the rights of slaveholders in the state. A generation older than Broadhead, Gamble had moved to Missouri in 1818 and formed a law partnership with his brother-in-law Edward Bates. As a justice on the Missouri Supreme Court in 1851, Gamble had delivered a dissenting opinion in the court's proslavery decision in the Dred Scott case. He retired from the state court in 1854 and from his law practice in 1858, moving east to Philadelphia; but the secession crisis brought him back to Missouri and into public life, first as the commanding figure at the convention and later as provisional governor of the state.[51] The younger of the Unionist leaders, James Broadhead, had moved from Virginia to Missouri in 1837. By 1859, he was practicing law in St. Louis. Although he voted for Lincoln in 1860 he distanced himself from what he regarded as the radical elements in the national party. He did not support the Black Republicans, presumably meaning men like Charles Sumner in Massachusetts, who made up what he described as the abolitionist element in the Republican Party. He also opposed those he called Red Republicans, the former Jacksonian radicals (like Benjamin Butler of Massachusetts) who promoted hostility between labor and capital. After the war Broadhead gained national distinction as a lawyer and returned to the Democratic Party as a conservative, winning election to the U.S. House of Representatives in 1882.[52]

By the time the state convention adopted Gamble's report and adjourned (21 March 1861), a majority in the general assembly had become sufficiently hostile toward St. Louis to agree with Governor Jackson that its mayor should be stripped of any direct authority over the city police and the militia in the St. Louis Military District.[53] Acting on his own authority, Lyon responded to the new threat by directing the defenses of the Arsenal. Major Hagner found himself increasingly isolated within his command. As Captain Tracy observed in his journal on 31 March, "Hagner is wholly out of the court." Tracy noted frequent visits to Lyon by Frank Blair "and a German named Sigel." These men, not Hagner, exercised effective authority over the federal forces at the Arsenal. Franz Sigel was a native of Baden and an officer in the failed liberal revolution in Germany in 1848. He then joined the exodus of German liberals to the United States and settled in St. Louis in 1857. One of the most popular leaders of the German community, Sigel worked closely with Blair and Lyon to organize and arm the Home Guard. He was soon appointed brigadier general commanding the German Third Regiment of U.S. Volunteers. In case of an attack on the Arsenal, Blair and Sigel assured Lyon that they would launch an "onslaught at the rear upon the enemy." Tracy thought that the number of organized and armed Germans available to Blair and Sigel numbered about 400. Hagner, in Tracy's view, had become a disgrace to the army: "Hagner objects to firing over the walls in case of attack. 'Think,' says this hypocrite, this military Pecksniff, 'of the innocent women and children, who might be slaughtered by the balls.'"[54] General Harney continued to support Hagner and to insist that Lyon had no authority over the defense of the Arsenal. But Blair had effectively set in motion the events that led to Harney's removal and to Lyon's elevation as commander of the Department of the West.[55]

In early spring 1861, Republicans in St. Louis faced a shocking reversal of fortunes. On 1 April, Daniel G. Taylor defeated Republican John How in the election for mayor. A native of Ohio, Taylor established himself first in St. Louis as a riverboat captain and later as an owner of a steamboat company. In his days as a riverboat captain, he had been associated with Pierre Chouteau Jr. in the fur trade and had married into the proslavery Creole aristocracy of the city (his first wife, Angelique Henri, died in a steamboat explosion in 1858; soon thereafter, in 1860, he married Emilie Lebeau). Taylor won by running on a "Union Anti-Black Republican" ticket. His victory was decisive and a stunning rebuke for the Republicans. In the February election of delegates to the Missouri State Convention, Republicans had maintained their alliance with conditional Unionists and had carried the city with a majority of 5,000. Now, as large numbers of conditional Unionists voted for Taylor, the anti-Republican coalition won with a majority of over 2,600 votes. Thomas Snead believed that this reversal of political fortunes reflected a growing fear of the German Home Guard. With an anti-Republican mayor in office and the city police controlled by Governor Jackson's new Police Board, the tide of sectional conflict in St. Louis seemed to have changed. The composition of the new Police Board revealed the new political alignment. John A. Brownlee, a conditional Unionist leaning toward secession, presided. Daniel Taylor, calling himself an anti-Republican Unionist, sat on the board in his capacity as mayor. In addition to Brownlee, Governor Jackson had appointed Minute Men leader Basil Duke and two more open secessionists, James H. Carlisle and Charles McLaren.[56]

A few days after Taylor's election, Captain Tracy, Captain Rufus Saxton, and Colonel Benjamin L. E. Bonneville (all staunch Unionists) attended a dinner party at General Harney's home in St. Louis. The French-born, West Point–educated Bonneville commanded an infantry regiment stationed at Benton Barracks, north of St. Louis. He had served in the Mexican War, but he was best known as an army explorer in the Southwest. (Utah's Lake Bonneville and Bonneville Salt Flats bear his name.) He impressed Tracy with his gracious manners. Another guest, *St. Louis Bulletin* publisher Samuel Bullitt Churchill, did not. Churchill served as a colonel in the State Guard and, with General Frost, represented St. Louis in the state senate. (In mid-

May Churchill joined other secessionists in the legislature to recommend that all state funds, including those set aside for public education, be spent to arm the state.) Tracy thought that Harney intended to foster camaraderie among federal and state military officers; the effort failed, as far as he was concerned. He described Churchill as "a sallow, black-haired Secessionist, who if he were not employed to ascertain our temper about [secession], certainly succeeded in developing it." Arrested as disloyal later in 1861, Churchill was banished by federal authorities from St. Louis in 1863. He returned to his native Kentucky.[57]

If there was a political purpose to Harney's dinner party it was surely to try to isolate Nathaniel Lyon. For his part, Lyon relied on Gratz Brown and Frank Blair to maintain a close and cordial relationship with the Germans. The liaison worked well, and the *Mississippi Blätter* (the weekend supplement of the *Westliche Post*) sang the praises of Lyon, who had "distinguished himself since youth through bold deeds of war." The paper summarized for its German readers the federal officer's career: he had attended West Point, had fought against the Seminoles in Florida, and had served under Zachary Taylor and Winfield Scott in the Mexican War, where he distinguished himself at the battles of Vera Cruz and Cerro Gordo. St. Louis Germans could feel confident under Lyon's leadership: "If the secessionists give him a chance, they will certainly get an opportunity to feel his valiant hand." The editor described the defenses of the Arsenal and assured German readers that General Frost and Governor Jackson "would have a hard time getting anywhere with their Minute Men, should they be seized with the desire to try to take it."[58]

While Harney continued to oppose Blair's and Lyon's efforts to fortify the Arsenal and other strategic points against secessionist attack, the newly organized Confederacy dispatched General P. G. T. Beauregard to South Carolina to direct an assault on the Union garrison at Fort Sumter. Confederate cannon opened fire on Sumter in the predawn darkness of 12 April 1861. On the same day, the defenders of the St. Louis Arsenal received reports that they were about to be attacked. Captain Tracy noted at the time that Lyon "exhibits restlessness and even anxiety." At 11:00 P.M. on 12 April, Lyon held a conference with Tracy and other trusted commanders. Four officers were excluded from the meeting: two were not fully trusted by Lyon; two were known to be disloyal. Moses Wright of Tennessee resigned in May to join the Confederacy; Richard Bland Lee of Virginia had been placed under arrest, as Tracy noted, "as a secessionist, giving entrance to spies." At the meeting it was decided that Captain Thomas Sweeny would place riflemen (protected by sandbags) on the north wall. He also had charge of a howitzer aimed at the gate on that side. Saxton commanded the defense of the west side, including the main gate to the street. Tracy held several brick buildings, fortified with sandbags at the windows, which faced south. He had a howitzer ready to rake the west wall if attackers gained entrance on that side. Lyon expected the enemy to mount an artillery battery on a rise of ground facing the west wall, and it was agreed that if the secessionists deployed cannon in that manner, Tracy's force would storm the battery before it could go into action. Lyon took command of guns dug in at the center of the parade grounds, near the guardhouse. At the end of their conference, Lyon rose, struck the table with his fist, and declared, "Gentlemen, if that man Hagner, interferes with you in any way, put him in irons, and in the guardhouse. And if he interferes with *me* I'll shoot him in his tracks." Under the circumstances, with Hagner all but unwilling to defend the Arsenal, Tracy and his fellow commanders understood and accepted Lyon's judgment.[59]

Although the expected attack did not come, an atmosphere of crisis persisted. On 13 April, the day Major Anderson surrendered the federal garrison at Fort Sumter, Lyon transferred Tracy's force to the powder magazine at Jefferson Barracks. There, for several days, Tracy eyed with nervous suspicion groups of armed men gathered on the riverbank, apparently scouting the magazine and its defenders.

The anti-Republican political reaction in St. Louis, together with Governor Jackson's successful effort to place the city's police under secessionist control, left the German community fearful of repression. When Mayor Taylor ordered the closing of saloons and other places of entertainment on Sundays, the Police Board enforced the order first by shutting down Henry Boernstein's German-language opera house (in the old Varieties Theater on Pine Street) and Anton Niederwieser's restaurant, Tony's Tivoli, at Elm and Fourth. The *Anzeiger des Westens* noted that Governor Jackson had been a guest at Tony's place (evidently enjoying food and drink) when the police closed it at midnight on Saturday 14 April. The editor saw in the police action a revived and redirected nativism. A familiar bigotry was now disguised as moral reform: "To the curses of life in the South, which we have long since learned to live with, are now added the curses of life in the narrow-minded North." In this climate, the editor feared that "soon we shall lose the freedom of the press," and the forces of despotism would prevail. "Austria and South Carolina," he warned, "will be at home in Missouri."[60]

On 16 April Governor Jackson received from Secretary of War Simon Cameron a call for 4,000 Missouri troops to be made available for service under the authority of the United States. The next day Jackson announced his refusal to comply. "Your dispatch of the 13th instant . . . has been received," responded the governor sternly. "Your requisition . . . is illegal, unconstitutional, and revolutionary in its objects, inhuman and diabolical, and cannot be complied with." On 17 April Jackson journeyed to St. Louis to meet with state militia commander Daniel Frost, with Police Board president John Brownlee, and with Minute Men leader Basil Duke, among others sympathetic to or leaning toward the Southern cause. The group discussed Frost's plan to locate a militia encampment on the bluffs south of the Arsenal and from these heights to force a federal surrender. Following the meeting, at Frost's suggestion, Jackson secretly dispatched Minute Men Colton Greene and Basil Duke to the Confederate capital at Montgomery, Alabama, to ask President Jefferson Davis for siege guns and mortars for an attack on the St. Louis Arsenal.[61]

Also on 17 April, Frank Blair returned to St. Louis from Washington, D.C., with authority from the War Department to draw 5,000 guns from the Arsenal to arm the Home Guard. Although Blair had not obtained Harney's ouster, his return strengthened Lyon's hand. Lyon immediately sent out patrols to control the area around the Arsenal. The Police Board protested, and Harney ordered Lyon to keep his men within the Arsenal. On 19 April Blair dispatched a letter to his brother Montgomery, urgently requesting Harney's removal.

Although he was privately maneuvering toward secession, Governor Jackson maintained a public stance of constitutional propriety. This deception served a purpose. As long as General Harney believed that Jackson acted in good faith and sought only to maintain the neutrality of the state, it was possible for the general to justify (to himself and to his supporters in Washington) his own neutrality. When Jackson denounced Lincoln's call for troops as unconstitutional and revolutionary, he evidently had in mind John C. Calhoun's views on the reserved rights of the states and former president Buchanan's argument that the federal government had no constitutional authority to compel states to remain in the Union. Lyon and his supporters regarded Jackson's refusal as an act of treason. Harney, clearly, disagreed. Under the circumstances it behooved Jackson not to associate himself with overt aggression against the United States until it was necessary to defend his state from military coercion by the federal government. The governor worked to maintain Harney's confidence. When a state militia force seized the small federal arsenal at Liberty, Missouri (on 20 April), it did so without direct orders from the governor. Moreover, when the Confederate secretary of war called on Jackson to supply his government with troops, the governor replied that he could not yet do so. "Missouri, you know, is yet under the tyranny of Lincoln's Government," he wrote in response to the Confederate request, "so far, at least, as forms go." But he explained his intentions: "We are using every means to arm our people and, until we are better prepared, must move cautiously."[62]

While Harney continued to respect what he believed to be the governor's neutrality, Lyon worked with Blair to circumvent Jackson and to raise volunteer troops. On 21 April Lyon learned that Lieutenant John M. Schofield (on leave from the army to deliver a series of lectures in physics at Washington University) had received orders from the War Department to muster Missouri volunteers into federal service. Lyon urged Blair to meet with Schofield, insisting that "something should be done if possible today." At Blair's direction, James Broadhead located Schofield and brought him to Blair's residence on Washington Avenue. Schofield, Lyon, and Blair then met with General Harney but found him opposed to admitting volunteers into the Arsenal grounds. Further, Harney refused to arm any volunteers with munitions from the Arsenal. To break this impasse, Blair wired Governor A. G. Curtin of Pennsylvania, urging him to ask his friend, Secretary of War Cameron, to instruct Harney immediately to arm the volunteers. That evening, bowing to pressures from Washington, Harney relented and admitted the volunteers and their officers to the Arsenal. In the next few days, the volunteers were mustered in as four regiments commanded by Blair, Henry Boernstein, Franz Sigel, and Nicholas Schuettner.[63]

On 22 April Governor Jackson issued orders for the militia to muster throughout the state. The state Militia Act (1859) clearly gave the governor the authority to call such a muster in all the military districts of the state. Still, Jackson continued to avoid any overt act of aggression against the United States, and General Harney continued to regard the state government as neutral. With the high ground near the Arsenal occupied by Lyon's growing forces, General Frost located his encampment on the western edge of the city, in an area known as Lindell Grove. Several of Frost's officers promptly resigned their state militia commissions, protesting Governor Jackson's refusal to comply with the War Department's call for troops. Included in this group was Major Frederick Schaeffer, a native of Germany, who protested in his letter of resignation that elements of Frost's command had "hoisted another flag than the only true flag of these United States." Schaeffer later joined the federal army and died at the Battle of Murfreesboro in December 1862. Frost's adjutant, John S. Cavender, also resigned and joined the U.S. Army. A native of New Hampshire, Cavender was promoted to brevet brigadier general at the end of the Civil War and commended for his "gallant and meritorious service" in the capture of Fort Donelson and at the Battle of Shiloh.[64]

On 23 April the orders that Blair had so fervently sought arrived. Secretary Cameron recalled Harney to Washington to respond to the complaints that Blair had been leveling against him. Harney left immediately to argue his case. In his view, Blair and Lyon had unnecessarily alarmed the citizenry of St. Louis; peace and tranquillity could best be maintained by keeping the volatile German population as quiet as possible. In Harney's absence, Lyon assumed command and immediately began organizing the four regiments of volunteers. On 26 April he shipped surplus arms and munitions from the Arsenal across the Mississippi River to the safety of Illinois.[65]

The same day a group of Minute Men took violent action against the German volunteers, evidently in the hope of sparking a confrontation with the Dutch that would galvanize General Frost's militia into active support of secession and perhaps bring the city's Irish immigrants into confrontation with the German Home Guard. As a group of German volunteers traveled by the rail line on Fifth Street from the Arsenal to their temporary barracks in north St. Louis, armed Minute Men stopped their car in front of the Berthold mansion. After some rough treatment and loud cheers for Jeff Davis from the armed group, the Germans were told to go to their homes.[66]

Privately, Governor Jackson expressed his hope that Missouri would leave the Union in a coordinated fashion with Tennessee and Kentucky. "Missouri should act in concert with Tennessee and Kentucky," he wrote on 28 April. "They are all bound to go out and should go together if possible. . . . Let us then prepare to make our exit."[67] Meanwhile, the militia began to assemble throughout the state.

On 30 April Lyon informed Secretary of War Cameron that he had occupied the hills near the Arsenal with infantry and with Captain Totten's battery. In addition, Lyon had rented several buildings near the Arsenal where riflemen were positioned to protect all approaches. That same day he received authorization from Cameron (bearing endorsements by General Scott and President Lincoln) to work in consultation with the St. Louis Committee of Safety—the order specifically named Oliver D. Filley, John How, James Broadhead, Samuel T. Glover, J. J. Witzig, and Francis P. Blair Jr.—to raise up to 10,000 troops as a reserve force. These troops were not to be mustered into the U.S. Army but would be organized as a "United States Reserve Corps," with Captain Thomas Sweeny commanding. The German Home Guard and the Committee of Safety now had the official sanction of the War Department. As General Scott noted in his endorsement, the "revolutionary times" justified such an extraordinary measure. The order also authorized Lyon to declare martial law if he thought it necessary, and it directed him to remove from the Arsenal weapons not needed by the "forces of the United States in Missouri," a task that he had already accomplished.[68]

In the Reserve Corps, Broadhead received a commission as major and served as Sweeny's quartermaster. Regimental commanders included a number of Germans: Colonel Herman Kallmann, whose men came from the German neighborhood between Soulard and Chouteau Streets; Colonel Charles G. Stifel, the wealthy owner of Stifel's brewery at Fourteenth and Chambers Streets; and Colonel Henry Almstedt, a German native who had served with the U.S. Army during the Mexican War. Also commanding regiments in the Reserve Corps were John McNeil and Gratz Brown. McNeil, a native of Nova Scotia, had risen to prominence in St. Louis through the fur trade (he was later remembered for his role in the execution of Confederate prisoners at Palmyra, Missouri, in October 1862).[69]

Lyon now had the resources he needed to confront Frost's state militia at the encampment they had named Camp Jackson, in honor of Missouri's governor.

4

"This Means War"

O N 1 MAY 1861 the German community in St. Louis appeared united and exuberant. The *Anzeiger des Westens* expected that within the week the four regiments allotted for Missouri in Lincoln's call for troops would be filled, and progress would be made quickly to enlist the Reserve Corps (or Home Guards as they were called locally) recently authorized by Secretary of War Cameron. Most of the Volunteer and Reserve Corps soldiers would be Germans. Within that community, support for enlistments came from all sides. The brewer Julius Winkelmaier made sure that the volunteers were well supplied with beer. Tony Niederwieser sent the soldiers several cartons of cigars. His restaurant had been closed on Sundays by the anti-Republican mayor and the secessionist Police Board, and Niederwieser undoubtedly relished the opportunity to resist what he viewed as the forces of repression in the city (he himself soon led a company in the Home Guard). Carl Ludwig Bernays, editor of the *Anzeiger des Westens,* reported approvingly that Niederwieser "continued to pay the wages of two of his people who have joined the artillery. A splendid example!"[1]

The *Westliche Post* also praised the Germans for their display of patriotism, and its editor, Theodor Olshausen, positively welcomed war. "What we have long predicted . . . has at last come to pass," he announced. The spirit of freedom had awakened, and "the earth shakes under the tread of its legions and the South trembles." The time for debate had ended; the time for determined action had arrived. Olshausen acknowledged that war would bring "much suffering and tribulation." Indeed, war "is often gruesome and destructive." But this war would also advance "the great goal of mankind—the demand for freedom." Let freedom be the battle cry, and the loftiest sentiments of humanity will "flow like gold in the heart of the fire of battle." War promised other benefits as well. It served as a "school, a strict educational institution from which the right men emerge." In fact, continued Olshausen, long periods of peace produced a lower order of leaders. The perils of war "bring to life noble feelings of self-sacrifice, valor, and magnanimity toward the conquered and the prisoner." Out of the carnage of war rose greatness.[2]

The arming of the German Reserve Corps proceeded apace with a rising war fever. On the morning of 2 May, 1,300 volunteers from the Third, Fourth, and Fifth Wards marched to the Arsenal to receive arms. The *Anzeiger* identified in this body of men three companies of "Americans," one company of "French," and the rest "naturally all German." The paper took special note of Captain Niederwieser's company and a decorative company of Turner Zouaves. As the Home Guards received their weapons, Franz Sigel's Third Regiment paraded past the Arsenal to the rousing cheers of the reserve troops. From the Seventh and Eighth Wards Colonel Gratz Brown brought 1,100 men to the Arsenal to join the Reserve Corps. Later in the evening, bearing their newly issued arms, Brown's men marched through the city to their headquarters "to rousing music." At Turner Hall, which served as headquarters for many of the Home Guards, the *Anzeiger* reported that "the forest of shining bayonets excited great enthusiasm."[3]

The excitement of raising and arming the regiments of U.S. Volunteers and the Reserve Corps obscured for the moment just how untrained and untested these men and their commanders were. This point was underscored for Captain Tracy on 2 May when elements of Blair's First Regiment arrived at the powder magazine at Jefferson Barracks to move 400 barrels of rifle powder to the St. Louis Arsenal. The operation should have been a delicate one. Whenever the barrels were moved, powder sifted from cracks; and the risk of an explosion was high if the loose powder came into contact with a spark. The veteran ordnance sergeant moved about carefully in his straw shoes and looked on with startled alarm as Blair's boisterous men, wearing hobnailed boots, wrestled the barrels into the waiting railway cars. The men were spared an explosion, but Tracy recognized that these raw recruits and their raw commander could be a danger to themselves and to those around them.[4]

Governor Claiborne Jackson also directed preparations for war. On 6 May, about 700 men in St. Louis answered his call for a state militia muster. Scheduled to last for eleven days, it included Colton Greene's Minute Men and members of several pro-Southern private militia companies, including the St. Louis Grays, The Laclede Guards, the Washington Blues, and Basil Duke's Missouri Videttes. Access to the heights near the Arsenal had been denied to the state militia by Lyon's deployment of infantry and artillery. The militia mustered instead in the tree-shaded fields known as Lindell Grove, located just west of the row houses that lined Laclede, Chestnut, Pine, and Olive Streets. Camp Jackson, commanded by General Daniel Frost, was bordered by Olive Street to the north, Garrison and Ewing Avenues to the east, Laclede Avenue to the south, and Grand Avenue to the west. The men named some of its streets for leading Confederates, most prominently General P. G. T. Beauregard, who had so recently presided over the bombardment and surrender of Fort Sumter.[5]

According to Thomas Snead, the secessionist editor of the *St. Louis Bulletin* who had moved to Jefferson City in February 1861 to serve as an aid to Governor Jackson, Frost knew that the arms and munitions that had been stored in the Arsenal had either been distributed to the Volunteer regiments and to the Reserve Corps or had been shipped across the river to Illinois. The original reason for the militia muster in St. Louis no longer existed, but, recalled Snead, "It was determined to hold that encampment, nevertheless."

William Tecumseh Sherman watched Lyon's preparations with great interest. Sherman had recently arrived in St. Louis, where he became president of the Fifth Street Railroad. He knew Lyon from the Mexican War, and as a frequent visitor to the Arsenal, he had had several opportunities to commend Lyon for his vigorous preparations to defend federal property. Nevertheless, for the time being Sherman occupied (and seemed to wish to occupy) an ambiguous position in the sectional crisis. The business associates who had brought him to St. Louis included the banker Henry S. Turner and the leading stockholder in the Fifth Street Railroad, James H. Lucas. Both men were well known for their Southern sympathies. Moreover, Sherman had turned down an offer of a senior clerkship in the U.S. War Department (an offer made in Washington by Montgomery Blair when, earlier in 1861, Sherman had visited his brother, John Sherman, the newly elected senator from Ohio). He also had rebuffed an offer from Frank Blair to try to make him Harney's successor as commander of the Department of the West. The Blairs wondered if Sherman's commitment to the Union should be questioned. In retrospect it is clear that he simply wanted more than a clerkship or a command composed principally of volunteers and Home Guards. He saw the clouds of war gathering on the horizon, and he held out for a better position. In mid-May he accepted an appointment as colonel of a regiment of regular U.S. troops, the Thirteenth Infantry.

Sherman visited the Arsenal on 9 May and found the federal soldiers busily distributing cartridges. Lyon was "running about with his hair in the wind, his pockets full of papers, wild and irregular." Sherman knew that Lyon "meant business," and he approved of the commander's resolve. He did not yet know that Lyon planned to attack Camp Jackson, but he certainly must have suspected as much.[6]

Later that day, Lyon visited Camp Jackson and reported his findings to the Committee of Safety. Franklin Dick recalled after the war that Lyon had dressed himself as an old woman. Dick's wife "Midge" was the sister of Frank Blair's wife "Apo," and Dick recalled that it was Blair who had borrowed the dress from their mother-in-law. The disguise, he said, enabled Lyon to be driven in a carriage undetected through the state militia encampment, though Dick may have embellished his tale over the years. Henry Boernstein recalled that the colonels of the Volunteer regiments met with the Committee of Safety on the evening of 9 May and that at dusk Lyon appeared "in clothing completely covered with dirt and mud from his reconnaissance (having crept though a ditch into the encampment)."[7] What is clear is that Lyon had learned of a shipment of arms to the camp and had decided that it was necessary for him to move against it.

Knowing that General Harney had not been relieved of duty and that he would soon return to St. Louis to resume his command, Lyon urged immediate action. He reported to the committee that General Frost's force had in its possession cannon taken by Confederates from the U.S. Arsenal at Baton Rouge. The discussion of Lyon's plan to capture Camp Jackson continued until midnight. Samuel Glover offered the most strident opposition, arguing that the muster was entirely legal, that the U.S. flag flew over the encampment, and that the proper method for recovering stolen federal property was for the federal marshal to deliver to General Frost a writ of replevin, which would initiate a legal procedure for the reclamation of misappropriated property. If Frost failed to respond to the federal writ, Glover agreed that Lyon could then properly use military force. The committee directed Glover to draft a declaration of replevin; but Blair strongly supported Lyon, who remained determined to proceed immediately before Harney returned.[8]

When the meeting broke up at midnight, Blair returned to Jefferson Barracks to prepare his regiment for action. Broadhead walked with Glover from the Arsenal to Glover's office at Fourth and Pine. Along the way they met pickets from Camp Jackson. As Broadhead recalled, their presence on the city streets indicated to him and to Glover that General Frost expected a movement against him. As the morning of 10 May approached, a heavy

rain prevented Blair from moving his regiment to the Arsenal by river transport as he and Lyon had planned. Instead Blair marched his men into the
city, and Lyon waited until early afternoon to begin his move against the
state militia.[9]

Although the heavy rain undoubtedly dampened the militiamen's spirits, Camp Jackson had worn a festive face for nearly a week. In one sense, it
represented a typical militia muster in the mid-nineteenth century. These
affairs mixed a bit of military training with a great deal of frolicking. Militia
musters provided an opportunity for young men to dress in their colorful
uniforms as the community gathered to witness their display of martial pomp.
The Olive and Market Street streetcar lines carried visitors to the edge of
Lindell Grove, and men, women, and children made regular visits to the
encampment. The Missouri Militia Act of 1859, the law that empowered
Governor Jackson to call the statewide militia muster, had been passed in an
attempt to bring greater order and discipline to the tradition of the citizen-
soldier. Nevertheless, visiting Camp Jackson became a grand social occasion
among the anti-Republican and anti-German citizens of St. Louis. Wit-
nessing events from Illinois, Ulysses Grant thought that St. Louis Unionists
were cowed and inactive. He had recently left St. Louis to work briefly in his
brother's leather business in Galena, and the secession crisis promised to revive his military career. Grant's patron in this regard was Congressman Elihu
B. Washburne of Belleville, Illinois. A visit to Belleville brought Grant within
a dozen miles of St. Louis, and he decided to visit the city. He knew Lyon from
his West Point days and from the Mexican War. On 10 May he watched with
approval as Lyon moved his forces out of the Arsenal to break up the state
militia encampment at Lindell Grove.[10]

Samuel Glover had emphasized the legality of the militia muster. General Frost stressed the same point in a letter he sent to Lyon on the morning of 10 May, a letter that Lyon refused to receive. Every officer and soldier
at the camp, wrote Frost, "had taken, with uplifted hand, the following
oath": "You, each, and every one of you do solemnly swear that you will . . .
serve the State of Missouri against all of her enemies, and that you will
. . . sustain the Constitution and laws of the United States and of this State
against all violence . . . so help you God."[11] But Frost's oath fell far short of
affirming unconditional support for the United States. Governor Jackson
had already declared Lincoln's call for troops unconstitutional, and it would
be surprising if many of the officers and men at Camp Jackson did not view

the Republican administration as a violator of the Constitution, an initia-
tor of violence against the states, and as the principal enemy of the State of
Missouri.

Perhaps Lyon exaggerated when he described "the camp of what is called
the State militia" as being composed "for the most part" of "rabid and violent opposers of the General Government." But he was undoubtedly correct
to characterize Camp Jackson as "a terror to all loyal and peaceful citizens."[12]
Secessionists were prominent there, and a spirit of rebelliousness pervaded
the encampment. Yet some men who answered Governor Jackson's call to
arms harbored little more than a vague attachment to Southern Rights and
to the neutrality that Jackson vowed to defend. For example, John Knapp,
commander of the First Regiment of the state militia was an editor, along with
Nathaniel Paschall, of the conditional Unionist newspaper, the *Missouri Republican*. He did not view his role in the militia muster as an act of rebellion
against the United States, and after the capture of Camp Jackson he supported
the Union. Later, when provisional governor Hamilton Gamble convinced
Lincoln that an "enrolled militia" in the state would provide greater security
to persons and property (including slave property) than the federal army,
Gamble called on Knapp to command the Eighth Regiment of the Enrolled
Missouri Militia. In 1864 Knapp led a brigade of militia troops in the pursuit
of Sterling Price's raiders.[13]

The "rabid and violent" enemies of Lincoln's administration were clearly
present at Camp Jackson, however. Daniel Frost, despite his Northern birth,
became a brigadier general in the Confederate army in March 1862 and served
with rebel forces in Arkansas until fall 1863, when he joined his wife and family (who had been banished from St. Louis) first in Mexico and, later, in
Canada. Colonel John S. Bowen, commander of the Second Regiment in
Frost's force, also wholeheartedly embraced the Confederate cause. A native
of Georgia, Bowen had graduated from West Point in 1853 and had been stationed for a time at Jefferson Barracks. There he met, courted, and married
Mary Kennerly, whose family shared Bowen's Southern values. As a resident
of St. Louis, he had served with the Missouri militia during the border war
with Kansas Jayhawkers. After the capture of Camp Jackson, he fought with
the Confederacy before dying of disease in 1863.[14]

During the late morning hours of 10 May Blair arrived at the Arsenal from
Jefferson Barracks with his First Regiment of Volunteers and with Captain
Sweeny's two companies of regular U.S. troops. At about one o'clock that

afternoon, Lyon began to deploy his forces. Seven columns of Union troops, perhaps numbering 8,000 men in all, advanced against the 700 men in the state militia encampment. Lyon took personal command of Blair's regiment, Sweeny's two companies, and Major Johann Backhoff's artillery battery and led the first column. As it happened, Grant arrived at the Arsenal just as Lyon began his advance. Grant greeted Lyon, introduced himself to Blair, and wished both men well in their afternoon's undertaking. Lyon's column then moved west on Laclede Avenue to the western end of Lindell Grove. There, a lane led north to Olive Street. Lyon followed it and turned east on Olive to deploy his men along the northern edge of Camp Jackson.[15]

Originally stationed at the Arsenal, Henry Boernstein's Second Regiment of U.S. Volunteers had moved at Lyon's direction to the vacant Marine Hospital, a building owned by the United States and located on a hill south of the Arsenal. Boernstein led his regiment west on Pine Street to Lindell Grove, where he linked up with Lyon's column and deployed his forces on the west side of the camp.

Franz Sigel's Third U.S. Volunteers and Nicholas Schuettner's Fourth U.S. Volunteers moved out of the Arsenal and marched north on Broadway toward Olive. Sigel turned his regiment west on Elm, then north on Tenth Street and passed Turner Hall (at Tenth and Walnut Streets). In the hall Colonel John McNeil's Third Reserves shook the building with their impassioned cheers. The *Westliche Post* reported that McNeil's men wept tears of joy and gripped their weapons tightly as they waited their turn to advance against the state militia. Editor Theodor Olshausen compared the emotional scene in St. Louis to the Paris uprising of 1848 and to the Baden-Palatine Revolution of 1849: "It was one of those splendid moments when emotion glowing deep in the heart of the masses suddenly breaks into wild flames."[16] Sigel then moved west on Olive while Schuettner's Fourth Regiment formed a parallel column and moved west on Market Street.

In addition to the U.S. Volunteers, Lyon ordered into the field four regiments of the newly enlisted Home Guards. The First Reserves, commanded by Henry Almstedt, marched up Jefferson Avenue from their headquarters in the first ward on the city's south side. Arriving at Lindell Grove on Laclede Avenue, Almstedt's men took up positions south of Sigel's regiment on the east side of Camp Jackson. Herman Kallmann's Second Reserves assembled at Soulard Market and marched north to Olive and then west to the camp. Kallmann deployed his men alongside Sigel's regiment at the northeastern corner of Lindell Grove. McNeil's Third Reserves gathered at Turner Hall and marched west (probably on Clark) to take control of the southeastern corner of the camp, three blocks south of Schuettner's regiment. Gratz Brown led the Fourth Reserves west from the center of the city to the northeastern corner of the camp, on Garrison Street, three blocks north of Sigel's regiment and Kallmann's Second Reserves.[17]

Outside the German neighborhoods, civilians watched the Union troops advance and showered them with derision. Among the hostile civilians was a young man of fifteen, Philip Dangerfield Stephenson. He and his older brother had made a number of trips to Camp Jackson to enjoy the festivity of a militia muster but also, in this springtime of secession, to imbibe the spirit of rebellion. On 10 May Stephenson and his brother were dismissed as usual from St. Louis High School at about two in the afternoon. They usually went home for supper, but the scene they encountered at Fifteenth and Olive generated a level of excitement that swept them into the developing confrontation. When Stephenson came onto Olive Street he looked east and saw "a solid body of troops, extending as far as the eye could track coming towards us." This was Sigel's Third U.S. Volunteers followed by Kallmann's Second Reserves. Word quickly spread that thousands of men were marching toward Camp Jackson on several other streets as well. Stephenson thought that the men marched somewhat awkwardly, bunched tightly together from sidewalk to sidewalk. He joined the curious and mostly hostile citizens who lined the streets watching and taunting the "damned Dutchmen."[18] Sigel's and Kallmann's soldiers were without uniforms but they were armed, and they had been trained in a rudimentary way to follow orders (in German) to march and maneuver in the field. Stephenson thought they were nervous as they passed Fifteenth Street, and he noted that they occasionally turned their weapons toward hecklers in the civilian crowd. As the Volunteers and Reserves advanced westward toward the camp, Stephenson and other onlookers followed them for more than a dozen blocks. Sigel meanwhile followed Olive Street west to Lindell Grove and took control of the roads leading to Camp Jackson from the east, positioning his six artillery pieces on high ground at its northeastern corner.

As word of Lyon's advance spread through town, Sherman quickly finished his work at the railroad office and went home to the three-story residence he rented from James Lucas on Locust Street between Tenth and Eleventh. There, he paced in front of his house listening for gunfire and for the roar of cannon. He heard nothing. Across Locust Street, his neighbor, Eliza Dean, called to him to say that she feared for the safety of her brother-in-law, who was a surgeon at Camp Jackson. Sherman tried to reassure her that Lyon would confront the militia with such a large force that surrender would be the only option. Mrs. Dean replied that the young men at the camp were from the first families of St. Louis and that they would surely put up a fight. "I explained," recalled Sherman, "that young men of the best families did not like to be killed better than ordinary people." He then walked over to Olive Street on Twelfth and encountered a man running from the direction of the camp, calling out, "They've surrendered, they've surrendered." Sherman returned to Mrs. Dean's house to deliver what he thought would be reassuring news. But the report of the surrender caused her to slam her door in his face. "Evidently," he concluded, "she was disappointed to find she was mistaken in her estimate of the rash courage of the best families."[19]

Within two hours Lyon had deployed his large force around Camp Jackson. Sigel's artillery threatened it from the high ground to the east, and Union troops controlled every road leading into and out of it. Frost was angered but not surprised by the federal movement against him. On the day of the attack, in the letter that Lyon refused to accept, Frost had reported that he was "constantly in receipt of information that you contemplate an attack upon my camp. . . . I understand that you are impressed with the idea that an attack upon the arsenal and the United States troops is intended on the part of the militia of Missouri." He then denied any such intention and protested that there was no justification for Lyon to attack "citizens of the United States who are in the lawful performance of duties devolving upon them under the Constitution in organizing and instructing the militia of the State." Frost had offered to Major Bell at the Arsenal and to General Harney the use of the state militia "to protect the United States in the full possession of all her property." Lyon, had he accepted the letter, would not have been comforted by Frost's willingness to work closely with Harney. More important, Frost did not bother to mention that Jackson had called the militia muster after refusing to comply with President Lincoln's call for troops.[20]

Lyon would not read or reply to Frost's letter, but he did send him a letter of his own, observing that Frost's command was "evidently hostile towards the Government of the United States." Lyon characterized the state militia as being "made up of those secessionists who have openly avowed their hostility to the General Government, and have been plotting at the seizure of its property and the overthrow of its authority." He charged that Frost's command was "openly in communication with the so-called Southern Confederacy, which is now at war with the United States" and that Frost had received "large supplies of material of war, most of which is known to be the property of the United States." Moreover, he continued, Frost operated under the orders of the governor of Missouri, who had urged the state legislature to prepare for hostilities with "the General Government and in co-operation with its enemies." Finally, Frost himself had refused to "disperse in obedience to the proclamation of the President"; that is, he had failed to place himself and his troops under the command of the U.S. Army as Lincoln's proclamation required. At 3:15 P.M., with his troops surrounding Camp Jackson, Lyon delivered his ultimatum:

> HEADQUARTERS UNITED STATES TROOPS
> Saint Louis, Mo., May 10, 1861
>
> Sir: . . . it is my duty to demand, and I do hereby demand, of you an immediate surrender of your command, with no other conditions than that all persons surrendering under this demand shall be humanely and kindly treated. Believing myself prepared to enforce this demand, one-half hour's time, before doing so, will be allowed for your compliance therewith.
>
> Very respectfully, your obedient servant,
>
> N. LYON
> Captain, Second Infantry, Comdg. Troops
>
> General D. M. Frost, Commanding Camp Jackson.[21]

To this demand Frost bitterly replied:

> CAMP JACKSON, MO., May 10, 1861
>
> Sir: I never for a moment having conceived the idea that so illegal and unconstitutional a demand as I have just received from you would be made by an officer of the United States Army, I am wholly unprepared to defend my command from this unwarranted attack, and shall therefore be forced to comply with your demand.
>
> I am, sir, very respectfully, your obedient servant,
>
> D. M. FROST
> Brig. Gen., Comdg., Camp Jackson, M.V.M.
>
> Capt. N. Lyon, Commanding U.S. Troops.[22]

Stephenson and the other civilians who had followed the Union troops to Camp Jackson had expected to witness a firefight, not an immediate surrender. At first he and his mates took up observation posts on the roof of a building some distance from the camp. But when they heard no shots being fired, they went forward and with other civilians passed through the Union lines into Camp Jackson. There they discovered that the State Guard had already surrendered to Captain Lyon. The Union soldiers divided the prisoners into two groups and marched them onto the Olive Street plank road while Lyon secured the captured camp and prepared for the return march to the Arsenal. Schuettner's and Sigel's regiments remained at Camp Jackson to guard the captured weapons. On orders from Lyon's adjutant, Franklin A. Dick, Boernstein marched his regiment east along the north side of the camp and formed a column behind Blair's regiment. Blair's troops enclosed half the prisoners; Boernstein's regiment enclosed the other half. A band, followed by Frost and his staff, led the procession of captives. To the rear was a rather forlorn group of Germans who had served with the state militia during the border war with Kansas Jayhawkers and who had answered Governor Jackson's call to muster; now they were the captives of fellow Germans who had joined the U.S. Volunteer regiments. At about six o'clock in the afternoon, the band struck up "The Star Spangled Banner" and the column began to move forward.

After learning of the surrender, Sherman walked out Olive Street to Lindell Grove with his seven-year-old son, Willie. He arrived to find the militiamen assembled on Olive between two lines of federal troops. As the band began to play, the column of troops and prisoners "made one or two ineffectual starts, but for some reason halted." During the delay, Sherman recognized and greeted Major Rufus Saxton, who commanded a battalion of regular troops. Sherman gave him a copy of an evening paper that he had bought on the walk down Olive Street. Waiting for the column to move, Saxton sat reading the news on horseback.[23]

Suddenly gunfire erupted. Sitting at her home "quietly sewing," Sarah Hill heard the musket fire and attributed it to practice drills at Camp Jackson. English-born and married to a native of Vermont, Hill strongly supported the Union cause. She learned of the violence from a neighbor, also a woman of English birth but sympathetic to the secessionist cause. The neighbor burst into Hill's room, fearfully denouncing "the Black Dutch" who, she said, were killing the men at Camp Jackson.[24] At the camp, federal officers quickly restored order but scores of civilians and soldiers lay dead and dying. Different observers saw (and recalled) different sequences of events. But there are enough common elements in their accounts to permit an objective examination of the incident.[25]

Theodor Olshausen witnessed the shooting and reported that the first shots had been fired after prosecessionist hecklers shouted insults at the German soldiers. Some of the soldiers were "so upset that they fired their weapons, admittedly over the heads of the onlookers." He reported that officers immediately identified the weapons that had been fired and arrested the offending soldiers. Stephenson also recalled that the first volley had been fired over the heads of the crowd; but he thought that it had been fired after a soldier, reacting to clods of dirt being thrown at his commander, Captain Constantin Blandowski, fired a single shot toward the crowd. In the melee that followed, Blandowski fell to the ground, shot in the leg by one of the federal soldiers (he later died of the wound).[26] In Stephenson's recollection, the federal troops had mistaken the shot by the startled soldier for hostile fire; it was then, he said, that the federals fired over the heads of the crowd. Sherman also reported that the first shots passed over the crowd's heads. "I heard the balls cutting the leaves above our heads," he recalled, "and saw men and women running in all directions."[27]

Frost, at the head of the first column of prisoners, recalled a single shot followed almost immediately by a volley, although in his account the federal troops had not acted recklessly but "with precision considering the rawness of the troops."[28] Boernstein, at the head of the second column, recalled that his troops advanced about 100 paces and then halted. Then, from a construction site on the south side of the street, "shots came from the building, from the trees, and from the camp fences, and bullets went whistling past our heads." As he looked around he saw "fifteen or twenty men with revolvers." It was then that the German troops opened fire on their civilian attackers.[29]

In all likelihood it was not a single event that prompted the shooting at Camp Jackson but a number of separate occurrences. All accounts attest to the verbal abuse heaped upon the German soldiers by many of the onlookers and by the captured militiamen. All accounts also describe missiles being thrown at the federal troops. But pistol shots were almost certainly fired as well. All accounts agree that the warning volley gave way to a deadly fusillade. The *Republican,* while defending the legality of the militia muster and denouncing the slaughter of "unoffending spectators," reported that the "conduct of a few . . . desperadoes" preceded the deadly volley from the troops.[30] In Stephenson's view, the gunfire turned deadly when the crowd of militia-men and camp followers (himself included) surged away from the warning volley and were fired upon by soldiers guarding the other side of the column. After the warning volley, Olshausen reported that a pistol shot rang out, "ac-companied by several flying rocks." This occurred just as the last of the cap-tured soldiers were turned onto Olive Street. Quickly "the fire spread to where we stood," the editor wrote. "Bullets whined to our left and right," he reported. "Right next to us a man fell dead." Not far away a second man fell to the ground with a shattered knee. The shooting stopped as abruptly as it began. By all accounts Lyon's regular troops held their fire, and aided by this re-straint, officers were soon able to stop the German soldiers from shooting. As Olshausen surveyed the field "where the dead and wounded lay," he counted fourteen who were "killed outright" and another forty who were wounded, some seriously. Women and children lay among the dead and wounded, and Olshausen was "convinced that there were more Unionists among the victims than secessionists." In addition to the civilian deaths, he reported that three soldiers in Boernstein's Second Regiment were wounded, along with Captain Blandowski of Sigel's Third Regiment. One volunteer in Company H of Sigel's regiment had been killed, as was Nicholaus Knobloch "of the regulars." The *Missouri Republican* reported that three members of the militia had been killed. In Boernstein's regiment, the paper reported two killed and six wounded. For the editor of the *Westliche Post,* "This sad final act cast a dark veil over an otherwise glorious day."[31]

Sherman, standing with his son Willie near the edge of Lindell Grove, saw a drunken bystander attempting to make his way through the federal line to cross Olive Street. A sergeant in a company of regular troops ordered him back. The "drunken fellow" continued to advance, and the sergeant blocked his passage, raising his musket "a-port," or across his chest. When the man grabbed the musket, the sergeant knocked him back, and he tumbled down the embank-ment by the side of the road. When he regained his footing and picked up his hat, the column had moved forward and the regular troops had passed. Ger-man troops then passed along this section of Olive Street.[32] The drunkard made his way back up the embankment brandishing a small pistol, which he fired at the U.S. troops. Sherman reported that the shot brought the column to a halt in momentary confusion. The soldiers then began firing over the heads of the bystanders in Lindell Grove. Soon, however, they fired directly into the crowd.

Some of those that Sherman watched running about in a "general stampede" were bleeding from wounds. Sherman and Willie lay on the ground, partially protected by the embankment that rose from Lindell Grove to Olive Street. When the soldiers paused to reload their muskets, Sherman "jerked Willie up" and ran away from the road to a gully in the grove. There they remained until Sherman was certain that the troops had passed. Father and son then made their way home, carefully, avoiding the troops and their captives.[33]

Over the years, historians have criticized Lyon and Blair for their actions at Camp Jackson. Writing in 1888, Lucien Carr (married to Cornelia L. Crow, the daughter of the St. Louis business leader and philanthropist Wayman Crow) deemed its capture a "blunder." In his view, the federal movement had been an act of war against a state that remained in the Union, just as neighboring Illinois and Iowa remained in the Union. Carr did not mention the fact that the governors of those two states, in contrast to Missouri's Governor Jackson, had responded positively to Lincoln's call for troops.[34] Writing in 1998, William E. Parrish, a leading historian of Civil War Missouri and the biographer of Frank Blair, concluded that "the move against Camp Jackson was a colossal blunder," presumably because of the bitterness the federal action left in its wake.[35]

To be sure, by the time Lyon moved against Camp Jackson, secessionists in St. Louis could no longer reasonably hope to seize control of the Arsenal or the powder magazine at Jefferson Barracks. Fewer than 1,000 men answered the call to muster at Camp Jackson, and they faced a federal force that approached 10,000 men. Moreover, as Hamilton Gamble and others had warned during the deliberations of the state convention, free states surrounded Missouri on three sides. Federal troops in Illinois, Iowa, and Kansas could (and would) invade if secessionists took up arms against the forces of the United States in Missouri. Governor Jackson may have initially hoped that a militia muster in St. Louis could lead to the seizure of the Arsenal, but by the time it gathered at Camp Jackson the significance of the encampment clearly lay elsewhere.

The militia muster across the state served a distinct purpose in permitting Jackson and Price to begin to gather their resources and to mobilize their forces to resist federal authority without directly challenging U.S. troops. Moreover, a state military presence in St. Louis supported the anti-Republican mayor and the secessionist Police Board. St. Louis could also give militia forces in the interior of the state access to weapons shipped up the Mississippi from the Confederate garrisons just below Cairo, Illinois. The eleven-day militia muster offered Governor Jackson an opportunity to begin preparations for war at a time when he could not yet directly threaten the U.S. military forces stationed in Missouri.

Jackson's plan very nearly worked. The major weapons shipped to Camp Jackson probably arrived because Lyon and Blair allowed them to. Nevertheless, at the camp and in the military districts across the state, officers and men made serious preparations for war. In that context, Lyon had very little room within which to maneuver as events unfolded. The muster began while General Harney was in Washington and while Lyon was free to work without hindrance to raise and arm the regiments authorized by Cameron, Scott, and Lincoln on 30 April. But when Lyon learned that Harney had retained his command and that the general would return to St. Louis on 11 May, Lyon faced the prospect that Camp Jackson would finish out the last week of its existence unchallenged by federal authority. Lyon, of course, was eager to move against it. In his eyes, the governor's call for a militia muster immediately after his refusal to comply with Lincoln's call for troops made the camp an intolerable act of defiance against the United States. The secret shipment of weapons to the camp from the Confederacy gave Lyon a reason to take action. Even so, he had to overcome strong resistance from Samuel Glover, when he presented his plan to the Committee of Safety. Only Blair's strong support for immediate action made it possible for Lyon to proceed. Without it, the committee would have been deeply divided.

Blair knew the temper of the city. Specifically, he knew that the recent election added significantly to the power of the enemies of the Union. Perhaps, as Snead believed, the election had reflected a nativist reaction to the German Home Guard activity.[36] Perhaps it simply revealed the caution of conditional Unionists. In either case, with the Police Board in secessionist hands and with the mayor an avowed enemy of Lincoln and the Republicans, the state militia force at Camp Jackson posed a distinct threat, not to the Arsenal but to the Republicans and to other stalwart Union men. The closing of Niederwieser's restaurant and Boernstein's opera house on Sundays seemed to the German community to be a dangerous beginning to what could become, with the support of the state militia, a chilling climate of repression. Moreover, the festive nature of the muster made it clear that the encampment emboldened and empowered secessionists, focusing their enthusiasm for the cause of the South against the "damned Dutch" and the "black Republicans" in St. Louis. These were not sentiments that Blair wished to see encouraged because they demoralized Unionists and rendered them (as Grant had noted) timid in the face of secessionist posturing. If the Unionist majority in St. Louis could be cowed, secessionists could make the city a conduit for arming their recruits elsewhere in Missouri.

Grant noted that pro-Southern sentiment was muted and sullen after the capture of Camp Jackson. "The secessionists became quiet," he recalled, "but were filled with suppressed rage." Earlier it was the camp's supporters who "had been playing the bully," he wrote. Now "Union men became rampant, aggressive, and, if you will, intolerant." Wishing to congratulate Lyon after the capture of Camp Jackson, Grant boarded a streetcar at the corner of Fourth and Pine to make the trip south to the Arsenal. On the car he encountered "a dapper little fellow" full of outrage that Unionists had successfully demanded the lowering of the "rebel flag" from the nearby Berthold mansion. The dandy declared that where he came from any man who would dare to act in such a manner would be hanged from the nearest tree. Grant interjected that "after all we were not so intolerant in St. Louis as we might be." He "had not seen a single rebel hung yet, nor heard of one." But, he added, "there were plenty of them who ought to be, however." The little fellow, said Grant, "subsided."[37]

Lyon, in his official report to the War Department, did not elaborate on the loss of civilian lives after the capture of the state militia. He simply reported that, under orders from the adjutant general's office, he had "accepted, swore in, and armed 3,436 men and 70 officers of the loyal citizens of St. Louis, as a 'reserve corps,' for the protection of Government property and enforcement of its laws." He had done this on 7 and 8 May and would have continued to enroll the reserves if the events leading to the surrender of Camp Jackson had not intervened. On the night of 8 May, Lyon reported, the steamer *J. C. Swon* had arrived in St. Louis with a large cargo of military stores including, as he had been informed, "muskets, ammunition, and cannon taken on board at Baton Rouge" by Confederate forces. Under cover of darkness the weapons were transported to Camp Jackson, providing the justification he needed to move against the state militia. In all likelihood, Lyon could have intervened but chose not to:

> The boat arriving in the night, great industry was used to transport these stores during the night (and before being likely to be exposed in the morning) to the camp of what is called the State militia.

Their extraordinary and unscrupulous conduct, and their evident design, and of the governor of this State, to take a position of hostility to the United States, are matters of extensive detail and of abounding evidence. . . . It was therefore necessary to meet this embarrassing complication as early as possible, and accordingly I proceeded yesterday with a large body of troops, supported by artillery, to the camp above referred to . . . and demanded of General Frost, the commander, a surrender of his entire command.[38]

After the surrender of Camp Jackson, Lyon gathered the evidence he sought to demonstrate U.S. munitions had been secreted into the camp. From the Baton Rouge Arsenal he found three thirty-two-pound guns, one mortar (and three mortar beds, suggesting that the missing mortars were somewhere in the city), "and a large supply of shot and shells in ale barrels." The artillery pieces were still packaged in heavy planks and labeled for delivery to "Greeley & Gale, St. Louis." The merchants named—Carlos Greeley and Daniel B. Gale, both New Hampshire natives—were well known for their strong Unionist convictions. Since no delivery of military materials had been made to them, Lyon concluded his report by observing that the weapons had been shipped in this way to protect them from "close scrutiny."[39]

Lyon said only this about the violence that followed the surrender: "During the surrender of Camp Jackson and their passage into our lines a mob attacked our force, a published account of which will be transmitted." The day after the surrender, he reported that the 639 men captured were released "on their parole of honor not to fight against the United States during this war." With one exception, the 50 officers were also released on the same oath. The one holdout, Captain Emmet McDonald, a cavalry commander at Camp Jackson, declined the parole and challenged the constitutionality of the federal action. Lyon closed his report by observing that the volunteer brigade that he had raised upon order of President Lincoln had elected him brigadier general. He had accepted the position, he reported, and awaited confirmation of his new rank from the War Department.[40]

Lyon's circumspection regarding the loss of life at Camp Jackson was matched by Frost's outrage. To General Harney, Frost directed a detailed complaint. Lyon had illegally attacked his camp and required his surrender. Once disarmed and surrounded by Lyon's men, "a fire was opened upon a portion" of his troops "and a number of my men [were] put to death, together with several innocent lookers-on,—men, women, and children." When his camp was attacked "in this unwarrantable manner," and during all the days of its existence, "the only flags that floated there were those of the United States, with *all* the stars, and its fellow, bearing alone the coat of arms of the State of Missouri." Frost protested the terms of the parole as illegal and demanded the return of confiscated equipment that had been purchased by himself and his men. On 18 May Harney forwarded Frost's protest to the adjutant general's office in Washington, D.C., recommending that private property be restored to Frost and his men ("munitions of war excepted") and requesting instructions "respecting the transaction to which General Frost invites attention."[41]

After the capture of Camp Jackson, sporadic fighting left several more dead and wounded. As James Broadhead recalled, "The night after the Camp Jackson affair was a bad night for mobs."[42] More violence erupted on 11 May, as the 1,200 men of Stifel's Fifth Regiment presented themselves at the Arsenal to receive their arms. On their return to Stifel's Brewery on the city's north side, the troops were greeted with cheers in the German southside neighborhoods as they marched north on Second Street. But as the regiment turned west on Walnut Street and made its way to Seventh Street, a large gathering of hecklers cursed the troops, stoned them, and threatened them with knives. At the corner of Walnut and Fifth and again at Seventh Street, shots were fired at the rear of the column and several soldiers fell. The soldiers then turned and fired at the crowd, killing a half dozen as the rest fled. Lyon reported to the War Department that two soldiers had been killed, together with ten of the civilian assailants. Governor Jackson's aide, Thomas Snead, believed that the two soldiers had been killed by their own fire. He reported six civilians killed.[43]

Shortly after this attack, the paroled captives from Camp Jackson were freed. Fearing that they would be attacked if they passed through the German southside neighborhoods, Harney had them transported by boat to Chestnut Street, in the center of the city. From there they made their way without further incident to their homes.[44]

The capture of Camp Jackson abruptly altered the balance of power in St. Louis. The supremacy of federal authority in the city had been asserted decisively. The threat posed by the mayor and the Police Board evaporated as Lyon disarmed and dispersed the militia. Broadhead, who had been sympathetic to Glover's legal arguments against attacking Camp Jackson, had supported Lyon's actions with reservations (as had Glover). Despite the shocking loss of life—perhaps, in part, because of it—Broadhead noted the effect that Lyon's action had on many St. Louisans who previously had felt free to voice their support for the Southern case. Like Sherman's neighbor, these people now kept their opinions to themselves, behind closed doors. The capture of Camp Jackson, Broadhead wrote a friend, had "operated like a poultice, the inflammation has been drawn out of a great number of men who were heretofore rampant secessionists."[45]

What very nearly made the Camp Jackson affair a blunder as far as Blair and Lyon were concerned was the concerted opposition it generated against them. In its immediate aftermath Lyon's long-standing dispute with General Harney erupted into an open and bitter conflict. Within the month, it ended with Harney's removal and Lyon's appointment as commander of federal forces in Missouri. But a number of prominent St. Louisans ardently advocated the opposite outcome, and it was not immediately clear that they would not succeed. Harney counted among his supporters the conservative Unionists of the city. Immediately after the capture of Camp Jackson, a group of leading citizens, including James Yeatman, Wayman Crow, Hamilton Gamble, and Robert Campbell, met with Mayor Daniel Taylor to discuss how they should proceed to sustain Harney and obtain Lyon's removal. The group ended its meeting by deciding that Yeatman and Gamble would go to Washington and work with Gamble's brother-in-law, Attorney General Edward Bates, to support Harney's conciliatory policy and to seek Lyon's removal.[46]

Harney returned to St. Louis as planned on 11 May and met immediately with Wayman Crow and other conservatives who also urged Lyon's removal and demanded the suppression of the German Home Guard. Shocked by the loss of life that followed the camp's capture and alarmed by the volatile mood of nativists and Germans in St. Louis, Harney expressed support for the conservatives' position. But he had learned during his consultations in Washington that the continuance of his command in the Department of the West depended on his ability to work with Frank Blair. Well aware that Captain Lyon (and the capture of Camp Jackson) had Blair's full support, Harney publicly approved of Lyon's actions. He told the conservatives, however, that he would attempt to disarm the Home Guard; failing that, he would try to have them stationed at Jefferson Barracks, safely outside the city. To quiet fears of a German insurrection, he ordered all the regular U.S. troops (except Lyon's company) into the city, where, with four pieces of artillery, they were deployed to contain the German wards.[47]

In a proclamation issued 12 May, Harney outlined the cautious course that he intended to follow. "I have just returned to this post," he announced, "and have assumed the military command of this department." He expressed his regret for "the deplorable state of things here" and promised to discharge his "delicate and onerous duties . . . to preserve the public peace." Emphasizing his sharp disagreement with Lyon, he announced, "I shall carefully abstain from the exercise of any unnecessary powers and from all interference with the proper functions of the public officers of the State and city." He would use the military forces under his command only "in the last resort to preserve the peace." He had, he acknowledged, "no authority to change the location of the Home Guards," but he would act to "avoid all cause of irritation and excitement" by using regular soldiers when called on by the local authorities to assist in preserving the public peace.[48]

As Harney resumed his command, he attempted to isolate Lyon, who briefly feared that the general might succeed and in the process reverse an important victory over the disloyal elements in St. Louis. Writing to the War Department on 12 May, Lyon stressed that "the energetic and necessary measures" that he had taken to capture Camp Jackson "require persevering and consistent execution" to prevent the formation of further "combinations" hostile to the federal government. He protested that the "authority of General Harney under these circumstances embarrasses, in the most painful manner, the execution of the plans I had contemplated, and upon which the safety and welfare of the Government, as I conceive, so much depend."[49]

As Lyon drafted his letter of protest to the War Department, Frank Blair lodged a protest of his own directly with General Harney. Meeting with Harney on 12 May, Blair reminded him that the Reserve Corps (i.e., the Home Guard) had been raised and armed by an order endorsed by President Lincoln. Moreover, Lyon had been instructed in that order to raise the Home Guard in consultation with the St. Louis Committee of Safety. Blair assured Harney that the committee wanted the Home Guard armed and in the city. Harney had little choice but to acquiesce. Nevertheless, Blair sensed that Harney continued to favor a conciliatory policy toward the city's disloyal elements. At Blair's direction, Franklin Dick traveled to Washington to support Lyon and oppose Harney.

At Lyon's request, *Anzeiger des Westens*'s editor Carl Ludwig Bernays visited Washington on a similar mission.[50]

In what proved to be Harney's most effective move, he secured from the War Department permission to raise a sixth regiment of U.S. Volunteers. "I think it of the utmost importance," he wrote Cameron on 15 May, "that an additional regiment, consisting exclusively of Irishmen, should be raised in Saint Louis." As Harney noted, the federal troops raised by Lyon, in consultation with the Committee of Safety, "consist almost exclusively of Germans." He believed that the new Irish regiment would help to "settle matters" in St. Louis and "do away with the prejudice against the Government troops."[51] Certainly he knew that an Irish regiment would not contribute to the influence of Lyon and Blair, and he may have hoped that it would serve to weaken their control over the direction of federal policy. Although Bernays strongly supported Lyon over Harney, he publicly welcomed the new regiment as evidence that the struggle to keep St. Louis in the Union would not be made by Germans alone. "With almost all the Irish on our side under General Lyon's command," he observed in the *Anzeiger des Westens,* "the war will have a happy conclusion." He continued to urge Germans to demonstrate their support for the Union cause, prompting his readers to sign up "to serve until the end of the war," and he hoped that a seventh and eighth regiment would make room for even more German recruits.[52]

Meanwhile, the governor continued to organize the military forces of the state. He regarded the attack on Camp Jackson as an act of aggression, and, as Lyon had observed at the 9 May meeting of the Committee of Safety, Jackson had secretly presented the general assembly with a military bill that would place Missouri "in a complete state of defence." When news reached Jefferson City late in the afternoon of 10 May that Lyon had captured Camp Jackson and that he held state militiamen as prisoners in the U.S. Arsenal, all resistance to the bill evaporated, and it quickly passed. The general assembly adjourned on 15 May after creating a military fund with all the state's available resources. On 18 May Jackson appointed Price major general commanding the military forces of Missouri. Of the nine brigadier generals Price appointed, only one, Meriwether Lewis Clark, was a St. Louisan. Named in honor of his father's partner in the epic Lewis and Clark expedition from St. Louis to the Pacific and back, Clark, a graduate of West Point, had fought in the Black Hawk and the Mexican Wars and by the 1850s made his living in St. Louis as an engineer and an architect. Price appointed the fifty-two-year-old briga-dier general of the Missouri State Guard. Clark later transferred to the Con-federate army and served as an artillery commander with Price, Van Dorn, and finally with Lee in the Army of Northern Virginia.[53]

Harney issued a proclamation on 14 May that declared the military bill to be in violation of the Constitution and laws of the United States and there-fore "a nullity." "This bill," he said, "cannot be regarded in any other light than an indirect secession ordinance." The general implored the citizens of Missouri not to heed its call to arms.[54] But he soon returned to his concilia-tory ways.

Meanwhile, Franklin Dick arrived in Washington ahead of James Yeat-man and Hamilton Gamble. Hurriedly, Montgomery Blair arranged a meet-ing with Dick, President Lincoln, and Secretary of War Cameron. Dick urged that Harney be removed and that the War Department quickly confirm Lyon's new rank as brigadier general. At Bates's request, Lincoln delayed his deci-sion in the matter until after he had met with Yeatman and Gamble. Lincoln sided with the Blair faction, however, and approved Lyon's promotion to brigadier general (on 17 May). Perhaps as a concession to Bates, Lincoln con-tinued to support Harney's policy of conciliation, although the President decided to leave the final disposition of the matter in the hands of Frank Blair.[55]

On 20 May Blair received an order (dated 16 May) removing Harney from command, accompanied by a note from Lincoln (written 18 May). The president expressed his hope that it would not be necessary for Blair to deliver the removal order to Harney. Lincoln bowed to the arguments that the Blairs had put before him, but he did not oppose Harney's conciliatory policy if it worked to keep the peace in Missouri. After expressing his con-cerns, Lincoln left the matter entirely to Blair: deliver the order if "in your judgement it is *indispensable*."[56]

Unaware that the fate of his command had been placed in the hands of his leading critic, Harney continued on his conciliatory course. Notwithstand-ing his proclamation of 14 May declaring the military bill an indirect seces-sion ordinance, and notwithstanding Governor Jackson's appointment of Sterling Price as commanding general of the state militia, Harney agreed on 20 May to meet in St. Louis with Price to consider an agreement that could preserve the peace. On 21 May, Harney and Price conferred and agreed to cooperate to restore and maintain "peace and good order to the people of the state." If, as Harney's proclamation had stated, the general viewed the military bill as an act of secession, the Harney-Price agreement reflected Price's ability to convince Harney that the issue of peace should take precedence over the question of loyalty. The agreement stated that "General Price . . . undertakes, with the sanction of the governor of the state . . . to direct the whole power of the state officers to maintain order within the state among the people thereof." Further, the agreement declared that, as commander of federal forces in Missouri, Harney "can have no occasion, as he has no wish, to make movements which might otherwise create excitement and jealousies which he most earnestly desires to avoid." In concluding their agreement, Price and Harney expressed their hope that "the unquiet elements, which have threatened so seriously to disturb the public peace, may soon subside, and be remembered only to be deplored."[57]

After the Harney-Price agreement was signed, Governor Jackson relaxed his preparations to defend Jefferson City from federal attack and sent the state militia to remain in readiness in its several home districts. Price had obtained from Harney a valuable breathing space for Jackson and his fellow secessionists.[58] Respecting Lincoln's wishes not to remove Harney unless absolutely necessary (and, perhaps, waiting for Harney to thoroughly discredit himself), Blair expressed his "disgust and dissatisfaction" with the agreement but otherwise left matters alone.[59] A great deal of work remained to be done to secure the St. Louis region from disloyal elements. A federal advance against Sterling Price and Claiborne Jackson could wait.

While Harney's fate was being decided, Lyon moved aggressively to deploy the forces under his command in a manner that gave him full control of the city. On the evening of 16 May he ordered Boernstein's Second Regiment to occupy the waterworks on the city's north side. Boernstein made his headquarters at the reservoir while a rifle battalion commanded by Major Osterhaus camped on the heights between Hyde Park and Bremen Avenue, where they controlled the North Missouri Railroad and the Mississippi River with two cannon. Major Bernhard Laibold also served (he was later a brigade commander at Chickamauga). Boernstein's artillery commander, Major Johann Backhoff, had served with Franz Sigel in the Baden army before emigrating to the United States. Lyon directed Sigel's Third Regiment to occupy Neuer's soap factory alongside the Pacific Railroad. From that point they also controlled the St. Charles and Manchester streetcar lines. Blair's First Regiment moved onto the island near the Arsenal and there controlled passage up and down the Mississippi. A detachment of his regiment controlled Gravois Road, which led to the countryside south of the city.[60]

Lyon also took action to rout rebels from Potosi in nearby Washington County, which he reported had been prompted by "the frequent arrivals at this place of persons from Potosi, complaining of revolting outrages, and being driven from their homes because of their loyalty to the General Government." To meet this threat Lyon dispatched two infantry companies from the Fifth Missouri Volunteers (commanded by Captain Nelson Cole) and a rifle battalion from the First Missouri Volunteers. The force arrived by rail at Potosi before dawn on the morning of 16 May and surrounded the town. Squads of soldiers entered the houses of all persons suspected of disloyal activities and arrested and gathered them together at the town's courthouse. Homes were searched, but no arms were found. Of the fifty-six men arrested, forty-seven were paroled on their oath not to take up arms against the United States. The nine recalcitrants were taken as prisoners to the St. Louis Arsenal. Cole then led his force to two smelting furnaces whose owners had supplied lead to suspected rebels. There they seized 100 pigs of lead; another 325 were confiscated at the railroad depot. Also at the depot, the troops found partly manufactured rebel uniforms. At noon Cole's force began its return trip to St. Louis, stopping briefly at De Soto to disrupt a "large secession meeting." Learning that a force of mounted men was nearby, Cole dispatched a platoon of forty soldiers to engage them. The suspected rebels dismounted and ran into the woods as the soldiers approached. Cole's men captured fifteen horses, some firearms, and a secessionist flag. They then raised the American flag over De Soto, and Cole left a guard of thirty men in the town as he continued to St. Louis, arriving at 6:00 P.M.[61] If Lyon thought a patrol of this kind could effectively suppress disloyal activities in the countryside, he very quickly learned otherwise.

As Blair undoubtedly expected, it did not take long for Harney to discredit himself in Lincoln's eyes. On 22 May James Broadhead wrote the War Department for the Committee of Safety, denouncing the Harney-Price agreement. On 24 May Frank Blair wrote the Secretary of War, denouncing Governor Jackson as a traitor and arguing that his agreement with Price made Harney an accomplice of traitors.[62]

As reports from across the state reached St. Louis concerning secessionist activities, Blair sent them to his brother in Washington, and the War Department sent two back to Harney. In one, a correspondent of Oliver Filley reported from Saint Joseph on 22 May that "secessionists have seized fifteen thousand pounds of lead at Lebanon." Secessionists had also reportedly taken control of "seventeen kegs of powder." From Springfield on 21 May Frank Blair received a report that the "American flag floating over the post-office was to-day taken down by a mob . . . and the States rights flag hoisted in its place." The mob then tore the American flag to pieces. Harney also received information that troops and military supplies were being moved into southwestern Missouri from Arkansas. He sent this information to Price and asked, "Would it not be well for me to station a regiment in the southern frontier of Missouri?" Price telegraphed in reply that he had "attended" to the dispatches from Saint Joseph and Springfield and answered the question: "I advise that you do not send a regiment into the southwest; it will exasperate our own people."[63]

Harney's solicitude toward Price prompted a stern lecture from President Lincoln. Through the adjutant general of the army, Lincoln warned Harney of his growing concern: "It is immaterial whether these outrages continue from inability or indisposition on the part of the state authorities to prevent them," he observed. "The authority of the United States is paramount," the president continued, "and whenever it is apparent that a movement, whether by color of State authority or not, is hostile, you will not hesitate to put it down." Harney replied to these stern instructions by arguing that the agreement with Price was essential to "the loyalty now fully aroused in the State and her firm security in the Union. . . . I entertain the conviction," he concluded, "that the agreement between myself and General Price will be carried out in good faith."[64]

Reports of hostile action continued to reach Harney, who then informed Price but received assurances that all was well. Price acknowledged that Union men might have suffered at the hands of "irresponsible individuals," but he insisted that they had not participated in any "meetings or organizations." How Price had arrived at this conclusion he did not say. He appealed (evidently with good effect) to Harney's sense of honor as an officer and a gentleman: "General, it is my unchanged and honest intention to carry out the letter of the agreement entered into between us." Fearing that Harney might feel compelled to move federal forces into the interior of the state—as Lincoln had insisted that he should—Price added that he felt certain that Harney, "from the high sense of honor that has always attended your public acts . . . will, with equal fidelity, observe the same on your part."[65]

If these were reassuring words for Harney, they were not so for Lincoln or Blair. On 30 May Blair delivered to Harney the orders for his removal. Stunned, Harney protested to the War Department, but to no avail. On 31 May Lyon announced that he had assumed command of the Department of the West as brigadier general of the Missouri U.S. Volunteers.[66]

Two days before Harney's removal, on 28 May at 3:30 P.M., Captain Blandowski died from the wound he had received at Camp Jackson. Surgeons had amputated his shattered leg in an attempt to save his life. Although probably hit by a minié ball from one of the muskets of the federal troops, Blandowski became in death a martyr to the Union cause. His death lifted the dark veil that had fallen over German troops after the killings at Camp Jackson. A Polish patriot born in Prussia, Blandowski had had extensive military experience in Europe fighting with Poles, Sardinians, and Hungarians against the Austrian Empire. With the collapse of the Hungarian revolution in 1849, he fled to the United States, settling eventually in St. Louis, where he made his living as a fencing instructor. He established close ties in the German community, and in 1861 he commanded Company C of Sigel's Third Regiment, U.S. Volunteers. For the funeral procession Sigel ordered Companies A, B, and C to assemble at Turner Hall at 8:00 A.M. on 29 May. Joining the three companies were a contingent of Turner Zouaves carrying the Turner flag. Blandowski had demonstrated his and his students' prowess in fencing at Turner Hall and probably had been a member of the organization himself. Sigel led the procession to Samaritan Hospital, where the captain's body lay. The procession then made its way to Picker's Cemetery as a large crowd of federal soldiers and Unionist civilians watched. "Never," reported the *Westliche Post,* "had anyone ever seen so many soldiers or such good ones." In quiet procession the funeral party marched to the beat of muffled drums down Franklin Street. Blandowski's company, with two pieces of field artillery and a band, escorted the coffin and led the procession. His relatives, army officers, representatives of the Turner Society, and a rear guard of troops completed it. At the grave, Captain John F. Hohlfield (who died of wounds received at the Battle of Wilson's Creek in August) delivered a stirring eulogy. Unionists in St. Louis believed that Blandowski had been shot by a pistol fired from the crowd of onlookers at Camp Jackson; the physician's report that the wound had been caused by a minié rifle ball did not appear in the *Republican* until after the funeral. Blandowski's death, said Hohlfield, strengthened the resolve of Unionists to put down the murderous spirit of secession. The

Westliche Post reported that Hohlfield "reminded his listeners that the first victims in this war had been brought down by cowardly assassins" and that "earnest oaths of revenge against the cowardly snipers flitted toward heaven from this open grave." An honor guard fired three volleys "over the freshly covered grave."[67]

On the day of Blandowski's funeral, a St. Louis woman, uncertain of her loyalty toward the Union, wrote in anger reporting the aggressive activities of the Home Guard. Proud of her family's Southern heritage and deeply hostile toward the Dutch and the Republicans, Bethiah Pyalt McKown complained that "our City is encompassed with armed *Goth* and *Vandals,* for they are Dutch and Poles that cannot speak our language and they are searching every carriage as it passes, and every house in the environs of the City for arms and ammunition." The Home Guards were seizing not only military weapons but "*shot guns, and pistols,* whenever they can lay their lawless hands upon them."[68]

Harney's removal from command threatened Governor Jackson's efforts to maintain a truce between federal and state armed forces as he worked to amass sufficient military strength openly to declare Missouri a state in the Confederacy. Aware that Attorney General Bates and his conservative allies in St. Louis strongly supported the Harney-Price agreement, Lyon did not immediately revoke it. But unless Jackson could reach an understanding with the new commander, Price's ability to organize the state's military forces free of federal interference became problematic. Richard Barrett, recently paroled after the surrender of Camp Jackson, pressed Jackson and Price to seek a meeting with Lyon in the hope that the agreement could be extended indefinitely. Lyon agreed to a meeting and wrote a letter of safe conduct. Jackson and Price left Jefferson City on 10 June and the next morning they informed Lyon that they were at the Planters' House and would meet him there. At first Lyon insisted that they meet at the Arsenal, but Jackson wanted it to take place on more neutral terrain. Lyon agreed to meet at the hotel and arrived with his aide-de-camp, Major Horace Conant, and with Colonel Frank Blair. Thomas Snead attended as aide-de-camp to Price and recalled that Lyon opened the discussion by saying Blair would represent the government. After half an hour Lyon began to participate in the discussions, and gradually he eclipsed Blair. In a proclamation issued from Jefferson City on 12 June, Jackson explained what had been discussed. He had proposed to disarm the State Guard, to suppress all insurrectionary activity in the state, and to call on the aid of the U.S. troops, if necessary, to maintain the neutrality of the state. In exchange for this, he had demanded that Lyon disarm the Home Guard. In Jackson's view the Reserve Corps usurped his authority over all state militia forces. The governor also sought a pledge from Lyon not to deploy federal troops in areas where they were not then stationed. After what Snead remembered as "four or five hours" of fruitless discussion, Lyon suddenly declared the meeting closed.[69]

Lyon remained seated, but he spoke "deliberately, slowly, and with a peculiar emphasis," as Snead recalled. He emphasized the supremacy of federal authority in the state, having clearly grown irritated with Jackson's demands. He vehemently refused to "concede to the State of Missouri the right to demand that my Government shall not enlist troops within her limits, or bring troops into the State whenever it pleases, or move its troops at its own will into, out of, or through the State." He then rose to his feet to deliver his philippic. "Rather than concede to the State of Missouri for one single instant the right to dictate to my Government in any matter however unimportant"—as he spoke he pointed in turn to Price, Snead, Blair, and Conant—"I would see you, and you, and you, and you, and every man, woman, and child in the State, dead and buried." Turning to Governor Jackson, Lyon then added, "This means war." In an hour, he said, "one of my officers will call for you and conduct you out of my lines." He left the room abruptly, as the others, men who had known each other for years, said their good-byes.[70]

Harney's removal and the collapse of the Harney-Price agreement came as a bitter blow to Attorney General Edward Bates, who had worked closely with his young St. Louis law partner, Charles Gibson, to support Harney's command. Bates was outraged by the Camp Jackson affair and wholeheartedly approved of the Harney-Price agreement. When Lyon assumed command and ended the agreement, Bates and Gibson worked successfully to nurture a civil government in Missouri that could limit the impact of military authority. A native of Virginia, Gibson shared Bates's view that the war should not disrupt slavery in Missouri. Family ties also united the men in a common political pursuit. Gibson was married to a niece of Bates's brother-in-law, Hamilton Gamble. It was to Gamble that Gibson and Bates turned to maintain Missouri on a conservative and proslavery Unionist course. Bates secured for Gibson a position as solicitor of the court of claims in Washington, but frequent trips to St. Louis kept him in touch with political matters.[71]

With the demise of the Harney-Price agreement, claims of neutrality quickly came to an end. Battle lines had been drawn between the military forces of the United States and those of its enemies. When John C. Frémont assumed command of the Department of the West (in late July) he arranged the first exchange of prisoners in his military district. Ulysses Grant recalled that soon after he took command at Cairo, Illinois, "General Frémont entered into arrangements for the exchange of the prisoners captured at Camp Jackson in the month of May." Grant received orders from Frémont "to pass them through my lines . . . as they presented themselves with proper credentials." Prominent in this group headed for Confederate lines in Kentucky was Richard Barrett, who had been instrumental in arranging the fateful meeting at the Planters' House that ended the Harney-Price agreement. Grant knew Barrett and several others in the group from St. Louis and received them at his headquarters "as old acquaintances." While Grant conversed with Barrett and the others, an aide entered the room to remind Grant that he was to travel the next day to Cape Girardeau to inspect troops stationed there. Later, after his guests had left, Grant decided to postpone the trip. The next day, rebels supported by artillery stopped a government boat on the Mississippi a few miles above Cairo; Richard Barrett led the Confederate boarding party. "It was hard to persuade him that I was not there," observed Grant, who left the story of Barrett's deception to speak for itself.[72]

Although a sense of honor in the parole of prisoners remained strong early in the war, the code did not hold with Barrett or, presumably, with the other veterans of Camp Jackson. With the exception of Emmet McDonald, Barrett and the others had pledged not to take up arms against the United States. Grant had entertained the parolees with the implicit understanding that they were no longer enemies of the federal government. Like General Frost, Barrett undoubtedly regarded the action taken against him at Camp Jackson and the subsequent parole as unconstitutional. Perhaps, too, the enmity of neighbors divided by civil war made honor seem a hollow sentiment. Humorous as Barrett's deception proved to be, the contempt he displayed for the code of honor held ominous implications for the course of the war in Missouri.

5

"A Passion for Seeming"

IN THE NATION'S EYES, the events surrounding the Camp Jackson affair had been foreshadowed—and to a large extent obscured—by an outbreak of violence in another border city, one far closer to the nation's capital. Early on the morning of 19 April 1861 the Massachusetts Sixth Infantry regiment arrived in Baltimore, Maryland. They had come by rail from Philadelphia en route to Washington, D.C., a journey that required a transfer across Baltimore from one station to another. To make the transfer, teams of horses drew railcars singly through the city. Seven cars made it without incident, but a mob halted the last three. The troops left the cars and marched in columns toward the station. Insults filled the air, and a shower of stones soon followed. Pistol shots rang out, and a soldier in the front ranks fell dead. On an officer's command, the troops fired a volley into the crowd, opening a pathway through which they advanced in quick step. But scattered shooting from the crowd continued. By the time the regiment completed the transfer, six soldiers lay dead and thirty had been wounded. Twelve civilians died in the affray.[1]

The federal response to the bloodshed in Baltimore soon reverberated in St. Louis. At Lincoln's request, Attorney General Edward Bates confronted the complex issue of martial law. The president asked him to assemble opinions regarding the applicability of martial law in Maryland for the specific purpose of suspending the federal Constitution's Fifth Amendment requirement that a grand jury issue indictments in cases of "capital or otherwise heinous crime." Bates assigned the task to Assistant Attorney General Titian J. Coffey, who prepared a digest of opinions on the matter, which Lincoln received on 20 April. The document outlined the problem of military authority and civil law that soon plagued St. Louis. Military law applied only to troops, not to civilians, the digest noted. The president, as commander in chief, had authority over the armed forces, but he possessed no direct authority over citizens in the states. The Bates-Coffey digest also contained the opinion expressed by the late Supreme Court justice Joseph Story, in his influential

Commentaries on the Constitution of the United States (1833), that only Congress could suspend the writ of habeas corpus and thereby set aside the fundamental judicial protection against arbitrary arrest. Lincoln knew that commanders in the field had imposed martial law on civilians in the past—as Andrew Jackson had done in New Orleans at the close of the War of 1812—and that such actions effectively suspended the writ of habeas corpus and, indeed, all civil law. These actions had been based on arguments of military necessity, and it remained to be seen how persuasive similar arguments would be in the suppression of domestic insurrection.[2]

The clearest course to follow, and the one anticipated by the drafters of the Constitution, involved a suspension of the writ of habeas corpus. Notwithstanding the Bates-Coffey digest and Justice Story's opinion, Lincoln did not immediately seek congressional suspension of the writ. Undoubtedly he recognized that a universal suspension of the writ would heighten fears of federal tyranny and strengthen the appeal of secessionists. The course that he pursued met the political exigencies of the secession crisis, although it raised fundamental questions of constitutional law. Following historical precedent, Lincoln privately authorized General Winfield Scott, general in chief of the U.S. Army, to empower commanders in the field to suspend the writ wherever hostile individuals threatened to impede or interrupt lines of transportation and communication connecting Washington with Philadelphia and the rest of the Northeast. The president's first public pronouncement of a suspension of the writ came on 10 May 1861 (the day that Nathaniel Lyon captured Camp Jackson in St. Louis). He authorized commanders in Florida "to suspend there the writ of *Habeas Corpus* and remove from the vicinity of the United States fortresses all dangerous or suspected persons."[3]

Throughout the war, Lincoln relied primarily on commanders in the field to act on their own authority to arrest persons suspected of disloyal activity. The view, widely circulated by antiwar Democrats, that Secretary of State William H. Seward masterminded military arrests from his office in Washington has been thoroughly discredited by historian Mark Neely. Early in the war, Seward recorded the military arrest of 864 persons, many of them in the District of Columbia. By February 1862, the War Department assumed bureaucratic responsibility over military arrests and prisons. The ad hoc nature of military arrests continued throughout the war and left in its wake a confusing documentary record that makes it impossible to measure precisely the impact of the suspension of the writ. Following a close examination of this record, Neely has concluded that no more than 13,000 civilians experienced military arrest during the war. But the largest number of these occurred in Missouri, and the military prisons in St. Louis soon stood at the center of a wartime controversy over civil liberties.

The suspension of civil liberties did not go unchallenged. Lincoln's revocation of the writ of habeas corpus in Maryland prompted Chief Justice Roger B. Taney's decision in *Ex parte Merryman* (1861). In that case, federal military authorities arrested John Merryman, a citizen of Maryland, on suspicion of disloyal activity. Merryman applied to and received from Taney (sitting at the time as a federal circuit judge in Baltimore) a federal writ of habeas corpus. In his decision, Taney followed Story and argued that only Congress had the authority to suspend the writ under the conditions cited in Article 1, section 9 of the Constitution.[4] Citing Lincoln's suspension of the writ, the commanding general in Baltimore refused to respect Taney's court order. Lincoln also ignored Taney's order, although Congress authorized the president's action in suspending the writ in 1863 and thereby rendered the constitutional issue moot.

An earlier judicial challenge to martial law had arisen in St. Louis as a consequence of the capture of Camp Jackson. Of the state militiamen taken to the federal Arsenal by Nathaniel Lyon, only one, Emmet McDonald, refused to take the offered parole. McDonald argued that his arrest by federal authorities had been illegal. Furthermore, the parole required him to promise not to bear arms against the United States. That promise implied that the Camp Jackson muster had been an act of rebellion, a point that he denied. Acting for McDonald, St. Louis attorney Uriel Wright, later a secessionist, sought and received a federal writ of habeas corpus from U.S. District Court judge Samuel Treat. A Harvard-educated New Englander, Treat had moved to St. Louis in 1841 and first became prominent as editor of the Democratic *Missouri Reporter*. When Montgomery Blair resigned as judge of the Missouri Court of Common Pleas in 1849, Treat accepted an appointment to fill the post, later winning election to a six-year term. In 1857 President Franklin Pierce appointed Treat judge of the newly created federal District Court for the Eastern District of Missouri. In the developing sectional crisis, Treat allied himself with the Southern Rights enemies of Benton and Blair, notably Senator David Atchison and Lieutenant Governor Thomas C. Reynolds. In his habeas corpus decision, *In re McDonald* (1861), Treat argued that "every one who is illegally restrained of his liberty, under the color of United States authority, has the fullest redress in the United States courts." Treat sent a copy of his decision to Chief Justice Taney, who returned the favor by sending Treat a copy of his decision "in a similar case" (undoubtedly *Merryman*). Taney lamented the "sad & alarming condition of the public mind when such a question can be regarded as open to discussion." The chief justice felt gratified, however, that "the Judiciary" resisted "all attempts to substitute military power in the place of judicial authorities." But in St. Louis as in Baltimore, military power prevailed over judicial authority. In response to Treat's writ, General Harney acknowledged his duty to uphold the Constitution but cited a "higher law" that required him, in this case, to reject "the forms of law."[5]

The suspension of the writ of habeas corpus by military authority in Baltimore and in St. Louis marked the beginning of a gradual transformation from Unionist to Confederate for Uriel Wright and for the former mayor of St. Louis, John M. Wimer. Neither Wright nor Wimer identified with the proslavery Southern Rights ideologues during the 1850s. Indeed, Wimer had won election as mayor in 1857 as an antislavery Democrat of the Benton school, and in the late 1850s he maintained close political ties to the city's emerging Republican leadership. After Camp Jackson, however, it seemed increasingly clear to both men that Lincoln's administration, in the name of securing the Union, intended to suppress all dissent, subvert republican institutions, and establish a military despotism. Wright and Wimer testify to the often-complex motives that led some men to take up arms against the United States.

A Virginian by birth, Wright attended West Point for a time and studied law in Virginia with one of the Old Dominion's leading jurists, the unbending advocate of states' rights Judge Philip Pendleton Barbour of Orange County. (President Jackson appointed Barbour judge of the U.S. District Court of Eastern Virginia in 1830 and in 1836 elevated him to the Supreme Court.[6]) Wright married in 1833 and moved to Palmyra, in northeast Missouri, where he established a successful law practice and won election to the state legislature. He then relocated to St. Louis and continued his distinguished career as a lawyer. One antebellum case gained him a degree of national recognition. In 1859 he represented Miss Effie Carstang in her breach of promise of marriage suit against the wealthy St. Louis merchant and botanical garden patron Henry Shaw. Wright's eloquence helped to win for Miss Carstang an astonishing $100,000 judgment against Shaw. Shaw gained a second trial, however, in which he prevailed against Wright's advocacy. Nevertheless, Wright's defense of Miss Carstang's honor and the initial $100,000 judgment added greatly to his local prominence, and the story of the suit attracted the attention of the eastern press.[7]

Wright, a Whig in politics, joined other luminaries to address a pro-Union rally in the east yard of the St. Louis Courthouse on 12 January 1861. As a staunch Unionist, he won election to the Missouri State Convention, the body that secessionists hoped would carry Missouri out of the Union. Later in March, Wright joined a group of prominent St. Louisans at a Unionist rally in Carondelet, a village directly south of St. Louis. There he vigorously denounced secessionist Basil Duke and his Minute Men followers. Raising his cane over his head, he vowed to thrash any man who insulted his country's flag or who attempted to replace it with another.[8] Over time, however, his hostility toward federal coercion overcame his early sympathy for the Union. The secession of his native state of Virginia on 17 April 1861 undoubtedly affected him deeply. He angrily denounced Lyon's actions at Camp Jackson in May and blamed him for the bloodshed that followed the capture of the state militia. Before a crowd gathered at the steps of the Planters' House Hotel following the Camp Jackson affair, Wright expressed his mounting disaffection: "If Unionism means such atrocious deeds as have been witnessed in St. Louis, I am no longer a Union man."[9]

The suspension of the writ of habeas corpus further strained the bonds that tied Wright to the Union. In a June letter to the *Missouri State Journal,* Wright took aim at Lincoln and at the members of the St. Louis Committee of Safety, who worked with Lyon to suppress dissent. By suspending the writ "whenever he feels like it," Wright argued that Lincoln "usurps authority delegated only to Congress." At Lincoln's behest, federal military officers in Baltimore and in St. Louis disregarded the rule of law: "The Government of the United States is now at this moment a military mob, and if the president had been declared by the people a dictator, he could not exercise more arbitrary power than he has already assumed."[10]

Wright dated his letter 15 June 1861, several days after the collapse of the Harney-Price agreement and after Governor Jackson's evacuation of Jefferson City. When the state convention reconvened in July, Wright opposed its decision to declare the state's executive offices vacated, and he refused to vote when the convention elected Hamilton Gamble provisional governor. Still, he expressed his admiration for Gamble as a conservative Unionist, and as late as August 1861, he wrote to the St. Louis *Missouri Republican* that "there is no man in the limits of the State upon whom I more readily confer the important trust which must devolve upon a chief executive."[11] But for Wright, the painful time for decision had arrived, and he shortly joined Sterling Price and served as a Confederate staff officer throughout the war.[12]

For John Wimer, the decision to fight for the Confederacy required an abrupt repudiation of antislavery political ties. A native of Virginia, he moved to St. Louis in 1828, opened a blacksmith shop, and became active in city politics. Closely identified with the Benton Democrats and the emerging Republican Party, he won election for two terms as mayor, succeeding John How in 1857. His political associates viewed him as a leading figure in the city's emancipation party. Like Uriel Wright, however, the secession of his native Virginia deeply affected him. He fiercely opposed Lyon and Blair in the Camp Jackson affair, and he refused thereafter to take the loyalty oath required of him. In spring 1862, federal authorities jailed him for disloyal activity. Held first at the Gratiot Street prison, he escaped while being transferred to the Alton military prison. He made his way through Union lines to southwestern Missouri and fought with General Emmet McDonald's Confederate cavalry force. Both Wimer and McDonald died in July 1863 in the Battle of Huntsville, Missouri.[13]

Lincoln's policy of allowing commanders in the field to decide issues of habeas corpus and martial law resulted in a patchwork of policies in Missouri and elsewhere in the border states. When General Harney ignored the federal writ of habeas corpus in the McDonald case he did so without seeking or having received instructions in the matter from the War Department. Harney, like most commanders, simply assumed that military authority superseded civil authority whenever the two came into conflict. Yet he showed surprising solicitude toward state authorities in his agreement with Price. By contrast, Ulysses S. Grant gave his officers wide latitude to seize printing presses, arrest disloyal persons, and confiscate property whenever it seemed appropriate to do so.

When John C. Frémont took command in the newly formed Department of the West late in July 1861, he rivaled Lyon in his eagerness to suppress disloyal acts and expressions. Frémont promptly ordered the pro-Southern *Missouri State Journal* closed. When the paper's editor, Joseph W. Tucker, continued to print emergency sheets to denounce federal policies, Frémont had him arrested and tried for treason. Bethiah McKown, a pro-Southern resident of the city, took bitter notice of the event in a letter to her son: "Yesterday morning a band of the Hessians surrounded the Office of the only manly independent journal we had, and carried away all the type." Surely such an assault on the liberty of a free people provided just cause for "independent Missourians" to "rise in their majesty & might to crush out these *vandal Lincoln hordes*."[14] On 14 August Frémont declared martial law in St. Louis. "Our city is now under *martial law*," noted Mrs. McKown; "persons are not allowed to stand in groups to talk." Men were being arrested for treason and "the no's [numbers] of all the houses and the names of all the occupants has been taken down, in order to tell who are Federals and who Secessionists."[15] On 30 August Frémont extended martial law throughout the state in a proclamation that also announced the summary execution of guerrillas and the emancipation of slaves as punishment for the disloyal activity of masters. These additional measures embroiled him in a test of wills with Lincoln, but on the issue of martial law and the consequent suspension of the writ of habeas corpus the president never questioned Frémont's authority.

Frémont had introduced a powerful extension of military law over civilians: civilian trials before military commissions. This procedure, soon used by military authorities throughout the country, raised fundamental constitutional questions, although they were obscured by the uncertain boundary separating military and civil law. Salmon P. Chase, Lincoln's secretary of the treasury, exemplified the uncertainty surrounding the issues of habeas corpus and martial law. He warmly supported Frémont's radical course in Missouri and urged Lincoln to add presidential support to it. Later, as Taney's successor as chief justice, Chase joined a unanimous Supreme Court decision in *Ex parte Milligan* (1866), ruling that military commissions did not have the power to try civilians when the offenses charged against them had not been committed in areas of military activity. Specifically, the Court overturned the military conviction of a civilian in Indiana. But a majority of the Court went further, to rule that neither Congress nor the president could authorize military trials of civilians in areas where civil courts functioned. On this point, Chase joined a minority of four justices who argued that the existence of a public danger empowered Congress to order military trials.[16]

Milligan did not deal directly with habeas corpus, and consequently it did not dispute the manner in which Congress assented to Lincoln's suspension of the writ. But the decision did reverse the weak position enunciated by the Court in *Ex parte Vallandigham* (1864), when a majority of the justices refused to review a civilian conviction by a military commission. During the war, the absence of the *Milligan* distinction between civil and military law left federal authorities free to try civilians before military commissions. But in retrospect, it can be asked whether Missouri passed the threshold set in *Milligan* to justify civilian trials by military commissions. The answer further underscores the ambiguity of federal policy there.

A strong case can be made that Missouri did meet the threshold set in *Milligan*. In nearly every county, guerrilla activity required federal military action. By this measure, Lincoln had acted within his constitutional powers when he allowed Frémont's application of martial law and the trial of civilians by military commissions. At the same time, however, Lincoln's administration recognized the legitimacy of civil authority in Missouri and frequently intervened to protect it from the effects of military edicts and actions. By the standard later set in *Milligan,* these conditions could be construed to argue that civil law prevailed and that military commissions had no authority to try civilians.

What made the issue of civil liberties especially problematic in Missouri was the coexistence of martial law and civil law. The distinction that the Supreme Court drew in *Milligan* suggested that a consistent course in Missouri required federal authorities either to suspend all civil government and rule through martial law or to extend to all citizens the full protection of civil liberties, regardless of the outcome. All Unionists rejected the second alternative because it played directly into the hands of rebels. But conservative Unionists labored hard to limit the sphere of military rule in the state, and they generally found Lincoln to be sympathetic to their cause. As far as Lincoln and most Missouri Unionists were concerned, clear distinctions of law could await the end of the war and the restoration of the Union.

The legitimacy of civil authority and the sanctity of civil liberties lay at the heart of the roiling dispute that began with the Camp Jackson affair and intensified when Claiborne Jackson fled Jefferson City with Nathaniel Lyon in close pursuit. It has been argued, by secessionists at the time and by some historians since, that Lyon led a "coup d'etat" at Camp Jackson and that Missouri Unionists subsequently acted illegally to establish a provisional government for the state after Claiborne Jackson evacuated Jefferson City. Michael Fellman, for example, has invoked this argument to insist that Missouri descended into a state of lawlessness during the Civil War as vengeful guerrillas and Union troops terrorized the plain folk of the countryside.[17] The argument is misleading, in the first place because the capture of Camp Jackson simply ended a militia muster and did not overthrow the existing state government. It is also misleading regarding the formation of the provisional government. It was the elected state legislature of Missouri, at the urging of Governor Jackson, that established the institutional framework for a fundamental restructuring of state government. On 18 January the Missouri General Assembly provided for the election of delegates to a state convention, authorized by law to "consider the then existing relations between the government of the United States, the people and governments of the different States, and the government and people of the State of Missouri." The legislature further authorized the convention "to adopt such measures for vindicating the sovereignty of the State and the protection of its institutions as shall appear to them to be demanded."[18] Jackson, of course, had hoped that the convention would carry Missouri out of the Union. Instead, the legislature's broad mandate legitimated the establishment of a provisional government to replace Jackson's government in exile.

Before the first session of the convention adjourned on 22 March it appointed a committee of seven (representing Missouri's seven congressional districts) with authority, through a majority vote, to call the convention back into session in the event of an emergency. After Governor Jackson evacuated the state capital in June, five members of the committee agreed that a state of emergency existed. In a proclamation issued on 6 July, the committee called for the convention to reconvene in Jefferson City on 22 July. With the convention's original presiding officer, Sterling Price, commanding secessionist forces in southwest Missouri, the delegates declared the convention presidency vacant and promptly elected a Unionist to the post.[19]

The argument of usurpation and illegality is flawed for another reason as well. It obscures a fundamental struggle taking place in Missouri over the capacity of the federal government to impose law and order in a state. St. Louis Unionist leaders favored a dominant federal presence throughout the state. Outside the city, however, conservative Unionists, many of them slaveholders, insisted on the autonomy of state government. This conflict between civilian and military authority—between the authority of the state, dominated by agrarian and slaveholding interests and the authority of the federal government, supported by St. Louis merchants and manufacturers—reached a level of national crisis during Frémont's tempestuous command. The outcome of that crisis deepened the divide between St. Louis, the wartime citadel of federal power, and the central and southern regions of the state, where loyalty to the state took precedence over loyalty to the United States.

In the reconvened state convention, pro-Southern delegates had been reduced to a small minority, led by Uriel Wright. His group numbered about twenty delegates, and they were easily defeated on most matters by the more than fifty Unionist delegates. The Unionist majority, initially led by James O. Broadhead of St. Louis, adopted a resolution creating a new committee of seven to report to the convention a method of reorganizing the state government. Broadhead served on the committee and argued that the general assembly's charge to the convention authorized it to amend the state constitution to provide for the replacement of "abandoned" state offices and "abandoned" seats in the state legislature. The report further recommended that the vacant executive offices of governor, lieutenant governor, and secretary of state be filled immediately on a provisional basis by the convention. And it proposed that the convention grant the appointed officers full constitutional power until the next state election, then scheduled for August 1862. Broadhead's report also recommended that the state supreme court be increased in size from three to seven to override its proslavery majority.[20]

Hamilton R. Gamble, though delayed by a visit to Attorney General Edward Bates in Washington, lent strength to conservative Unionists at the convention and introduced a number of changes in the draft report. Broadhead, and much of the convention, deferred to Gamble's leadership because he spoke with the authority of the Lincoln administration. In effect, Gamble rewrote the report. Broadhead's St. Louis law partner, Samuel T. Glover, successfully urged the committee to strike the provision regarding the expansion of the supreme court. But more broadly, the conservative course outlined by Gamble worried Glover. Of particular concern was the role to be played by the voters of Missouri. Governor Jackson had hoped that the electorate would approve an ordinance of secession, and Glover feared that voters would reject a resolutely Unionist provisional government. Gamble added to the report a recommended test oath, to identify an eligible electorate; he also pushed back the date of the state election from August to November 1862. Neither provision satisfied Glover, however. When the revised report received the approval of the full convention on 29 July, Glover reacted with alarm, fearing that the St. Louis Unionists had given up too much ground to the states rights' interests in the rural counties. In his view, the state's loyalty to the Union should not, even indirectly, be subject to a popular referendum. "The ordinance which I read this morning," he wrote to Broadhead, "actually proposes to submit to the people the loyalty of Mo. In this way the relations of Missouri to the Union is to be balloted upon!!" "I thot [*sic*]," continued an outraged Glover, "these were the points we could not yield—I thot we intended to fight over these no matter what the people said." Although a conservative in many respects, Glover insisted on the supremacy of federal authority. "How in the name of God could you consent to such a miserable giving up the constitution of the United States?" he demanded. "Put it to a vote!! God damn it, don't you know how to vote no." Glover blamed Gamble for the states' rights tendency of the convention. "I feared when you got Gamble on that committee trouble would come—how afraid you all are of him."[21]

As conservative Unionists shaped a provisional government and as Nathaniel Lyon pressed on against Sterling Price's forces in southwest Missouri, Major General John C. Frémont assumed command in Missouri on 25 July, and conflicting views regarding civil authority and civil liberties burgeoned into a crisis with national implications. Frémont came to St. Louis with the strongest possible credentials. Famous in his own right as a western explorer and as the 1856 Republican candidate for president, he was also the son-in-law of the late Thomas Hart Benton and thus intimately tied to the family of Francis P. Blair. Although the elder Blair was ostensibly retired on his Silver Spring estate in Maryland, he remained an active and powerful political presence in Washington. He thought well of Frémont and had taken a leading role in the Pathfinder's 1856 presidential campaign. Now, with his son Montgomery in Lincoln's administration as postmaster general and son Frank a Unionist leader in St. Louis, Blair had every reason to believe that Frémont would build on his strong political foundations to establish an effective federal presence in Missouri.

Frank Blair was in Washington when Frémont took command in St. Louis. When news of Lyon's death and the federal defeat at Wilson's Creek reached him, Blair promptly returned to St. Louis and accompanied Lyon's casket to his Norwich, Connecticut home for burial. In the heightened sense of crisis that followed the Wilson's Creek defeat, Blair regarded Frémont's appointment a propitious one. "Affairs here are rather threatening," he wrote to Montgomery on 15 August, "but if the Government will send Frémont a strong reinforcement & at once he will turn the tables on the enemy & make him sorry that he left home."[22] He had not yet discerned how far Frémont had moved away from his old family and political ties or sensed that his commission as major general and his appointment to command the Department of the West had inflated his already expansive ego.

From the beginning of their marriage, the Frémonts had formed a partnership in which his ambition and her imagination merged so that John Frémont became the embodiment of Jessie Benton's dreams and aspirations. He the illegitimate son of a French Royalist émigré and she the spirited daughter of Missouri's powerful senator, the Frémonts' personal history became one of their generation's leading legends of adventure and romance. They met in Washington where Jessie, a teenager, attended a fashionable Georgetown boarding school and John, in his mid-twenties, worked as a surveyor in the War Department's Corps of Topographical Engineers. After an 1838 expedition with Joseph N. Nicollet to survey the northern plains, Frémont returned to Washington late in 1839. Benton's passion for western exploration soon brought the two men together. After several dinners at the Benton home, Frémont began courting Jessie, but her parents were not pleased with the older man's display of affection. Jessie later recalled that her mother prevailed upon a family friendship with Secretary of War John R. Poinsett to have Frémont removed from Washington and distanced from her sixteen-year-old daughter. An assignment in Iowa kept him out of the capital for six weeks, but when he returned, the couple eloped. Senator Benton's anger subsided only gradually. His acceptance of the union appeared first in a curt announcement in the Washington, D.C., *Globe,* published by Benton's close friend Francis P. Blair. The announcement read that "Miss Jessie Ann Benton, second daughter of Col. Benton," had been joined in matrimony "to Mr. J. C. Frémont of the United States Army." The story was later told that when someone at the *Globe* noted that it was customary to announce that the man married the woman, Benton replied, "Damn it, sir! It will go in that way or not at all! John C. Frémont did not marry my daughter; she married him."[23]

For a time the young couple lived under a cloud of social disapproval. Finally, as Benton's love for Jessie combined with a genuine affection for John, Washington society soon added its blessing to the union. On 1 January 1842, President John Tyler held a New Year's Day reception at the White House. Jessie and John Frémont took the opportunity to make a conspicuous appearance with Senator Benton and his wife. John arrived in his dress uniform; Jessie appeared in a blue velvet dress with a matching bonnet topped with yellow ostrich feathers.[24] The event marked the beginning of the Frémonts' public life.

In the decade of the 1840s the name Frémont became synonymous with western empire and with Benton's grand plans for St. Louis to become the gateway to the West, to the Pacific, and to India and the Orient. Frémont's published accounts of his expeditions (written by Jessie) added to his renown, although not everyone found the self-styled hero an engaging figure. Part of the rationale for the expeditions had been scientific, to gather the botanical specimens that were proving to be essential components in the developing science of morphology and in the developing theory of biological evolution. The Harvard botanist Asa Gray and his St. Louis associate, the German immigrant botanist George Englemann, eagerly awaited the plants and seeds that Frémont brought back from the West. But he refused to allow a botanist to join him on his expeditions. Englemann found Frémont frustratingly self-centered. Writing Gray, he complained that Frémont "appears to me rather selfish—I speak confidentially—and disinclined to let anybody share in his discoveries, anxious to reap all the honour, as well as undertake all of the labour himself."[25] After Frémont repeatedly rebuffed Gray's efforts to allow a botanist to join his expeditions, Gray arrived at the same conclusion. Similarly, when the New England sage Ralph Waldo Emerson read Frémont's accounts of his discoveries, he sensed an overweening vanity. Frémont's "passion for seeming must be highly inflamed," Emerson wrote in his journal. The entire exploration enterprise seemed to be intended to promote the greater glory of John C. Frémont. The dangers of Indian warfare, the trials of hunger and thirst, the physical exhaustion, even the terror of the unknown could not "repress this eternal vanity of *how we must look.*"

The Mexican War added further to Frémont's fame, and the California gold rush made him a wealthy man. Early in May 1847, Jessie celebrated American victories in Mexico at her father's house on C Street in Washington. With other residents of the city she decorated three windows of the house with colored-paper transparencies to be illuminated at night with candlelight. The central window displayed the names "Santa Fe, Chihuahua, and the Missourians," references to General Stephen W. Kearny's advance across the southwest; the two side windows celebrated the American victories at Buena Vista and Cerro Gordo.[26] Jessie was unaware that a dispute between Kearny and Frémont would lead to her husband's court-martial for insubordination. The dispute proved to be illustrative of Frémont's incapacity for compromise. In deference to Senator Benton, President Polk tried to soften the blow of the court-martial conviction by encouraging Frémont to continue in his command. But he would not tolerate the rebuke and promptly resigned his commission.

The resignation came in fall 1848, and the Frémonts set out as private citizens to make California their home. As Jessie took the isthmus passage to the Pacific, Frémont planned to regain his popularity as a western explorer by identifying a railroad route from St. Louis to San Francisco. Benton encouraged the expedition, which gained the support of wealthy St. Louisans, including Robert Campbell, Oliver D. Filley, and Henry T. Blow's father-in-law, the saddler Thornton Grimsley. Frémont decided to make a dramatic and daring crossing of the Rocky Mountains in midwinter to demonstrate that the route he located would be passable by rail throughout the year. Although warned by mountain men and by Indians that unusually heavy snows made a crossing impossible, he pressed forward with his party of thirty-three men. Frémont survived the ordeal, but eleven of his party died.[27]

The expedition failed to mark the intended railroad route to San Francisco, but it did place Frémont in the public eye once again. In December 1849 he won election as one of California's first senators. The Frémonts returned to Washington newly wealthy with California gold and at the forefront of the political movement to restrict the westward expansion of slavery. Frémont's first foray into politics proved to be a short one, however. He had received a one-year term determined by drawing lots, and he did not win reelection to a full term. Nevertheless, Senator Benton kept Frémont's name before Congress, seeking the appointment of his son-in-law as director of a transcontinental surveying team. As Frémont and Benton lobbied for the position during early summer 1853, Jessie and her children sought relief from Washington's oppressive heat at the Silver Spring estate of the Blair family. There, Elizabeth ("Lizzie") Blair Lee helped Jessie nurse her sick baby girl. Through the hot July night Lizzie and Jessie took turns holding the dying child. A long-standing family friendship had deepened into an intimate personal bond.[28]

Benton and Frémont did not secure from Congress the authorization they sought for a western expedition. Again, with private support and again during the winter (1853–1854) Frémont headed west to mark the path for a railroad from St. Louis to San Francisco. With each expedition his fame grew, and the popular association of Frémont with Free-Soil had grown so strong that Francis P. Blair began to advance the Pathfinder's name as the presidential candidate of the emerging Republican Party. On 17 May 1855, when Jessie bore her fifth and last child, the Frémonts named the boy Francis Preston in honor of the elder Blair. A year later in June, delegates to the Republican National Convention met in Philadelphia, with Blair presiding, and chose

Frémont as their presidential candidate. Despite his son-in-law's candidacy, Benton refused to disavow the party of Jackson and campaigned actively for his old friend James Buchanan. Benton opposed the sectional orientation of the Republican Party. Its victory, he correctly predicted, would lead to Southern secession and to civil war. "We are treading," Benton told the *New York Tribune* in August 1856, "upon a volcano that is liable at any moment to burst forth and overwhelm the nation."[29] Jessie, with the help of the Blairs, managed to maintain the family's cohesion during this divisive campaign, but Benton's active opposition to Frémont's candidacy left the Pathfinder at once less certain of his capabilities and more determined than ever to prove himself a great man. Although the Republican Party justifiably considered the election returns of November 1856 a harbinger of future victory, Frémont felt the pangs of defeat once again, and more deeply.

Jessie saw her father for the last time on the occasion of his seventy-sixth birthday, on 14 March 1858. As the Frémonts prepared to return to California, Benton successfully disguised his infirmity and cheerfully bid his daughter farewell. He died on 10 April, two days before the Frémonts arrived in San Francisco.[30] It was impossible for them to return in time for the funeral in St. Louis. The decision to return to California, coupled with Benton's death, disconnected the Frémonts from the political world that Jessie's father had so prominently occupied. The full meaning of this break became apparent in 1861 when the Frémonts returned to St. Louis, determined to hold the city and the West for the Union.

During winter 1860–1861, John left Jessie in California and traveled to Europe, by way of New York, in search of investors for his Mariposa gold mining project. In New York in February, he met briefly with president-elect Lincoln. When news of war reached Frémont in Paris he immediately offered his services to the Union cause. He soon learned he had been appointed major general and hastily returned to the United States to assume a command.

The political wisdom of appointing Frémont commander of the newly created Department of the West seemed self-evident. The military district included Illinois and the states and territories between the Mississippi River and the Rocky Mountains. The Pathfinder would save the West for the Union. With his headquarters in St. Louis, Frémont could count on the support of the friends of his late father-in-law as well as on the influential Blair family. Although the Frémonts had visited St. Louis only briefly over the years, their ties to the city's Unionist leadership had been exceptionally strong.

Jessie joined her husband in St. Louis, serving as his secretary and closest adviser. Much later, writing her memoir, *Souvenirs of My Time* (1887), she recalled a hostile, shuttered city with few signs of commercial or social intercourse. She described intimidated Union soldiers, fearful of venturing far from the fortified Arsenal. She reported that Confederate flags flew prominently from the houses of leading citizens and that Confederate recruiters worked openly to fill the ranks of the rebel army. There was some truth to this characterization of the city. Pro-Confederate elements, led by Basil Duke, had made the old Berthold mansion a recruiting center of sorts. Previously, it had been the headquarters of the Missouri Democratic Party, and Duke's pro-Southern Minute Men had gathered there in a brief show of opposition to the far more numerous (and largely German) Wide Awakes.[31] It was also true that the beginning of war brought a sharp decline in riverborne commerce and that German soldiers and proslavery civilians confronted one another angrily and even violently on the city's streets. On 17 June, for example, a detachment of German troops reacted rashly to a civilian attack and left three innocent bystanders dead as they unleashed a volley of musketfire into an open session of the Recorder's Court.[32] In the wake of this incident, pro-Southern sentiments continued to smolder in the city, and hostility toward the Germans and their Unionist allies ran high in certain groups. But it was also true that Southern sympathizers had been distinctly quieted by Lyon's capture of the state militia at Camp Jackson. When Henry Boernstein returned to St. Louis from military duty in Jefferson City in July 1861, he found the town "literally desolated." Many of the Southern sympathizers had left St Louis, and many of the German men were under arms in the field.[33]

Jessie Frémont may have exaggerated the level of overt disloyalty in St. Louis to provide a dramatic backdrop for the hard work that lay ahead for her husband. However, much of the task of securing the city for the Union had been accomplished three months before the Frémonts arrived. By summer 1861, St. Louis had become the staging ground for federal military operations in the lower Mississippi Valley. Unionists were not quiet in the city. The husband of Sarah Hill, a builder by trade, had joined the federal army and served throughout the war as an engineer. She visited him at his camp in Lafayette Park, located in one of the city's most fashionable neighborhoods. "Beautiful Lafayette Park," recalled Hill, "with its brilliant flower beds and stretches of green sward, looking like emerald velvet, was turned into a great military camp." She came to the camp with a basket of food and enjoyed an afternoon picnic with her husband. But it seemed strange to see the park filled with tents and campfires. "On the grassy lawns that policemen had so watchfully guarded," she noted, "now campfires were burning and men were cooking the evening meal."[34] The sullen Southern sympathies that Jessie Frémont sensed when she arrived in St. Louis were real. So, too, were unmistakable signs of federal power and control.

Frémont established his headquarters at Colonel J. B. Brant's mansion on Chouteau Avenue, owned by Jessie's cousin, the widowed Sarah Benton Brant. Frémont paid her $6,000 a year in rent from the army. Located on the building's first floor were printing facilities, a telegraph office, and Frémont's staff officers. The second and third floors were closed from the rest of the house. Jessie and John had their residence on the upper floors, as did their closest advisers. Guards carefully screened all guests to the upper floors and effectively insulated the Frémonts and their inner circle from all unannounced and uninvited visitors.[35] The commander's critics resented their isolation and criticized the rental arrangement as a form of family graft.

It would have been foolhardy for the Frémonts to attempt to avoid all controversy and criticism in St. Louis. But summer 1861 was an inopportune time for them to isolate themselves from the city's Unionist leaders. Just a few days before the Frémonts arrived in St. Louis, the Missouri State Convention reassembled in Jefferson City to create a provisional government. Fully under the control of Unionists, the convention reestablished the authority of the state. Although the supporters of Governor Claiborne Jackson charged that the legitimate government of the state had been overthrown by federal military force, the conservative provisional government installed by the state convention soon established a sphere of state authority that frequently frustrated federal military commanders. If Frémont had been more effectively engaged with St. Louis Unionist leaders, including Blair, Broadhead, and Glover, he might have forestalled the states' rights and proslavery course that Hamilton Gamble fashioned for Missouri with the aid of Attorney General Bates. As it was, the only significant opposition to Gamble's initiative came from Uriel Wright. "I do not think the people will stand your dictation of a government," he warned the convention delegates. "They won't stand the government you make for them." Nevertheless, the convention majority elected Gamble provisional governor. He delivered his inaugural address on the evening of his appointment, 31 July 1861, less than a week after General Frémont's arrival. The provisional governor reminded the delegates that it would require unity of purpose to begin to "pacify the troubled waters of the State."[36]

At the outset, the unity that Gamble sought prevailed. Bates believed that the new governor, "better than any extreme man," could "tranquillize the State." Even Uriel Wright, notwithstanding his charges of usurpation against the state convention, accepted Gamble with "unqualified approbation." Once President Lincoln recognized Gamble as Missouri's chief executive, the work of the convention had ended: state government had been restored in Missouri, and Gamble pressed forward to reestablish the state militia.[37] Because Frémont initially enjoyed the enthusiastic support of the Blair family, Glover and other critics of Gamble's conservative course had reason to believe that the new federal commander would curtail the authority of the provisional governor, particularly in matters relating to the military security of the state. Like Nathaniel Lyon before him, Frémont viewed federal authority as supreme, and he envisioned no legitimate role for an independent state militia. Like Claiborne Jackson, however, Gamble distinguished between federal and state spheres of authority, and as provisional governor, he intended to command a state military force. By the end of August, as the relationship between the Frémonts and the Blairs began to sour, Gamble became the unintended and unexpecting beneficiary of a remarkable political turnabout. On 29 August, when he traveled to Washington, D.C., to argue that the War Department should allow him to organize a state militia, he carried with him Frank Blair's letter to his brother Montgomery containing the first sustained criticism of Frémont. In the fight against the commander, Frank Blair became the reluctant ally of Hamilton Gamble.[38]

Frémont offended Blair and other St. Louis Unionists with his mixture of overt arrogance and detachment, which struck some observers as a form of condescension and others as a manifestation of incompetence. Blair found both elements of the commander's personality markedly evident during a meeting with Frémont held a few days before Gamble's departure for Washington. Blair arrived at Frémont's headquarters accompanied by John M. Schofield, chief of staff to the late Nathaniel Lyon. Blair and Schofield planned to discuss with Frémont the consequences of the federal defeat (and Lyon's death) at the Battle of Wilson's Creek earlier in August. Not only did Frémont keep the two men waiting for some time, but when he finally admitted them to his office he spoke grandly of his plans to drive the Confederates from Missouri. Frémont made no mention of Lyon's death or of the Battle of

Wilson's Creek.[39] His court-martial conviction after the Mexican War had left him contemptuous of West Point–trained officers, like Schofield, but the fact remained that he had no significant military experience of his own. The Pathfinder had demonstrated a good deal of bluff and bravado in California, but there had been no important military engagements.

Once in St. Louis, Frémont's indecisiveness had surfaced almost immediately. General Lyon in Springfield, Missouri, and General B. M. Prentiss in Cairo, Illinois, requested reinforcements from the new commander as they both faced superior Confederate forces. Lyon's needs were particularly pressing. Sterling Price's untrained Missourians had joined forces with regular army troops in Arkansas that had defected with their commander, General Ben McCulloch, to the Confederacy. Despite McCulloch's reluctance to go into battle with the Missourians, the numerically superior Confederate force prepared to engage Lyon's army in southwestern Missouri. Prentiss's fears concerning Confederate capacities to seize control of the confluence of the Ohio and Mississippi Rivers proved to be somewhat exaggerated. At the time, however, Frémont could not safely ignore them. Prentiss had correctly discerned that Confederates in Arkansas, Kentucky, and Tennessee had put forward a plan to invade southeastern Missouri and take control of Cairo. Confederate general Leonidas Polk in Memphis moved about 6,000 troops across the Mississippi to occupy New Madrid, Missouri. "Now is the time to operate in Missouri," he wrote the Confederate secretary of war late in July. Polk believed that after the federal "experiences at Manassas," the Union troops in northern Virginia "will make no forward movement there very soon." The Confederates could safely concentrate their energies in the West. Polk proposed to fortify New Madrid, and with fresh troops he believed he could repel any federal effort to enter Kentucky at the same time that he would "act vigorously in Missouri."[40] With only Colonel B. Gratz Brown and his Fourth Regiment of German Home Guards standing between Confederate forces in southeastern Missouri and the city of St. Louis, the Confederate commander at New Madrid, General Gideon J. Pillow, reported that his men were exuberant with the prospects that lay ahead of them. "The whole force," Pillow informed Polk, "is full of enthusiasm and eager for the '*Dutch hunt.*'" Pillow's experience at New Madrid convinced him that Missouri could be liberated from federal control: the "whole population of New Madrid and the country around met me with a thousand cheers."[41]

Watching developments from St. Louis, Frémont had reason for concern. As McCulloch joined with Price to move against Lyon near Springfield, Pillow might join forces with Confederate general William J. Hardee in north-central Arkansas to move north and block a federal retreat. A coordinated movement of this sort could succeed in placing a Confederate army at the defenses of St. Louis.[42]

In reality, however, a concerted Confederate attack was unlikely. Hardee, for his part, never ceased insisting that he lacked the supplies necessary to move his troops into Missouri. Nevertheless, Frémont's exaggerated fears of a Confederate thrust toward St. Louis led him to conclude that the greatest danger to his command lay in a Confederate movement against Cairo, opening an invasion route up the Mississippi. He therefore advised Lyon to remain cautious in confronting Price near Springfield and to retreat, if necessary, to the railhead at Rolla. Frémont then chartered eight steamboats, loaded them with a well-equipped army of 4,000 men, and set off on his flagship, the *City of Alton,* to reinforce Cairo.

Despite Frémont's overreaction to the Confederate threat at Cairo, the blame for the Union defeat at Wilson's Creek lay squarely with the commanders in the field. The popular German general, Franz Sigel, persuaded Lyon to attack Price and McCulloch over the objection of Schofield, who cautioned the commander to follow Frémont's advice and retreat to Rolla. Sigel also convinced Lyon to divide his small force (about half the size of the Confederate force he faced) and attempt to surprise and destroy the enemy in a well-coordinated pincer movement.[43]

In the loss of a federal brigade at Lexington, Missouri, several weeks after the Confederate victory at Wilson's Creek, Frémont bore considerably more responsibility. Evidently preoccupied with Confederate activity south of St. Louis, he seemed to ignore Price after Wilson's Creek. Price was hardly in a strong position, despite his victory. McCulloch distrusted him and also feared moving too far north and exposing his force to larger concentrations of Union troops in Kansas, Iowa, and northeastern Missouri. Soon after the victory at Wilson's Creek, McCulloch moved his men back into Arkansas and left Price to advance northward alone. Rather than pursue the retreating federal army toward Rolla, he moved his army into central Missouri, seeking fresh recruits. There, he encountered an isolated federal force at Lexington and achieved another stunning victory.

Colonel James A. Mulligan commanded an Irish brigade from Chicago at Lexington, augmented with troops from Illinois and Missouri. Mulligan took possession of the town on 9 September and found himself confronted by Price's army a week later. Belatedly, Frémont directed reinforcements to Lexington. The effort failed. General John Pope, in Mexico, Missouri, dispatched 4,000 troops to rescue Mulligan, but confusion regarding transportation kept them from arriving on time. General Samuel D. Sturgis, advancing from Palmyra in northeast Missouri, came close to relieving Mulligan, but fearing that he, too, would be overwhelmed by Price, held back. Elements of a force sent by General Jefferson C. Davis from Jefferson City fired on one another as they advanced in darkness and failed to arrive in Lexington before Mulligan surrendered to Price on 21 September.[44]

Frémont's arrogance stood out in sharp contrast against the backdrop of these federal defeats. He demonstrated little or no regard for the opinions of St. Louis Unionists, including Frank Blair. He relied instead on the advice of Jessie and a tight circle of friends who were loyal to the couple. Frémont counted among his closest advisers a cluster of Hungarian and Italian exiles from the failed European revolutions of 1848. An elite cavalry unit, Frémont's Body Guard, received the general's special attention. He chose Charles Zagonyi as the unit's commander. A veteran of the Hungarian revolution, Zagonyi had settled in New York in 1851. Summoned to St. Louis by fellow Hungarian revolutionary General Alexander Asboth, Zagonyi impressed Frémont with his skill as a horseman. The Body Guard wore plumed hats and a distinctive dark blue uniform. Mounted on matching chestnut horses and bearing German-manufactured sidearms, the 150-man Body Guard accompanied Frémont's movements through the city with a formality worthy of a European prince.[45] The flamboyant Body Guard, and Frémont's insularity at his headquarters, offended the men he badly needed as supporters. "I am beginning to lose my confidence in Frémont's capacity," wrote Frank Blair in his 29 August letter to Montgomery. "He seems to occupy himself with trifles and does not grasp the great points of the business." Frémont's insularity troubled and mystified Blair. "Men come with affairs of regiments and go away without seeing him or without an answer." Blair had urged him to set aside an hour a day to receive "all who come, without making them run the gauntlet of his desks & orderlies." But Frémont ignored the suggestion, and Blair sensed that the old family friend feared "some sort of rivalry with me." "I know very well that it will pain you to hear these things of Frémont," Frank concluded, "but I cannot be silent."[46]

Frémont's unwillingness or inability to work effectively with Frank Blair in St. Louis set in motion the events that cost him his command. But his aloofness did not prevent him from finding some supporters in the city. The general consulted frequently with James B. Eads concerning the construction of gunboats, and he worked effectively as well with the riverboat captain Thomas Maxwell in the organization of a "marine corps" of river pilots, engineers, firemen, and sailors. Eads and Maxwell provided Frémont with the expertise he needed to reinforce Cairo by river.

Frémont's fondness for European revolutionaries may have accounted for his popularity among St. Louis Germans, even as he fell into disfavor, first with the Blair family and later with President Lincoln.[47] This group also tended to support him because they shared his views regarding wartime emancipation. It is revealing in this regard that while Frémont shut out Frank Blair from his inner circle he consulted closely with several Radical Republicans, including Congressman Owen Lovejoy, the brother of the martyred abolitionist Elijah P. Lovejoy. For the most part, Frémont sought advice from people with few if any ties to St. Louis; Jessie and the foreign-born aides dominated his inner circle. Along with Zagonyi, Frémont consulted with Asboth, who served as his chief of staff.[48] Frémont also turned for advice to Colonel John Fiala, another veteran of the Hungarian revolution and a topographical engineer, and to staff member Gustav Koerner, a German-American confidant of the Illinois governor Richard Yates.

To those outside Frémont's inner circle, perhaps the most unpopular figure in the commander's entourage was the provost marshal and quartermaster, Major Justus McKinstry. McKinstry's presence in St. Louis predated Frémont's; indeed, he originally had been appointed provost marshal at the urging of Frank Blair. But in McKinstry's dual role as quartermaster and provost marshal, he became a conspicuously unpopular figure. Under martial law he severely restricted freedom of movement into and out of the city; citizens could not enter or leave St. Louis without a pass issued by him. McKinstry also decreed that no one should be on the city's streets after 9:00 P.M., and he used his police powers to suppress the press, particularly the *Missouri Republican,* a newspaper supportive of Blair and critical of Frémont.[49] To Blair and his supporters, McKinstry became emblematic of the corruption and tyranny that they associated with Frémont's command. Sensing trouble, Frémont requested and secured from Quartermaster General Montgomery C. Meigs (brother-in-law to Frank and Montgomery Blair)

McKinstry's removal as quartermaster. But the damage had been done. Frémont kept McKinstry as provost marshal, and when Lincoln removed Frémont from command, McKinstry returned to St. Louis under arrest. He was tried by court-martial in St. Louis in October 1862 and found guilty of selling government war contracts.[50]

By mid-August 1861, the Department of the West seemed badly confused under Frémont's leadership. Lincoln's secretary, John Hay, visited St. Louis late in August and met frequently with the Frémonts. He proclaimed Jessie too talkative, and he found the general "imperious" but "quiet, earnest, [and] industrious." Overall, Hay remained his supporter.

As the political climate worsened for Frémont during late summer and early fall 1861, so too did military conditions in the field. Outside St. Louis, disloyal sentiment ran high. Writing from his headquarters in Mexico, Missouri, in the heart of Little Dixie, the veteran soldier Brigadier General John Pope described the unsettled conditions that he found early in August 1861. Small groups of "reckless and violent men" roamed the countryside in "parties of twenty or thirty" and kept the entire region in a state of "apprehension and uneasiness" as they committed "depredations upon all whose sentiments were displeasing." Most troubling for him was the fact that men who appeared to be quiet, peaceful citizens took no action to prevent these depredations and showed no interest in providing federal authorities with information that would lead to the capture of the guerrillas. "The mass of the people stood quietly looking on at a few men in their midst committing all sorts of atrocious acts," he observed. Worse still, he suspected that many of these quiet men were themselves guerrillas. "When troops are sent out against these marauders," he reported, "they found only men quietly working in the field or sitting in their offices, who, as soon as the backs of the Federal soldiers were turned, were again in arms and menacing the peace."

Pope believed that he had two courses open to him to meet these circumstances. The first option was to dispatch "small bodies of troops, to hunt out the parties in arms against the peace, and follow them to their homes or places of retreat." Pope rejected this because it would lead to "frequent and bloody encounters, to searching of homes, and arrests in many cases of innocent persons." Such a policy would contribute to the public's distress and probably strengthen the guerrillas. The alternative policy was to encourage "Union men and sessessionists" to act together to end the violence in order to protect their own property. To this end Pope ordered the appointment of committees of public safety, "selecting for that purpose the most wealthy and prominent men in the county, preferring mostly the secessionists." The members of these committees would either secure peace in their communities or risk the confiscation of their property. "I have not the slightest disposition to play the tyrant to any man on earth," he concluded. A Kentuckian by birth, he understood that the citizens under his command were unlikely to express enthusiastic loyalty to the Union. "I only ask the people of North Missouri to keep the peace," he wrote.[51] Pope's policy probably worsened a bad situation. Soldiers from Kansas, Illinois, and Iowa, frustrated by guerrilla attacks and predisposed to distrust the loyalty of all Missourians, confiscated and destroyed property with what seemed to the local citizenry an arbitrary hand. An official of the Hannibal and St. Joseph Railroad (constructed in the 1850s with a combination of federal land grants, state bonds, and eastern capital) complained—to Governor Gamble, to General Frémont, and, through an officer of the company in Boston, to the Secretary of War—that indiscriminant acts by federal troops in northern Missouri added to the sympathy and support of the guerrillas.[52]

The presence of Price's army in central Missouri encouraged guerrilla attacks on Unionists and on federal detachments throughout the state. In frustration, Frémont issued his famous counterinsurgency and emancipation proclamation. Characteristically, he drafted the document in the privacy of his headquarters, consulting no one except Jessie. He began by describing the "disorganized condition" of the countryside that left the civil authority largely helpless. He determined to take "the severest measures" to suppress the "bands of murderers and marauders, who infest nearly every county of the State, and avail themselves of the public misfortunes and the vicinity of a hostile force to gratify private and Neighborhood vengeance." He resolved to bring an end to the "daily increasing crimes and outrages" that were driving Unionists out of the countryside "and ruining the State." To this end, he declared martial law "throughout the State of Missouri." He then defined a line of federal occupation in the state that extended east from Leavenworth, Kansas, to Jefferson City, and then southeast to the railheads at Rolla and Ironton, ending at Cape Girardeau on the Mississippi River. Frémont then declared that "all persons who shall be taken with arms in their hands" north and east of this line "shall be tried by court-martial, and if found guilty will be shot." He further declared that all property of persons who had taken up arms against the United States, or who actively supported those who did so, "to be confiscated to the public use, and their slaves, if any they have, are hereby declared freemen." Where law and order could be administered "by the civil officers in the usual manner," the proclamation would not "suspend the ordinary tribunals of the country." But where the civil authorities could not or would not maintain order, the proclamation placed "in the hands of the military authorities the power to give instantaneous effect to the existing laws, and to supply such deficiencies as the conditions of war demand."[53] It was a stunning proclamation and fundamentally a misguided one.

When, on 8 September, Frémont received Lincoln's critical response to his proclamation, Jessie (with her French maid) set out immediately for Washington to deal directly with the troublesome president. In his letter, Lincoln politely but firmly urged the general to amend his proclamation in two important ways. First, he observed, "Should you shoot a man, according to the proclamation, the Confederates would very certainly shoot our best men in their hands in retaliation." The president therefore directed that Frémont not allow executions "under the proclamation without first having my approbation or consent." Second, Lincoln expressed his belief that the emancipation provision "will alarm our Southern Union friends and . . . perhaps ruin our rather fair prospect in Kentucky." After making this second point, Lincoln asked Frémont "as of your own motion," to modify the confiscation provision to conform with the First Confiscation Act recently passed by Congress on 6 August 1861. The president enclosed a copy of the act and closed his letter in a tone of conciliation: "This letter is written in a spirit of caution and not of censure."[54]

Lincoln's gentle rebuke provoked a fiery response. Frémont simply refused to comply with the president's order and suggestions. "I acted with full deliberation," he instructed the president sharply, "and upon the certain conviction that it was a measure right and necessary, and I think so still." Concerning the proclamation's emancipation provision, Frémont insisted that Lincoln reconsider his own position. "If, upon reflection, your better judgment still decides that I am wrong in the article respecting the liberation of slaves, I have to ask that you will openly direct me to make the correction."[55] Perhaps he believed that Lincoln would be unwilling publicly to express opposition to the emancipation order. In fact, however, the president did not hesitate to make public his desire to rescind Frémont's order:

Your answer, just received, expresses the preference on your part that I should make an open order for the modification, which I very cheerfully do. It is therefore ordered that the said clause of said proclamation be so modified, held, and construed as to conform to, and not to transcend, the provisions on the same subject contained in the act of Congress entitled, "An act to confiscate property used for insurrectionary purposes," approved August 6, 1861, and that said act be published at length, with this order.[56]

On 10 September, Jessie arrived in Washington, took her rooms at Willard's Hotel, and sent her card to Lincoln, requesting an interview. The president immediately replied, "Now, at once, A. Lincoln." Chagrined that she had not had time to rest, bathe, or change her clothes, she nevertheless complied with the directive and arrived at the White House at about nine o'clock in the evening. She found Lincoln in a stern mood. Jessie handed him the letter she carried from John, outlining his accomplishments in securing the confluence of the Ohio and Mississipppi Rivers and his plans to advance on Memphis. Lincoln took the letter but did not respond directly to it. Instead, according to Jessie's recollections, he criticized her husband for not consulting with Frank Blair before issuing the proclamation. Had he done so, said Lincoln, the proclamation would not have been issued as it had been. The war was being fought to preserve the Union, he continued. Jessie remembered his tone as "mad" and "repelling": *General Fremont should not have dragged the Negro into it— . . . he never would if he had consulted with Frank Blair."*[57]

The next day Jessie met with Francis P. Blair. She found him to be furious with her for meddling in these affairs and for making an enemy of the president. The elder Blair had known Jessie since her childhood; his own daughter Lizzie had been one of Jessie's closest friends. But Jessie had not seen Blair since leaving for California in 1858, and she seemed not to comprehend the source of his anger. Why had Frémont defied Lincoln, Blair asked. Why had Jessie come to Washington to "find fault with the President"? Blair found Jessie to be stubborn and unyielding, displaying no deference toward her father's old friend. Instead, she assumed "a very *high* look," Blair reported to Lizzie. "In a word," he concluded, the Frémonts "hate & fear Frank & are hostile to everybody in the administration who is supposed to stand between them & imperial power." Blair had talked with Jessie for the better part of three hours and "sounded her to the bottom." The two parted company knowing that the intimacies of their past could no longer overcome the accumulated antagonisms. Lizzie recoiled at the developing feud. She did not believe that the emancipation issue lay at the bottom of the fight: "Frank is so radical that I can't think that the source," she wrote. Both John Frémont and Frank Blair seemed to Lizzie to be "firm brave men." She concluded plaintively, "A formal quarrel fills me with a terror I can't articulate."[58]

Before returning to St. Louis, Jessie sent a note to Lincoln on 12 September demanding a copy of the critical letter concerning Frémont that Frank Blair had sent to the president through Gamble and Montgomery Blair. Not surprisingly, Lincoln refused to comply with the imperious demand: "I do not feel authorized to furnish you with copies of letters in my possession without the consent of the writers."[59] In all, it was an astonishing interaction, and one from which Jessie and John Frémont learned absolutely nothing.

The emancipation order and its revocation occurred while Hamilton Gamble also visited the nation's capital, gaining from Lincoln the control he sought over a reconstituted state militia, a force that he would use to try to maintain slavery in Missouri. To Gamble, the solution to the guerrilla problem seemed clear: a state militia under his command could more easily distinguish law-abiding from lawless citizens and thereby suppress the guerrilla insurrectionists.[60]

The militia issue opened an area of disagreement between Gamble on the one hand and Blair and Frémont on the other. Gamble resented the largely German Home Guard, officially a reserve force under federal control that functioned like a militia and that was viewed as a hostile force by many Missourians. Gamble wanted the Germans to be enrolled as regular federal troops or placed under his direction as a state militia force. When the provisional governor traveled to Washington late in August, Bates secured him an interview with Lincoln, who promised federal support to arm a state militia under Gamble's command, despite Frémont's emphatic suggestion to the president "that for the present no authority be given to Governor Gamble to raise regiments in Missouri."[61] In time, Lincoln's purposes became clear as the president worked to secure a measure of peace in Missouri that was consistent with the state's nominal loyalty to the Union. Eager to redeploy regular federal troops farther south, Lincoln saw in Gamble's plan a way to maintain Missouri's nominal loyalty without engaging large numbers of federal troops in the enterprise. At the time, however, it was clear only that Lincoln had empowered Gamble to organize the support of the most conservative Unionists in Missouri, a policy that disgusted Frémont and worried Blair.

Gamble returned to Missouri with a letter from Lincoln instructing Frémont to cooperate fully with the provisional governor. As a staunch defender of the state's constitutional prerogatives, Gamble focused his energies first on maintaining and directing a state militia and later on maintaining slavery. He was aided in both endeavors by the mounting hostility between Frémont and Blair. Blair and Gamble became allies in the fight to secure Frémont's removal, and Blair's hostility to the reconstituted state militia faded from view. Gamble generally played his role wisely and well, maintaining his authority as governor but avoiding confrontations with Frémont. On the issue of the St. Louis Police Board, Gamble acceded to Frémont's wishes by filling vacancies with nominees suggested by the general.[62] The governor experienced his greatest frustrations as he labored to arm the new state militia. Although authorized by Lincoln to obtain arms for it from Frémont, the general claimed that he had none to provide. In September Gamble sent a St. Louis ally, the real estate speculator and railroad builder William M. McPherson, east to attempt to secure arms. McPherson received from Lincoln an order of 4,000 weapons, but he could locate fewer than 3,000. These weapons and a handful of additional arms that he gathered up went to Gamble, who continued to press Bates for more help until he learned from that source that the scarcity of arms was real and not the product of federal evasion.[63]

The revoked emancipation order attracted national attention and gained Frémont a good deal of support among Radical Republicans. In Missouri, however, the proclamation had little more than symbolic importance. According to William Parrish, the only persons freed by Frémont's orders were two slaves owned by Thomas L. Snead. The slaves had been with Snead when he, Jackson, and Price had their last meeting with Lyon and Blair in St. Louis. Snead then took the slaves into the field. Evidently they made their way into federal lines, and were freed by deeds of manumission on 12 September 1861, just before Frémont received Lincoln's final directive on the matter.[64] Overshadowing all else in St. Louis, however, was Frémont's almost unimaginable blunder of alienating Frank Blair and his powerful political family. Most astonishing, the Frémonts never saw the developing breach for what it was: a sharp reversal of their fortunes in public life.

Because the federal defeats at Wilson's Creek and Lexington occurred between the highly visible federal defeats in northern Virginia, at Bull Run on 21 July and at Ball's Bluff on 21 October, Frémont's command in Missouri became associated with the military ineptitude that made Congress increasingly critical of Lincoln's conduct of the war. Frémont thus felt a good deal more pressure than he otherwise might have to strike a decisive blow against the Confederates in the West. In fact, he enjoyed some significant military successes while he commanded the Department of the West. On 28 August 1861, he appointed Ulysses S. Grant commander of a military district encompassing portions of southeast Missouri and southern Illinois and directed him to maintain control of Cairo, Illinois, on the Mississippi River at its strategic confluence with the Ohio. A few days before Jessie set off for her ill-fated confrontation with Lincoln, Grant acted on his own initiative to take control of Paducah, Kentucky, on the Ohio near the mouth of the Tennessee River. He was aware that Confederate general Leonidas Polk, headquartered in Memphis, was preparing to occupy the same position. A Confederate force at Paducah would menace the federal garrison at Cairo. Conversely, a federal force there opened a potential invasion route into Kentucky and Tennessee and limited the effectiveness of the Confederate defenses on the Mississippi, at Columbus in Kentucky and at Cape Girardeau in Missouri. Frémont made the most of Grant's aggressive action in the letter he sent to Lincoln with Jessie. "I have re-enforced, yesterday, Paducah with two regiments," he wrote, "and will continue to strengthen the position with men and artillery." He reported that the federal force at Paducah could move to the "rear and flank" of the Confederates at Columbus. He proposed to occupy Nashville and then launch "a combined advance" from central Tennessee and down the Mississippi River to take Memphis. "I trust," he concluded, "the result would be a glorious one to the country."[65]

By the time Jessie delivered John's letter to Lincoln, the president had lost confidence in him and had begun to look for a judicious way to bring an end to the Pathfinder's command in the West. Lincoln dispatched Montgomery Blair and Montgomery C. Meigs to St. Louis to begin the process of disengagement. The two men stopped first in Chicago to deliver a letter from Lincoln to General David Hunter explaining that Frémont needed help and that the president wanted Hunter to provide it. Hunter joined Blair and Meigs, and the three men arrived in St. Louis on 12 September. Two days later, Congressman Schuyler Colfax visited Frémont in St. Louis and found the general assuming the role of a martyr. When Colfax urged him to send troops to rescue Mulligan's force at Lexington, Frémont showed the congressman muster rolls purporting to prove that he had at his disposal only two regiments of properly equipped troops and fewer than 5,000 reserve troops in the Home Guard and in other detached units. He could not adequately defend St. Louis, he told Colfax, and he was powerless to assist Mulligan. Furthermore, he showed Colfax orders received from Secretary of War Simon Cameron and from General Winfield Scott ordering that five Missouri regiments be sent east to defend Washington, D.C. Frémont would comply with the administration's order as best he could, he said. The nation's capital "must be saved even if Missouri fall and I sacrifice myself." On 18 September, when Frank Blair publicly criticized Frémont's military paralysis in the face of Price's advance into central Missouri, the general ordered his critic jailed. In a telegram to the War Department, he explained that Blair had engaged in "insidious and dishonorable efforts to bring my authority into contempt with the government, and to undermine my influence as an officer." Montgomery Blair viewed the arrest of his brother as "Genl' Jessie's doing" and telegraphed Frémont, urging Frank's release. The postmaster general admonished his old friend: "This is no time for strife except with the enemies of the country." Frank, for his part, angrily demanded a court-martial to test the validity of Frémont's charges. On 26 September Frank filed formal charges of his own against Frémont with the War Department; when he published his rebuttal of the charges the offended commander had him arrested a second time. The imbroglio added to the pressures mounting against Frémont. The *New York Times* reported Blair's charges and joined the call for the general's removal.[66]

As the situation in St. Louis worsened, Montgomery Blair struggled to understand Frémont's motivation. "I confess I have never been so entirely deceived in respect to a man's faculties," he wrote a friend. "I do not vent upon him my indignation for Frank's arrest," he continued; Montgomery blamed the worst on Jessie. "I understand now that spies are set upon Frank by Jessie to see if she can't get hold of some talk to eke out the prosecution." Montgomery expected to see "a parcel of ridiculous lies trumped up to help out this woman's thirst for revenge. She is perfectly unscrupulous you know."[67]

By 27 September the pressure to remove Frémont had mounted steadily, but Lincoln, perhaps bowing to the views of Radical Republicans, voiced his inclination to give the general a final opportunity to repair the damage. In fact, Lincoln must have suspected that Frémont would fail, thereby placing the need for his removal beyond any serious doubt. Seeing only continued support for Frémont, a discouraged Attorney General Bates, an outspoken critic of the general from the start, wrote to Gamble, informing him that Frémont was to be given a second chance: "I thought . . . that Frémont would certainly be relieved, but this day I find that result is not probable, therefore I am in deep trouble on account of our poor betrayed and sacrificed state. . . . General Frémont is not to be removed—at least until he has had a full opportunity to retrieve his fortunes, or to ruin our state utterly and endanger our cause."[68] To James Broadhead, Bates confided that "I have demanded the recall of Genl. Frémont, possibly with too much emphasis & too often repeated."[69]

On the day after his reprieve, Frémont prepared to lead an army into the field to avenge the Confederate victories at Wilson's Creek and Lexington and to redeem his own reputation. In a private letter soon made public by a friend in New York, he complained that his enemies repeatedly hindered him as he faced the difficult challenge presented by Price and the guerrillas that supported him. The enemy he faced has "no posts to garrison and no lines of transportation to defend or guard." The "whole force" of the enemy "can be turned at will to any one post, while we have from Leavenworth and from Fort Scott to Paducah to keep protected." Frémont wanted his friend to know that he faced difficult circumstances, but he declared himself "competent to it." Nevertheless, it seemed unfair to him that he had to "meet the enemy in the field" at the same time that he was forced "to attend to the enemy at home." Because of the doubts raised by his critics, the good credit of the United States among St. Louis merchants "is shaken." Frémont promised that he would stand above the sordid fray. "To defend myself would require the time that is necessary to and belongs to my duty against the enemy," he proclaimed. The task before him was clear: "Everything that hurts, impedes, or embarrasses the work entrusted to me I strike at without hesitation. . . . I take the consequences," he concluded. "The worst that can happen to me is relief from great labor."[70]

Notwithstanding Lincoln's decision to give him another chance, the general's public posturing clearly did not sit well with either the president or the War Department. When Frémont informed General Winfield Scott that he intended to move against Price and that he expected to engage McCulloch as well, he closed with a familiar gesture of self-importance: "Please notify the President immediately." Scott replied tersely that Lincoln was pleased to learn that the general saw the need for action. "His words are," wrote Scott, "he expects you to repair the disaster at Lexington without loss of time."[71]

As Frémont's fortunes sank, Governor Gamble called the state convention into special session in St. Louis to advance his own plans to enforce a measure of law and order in the state. To meet the continued threat posed by guerrillas, the convention revised the militia law to create the Missouri State Militia (MSM), a volunteer force expected to draw to its ranks men who would serve the state to suppress guerrillas but who would not readily join the federal army.[72] In consultation with Lincoln and with the War Department, Gamble agreed that the MSM would function substantially under the authority of the federal government. Orders issued by the War Department on 7 November stipulated that "this force is to co-operate with the troops in the service of the United States in repelling the invasion of the State of Missouri and in suppressing the rebellion therein." The force would be governed by the regulations of the U.S. Army and would be held subject to the Articles of War passed by Congress. Moreover, the cost of raising and maintaining the force would be paid by the United States, and the commanding general appointed to the Department of the West by the president would "command the whole of the State forces." However, the governor would appoint all the field officers below the rank of major general. Most significantly, the state militia would not be ordered out of the state, "except for the immediate defense" of it.[73]

As Frémont prepared to pursue Price, he ordered five divisions (under Pope, McKinstry, Hunter, Sigel, and Asboth) to concentrate their forces at Springfield. A nervous president dispatched Secretary of War Cameron to St. Louis to confer with Frank Blair and with supporters of Governor Gamble. He then traveled with Adjutant General Lorenzo Thomas to Frémont's field headquarters at Tipton, Missouri. On 14 October Cameron wrote Lincoln that he had met with Frémont and found him "mortified, pained, and, I thought humiliated." Frémont asked Cameron for a chance to redeem himself. He had gone to Missouri at the urgent request of the president, he explained. He had faced and overcome great obstacles. If he were to be removed, the Union cause in Missouri would be left in shambles. Lincoln had given Cameron the authority to remove Frémont immediately if he thought fit; the secretary decided that he would withhold judgment until he returned to Washington. He told Frémont that he was "giving him the interim to prove the reality of his hopes as to reaching and capturing the enemy, giving him to understand that, should he fail, he must give place to some other officer."[74]

Frémont's campaign against Price and McCulloch generated consternation rather than enthusiasm among his corps commanders. John Pope wrote bitterly to David Hunter that "if we attempt to go south of the Osage [River] without supplies for at least a month, and without much better preparation . . . I do not believe that one half of these troops will ever return alive." With winter approaching, Pope reported that his men lacked overcoats and possessed only a single blanket. "Each division commander is left to himself," he complained. No provision trains or depots had been organized for the campaign, and none seemed to be planned for the future. Pope expected to establish a depot for his division at Otterville and carry what he could by advancing in short marches. "Altogether," he concluded, "this is the most remarkable campaign I ever saw, heard of, or read of."[75]

Despite the complaints, Frémont enjoyed some success as he moved against Price. At Springfield on 25 October 1861, Major Zagonyi led the Body Guard in a cavalry charge that gained the attention of *Harper's Weekly* and won national acclaim for Frémont.[76] But Pope continued to grumble. "Of course, Gen. Frémont and the men around him, whose official existence depends upon his not being superseded, are desperate," he wrote Hunter. "But should they be permitted to drag to destruction, or at least to great and unnecessary suffering, the 30,000 men of this army, for no other purpose than to save, if possible, their own official lives?" As Frémont prepared to pursue Price beyond Neosho into Arkansas, Pope asked, "What is to be accomplished, or rather what does any sane man suppose will be the result?"[77] Hunter had already told Cameron that he found Frémont unfit for his command. General Samuel Curtis wrote Lincoln that "General Frémont lacks the intelligence, the experience, and the sagacity necessary to his command." A congressional subcommittee led by Elihu B. Washburne of Illinois scrutinized government contracts let in St. Louis and found "robbery," "fraud," "extravagance," and "peculation" as "can hardly be conceived of."[78]

By this time, Lorenzo Thomas and Simon Cameron had completed their inspection tour of Frémont's command, and Thomas submitted to the secretary a sharply critical report that became public when published by the *New York Tribune*. It noted that General Hunter had been sent at Lincoln's direction to advise Frémont, but the commander had sought no advice. Instead he presented Hunter with his plan to occupy Springfield, which he described, undoubtedly with the advice of his Hungarian topographical engineer John Fiala, as the strategic point in the terrain lying between the Osage and Arkansas Rivers. "Why," asked Thomas in his report, "did not this enter the brain of the major general before the fall of Lyon, and he strain every nerve to hold that important key when in his possession?" When Hunter responded to Frémont's plan with the observation that it made less sense to move toward Springfield, "where there is no enemy and nothing to take," than it did to proceed to reinforce Lexington as Price advanced in that direction, Frémont sent Hunter without instructions to Rolla, then to Jefferson City, and finally to Tipton, where Thomas and Cameron interviewed him.[79] The day after Thomas filed his report, Lincoln's cabinet discussed the Frémont situation. Bates recorded in his diary on 22 October that Lincoln favored removal, but Secretary of State William H. Seward, joined by Treasury Secretary Chase and Cameron, "timidly yielded to delay."[80]

As more complaints reached Lincoln (including one from his friend Ward H. Lamon), the president finally acted and on 24 October sent the removal order to General Curtis in St. Louis. Curtis's messengers arrived at Frémont's camp near Springfield at 5:00 A.M. on 3 November. The president's order included one caveat to Curtis: "If when General Frémont shall be reached by the messenger . . . he shall then have, in personal command, fought and won a battle, or shall be in the immediate presence of the enemy in expectation of a battle, it shall not be delivered but, held for further orders."[81] The messenger found Frémont in his tent with no immediate plan to engage Price, and thus he delivered the removal order. David Hunter, designated as Frémont's replacement, arrived to take command at 10:00 P.M.[82] When Gustav Koerner learned that Frémont had been relieved, he offered Illinois senator Lyman Trumbull a balanced judgment of the commander he had admired and served. Although "there was a great amount of labor performed day and night" by Frémont, there seemed to exist "no proper system or method." Koerner found him "honest and honorable himself" but observed that some of his closest friends were devious and dishonest. "He is no judge of men at all," he concluded, "and he can readily be imposed upon by plausible knavery."[83]

To the end, St. Louis Germans remained supportive of Frémont. So too did the St. Louis Unitarian minister, William Greenleaf Eliot. In October he had met with Lincoln to explain his understanding of conditions in Missouri. As Frémont's removal seemed imminent, Eliot wrote to Treasury Secretary Chase defending the general against Frank Blair's charges. The minister admitted that to "unfriendly eyes" Frémont frequently "laid himself open to censure." He acknowledged that the commander demonstrated a "tendency to extravagant parade." But he also demonstrated a "boldness in taking responsibility . . . that has surprised and alarmed the semi-loyal." Although some "hearty Unionists have doubted his wisdom and desired a greater degree of conciliation and caution," Eliot warned that "we must consider the extreme difficulty of his position." When Frémont had arrived in St. Louis, a Confederate flag flew brazenly from the Berthold mansion. He closed the Confederate headquarters, and Union men from Iowa and Illinois as well as from Missouri eagerly joined the federal army to serve under the famous general. In Eliot's view, Frémont's "bold demonstration of strength created strength." The minister was not among Frémont's intimate circle; indeed, he had rarely met the man. But he clearly associated the security of the city with Frémont's presence and concluded, "It would not only be unjust and unfair but unwise, to supersede him until a battle is fought."[84]

With Frémont's removal, Lincoln's plan for Missouri became clear. The president would have Hunter secure the eastern portion of the state by fortifying the railheads at Sedalia and Rolla. Then, "in judicious co-operation" with James H. Lane in Kansas, it would be possible for federal forces in the region to meet and repel a Confederate invasion of the state. Lincoln would leave most of the state to Gamble's control and care. The rebellious spirit would soon subside, Lincoln believed: "The people of Missouri will probably be in no favorable mood to renew . . . the troubles which have so much afflicted and impoverished them." Lincoln conceded that "local uprisings will . . . continue to occur," but these disturbances could be suppressed by "local forces." Frémont's pursuit of Price had been fruitless and dangerous, and it should end. "You are not likely to overtake Price," Lincoln wrote Hunter. A federal force entering Arkansas could easily be swallowed up. "I feel sure that an indefinite pursuit of Price, or an attempt by this long and circuitous route to reach Memphis, will be exhaustive beyond endurance, and will end in the loss of the whole force engaged in it."[85]

Late in November, the Frémonts left St. Louis for New York City, where the political implications of his feud with the Blairs and with Lincoln became clear. Supporters paid their respects and condemned Lincoln's timidity on the slavery issue. Henry Ward Beecher invited the couple to his Brooklyn church, where he delivered a sermon praising Frémont: "Your name will live and be remembered by a nation of *Freemen*."[86] Bowing to political pressures, Lincoln almost immediately reassigned Frémont to the newly created Mountain Department, with responsibility over western Virginia, eastern Kentucky, and part of Tennessee. When the president later placed him under the command of his old Missouri adversary, John Pope, Frémont asked to be relieved of command; Lincoln quickly complied. Still, Radical Republicans pressed Lincoln to give him a new command and another chance to achieve military success. The president would no longer be swayed. When the old antislavery warrior George Washington Julian of Indiana visited Lincoln to make this plea, he appeared to agree with Julian's assessment of Frémont's capacities. But he then reminded Julian that to give Frémont a command would require the removal of another general. The situation reminded Lincoln of a story: when a father advised his son to take a wife, the lad asked, "Whose wife shall I take?" Frémont received no new command.[87]

For St. Louis, the effect of Frémont's failure had confined Unionist strength to the city and its outlying railheads. Elsewhere in the state, Lincoln acquiesced in conservative Unionist control, as much to keep the peace among the warring factions unleashed by Frémont as to implement a determined course. This outcome had not been inevitable. Though the break between the Blairs and the Radical Republicans over issues relating to emancipation would have occurred in time, it need not have occurred in 1861. The moment that St. Louis Unionists had anticipated, to exert a more complete control over the state, had been lost.

Entrance to the St. Louis Arsenal (*New York Illustrated News*, 15 July 1861)
St. Louis Mercantile Library Association at the University of Missouri–St. Louis

General Daniel M. Frost (carte de visite by J. A. Scholten, 1861)
Library of Congress

Franz Sigel
Library of Congress

John C. Frémont (steel engraving by J. C. Buttre, 1858)
Missouri Historical Society, St. Louis

Edward Bates
Library of Congress

Jessie Benton Frémont (carte de visite by Matthew Brady)
Missouri Historical Society, St. Louis

6

"A Friend of the Enemy"

A TTORNEY GENERAL EDWARD BATES secured the appointment of James Broadhead as assistant district attorney for the Eastern District of Missouri in June 1861 and instructed him to prosecute "offenders against the United States." Broadhead lost no time in doing so. Within the month, he ordered the arrest of Joseph W. Tucker, editor of the openly prosecessionist *Missouri State Journal,* on charges of treason. Broadhead secured a search warrant and found in Tucker's office (on Pine Street between Third and Fourth) a letter dated 28 April 1861, in which Governor Claiborne Jackson clearly set forth his prosecession sympathies and plans. A second letter (dated 16 July 1861) also fell into federal hands and reinforced Broadhead's conviction that Tucker was actively engaged in supporting the rebellion. Addressed to "Joseph Tucker, esq., *Editor of the State Journal,* St. Louis," a secessionist commander in Ripley County sought Tucker's assistance in contacting Governor Jackson with the news that he planned to position 5,000 men between Rolla and Ironton, with the expectation of joining with Price to drive the federal forces "north of the Missouri and into St. Louis in thirty days."[1] Tucker made it clear that his sympathies lay with the Confederacy, but his published opinions were not treasonous; and it is doubtful that the receipt of letters from secessionists by itself rose to the level of an "overt act," defined by the Constitution as the requirement for convictions in cases of treason.

Clearly, the constitutional definition of treason made it difficult for federal authorities to suppress disloyal activity among civilians. Declarations of martial law, the suspension of the writ of habeas corpus, and trials before military commissions provided broader avenues of intervention. On 14 August 1861 General Frémont declared martial law "in the city and county of Saint Louis" and appointed Major Justus McKinstry (then acting quartermaster) provost marshal. Frémont gave McKinstry sweeping powers: "All orders and regulations issued by him will be respected and obeyed accordingly."[2] Two weeks later Frémont extended martial law through most of the state and drew the censure of President Lincoln by authorizing summary executions and the emancipation of slaves. Although Frémont's more limited declaration of martial law on 14 August had been made without direct authorization from the War Department, Lincoln made no mention of it as he rescinded portions of the later order. In effect, he allowed Frémont's first declaration of martial law to stand. For conditional Unionists, the imposition of martial law created distinct new dangers. With Confederate and Union armies in the field, any opposition to federal policies became potential violations of military law. Angry denunciations of Abraham Lincoln and "black Republican" despotism—the familiar language of the Democratic Party just a few months earlier—now could be grounds for military arrest.

Early acts of confiscation determined the location of military prisons in St. Louis. Thus, the Myrtle Street prison was a converted slave pen operated by slave dealer Bernard M. Lynch at the corner of Fifth and Myrtle Streets. Lynch had moved south into the Confederacy early in the conflict, and in September 1861 federal authorities confiscated his two-story brick building and converted it for use as a prison. Among the initial group of twenty-seven inmates was Max McDowell, the son of Dr. Joseph McDowell, who had founded the McDowell Medical College on Gratiot Street. Active in politics, Dr. McDowell was well known for his proslavery and pro-Confederate sympathies. On 30 May 1861, German Home Guards searched the college as a suspected hiding place for weapons (they found none). Shortly after the search, Dr. McDowell, accompanied by his two sons, Max and Drake, left St. Louis for the Confederacy. Eventually, Dr. McDowell traveled to Europe, but Max returned to St. Louis in an effort to recruit troops for the Confederacy. Arrested in this activity, he became one of the first prisoners at the Myrtle Street prison, the "Hotel de Lynch," as the *St. Louis Missouri Democrat* dubbed it, obviously enjoying the fact that Confederate sympathizers were jailed in the former slave pen.[3]

In December 1861 McDowell's Medical College became the Gratiot Street prison. The old dissecting room became the mess hall, and sufficient bunks and cooking stoves were installed to accommodate from 500 to 700 prisoners. Early in 1862, Anne Ewing Lane (the eldest daughter of St. Louis's first mayor, William Carr Lane) reported to her sister that the federal authorities "have several hundred prisoners down at McDowell's College." The makeshift character of the place permitted a number of early escapes, two of which struck Anne Lane as particularly amusing. One prisoner borrowed the clothing and tool box of a friendly carpenter working in the prison and simply walked past the guards. Another prisoner took his cue from the minstrel stage: he "went to the chimney and blackened his face & hands, put on a head-handkerchief, took the coal bucket to get some coal, but has not yet made his appearance."[4]

The Department of the Missouri also used a newly constructed prison across the river at Alton, Illinois. In January 1862 the War Department and the governor of Illinois authorized General Henry Halleck to use it for military prisoners to be transferred from the overcrowded Gratiot and Myrtle Street facilities, beginning in early February. Federal authorities then used those two prisons as temporary holding facilities. The city's provost marshals determined who stayed in them and for how long.[5] Some of the prisoners awaited trial before a military commission at the Arsenal; others, convicted and sentenced to a prison term, awaited transfer to Alton. Within a week after the Alton prison opened, authorities there reported it full.[6]

The St. Louis prisons differed from military prisons elsewhere in the country because they housed not only prisoners of war but also political prisoners, deserters from the Union army, and federal soldiers awaiting trial for crimes. Federal authorities brought persons arrested for disloyal activity before military commissions for examination. Afterward they were either released on bond, banished, sentenced to prison, or sentenced to death. Prison terms were served at Alton.[7] Early in January 1862, Halleck appointed Colonel J. W. Tuttle of the Second Iowa Volunteers superintendent of the Gratiot Street prison. With that appointment came detailed instructions that suggested what earlier conditions might have been like. The prisoners would be allowed to receive from friends any articles of clothing and personal hygiene "usually provided for soldiers." However, "articles of luxury or ornament" would be excluded, and if friends offered prisoners pipes and tobacco, these would be "regarded as common stock and be divided among the prisoners generally." They would be required to show "proper respect" when officers visited for inspections. At the command "All attention," they were to stand "in the position of a soldier until the inspecting officer has passed."[8]

In December 1861 federal authorities held a group of sixteen black men in the city prisons. They had attached themselves to Frémont's army during his campaign against Price and had returned to St. Louis with the federal forces. According to state law, they were fugitive slaves to be held in jail until claimed by their master. If not claimed in three months, state law authorized the sheriff to sell them at public auction. When Halleck learned that the "colored prisoners of war" were collecting a fee for washing the clothes of the white prisoners, he ordered the practice stopped. The black men, said Halleck, "will be required to do so as prisoners of war without remuneration." At the same time, he saw no reason why the white prisoners should not be put to work as well. Under proper guard, the white men could "bring in fuel, &c."⁹

The black men presented Halleck with a more difficult problem than he at first realized. As Provost Marshal General Bernard G. Farrar pointed out to the commander, they were not prisoners of war. Moreover, Congress prevented the army from executing (or violating) the slave laws of the states. And because the men had been used by their disloyal masters in aid of the rebellion, the federal Confiscation Act of August 1861 provided that they be confiscated from them. Halleck, not a generous man in this arena, directed Farrar to free the men from prison but to transfer them to the custody of the quartermaster "for labor till they have paid the United States for the clothing and other articles issued to them at the expense of the Government."¹⁰ There are no further indications that blacks were held as prisoners of war.

Prisoners who became ill were to be removed to the prison hospital, a building next to the prison. There, Confederate doctors who were prisoners of war served as volunteers under the direction of a federal medical officer. The federal government cared for extremely ill prisoners at several city hospitals, including the New House of Refuge, the City Hospital on Fifth Street, and military hospitals on Fourth and Hickory Streets and at Jefferson Barracks. The hospital operated by the Catholic Sisters of Charity also treated military prisoners.¹¹

From the beginning of the war, martial law and the arbitrary power it gave to provost marshals produced problems. Frémont had placed enormous power in the hands of the tyrannical and corrupt Justus McKinstry. When Henry Halleck assumed command in mid-November 1861, he instituted a more cautious and bureaucratic policy. More accomplished as a scholar than as a field commander, he possessed a sophisticated understanding of law (he had written on the subject of international law). Unlike Frémont, Halleck insisted on establishing and following a clear line of command. On 20 November he telegraphed Lincoln (via General in Chief George B. McClellan), informing him that "no written authority is found here to declare and enforce martial law in this department. . . . Please send me such written authority, and telegraph me that it has been sent by mail." Lincoln left the matter to McClellan's discretion. "If General McClellan and General Halleck deem it necessary to declare and maintain martial law at St. Louis," Lincoln wrote McClellan, "the same is hearby authorized."[12] McClellan waited several days before drafting a reply to Halleck. On 25 November Halleck complained to the War Department that his telegram "still remains unanswered." Seeming to suspect that the restraints implicit in Lincoln's border-state policy complicated the matter, Halleck assured Adjutant General Lorenzo Thomas that "it is not intended to either declare or enforce martial law in any place where there are civil tribunals which can be intrusted with the punishment of offenses and the regular administration of justice." However, in those places where no such tribunals existed, "it devolves upon the military to arrest and punish murderers, robbers, and thieves." Halleck added that martial law already existed: "In this city, for example, it has existed for months, but by what legal authority I am unable to ascertain." "It certainly is not right," he complained, "to leave a public officer in a position where his duty requires him to exercise an authority which his superior can, but is unwilling to confer."[13]

As Halleck drafted his complaint, McClellan belatedly responded to the original telegram. He hesitated to grant Halleck the broad authority he sought and demanded specific information "as to the necessity of enforcing martial law." Halleck should demonstrate conditions "sufficiently pressing for such a step" and supply "the names and addresses of the officer to whom you think the power should be given." Again, Halleck tried to explain his situation: there was no organized enemy that had formed a "large gathering in any one place so that we can strike them." Instead, widespread lawlessness plagued his command and required not a military campaign but the imposition of martial law. A collapse of civil authority and attacks on Unionists and their property made refugees of loyal citizens. "To punish these outrages and to arrest the traitors . . . it is necessary to use the military power and enforce martial law." It "has been for months exercised here by my predecessor," he observed, but he demanded "written authority." "I mean to act strictly under authority," he explained. If the president and the general in chief refused to grant that authority, "the Government must not hold me responsible for the result."[14]

While Halleck awaited authorization to declare martial law he issued sternly worded orders on 4 December, vowing to enforce the "laws of war." He appointed Bernard G. Farrar provost marshal general for the department. Farrar, a St. Louis native just thirty years old, was the son of a prominent physician of the same name from Virginia. Educated at the University of Virginia, Farrar returned to St. Louis, where he and Franklin Dick engaged in a number of joint real estate enterprises. In April 1861 Farrar joined the federal army. He was a close friend of Frank Blair and served as aide-de-camp to Nathaniel Lyon, carrying Lyon's demand for the surrender of Camp Jackson to the state militia commander Daniel Frost. He served as provost marshal general under Halleck until October 1862.[15] In his orders, Halleck warned the citizenry that "mild and indulgent" treatment of disloyal behavior had come to an end. Anybody "giving information to or communicating with the enemy will be arrested, tried, condemned and shot as spies," he announced. "It should be remembered," he observed in a revealing addendum, "that in this respect the laws of war make no distinction of sex; all are liable to the same penalty." The wives and mothers of rebels could no longer communicate with their husbands and sons without risking arrest and severe punishment. Halleck ordered the arrest of women who displayed the Confederate flag and those who insulted Union troops, a common occurrence when Union soldiers escorted Confederate prisoners to the city's military prisons.

Halleck soon received the written authority he wanted. A directive signed by Lincoln and by Secretary of State William H. Seward "authorized and empowered" him "to suspend the writ of habeas corpus within the limit of the military division under your command and to exercise martial law as you find it necessary in your discretion to secure the public safety, and the authority of the United States." On 26 December 1861 Halleck declared martial law in St. Louis and "in and about all railroads in this State." He later added telegraph lines to the decree. The intent was clear: to define an area of military interest within which martial law applied and to leave the rest of the state in the hands of the civil government established under the authority of the state convention. Wherever civil courts "aid the military authorities in enforcing order and punishing crime," Halleck promised not to interfere with their jurisdiction. In General Orders, no. 1, issued on 1 January 1862, he authorized civilian trials by military commissions. St. Louis and the surrounding military district felt the full force of military rule for the rest of the war.[16]

Halleck also drew on the "laws of war" to institute a policy of assessing disloyal persons. His board of assessors (appointed 12 December 1861 and consisting of two officers and several loyal citizens) drew up a list of known and suspected secessionists and listed the value of their property, determined by scrutinizing tax records. Furthermore, those people who did not voluntarily donate money to the Western Sanitary Commission to assist in the support of civilian refugees in St. Louis would be required collectively to pay

$10,000. Halleck defined three degrees of disloyalty. He directed the board to levy the highest level of assessment against persons who had joined the Confederate army. Those who gave direct aid to the Confederacy constituted a second class of disloyal persons. The third class consisted of individuals who in print or in speech supported the Confederacy. Halleck's order provided for appeals, but he imposed a 10 percent fine on appellants who failed to establish their loyalty. If the assessments were not paid, his order provided for the seizure and sale of property.[17]

The first list drafted by the St. Louis board of assessment contained 300 names. The board selected an initial group of 60 from this list and levied fines of from $100 to $400 and gave the assessees five days to pay. Some of those assessed disavowed the Confederacy and, after taking the oath of allegiance, were relieved of their assessment and removed from the list. A group of 25 protested the legality of the assessments and pressed unsuccessfully for their repeal. The assessments were not simple to administer, however. St. Louisans were unwilling to serve on the board if they were to be publicly identified. Moreover, Halleck found that the initial assessments had been levied on lesser offenders. In orders issued on 7 January 1862, the commander reconstituted the board and instructed its members to revise downward the existing assessments. By 16 January the new assessments were ready, and Halleck ordered property seized and sold when those assessed refused to pay. Topping the new list in terms of the amount assessed and the value of property seized and sold was William McPheeters, a physician who had joined the Confederate army as a surgeon. He had been assessed $800, and federal authorities seized for sale a buggy, a table inlaid with Egyptian marble, and a rosewood piano, among other pieces of property. J. Kennard and Sons, merchants, were also assessed $800 and had carpets valued in that amount seized. D. Robert Barkclay, a lawyer, lost two library cases and the books they contained. Samuel Engler, a merchant, lost $700 worth of candles (although they sold at auction for about $400). In all, the assessment board levied fines of $16,340 and collected $10,913.45. About two-thirds of the amount collected came from the auction of seized property ($6,563.45). This first round of assessments ended early in March 1862, and Halleck dissolved the board as he relinquished command of the Department of the Missouri.[18]

The pro-Southern sympathies of St. Louis's old elite were pronounced, but increasingly they had to be kept private. One scion of an old family, Lucien Duthiel Cabanne, grudgingly took the oath of allegiance in order to enter

St. Louis from his residence near Belleville, Illinois, to attend his son's wedding in October 1861. Battles were being fought at every level of the city's commercial and cultural life. Albert Pearce, a staunch Unionist, had won election as president of the chamber of commerce early in January 1862, and he sought election as president of the Mercantile Library as well. Anne Lane noted with approval that Pearce lost his bid to control the Mercantile to John H. Beach. "The 'Union Ticket' as it was called had Albert Pierce [sic] over here for President, and all the members of it were out-and-out Black Republicans." The opposition's ticket included vice-presidential candidate "Charlie Miller, and one or two other 'Seceshers' were on the other ticket and they were elected."[19]

As federal authorities assigned assessments to prominent secessionists, the pressure on Anne Lane's friends increased considerably. She believed (correctly as it turned out) that her father would be closely watched, but due to his discretion and his age—and to his increasingly frail health (he died early in January 1863)—the family was spared an assessment. But Anne Lane noted that family friends were hard hit. Among them were Samuel Bullitt Churchill, a former St. Louis postmaster; Mrs. Orleana Wright Schaumburg, widow of Judge Charles Schaumburg; Mrs. Stephen Watts Kearny, widow of Frémont's nemesis General Kearny (who died in 1848); and Mrs. Joseph A. Sire, widow of a wealthy St. Louis fur trader.

It was a bitter period for Anne Lane to endure. "The dutch and the darkies are the only free people here now," she wrote to her sister in Germany early in May 1862. The Germans were particularly annoying to her. "If you in Germany have more music than we have here," she wrote her sister, "I am sorry for you." Through her open windows she heard the bands and singing from nearby beer gardens. The beer garden at Washington Hall (50 South Third Street) directly behind her house on Fourth Street "is in full blast." So, too, was Tony Niederwieser's restaurant at 17 South Fourth. General Harney's former residence, nearby on Fourth, had also been turned into a beer garden. "I was in hopes," she wrote, "the war would have killed off so many of the dutch that beer gardens would have suffered but it seems not." The liberties of Southern people were being systematically destroyed, she thought. "The Higher law doctrines" of the Republicans "have prostrated every safeguard," she wrote. But a sense of foreboding was not restricted to the old elite. The Southern-born wife of a St. Louis blacksmith wrote to her son in Saline County on 1 July 1862: "I dread to think of the coming winter; the Negro's [sic] are coming in by the hundreds."[20]

In July 1862 General Schofield, working with Governor Gamble, reinstituted assessments in St. Louis (and in September, across the state) to pay for the uniforms and arms of the new Enrolled Missouri Militia. Schofield placed his provost marshal general, Thomas T. Gantt, in charge of the new assessments. By the end of the year, William Greenleaf Eliot and Samuel T. Glover led the Unionist opposition to the revived assessments. Writing to Governor Gamble, Eliot noted that the citizens of the state exhibited "all shades of opinion" regarding secession and the war. Those who claimed neutrality were, in Eliot's view, little better than open traitors. But Eliot also discerned several "grades of lukewarmness" and those who exhibited a "hesitating zeal." These points of view fell short of "unqualified loyalty," but when military commissions tried to tailor assessments to degrees of disloyalty, "no two tribunals could agree upon the details of such an assessment, either as to persons or amounts to be assessed." The absence of consistency in their application made them seem unfair, and Eliot regarded it as "dangerous to the public peace" to keep persons in the community who had been "exasperated by fines and held up to public contempt." He favored banishment "'beyond the lines.'" Glover himself found the secret nature of the board's proceedings offensive. On 20 January 1863 the War Department suspended all assessments in Missouri, and the practice was not resumed until Sterling Price's marauding army caused a fresh flood of civilian refugees to descend on St. Louis for protection and subsistence.[21]

The policy of assessments served the intended purpose of raising money from disloyal families to support refugees, but it did not silence dissent in St. Louis or prevent disloyal activity in the city. When General Samuel Curtis (the victor at the Battle of Pea Ridge) took command of the Department of the Missouri in September 1862, federal policy on the critical issue of slavery had begun to change. Lincoln issued the preliminary Emancipation Proclamation on 22 September 1862 and the final Emancipation Proclamation on 1 January 1863. The prospect—so dear to the hearts of conditional Unionists in the first two years of the war—that the Union could be restored with the social values of the slaveholding South undisturbed, grew increasingly remote as federal forces began to enlist black troops in spring 1863. Curtis and his provost marshal general, Franklin A. Dick, sensed that the federal government had embarked upon a more resolute course to suppress the rebellion, and they inaugurated a policy of banishment that proved to be far more disruptive than assessments had been for the families of Confederate soldiers.

In April 1863 the War Department issued General Orders, no. 100, offering commanders in the field—for the first time—detailed instructions in matters relating to martial law, enemy property, prisoners of war, partisans and spies, parole, and insurrection. These "Instructions for the Government of Armies of the United States in the Field" had been prepared by the legal scholar Francis Lieber, revised by a board of army officers, and approved by President Lincoln. On the issue of loyalty and disloyalty, the orders instructed commanders to protect loyal citizens as much as possible from the "hardships of war" and to "throw the burden of the war, as much as lies within his power, on the disloyal citizens." Commanders should attempt to distinguish between disloyal citizens who are "known to sympathize with the rebellion without positively aiding it," and those who "without taking up arms, give positive aid and comfort to the rebellious enemy." Commanders could then determine how best to throw the burden of the war on the disloyal citizens. The orders empowered commanders to "expel, transfer, imprison, or fine the revolted citizens who refuse to pledge themselves anew as citizens obedient to the law and loyal to the government."[22]

By spring 1863, under the direction of General Curtis and Provost Marshal Dick, federal policy toward disloyal citizens in St. Louis relied substantially on banishments. But the practice had begun earlier under the more conservative commander, General Schofield. On 3 September 1862, Provost Marshal General Farrar had announced the banishment of "Mrs. Sappington, of Saint Louis County," Claiborne Jackson's mother-in-law. Farrar charged that she had "given information to the traitors of the movement of the U.S. forces" and had "harbored and aided men in arms against the United States Government." He ordered her to "give parole and bond in $2,000 for her future loyal conduct and conversation" and required that she leave Missouri within forty-eight hours. He directed that she "reside in the State of Massachusetts" and report to his office by letter each month.[23] On 14 May 1863, as Provost Marshal General Dick supervised the war's most extensive banishments in St. Louis, other members of the Sappington family—Mrs. David Sappington and Linton Sappington—were among thirteen men and five wives of Confederate officers banished to the Confederacy.[24]

Anne Lane lamented the banishments. "Several boat loads of southern sympathizers—mostly women & children" had been sent away from the city, she wrote to her sister, "and more are to go." Lane also believed that the "*Ladies*" of the Union Aid Society spied on those people whose loyalty they suspected. The members of the society, she believed, "are sworn to visit suspected sympathizers and report any thing they may be induced to say." In this way, she believed, the normal habits of hospitality and social intercourse had been corrupted by the Yankees to persecute those who were not sufficiently zealous in support of the Union cause. Among the most dramatic events for Anne Lane was the arrest of Mrs. Sallie McPheeters, wife of Confederate surgeon William McPheeters, and her children, who were lodged in the Gratiot Street prison for two days before being banished from the city. Sally McPheeters's efforts to communicate with her husband led to her arrest and banishment.

The hardships protested by Anne Lane were real, but so too were overt acts of espionage. Margaret McLure (later the first president of the first chapter of the Daughters of the Confederacy) used her home on Natural Bridge Road as a gathering place for Confederate agents—mail runners and spies—who penetrated Union lines. She was among those banished from the city in May 1863.[25] But banishment also resulted from what women of Southern sympathies regarded as simple acts of charity. Mrs. Fannie M. Coons, wife of Dr. A. J. Coons, provided aid to Confederate soldiers at the Myrtle and Gratiot Street prisons. She also organized a charity fair at the Mercantile Library that federal authorities regarded as a fund-raising event for the Confederacy. Federal authorities closed the fair, arrested its promoters, and banished Fannie Coons to Carlyle, Illinois, although she frequently made clandestine trips to St. Louis and resided for a time with her close friend (and staunch Unionist) Hannah Stagg. All the women arrested were quickly released on their parole—except for Fannie Coons, who accepted banishment rather than pledge her loyalty to the United States. Hannah Stagg marveled that her friendship with Fannie Coons survived the war.[26]

The May 1863 banishment list also included the Reverend David R. McAnally, editor of the *St. Louis Christian Advocate,* a Southern Methodist publication. He had been suspect for some time. In July 1861 a contingent of the Home Guard had ransacked his home, evidently searching for weapons. In August 1862 federal authorities arrested him and held him for more than a month at the Myrtle Street prison before he was interrogated by a military commission and released on his pledge "not to give aid or comfort to the enemies of the United States." On 10 May 1863, the anniversary of the capture of Camp Jackson, federal authorities again arrested McAnally and placed him in the Gratiot Street prison, where he learned that he would be banished.

On 13 May an armed guard marched him and a group of prisoners "through some of the principal streets of the city" to a steamer on the landing. Just before the boat left, Provost Marshal Franklin Dick summoned McAnally to his office and told him, with apology, that he had mistakenly been placed on the banishment list. Thereafter, McAnally suffered no more arrests.[27]

For the wives of Confederate soldiers who remained in St. Louis under martial law, the rigors of life in the field with their husbands may well have seemed preferable to the scrutiny of provost marshals. But as Mary Bowen (wife of Confederate general John Bowen) discovered, the fortunes of war could be very harsh. John Bowen had been elected colonel of the Second Regiment of the Missouri Volunteer Militia in March 1861 and with his men answered General Daniel Frost's call to muster at Camp Jackson. Bowen accepted the federal parole offered by General Lyon after the capture of the camp but immediately presented himself to the Confederate War Department in Richmond, where he received a commission as a colonel in May. In Memphis, Tennessee, Bowen organized the First Missouri Infantry Regiment, a unit that included a number of men from Camp Jackson. During the war, he steadily rose in rank, becoming brigadier general in March 1862 and major general in May 1863. Wounded at Shiloh, he recovered sufficiently to lead his brigade of Missourians in the defense of Vicksburg. Throughout the war, Mary Bowen remained close to her husband. She gave birth to her third child (a second son) at Camp Sterling Price in Mississippi in September 1862. She and her children remained with General Bowen during the painful siege of Vicksburg. A few days after the surrender of the fortress city, as the Bowen family made its way east into central Mississippi, General Bowen died of dysentery. Mary Bowen buried her husband and traveled to Atlanta, where she and her children lived until they were driven from the city by Sherman's advancing federal army. Mary Bowen returned to her Carondelet home at the end of the war, but evidently in pecuniary distress, she sold the property in 1867.[28]

In spring 1863, Anne Lane noted more family friends in the published lists of those to be banished, including Eliza ("Lily") Frost, wife of General Daniel Frost, and her mother, Mrs. Richard Graham (née Catherine Cecelia Mullanphy). Lily Frost offered a prominent example of the difficulties of living under martial law in St. Louis faced by the families of Confederate soldiers. After his capture at Camp Jackson, Frost accepted parole and returned to his Hazelwood estate in Florissant, Missouri, northwest of the city. He was assessed by General Halleck in 1861 and left his family at Hazelwood, making his way south to offer his services to the Confederacy. In St. Louis, Lily Frost was taken into custody for a time and held in the McClure mansion on Chestnut Street. Detained at the same location were the wives of Confederates Trusten Polk, William M. McPheeters, and Claiborne Jackson's former aide William M. Cooke (who won election to the Confederate Congress in fall 1861 and represented Missouri until his death in April 1863).[29]

Lily Frost used Confederate mail runner Absalom Grimes to send letters to her husband, and one was found on him when he was captured at Memphis. Provost Marshal General Franklin A. Dick charged Lily Frost and the other wives with "collecting and distributing rebel letters." More broadly, as Dick explained, "these women are wealthy and wield a great influence." Dick had sufficient evidence to convict the women of disloyal behavior before a military commission, but he then faced the "embarrassment" of deciding "what to do with them." It seemed best to send them through the lines to join their husbands and sons, so he requested authority to banish these "disloyal, avowed and abusive enemies of the Govt." On 23 April 1863 he received the authority he sought from Stanton. Lily Frost joined a group sent aboard the *Belle Memphis* on 13 May to Memphis. From that federally controlled city she traveled by rail to Okalona, Mississippi. With Mrs. Trusten Polk, Lily Frost journeyed west to Arkansas, where they rejoined their husbands.[30]

Mortimer Kennett and his nephew, James White Kennett, and the Philadelphia-born physician Simon Gratz Moses also were among the banished. Moses had moved to St. Louis in the early 1840s and practiced medicine at his residence at 22 North Eighth Street. Dr. Gratz A. Moses (probably the son of S. Gratz Moses) served as a physician with the Confederate army. The elder Moses may have returned to Philadelphia for the duration of the war; he died in St. Louis in 1897. The younger Moses also returned to St. Louis after the war and built a successful practice; he died there in 1901.[31] Frank Blair's cousin, Confederate cavalry commander Jo Shelby, angrily insisted that Blair help his wife relocate when she was banished from her St. Louis home. "I am surprised," wrote Shelby, "that any set of men should resort to such means as to vent their feelings on some innocent women." Shelby sent his best wishes to Frank's wife, Apolline, and promised to visit her when he returned to St. Louis with a Confederate army. Blair settled Mrs. Shelby in the Lexington, Kentucky home of Benjamin Gratz, Shelby's stepfather.[32]

Banishments served the purpose of getting troublesome folks out of the city and ended their capacity to influence and lead others in opposition to the United States. In an early episode, it was the presence of two dead men that provoked Provost Marshal General Dick to take preemptive action. One of the dead men was Emmet McDonald, the lone captive from Camp Jackson who had refused to give his parole. After that affair, McDonald fought with the Confederacy, commanding a Missouri artillery battery at the Battles of Lexington (Missouri) and Pea Ridge (Arkansas). Later in 1862 he raised a cavalry regiment in Arkansas and rose to the rank of colonel. McDonald rode with John Marmaduke during a raid into southwest Missouri early in 1863 and was killed by federal artillery fire near Springfield on 11 January. The other dead man was John M. Wimer, the former mayor of St. Louis. In many ways Wimer made an unlikely Confederate. As mayor in the mid 1850s, he stood with Frank Blair and Gratz Brown as a Free-Soil Democrat. With Blair and Brown, Wimer fought against Claiborne Jackson's Southern Rights Democrats and their effort to unseat Senator Thomas Hart Benton. But Wimer vehemently opposed Blair's and Lyon's actions at Camp Jackson. In spring 1862, federal authorities arrested Wimer for disloyalty and held him in the Gratiot Street prison. In August they transferred him to the Alton military prison, from which he managed to escape in December. He made his way to southwest Missouri and died with McDonald. In death, the two men raised troublesome issues for General Curtis and Provost Marshal Dick. Fearing that public funerals for them would encourage violent expressions of antifederal sentiment, Dick directed that the men's bodies be taken from their families' homes and quietly buried in the Wesleyan Cemetery near the site of Camp Jackson.[33] Their burials dramatized the problem federal authorities faced as they struggled to suppress and punish disloyalty.

This problem repeatedly required intervention by President Lincoln, who searched in vain to find a middle course for the border city. The case of two prominent brothers, the physician William M. McPheeters and the pastor Samuel B. McPheeters, illustrated the deep personal antagonisms that made the issue of loyalty and disloyalty in St. Louis a topic of ongoing concern to the president. William and his younger brother were natives of Raleigh, North Carolina, and graduates of the University of North Carolina, where Samuel and Frank Blair were classmates and roommates. For a time the career paths of the brothers diverged. William studied medicine in Philadelphia at the University of Pennsylvania. In 1841 he moved to St. Louis and in 1843 became professor of clinical medicine at the St. Louis Medical College. His 1849 essay, the "History of Epidemic Cholera in St. Louis," remains a standard account of that devastating event. Nearly four years younger than his brother, Samuel followed in his father's footsteps as a Presbyterian minister. After studying at Princeton Theological Seminary in the mid-1840s, he followed his brother to St. Louis and became pastor of the Westminster Presbyterian Church (which soon merged with another congregation to become, in 1853, the Pine Street Presbyterian Church).[34]

Notwithstanding their friendship with Frank Blair and Edward Bates, the McPheeters brothers did not share the sentiments of the unconditional Unionists. William openly sympathized with the Southern cause during the excitement of spring and summer 1861, while Samuel, who had taken a year's leave of absence from the Pine Street Church for reasons of health, worried and watched the unfolding of events from New Mexico, where he had taken a commission as an army chaplain. The violence that followed Lyon's seizure of Camp Jackson outraged William, who denounced it as the "St. Louis Massacre" and repeatedly refused to take the oath of allegiance required by the state convention to practice as a physician. In January 1862, General Halleck's assessment committee placed McPheeters on its list of disloyal persons. He refused to pay the fee assigned to him, and on 23 January Provost Marshal Farrar ordered the seizure of his household property, to be sold at auction. One of the McPheeters's children lay dying in the house when the federal troops entered it to take much of the family's furniture. Farrar announced in the city newspapers that on 3 February 1862 the government would offer for sale to the highest bidder "the chattels, property and effects of *Wm. M. McPheeters.*" This consisted of six rosewood damask chairs, two rosewood damask sofas, one rosewood marble-top table, a piano, and a buggy with harness. The property would be auctioned to raise the $300 assessed "upon said *Wm. M. McPheeters,* as a friend of the enemy, in aid of the suffering families, driven by the rebels from Southwest Missouri." When the sale occurred, the *Republican* reported "lively bidding" and took care to list the names of all buyers, even revealing the identity of one man who bid through a pseudonym. The paper reported, for example, that "Mr. English, carriage merchant" purchased the parlor furniture, and a "Mr. Bruder" bought the marble table. On 19 February Farrar announced a second levy against McPheeters.[35] In June he left St. Louis to join the Confederate army, serving with Sterling Price as a surgeon with the rank of major throughout most of the war.[36]

The departure of William for the Confederacy marked the beginning of a painful and complex struggle between Samuel and the staunchly Unionist members of his congregation. Before returning to St. Louis in summer 1861, the minister expressed to a friend his hope that he could keep himself free of the sectional contentiousness of the city. He took the oath of allegiance required by the state constitutional convention for the performance of marriages, but the open disloyalty of his brother brought suspicion upon himself. In June, as William McPheeters left St. Louis, angry members of Samuel's congregation confronted him on the issue of loyalty. Led by George P. Strong, these parishioners demanded to know why he had presided over the baptism of a child given the "name of that arch rebel and traitor, Sterling Price." Strong and his supporters regarded this activity to be "a premeditated insult to the Government, and all its friends in the Pine Street Church." The protesting members of the congregation demanded that Samuel McPheeters make his views on secession publicly known.[37]

McPheeters replied to Strong's letter on 8 July arguing that his political views were not the business of the congregation. He invoked Thomas Jefferson's famous comments on the separation of church and state and insisted that his role as pastor should be judged without regard to his views as a citizen. Letters continued to be exchanged between the two men during fall 1862, when Curtis succeeded Halleck as commander of the Department of the Missouri. Frustrated, Strong decided to make the matter public. In a letter to the *Missouri Democrat,* he called on Samuel McPheeters to state his views candidly and publicly. "As a man, called to be a minister of the Gospel, and our spiritual teacher and guide," he wrote, the public must know if McPheeters "is a friend or an enemy to our Government." This "is a question which does deeply concern us and our families. We have a right to know," he concluded, "and you have no right at a time like this to conceal it."[38]

Strong's public condemnation of McPheeters may have been intended to justify the actions soon taken by General Curtis against the minister. On 19 December 1862, the new provost marshal general, Franklin A. Dick, acted on orders from Curtis to banish McPheeters and his wife from the state. They were directed to relocate to a place of their choosing "North of Indianapolis and West of Pennsylvania" and to remain there for the duration of the war. In his order Curtis made no specific charges against McPheeters. The commander simply stated that McPheeters's "wife, his brother, and intimate associates" had "seduced" the pastor "from an open and manly support of the Government into active sympathy with the rebellion." Curtis also appointed a military commission to control the governance of the Pine Street Church.

On 23 December McPheeters left St. Louis for Washington to protest his banishment. On the eve of his departure he published his rebuttal to Strong and General Curtis: "As a pastor, and because I am a pastor, I have stood aloof from these things, even in my private relations."[39]

Attorney General Edward Bates, a devout Presbyterian and a close friend of the McPheeters family, arranged an interview for himself and McPheeters with President Lincoln. Lincoln responded to McPheeters's appeal by directing General Curtis not to banish him and his wife. James E. Yeatman and Giles F. Filley (members of William Greenleaf Eliot's Unitarian Church) promptly went to Washington to lobby the president to maintain the banishment order. Yeatman carried a letter from Curtis expressing the general's hope that Lincoln would give him "more rather than less discretion, especially as to the dispersal of persons disloyal and dangerous to the public peace." He explained that the relatively peaceful condition of his department "is mainly owing to a steady application of military power." The commander particularly recommended Yeatman to the president because he had been "raised in the South" and because "his inclinations are pro-slavery." Yeatman had earlier interceded with the president to support Harney over Lyon, and Lincoln knew him as a moderate Unionist. Curtis added that neither Yeatman nor Filley was a member of McPheeters's congregation, and thus they could speak with the president about the matter "without prejudice."[40]

After reviewing the case Lincoln attempted to chart a course that would appease McPheeters's Unionist friends (i.e., Bates) without alienating stalwart Unionists and General Curtis. He noted in his reply to Curtis that he could not find "anything specific" alleged against McPheeters. After his interview with the minister, however, the president agreed that "he does sympathize with the rebels." Lincoln questioned whether exile was warranted for "secret sympathies," but he left the final decision to Curtis's discretion. On one point, though, he gave the general explicit instructions: the United States should not, under any circumstances, take on the role of operating churches. Lincoln had long since accepted military commissions as the proper instrument through which executive authority could be wielded under martial law. But the creation of a military commission to administer the operations of a church carried the principle further than the president was willing to go. "The U.S. government must not, as by this order, undertake to run the churches," he wrote. "When an individual, in a church or out of it, becomes dangerous to the public interest, he must be checked; but let the churches, as such take care of themselves."[41]

Working through the church's governing board, George Strong continued his effort to remove McPheeters from the pulpit, which he achieved
after the church body had been purged of all disloyal elements by Provost
Marshal Dick. Defeated, Samuel McPheeters moved to a church in Kentucky.
After the war the Pine Street congregation voted decisively (but not unani-
mously) to invite him to return. By that time ill health plagued him, and he
returned to St. Louis only for a brief visit. He died in Kentucky in 1870 at the
age of fifty-one.[42]

Martial law and the use of military commissions to punish civilians clearly
denied Missourians ordinary civil rights. Efforts by Lincoln and his commanders in Missouri to distinguish between arenas of martial and civil law never
fully succeeded, nor did efforts to distinguish between criticism of the federal government and overtly disloyal acts. As Provost Marshal General Farrar
explained to a commander in Hannibal, Missouri, in March 1862, the contest between federal authority and civilian rights in Missouri "is now purely
a question of power not one of law." Those who had "discarded law . . . and
appealed to force" ought not to be allowed to find protection in ordinary civil
rights. "Do not hesitate to seize and hold their property," Farrar directed.
"Where there is no law there is no property," he continued. "If they deny the
power of the Government, they are without law and let them feel the consequences. We cannot," he concluded, "temporize with them."[43]

Nevertheless, there were clearly limits beyond which it was imprudent
for federal authorities to venture: Lincoln himself had specified churches. On
the one hand, commanders in Missouri repeatedly favored a stern suppression of dissent. On the other hand, as one of Frémont's aides expressed it,
federal authorities recognized that if "entertaining secession feelings" constituted an offense that justified imprisonment, "the Government would have
two-thirds of the State to feed at its expense."[44]

The perspectives and zeal of the various commanders of the Department
of the Missouri differed widely, but the suspension of the writ of habeas corpus in the state resulted in extensive and widespread civilian arrests throughout the war. Mark Neely, who has examined the military records of civilian
arrests, found that the U.S. Army arrested far more civilians in Missouri than
in any other state. The total number of arrests cannot be determined precisely
because no standard form of documentation existed. The commander at the
Gratiot Street prison complained in February 1863, for example, that a group
of eleven men arrived at his facility from Rolla with virtually no accompany-

ing documentary records: "There being no descriptive list sent with these prisoners it is impossible for me to give any explanatory notes concerning these men." The federal officer who brought them to the prison had made up a list of names; the provost marshal at Rolla had supplied no information. The existence of bureaucratic formalities did not guarantee careful documentation. Neely found in the National Archives a printed form filled out in the provost marshal's office in St. Louis, with the underlined entries filling in the blanks: "Prisoners at the *Gratiot* Street Military Prison the 2 day of *Feb* 1863, from *Corporal Willis Knight* sent forward from *Dont know where* on the *ditto* date of *Feb* 1863, by order of *Don't know who, as no papers came with guard of prisoners.*"[45] A careful examination by Neely of the records of the Gratiot Street prison for the period from April 1862 through October 1863 revealed that over 2,000 civilians "entered, passed through, or remained in that military prison." At that rate, the number of civilians imprisoned there, from the first suspension of habeas corpus by Frémont in September 1861 until the end of the war, numbered nearly 5,000. This figure does not include civilians held at military posts in Missouri or those imprisoned at the smaller Myrtle Street facility during its nearly three years of existence. Nor does it include Missouri prisoners transferred to the Alton military prison. By Neely's conservative calculations, it is clear that military authorities arrested and held at the Gratiot Street prison more than 1 out of every 100 men in the state. Given the large number of men enrolled in the Union and Confederate armies, this is, as Neely has concluded, "a formidable if not staggering figure."[46]

Conditions at the Myrtle Street and Gratiot Street prisons varied considerably, depending on the season of the year and the number of prisoners being held. For the most part, however, surviving accounts by prisoners do not describe harsh conditions. Among the first prisoners at Myrtle Street was the Confederate mail runner Absalom Grimes. Born in Kentucky in 1834, the son of a riverboat pilot, Grimes settled in St. Louis in 1850 and worked as a messenger for the Morse Telegraph Company. From 1852 until the outbreak of the war he worked as a riverboat pilot and lived in Hannibal, Missouri. There he counted himself one of the friends of Samuel Clemens (who briefly joined a rebel force before he moved west and began his career as Mark Twain). Federal authorities first arrested Grimes near Springfield in December 1861, but he managed to escape and rejoined Price before the Battle of Pea Ridge. He was captured there and transported by wagon to Rolla, by train to St. Louis, and was lodged in the Myrtle Street prison. "I had a good time while in the negro pen," he recalled, "as a large number of my friends, ladies and gentlemen, called on me." Regular visitors eased the rigors of prison life. Grimes's friends "brought me many presents of food, clothing, and money." Escape attempts were frequent and occasionally humorous. One of Grimes's fellow prisoners, Captain Hampton Boone, tried to escape disguised as a woman. A lady friend had visited Boone and brought him a dress. As he and his friend walked through the prison gate, a guard noticed that one "lady" wore cavalry boots and gave chase. Boone ran down Broadway, struggling to free himself of the dress. It was his misfortune, however, to become ensnared in the underlying hoop skirt, a birdcagelike apparatus. He tripped and fell and was recaptured.[47]

Federal authorities later transported Grimes to the Alton prison, which offered him a fresh opportunity to escape by riverboat with the aid of old friends. He stayed in St. Louis until April 1862 and then headed south. Arrested in Memphis, he was again incarcerated at the Alton prison and then, presumably because he was a civilian and not a prisoner of war, he was transferred back to the Myrtle Steet prison and placed in irons in an isolated cell under the sidewalk. Grimes described it as "an excavation in the ground which had been lined with boiler iron and this in turn with boards." This area had been divided into two cells "eight feet square and seven feet high." "I was well fed," he reported, "and friends brought me food and clothing." But, conditions were far from pleasant. The cell was very cold, and he had to be taken periodically to the commander's office to be warmed up. He briefly enjoyed more comfortable accommodations at the Gratiot Street prison, where he shared a room with half-a-dozen men. But rumors of a planned escape sent him back to Myrtle Street to the freezing cell. A letter from Grimes to Provost Marshal General Broadhead protesting the cold produced his transfer, on 19 December 1863, to Gratiot Street. It was during his stay there that he became acquainted with fellow prisoner Charles L. Hunt, one of the St. Louis leaders of the pro-Confederate secret society known to its members as the Order of American Knights.[48]

The night Grimes returned to Gratiot Street, sixty prisoners escaped through a tunnel they had constructed in a concealed cellar. The men cut through the brick wall near the cellar floor, dug a tunnel under the prison yard (a distance of about ten feet), and then under the sergeant's yard and house. The tunnel ran forty feet and opened into a cellar in a two-story house next to the sergeant's residence. The escapees crawled through, exited the cellar on Gratiot Street, and walked as leisurely as possible west, away from the prison. One prisoner mistakenly walked east, met a prison guard, and tried to reverse his course, but he was fired on and caught. The captured man revealed the location of the tunnel, and federal guards caught about fifteen men trying to make their way to freedom. Later in December, Grimes attempted to escape with his friend, Lieutenant William H. Sebring. They were caught and punished by being made to stand for a day, chained to a pole on the porch facing the prison yard. The punishment began favorably enough, with the temperature in the morning at seventy degrees. But by midday the wind switched to the north, and the temperature plummeted. By evening a heavy snowstorm had begun. The men suffered badly from the cold and began to fear that they would freeze. Two women friends could see into the prison yard from an office across the street. As the storm worsened, they got word to Broadhead, who directed the prison commander to take Grimes and Sebring inside. A second escape attempt, shortly before his scheduled execution on 10 July 1864, left Grimes wounded. His friend William Sebring, along with several others, made good their escape, but guards shot Grimes in the leg and captured him. He remained in prison, but his wound saved him from the hangman's noose long enough for Lincoln to commute his sentence to confinement in the state penitentiary in Jefferson City.[49]

Conditions in the St. Louis military prisons were a constant source of dispute and inquiry. Historian William Hesseltine concluded his study of the subject with the observation that "conditions in the prisons of St. Louis reveal only the natural defects of a makeshift prison." Overcrowding at times made conditions deplorable, however, and in general, the winter months produced hardships that had to be endured until spring. A protest by prisoners in May 1862 prompted the first official investigation into conditions at Gratiot Street. Investigators reported that prisoners received full army rations of one pound of fresh meat or one-third pound of bacon daily; this was supplemented with coffee, bread, beans, rice, peas, hominy, and soup. The investigators acknowledged that prisoners were served only two cooked meals a day, attributing this not to a shortage of food but to the limited cooking facilities at the prison.[50]

In May 1862 Colonel Thomas Gantt directed the refitting of the Myrtle Street prison, and by fall it was fully in use once again. An inspection of the Gratiot Street prison by Provost Marshal Farrar in June 1862 praised conditions at that location. But when Franklin A. Dick succeeded him early in November, he found that overcrowding and disease were serious problems.

Dick transferred 150 prisoners from Gratiot Street to the refitted Myrtle Street prison. Within days, however, the number of prisoners at Gratiot Street had swelled to over 1,000, and by mid-November sickness increased alarmingly. In one week over 200 sick prisoners lay on floors in city hospitals awaiting beds. Dick moved a number of prisoners to Alton, and by early December he reported the number at Gratiot Street to be at a manageable level of 570.[51]

The crisis had passed, but it prompted an investigation that involved the Western Sanitary Commission. In Special Orders, no. 16, issued 18 December 1862, General Curtis established a board of officers to examine conditions at the Gratiot and Myrtle Street prisons. The commander directed them to work with the Western Sanitary Commission and to consider whether new prison facilities were needed. The board found 471 prisoners at Gratiot Street and reported that the facility could hold 750. "The Myrtle Street Prison is in good order," the report continued. It held 145 prisoners at the time of the inspection, and the board reported that it could hold "150 prisoners through-out the winter." Reporting for the Western Sanitary Commission, however, James Yeatman described the Myrtle Street prison as overcrowded, with 155 bunks—the facility did not meet the commission's minimum standard for cubic feet of air space. In Yeatman's view, the population at Myrtle Street should be reduced to 100. Using the same standards for air space, he reported that the number of prisoners at Gratiot Street should not exceed 625. If there were to be a large increase in the prison population, Yeatman advised that new prison camps be constructed.[52]

An outbreak of smallpox at Gratiot Street in March 1863 prompted a new investigation by two physicians appointed by the U.S. Sanitary Commission, in many ways a rival of the Western Sanitary Commission. In April they sent their report to Secretary of War Stanton, who responded by ordering an inquiry of his own. In an implied critique of Yeatman's December 1862 report, these doctors found overcrowded and filthy conditions at the Gratiot Street prison. "The bunks in which the prisoners sleep are made to hold two persons in each tier and are three tiers high, and these are placed so close together that there is scarcely space to pass between them." The floors seemed to be earthen because they were so thickly covered with dirt. The men spent day and night in these unwholesome conditions since the prison yard "is scarcely sufficient to contain a foul and stinking privy." Stanton's investigation found tolerable conditions at Gratiot Street, but in October 1863, apparently in deference to the Sanitary Commission, the army assigned a medical officer to the prison. He found dilapidated conditions, particularly worn floors and collapsing ceilings resulting from repeated washing of floors. The medical officer also recommended increasing the ration of vegetables to ward off scurvy. Most important, however, with fewer than 1,000 prisoners at Gratiot Street and Myrtle Street, the worst of the overcrowding had passed; another investigation found that repairs had been made in the buildings and that excellent conditions prevailed.[53]

Clearly the winter months were not pleasant at the two prisons. In February 1864 the acting medical inspector of prisoners, Dr. A. M. Clark, reported to the commissary general of prisoners at the War Department that poor conditions also prevailed at Alton. Clark found that the "sinks" there (the sewage pits beneath the latrines) were located near the prison hospital and were in a "filthy and most offensive condition." The problem seemed to be a blockage in the connection between the sinks and the main sewer line leading to the river. He ordered the latrines "cleansed without delay" and the connection to the main sewer reopened. Clark found the bedding in the hospital section of the prison "sufficient and clean," but in the prison itself, the bedding was "filthy, and swarming with vermin." During his visit he found three unidentified women prisoners confined in a "damp, half-underground room, only partitioned off from an open cellar." He denounced their "present condition" as "an outrage on humanity" and urged the prison commander to "remove them to quarters better fitted to their sex." Throughout the Alton prison Clark found smallpox and measles "rapidly disappearing," but there were numerous cases of "pneumonia, bronchitis, catarrh, intermittent fever, [and] chronic diarrhea." He urged that the population of the prison, exceeding 1,800 at the time of his visit, be reduced to the 800 inmates that the structure had been designed to hold. To his report, Clark attached a table that recorded the size of the cells (eighty-eight "old cells" were 3'10" × 7' with 7'3" ceilings). In one room (approximately 13' × 50' with a 9' ceiling), Clark counted forty-two inmates. With 15 square feet of floor space for each prisoner, the room was barely large enough to permit the occupants to lie down on their sides.[54]

Clark found conditions considerably worse at the Gratiot and Myrtle Street prisons. "Neither of the buildings now in use are well adapted to their purpose," he reported. He suggested using the Alton prison for "sentenced prisoners" (those convicted of disloyal activities), with military prisoners relocated to healthier prison camps. At Gratiot Street, the two wings of the prison and the "dwelling houses" that were used as a hospital "may be said to be entirely unventilated." The only possible sources of fresh air were side windows, which were almost always kept shut. The Gratiot Street facility had been "bad enough at my last inspection," he reported. "It is many times worse now. . . . As to the Myrtle Street Prison, its sanitary condition is a disgrace to its commandant." The most appalling aspect of this facility was the manner in which it was "policed" (or cleaned). It seemed to Clark that this was accomplished "but one way: a hose is let into each room, which is then flooded with water, washing the rubbish and debris into the hall, while a large portion of water finds its way through the cracks and holes in the floor into the rooms beneath." Since all the bedding and blankets were left in place, "by the time the washing is over," the bedding on the lower floor was "as wet as the floor." In one of the lower rooms Clark found "a red-hot stove . . . in full blast" and the door and window "tightly closed." He tried to open the window but could move it no more than six inches. The "fetid steam" that pervaded the room sickened the doctor in a few minutes, "and this is but a type of the entire prison."

The sinks at Myrtle Street were located in the exercise yard, a plot of about seventy by twenty feet that also contained the fuel supply "and a variety of rubbish." Clark concluded: "I can say no word for this building except in unqualified condemnation." In closing he offered two examples of the horrible conditions he found there. First, he described a room holding the prison's two female inmates, "a white woman and a colored girl." They were housed on the second floor in a cell measuring about twelve feet by five feet, with two windows that were nailed shut. The only supply of fresh air came through a broken pane of glass. The atmosphere "was rendered still more foul" by a commode, "which bore evidence of not having been cleansed for some time." Clark believed that the white woman had been jailed for stealing from a soldier. The black woman, he thought, had committed no crime but was being held as a witness.

Second, Clark described the two "strong rooms" on the first floor. These were the cells that had housed Absalom Grimes. There were no windows. Air came in not from the outside but from inside the building through "a dozen inch auger holes . . . in one corner of the ceiling and the same number near the floor." He found the prisoners here "pallid and suffering severely from want of air."[55] The inspector recommended closing both prisons and transferring prisoners to Benton Barracks. By March 1864, the overcrowding had been relieved by transfers to Alton. General Rosecrans, who took command of the department in January 1864, ordered the construction of new buildings for prisoners at Jefferson Barracks, but Gratiot Street and Myrtle Street remained in operation. Under Rosecrans's direction, both buildings were repaired in summer 1864, and a system of weekly inspections began. One inspector reported conditions worthy of "public charitable institutions where the needy are cared for."[56] Conditions at a poorhouse were not intended to be pleasant; neither were those at a military prison.

Clearly, conditions at the two prisons could be extremely unpleasant, but prisoners seem to have been cared for as well as circumstances permitted. One inmate, Captain Griffin Frost of the Missouri State Guard, captured in Arkansas in January 1863, published a journal of his captivity at Gratiot Street in 1867, for the purpose of describing cruelties greater than those at the Confederate prison at Andersonville. When he was exchanged in April, Frost returned to the field of battle and was captured again and returned to Gratiot Street in October 1863. On his return, he and his fellow prisoners had not been fed for twenty-four hours, and as they stood in the bitter cold being searched for papers and weapons before being conducted into the prison, one of their number fell dead. Frost spent his first days at Gratiot Street in the "Round Room," which he described as sixty feet in diameter, where overcrowding required many prisoners to sleep on the floor. He found the rations dismal. "We are allowed only two meals a day," he recorded in his journal on 5 January 1863. With 800 prisoners at the prison, the cooks worked until dark to feed them all. Breakfast consisted of one-fifth of a loaf of bread, "a small portion of bacon," and a tin cup "of stuff they call coffee." For dinner prisoners again received one-fifth of a loaf of bread, a portion of boiled beef, and sometimes, boiled potatoes. Eating utensils, even spoons, were banned; prisoners ate with their hands. In a few days he and other officers were removed to more spacious quarters with bunk beds and windows. The worst treatment consisted of verbal abuse by guards, who outraged the Southerner's sense of chivalry when they spoke of Southern women as whores. Conditions at Gratiot Street could be unpleasant, but Frost's effort to compare the facility to Andersonville fell short of the mark.[57]

Far more revealing about the uncertainties of prison life was the correspondence of another prisoner at Gratiot Street, William J. Wooden of Carroll County. He had been tried by a military commission in St. Joseph on 15 May 1863, a procedure that ended, he claimed, without his knowing the verdict in his case or his sentence. After a month in prison in western Missouri, he still did not know his fate. "I suppose that the papers were sent to St. Louis," he wrote his sister. He expected to learn the decision soon, however, and he had a "strong hope that I will be released." By early July, however, federal authorities had transferred him to the Gratiot Street prison, and he reported to his family that "we have very comfortable quarters here." But he still did not know "when I shal leave here or where I shal be sento [*sic*]." Wooden tried to remain optimistic, however, telling his wife, "it is not half so disheartening to be in prison as what I expected."[58]

After three weeks at Gratiot Street (one of which he spent in the hospital), Wooden reported that while he had been sick he had received "very kind attention." He and the other prisoners got along "tollerable well." However, he feared that "it may be a long time before We see each other." He tried to advise his wife by letter on how to manage the farm, recommending that she turn the cow dry "and sell her this fall or beef her." He hoped that she could sell his watch for twelve dollars. At the same time he reassured her that there was plenty to eat: "Three times a day we have bacon and beef[,] wheat bread and coffee and potatoes." The prisoners were allowed to augment their prison fare by purchasing "pies and ginger bread[,] milk[,] onions and apple when we wish." But the fundamental uncertainty remained. He did not know "when I will be permitted to come home again." There had been an exchange of prisoners that day, but his name had not been called. He hoped to be exchanged and banished from the state: he "would be glad to be sent to nebraska."[59]

Early in August, Wooden wrote his sister from the military prison at Alton. He complained of his rheumatism. He had not known that he would be transferred to Alton until "about one hour before we were started." He hoped that some neighbors would "go before the Provost at Carrollton and state whether I was med[d]ling with government affairs or not." By mid-August he had been returned to Gratiot Street, perhaps due to his ill health. Although he did not know "how long I will be kept here or where I will be sent from here," he continued to hope that the authorities would banish him to "nebraska territory or washington territory." As the weather turned cold, his health declined steadily. Several prisoners had been released, and Wooden hoped that his sister could get a petition from neighbors to help secure his release. A period of warm, dry weather revived his spirits. "I am still in McDowels [*sic*] College," he joked to his wife, "and know not when I will get a diploma." With the return of cold weather, however, his health again declined. Late in January he told his wife that he had suffered a "spell of sickness" and revealed to her that "the boys here call me the old man Wooden and that does not suit." In March 1864 he reported that he had been removed from Gratiot Street to "what is called the branch hospittel." A friend wrote him encouragingly that "we are getting on with the case as well as we expected when you left if not better I hope to succeed in a short time." Wooden died on 20 March 1864, a little more than a month short of his thirty-eighth birthday.[60]

There had never been any shortage of disloyal sentiment or activity in St. Louis. But the issue of disloyalty took on wider significance by 1864. The Confederacy continued to stave off defeat, and war weariness in the North buoyed the hopes of Peace Democrats as they rallied around their candidate, George B. McClellan, in the presidential campaign of 1864. Lincoln had repeatedly urged his commanders in Missouri to give wide latitude to freedom of speech and press. When, for example, General Schofield, in September 1863, arrested William McKee, the radical editor of the *Missouri Democrat* (for the unauthorized publication of official correspondence, a letter to Schofield from the president), Lincoln expressed regret that the action had been taken. "I regret to learn of the arrest of the Democrat editor," he wrote Schofield. "I fear this loses you the middle position I desired you to occupy." Lincoln cared "very little for the publication of any letter I have written." He asked Schofield to "please spare me the trouble this is likely to cause." Later, in October 1863, Lincoln explicitly directed that Schofield "arrest individuals and suppress assemblies or newspapers" only when they produced a "palpable injury to the military in your charge." Otherwise, Schofield should not "interfere with the expression of opinion in any form, or allow it to be interfered with violently by others."[61]

The distinction that Lincoln asked Schofield to make was difficult; such inconsistency characterized federal policy. Political criticisms of the Republican administration and of the Union war effort could discourage young men from enlisting and thereby cause a "palpable injury to the military." The Union commander in Ohio, Ambrose E. Burnside, had made precisely this argument to justify the arrest of the outspoken Peace Democrat, former congressman Clement L. Vallandigham. Lincoln later banished Vallandigham to the Confederacy, although the Ohio Democrat soon made his way to Halifax and then to Windsor, Ontario. From there he made several forays into the

United States to campaign for governor of Ohio in 1864. Horatio Seymour's election as governor of New York in 1862, the New York City Draft Riots in summer 1863, Vallandigham's political prominence in 1864, and George B. McClellan's presidential nomination frightened many Union men, General Rosecrans among them, and created a fertile climate for rumors and perceptions of disloyal conspiracies.

When Rosecrans took command of the Department of the Missouri late in January 1864, he brought with him a tarnished reputation as a field commander and a problematic relationship with the War Department. Secretary of War Stanton disliked him, and Stanton's assistant, Charles A. Dana, suspected that the general's choice for provost marshal general, Colonel John P. Sanderson, had displayed cowardice at the Battle of Chickamauga. Dana's hostility initially delayed Sanderson's appointment. It was with the hope that they could boost their reputations in Washington that Rosecrans and Sanderson launched in St. Louis a zealous pursuit of disloyal individuals and organizations.[62]

What appeared to be the rising tide of the Peace Democrats' political activity, especially in the Midwest, fueled Rosecrans's and Sanderson's concerns about disloyal activity in St. Louis. Two St. Louisans—Charles L. Hunt and Charles E. Dunn—soon became the starting points for a widening investigation that convinced Rosecrans and Sanderson that they had uncovered a vast conspiracy to unleash a secessionist insurrection in Missouri and the Old Northwest. Sanderson's investigation reached far beyond the limits of the Department of the Missouri, and Stanton blocked the payment of his cadre of detectives. Fearing that Rosecrans intended to use a politically volatile conspiracy issue to elevate his stature in Washington and to circumvent Stanton, Lincoln dispatched his private secretary, John Hay, to St. Louis with instructions to review the evidence of a disloyal conspiracy and to advise the president. Hay dined with Rosecrans and sensed the general's hostility toward Stanton. He also met with Sanderson, who summarized the evidence he had collected. Hay thought that Sanderson hoped to impress Lincoln, perhaps in the expectation of securing promotion to brigadier general.

Hay gave some credence to Sanderson's allegations, but Lincoln did not interfere when Stanton ordered Rosecrans to release two St. Louis men arrested because of their alleged association with Hunt and Dunn. Angry and frustrated, Rosecrans released Sanderson's full report for publication in the *Missouri Democrat*. Other Radical Republican papers—including the *Chicago Tribune*, the

Illinois State Journal, and the *New York Tribune*—published the report as part of an election-season attack on Peace Democrats. In October, at Stanton's direction, Judge Advocate General Joseph Holt drafted a report on the Sanderson investigation and other allegations of anti-government conspiracies, which praised Sanderson's work. Stanton released the Holt report on the eve of the November presidential election. Lincoln and the Republicans won an overwhelming victory; the Peace Democrats had been crushed.[63]

The blatantly political purposes to which Stanton put Sanderson's and Holt's reports has raised questions among historians concerning their authenticity. Certainly Sanderson cast a wide net searching for "men of disloyal sentiments." Undoubtedly, men who were simply critics of federal policies were caught in it. Sanderson had angered many people in St. Louis by requiring suspected clergymen to take the oath of allegiance and by closing grog shops when he suspected them to be gathering points for the disloyal. But the evidence for his report came from a number of arrests and from subsequent interrogations. The partisan political purposes that his investigation ultimately served prompted the historian Frank L. Klement to suspect fraud and manipulation in all of it. If the goal of the men Sanderson investigated for disloyalty had been to assemble a vast conspiracy against the federal government, Klement has correctly concluded that no such organized activity ever existed. It was Sanderson's ambition that had fueled the conspiracy theory, Klement has argued. He "fabricated" the details of a conspiracy, the idea of which amounted to nothing more than a "fantasy" in the minds of a handful of Peace Democrats.[64]

There is no reason to doubt Klement's conclusion that a tendency to equate the Peace Democrats' political opposition with a disloyal conspiracy led Sanderson to some unwarranted conclusions. Lincoln and Stanton suspected as much, although both men willingly used the material he generated for partisan political gain. But as John Hay had noted, there were plausible and well-substantiated elements in Sanderson's story. Had the provost marshal general kept his focus on disloyal activity in St. Louis, his report would have been far more substantial than it was.

The disloyal activities Sanderson uncovered in St. Louis involved a secret society known to its members as the Order of American Knights (OAK). Shortly after Sanderson assumed his responsibilities as provost marshal general (in March 1864), he appointed two St. Louis men, known by him to be loyal, as undercover detectives. They assumed false identities, taking the names William Taylor and Edward F. Hoffman, and infiltrated the secret order. The St. Louis OAK had its origin in the states' rights and proslavery views of Phineas C. Wright, who lived in the city during the early years of the war.[65] Hostile toward what he regarded as the despotism of the Lincoln administration, he viewed the Emancipation Proclamation and the subsequent decision to raise black troops as the occasion for a secret effort to redeem the nation from "black Republican" rule. Among Wright's first initiates were Charles L. Hunt and Charles E. Dunn. By the time Sanderson's spies began their work, however, Wright had moved to New York City, where he worked with James A. McMaster, the editor of the Peace Democratic *Freeman's Journal*. Sanderson learned from the reports of undercover agent Taylor that "the O.A.K. has meetings in each ward of the city of Saint Louis." Taylor reported that he had attended a meeting of the organization on 15 April 1864 in the city's Tenth Ward. Thirty or forty men were present, and Alexander C. Durdee "presided as worthy grand senior." Green B. Smith performed the tasks assigned to the "ancient brother." Taylor also reported that the OAK members spoke of Charles E. Dunn as the ancient brother of the Fifth Ward organization. Also named in his report were Michael Leonard and "Hunt, hardware merchant on Fifth." A few days later Taylor claimed to have attended a meeting of the "Anthony Wayne Lodge" at Webster and Fifth Street. About one hundred fifty men were present, including Charles E. Dunn, Moses Rae, Robert S. McDonald, and Buck Carr. Taylor reported that Charles Hunt appeared to be the leader of the entire Missouri organization. "He has his headquarters as the commander of the State at his office on Sixth, between Olive and Pine." Charles E. Dunn "seems to be a sort of aide-de-camp to Hunt." On 1 May Taylor reported attending yet another meeting. About sixty or seventy men attended, and Taylor had no doubt from their demeanor that they would kill him if they learned his true identity.[66]

From late May to early July 1864, Sanderson ordered the arrest of OAK leaders, including Charles L. Hunt, Charles E. Dunn, and Green B. Smith. The men were held at the Gratiot Street prison and interrogated by Sanderson, who offered freedom in exchange for an admission of disloyal activity and a promise of future loyalty. In his questioning, he clearly hoped to be able to uncover a wide pattern of conspiratorial activity. He began with Hunt. Hunt's uncle, James Lucas, was the wealthiest man in St. Louis. He and Hunt's mother, Ann Lucas Hunt, were the surviving children of French-born John B. C. Lucas. (It was their brother, Charles Lucas, who had been killed in the duel with Thomas Hart Benton in 1817.) Hunt admitted to Sanderson that he had become a member of the Order on 8 March 1863 in St. Louis. He also acknowleged that he served as "grand commander of the State of Missouri," although he insisted that he had resigned sometime in mid-May 1864, several days before his arrest on 27 May. When Sanderson asked Hunt what change of opinion prompted him to leave the organization, Hunt replied only that he no longer wanted to be a member.[67]

Sanderson's interrogation of Charles E. Dunn proved to be somewhat more revealing. A forty-year-old native of Maryland, Dunn had lived in Missouri for fifteen years and worked for the St. Louis Gaslight Company. He denied having been a member of Basil Duke's Minute Men during the secession crisis, but he admitted to being a close friend of Charles L. Hunt. "Our political views are precisely alike," said Dunn, "both being Democrats." When asked if he visited Hunt's office, Dunn answered, "Yes, sir; two or three times a week." But when Sanderson's questioning turned in the direction of identifying a secret political organization meeting at Hunt's office, Dunn refused to answer:

> *Question.* Has not the office or building in which his office is situated been used for the past six months or year as the headquarters of a political organization?
> *Answer.* I decline answering that question.
> *Question.* Have you not been in the habit of visiting Mr. Hunt's office . . . for secret political purposes?
> *Answer.* I decline answering that question.
> *Question.* Do you or do you not know that secret political meetings have been held in Mr. Hunt's office?
> *Answer.* I must decline answering that question.

Dunn would not implicate Hunt in any secret political activity, but he admitted that he had been second in command in the Order in Missouri. Like Hunt, Dunn claimed to have resigned shortly before being arrested. What, asked Sanderson, was the purpose of the OAK. "A restoration of the Union," replied Dunn. "Were the objects and purposes of said organization hostile to the Federal Government," asked Sanderson. "In my estimation, no," replied Dunn. He agreed to take the oath of allegiance and to testify in court concerning the OAK if called upon to do so. Presumably, Sanderson permitted Dunn's release from Gratiot Street prison.

Of the arrested members of the OAK, only Green B. Smith fully cooperated with Sanderson's investigation. He was a native of St. Louis and, since

1850, a clerk in Thornton Grimsley's saddlery. Federal authorities arrested him on 8 May and Sanderson interrogated him on 2 August. Smith agreed to co-operate with Sanderson after admitting that he had earlier given false statements. He said that he had been initiated into the Order in spring 1863 in a room over Leitch's drugstore on the corner of Fifth and Market Street. His group called itself the George Washington Temple. He said that he joined the OAK "to aid and assist the Confederate Government, and endeavor to restore the Union as it was prior to the rebellion." Smith's arrest had followed the arrest of William M. Douglas, who had been caught by federal authorities carrying a cargo of revolvers and ammunition into north-central Missouri. Sometime before Smith's interrogation in August, Douglas had escaped from Gratiot Street prison, although several other prisoners had died in the attempt.

Smith admitted that he and other OAK members purchased "arms and ammunition" from friendly St. Louis merchants and sent them to "members in the country, where they could not be had," mainly revolvers shipped to north-central Missouri. Federal authorities prohibited the sale of arms without a special permit. Smith reported that without a permit he had purchased revolvers and ammunition from Julian and John Beauvais at wholesale prices; he had also made purchases from Dimick and Company on Fourth Street. He had carried the weapons to E. J. Rae's liquor store on Pine, between Second and Third Street; there he and Rae had packed the weapons for shipment into the country. After offering Sanderson a long list of alleged participants in the OAK, Smith renounced his connection with the Order, took the oath of allegiance, and vowed to become a law-abiding citizen after his release from Gratiot Street prison.

Sanderson's arrests and interrogations did not establish the existence of any widespread conspiracy, nor did they uncover an imminent insurrection. But he had assembled credible evidence of an actively disloyal secret society in St. Louis, the members of which engaged in illegal activity designed to support guerrillas and bushwhackers in the countryside.[68]

By fall 1864, Sterling Price's invasion of Missouri thoroughly absorbed the attention of General Rosecrans and his acting provost marshal general, Joseph Darr. On 21 October Darr transferred a number of female prisoners from their place of confinement on Charles Street to the Gratiot Street prison. "In view of this increase, and of the character of the prisoners," Darr warned, it was necessary to "take additional precautions against their attempting to escape." In a postscript, he noted that a "Mrs. Hardesty and children and the young boy, Woods, with his nurse, are held as hostages," evidently as a warning to Price's rampaging troops.[69]

Conditions at Gratiot Street worsened again in winter 1864–1865. From November to February over 800 prisoners needed to be hospitalized and 134 died. Now, however, federal authorities faced the consequences of victory. As the Confederacy collapsed, prisoners arrived malnourished and poorly clothed. Increasing numbers of prisoners were boys, ill suited to the hardships of military camps or of military prison.[70]

In December 1864, when General Grenville Dodge assumed command of the Department of the Missouri and sought to provide for refugees fleeing from Sterling Price's invasion, the military authorities levied their final assessments in Missouri. The two largest sums were assigned to Edward Bredell, a retired attorney ($1,000) and to the wealthy banker, L. A. Benoist ($2,000). All assessments ended in February 1865.[71] With the end of the war in April 1865, a board of examiners immediately released 200 prisoners from Gratiot Street and Alton. Prisoners of war who would take the oath of allegiance were released as quickly as they could be processed. By 1 May the population at Alton had dropped from 3,000 to 853; only 150 prisoners remained at Gratiot Street. By 13 June Alton's population dropped to about 100, and on 20 June the remaining federal prisoners there were transferred to Gratiot Street to be examined and released. On 31 August only 1 Confederate prisoner remained at Gratiot Street (there is no record of his release).[72]

7

"Curing Us of Our Selfishness"

L OOKING BACK on the Civil War more than a half century after the fighting had stopped, Hannah Isabella Stagg thought that the struggle had required of St. Louis women like herself extraordinary energy and innovation: "Above the roar of battle was heard a voice urging woman to assume a new and important role in the great drama that was being enacted." Women would not aspire to "fame and applause," but with quiet perseverance they would serve as "helper" to the soldiers in the field. When St. Louis women heard the call, she remembered, they soon answered it "by the formation of the Ladies' Union Aid Society."[1]

An 1870 commemorative lithograph suggests the variety of homefront activities that engaged the energies of the Ladies' Union Aid Society. In the foreground, a woman holds aloft the flag of the United States. On the ground in front of her, an eagle tears apart a Confederate flag and scatters its pieces over the dead body of a snake, the symbol of Copperhead disloyalty. In the background, women tend to a group of wounded soldiers—black and white, Union and Confederate. Other women offer aid to widows and orphans. A group of freedmen look on: one is kneeling and gestures to the women beseechingly.[2] Much of this imagery could have been anticipated by Stagg and other loyal women in 1861. Certainly they expected to assist soldiers and their families. Many of the women may have sensed that the developing conflict would bring with it the destruction of slavery. But none could have foreseen the extent of the carnage and the enormity of the task that lay ahead. For the loyal women of St. Louis, as well as for the men, the unanticipated consequences of the Civil War at first overwhelmed them and then transformed their perception of themselves and their society.

The membership of the Ladies' Union Aid Society drew heavily from the new northeastern-oriented mercantile class. Anna Lansing Wendell Clapp served as the organization's president. She and her husband, the merchant Alfred Clapp, had arrived in St. Louis from New York State in the late 1850s.

Active as well was Adaline Couzins, whose husband, John E. D. Couzins, was acting provost marshal under Nathaniel Lyon's command. Couzins's parents had immigrated to New York City from England during his infancy; he completed an apprenticeship as a carpenter and moved to St. Louis in 1834. John and Adaline Couzins farmed for one season in Pike County but soon settled in St. Louis, where he found work as a deputy sheriff. In 1842 he joined the police force and rose to the rank of captain, then the highest rank. In 1856 he resigned when he was passed over for the newly created post of chief. For a time he served as the city's fire and building inspector. When provisional governor Hamilton Gamble restructured the Police Board in 1861, the new members appointed Couzins chief, and he served in that capacity until the end of the war.[3]

Closely associated with Clapp and Couzins was Anna Filley. She and her husband, Chauncey I. Filley—the younger cousin of the wealthy manufacturers Oliver and Giles Filley—moved from their hometown of Lansingburg, New York, to St. Louis in 1850. Although it was Oliver Filley who served as the city's mayor during the secession crisis and joined the Committee of Safety, Chauncey became the most politically active among the Filley family. He was elected mayor in 1863, although he served only one year of his two-year term, due to poor health. A dedicated Republican, he attended the Chicago convention in 1860 (where he supported the nomination of Abraham Lincoln), and he led the Republican Party in St. Louis in the 1870s and 1880s. Chauncey Filley attended every Republican National Convention from 1864 to 1892.[4]

In the sphere of public education, as well as in the world of business, men and women from the Northeast exerted a significant influence. In the late 1850s, school board member Washington King (elected mayor in 1856 as a Know-Nothing) worked closely with the Massachusetts educational reformer, Horace Mann, to recruit principals and teachers for the expanding St. Louis public schools. Mann had become the first president of Antioch College in Yellow Springs, Ohio, in 1853, and King recruited a number of Antioch graduates as teachers. Mann's nephew, Calvin S. Pennell, took the post of principal of the St. Louis Public High School. Miss H. A. Adams, a recent arrival from New Hampshire, also became active in the Ladies' Union Aid Society. She had come to St. Louis as a schoolteacher in the late 1850s. Miss Adams attended the first meeting of the society and was elected secretary. After three years at that post, she became (during winter 1863–1864) the Western Sanitary Commission's agent in Nashville, Tennessee. She returned to St. Louis in spring 1864 and continued her work with the society and the Sanitary Commission until the end of the war.[5] Two other women recently arrived in St. Louis from the Northeast also took active roles in the Ladies' Union Aid Society. Mrs. C. R. Springer, a native of Maine, taught school in New Hampshire before her marriage to a St. Louis merchant in the late 1850s. Mary E. Palmer, a New Jersey native, settled in St. Louis with her husband, Samuel Palmer, in 1857.[6]

An enormous field of labor soon opened before these women as thousands of sick and wounded soldiers flooded St. Louis. Outbreaks of measles, scarlet fever, typhoid fever, and other infectious diseases took a heavy toll on the troops and overloaded the city's medical resources. But it was the multitude of wounded that truly shocked observers and initially overwhelmed those dedicated to caring for them. The nature of warfare had changed in fundamental ways, and no one anticipated the extent of the carnage to come.

With the collapse of the Harney-Price agreement in early June 1861, Nathaniel Lyon and Frank Blair boldly and confidently advanced against the militia forces loyal to Governor Claiborne Jackson and the governor's military commander, Sterling Price. Lyon and Blair shared their generation's understanding of warfare, shaped during the Mexican War. Advances in technology since that time made the Civil War a very different experience, however. Lyon and Blair left St. Louis having made no special preparations for the care of wounded soldiers. Dr. Samuel G. DeCamp, medical director for the Department of the West, had opened a general hospital in St. Louis, the New House of Refuge, on 6 August 1861, but it had yet to be fully equipped or supplied with nurses. There matters stood as Lyon's forces fought at Boonville and Wilson's Creek.[7]

Military men were well aware that the technology of warfare had changed, but none anticipated the devastating consequences of those changes. Put simply, the rifled musket had replaced the smoothbore musket as the standard infantryman's weapon. This had been made possible largely because of the introduction of the minié ball, a lead shot with a hollow core that enabled it to expand against the rifled wall of the musket barrel. The consequence of this innovation for soldiers in the field was enormous but only slowly understood. Armed with a smoothbore weapon—as soldiers had been during the Mexican War—troops holding a defensive position were trained to hold their fire until the attacking force came within 100 yards of their line. Only within that range could the tumbling shot fired from a smoothbore weapon hit a target with some degree of certainty. Under these circumstances, an advancing force of superior numbers would charge the 100 yards, brave the defensive fire, and expect to overrun the position before more than a volley or two had been fired. By contrast, the effective range of the rifled musket stretched out to 300 yards, enabling defensive fire to wreak tremendous damage on advancing troops. Because battlefield tactics—indeed, the very perception of the courageous officer and soldier—continued to emphasize the infantry charge, unprecedented carnage stunned soldiers and civilians alike.[8]

The real work of the Ladies' Union Aid Society began when traincars loaded with wounded soldiers descended upon St. Louis, in small numbers at first from the skirmish at Boonville and then in truly alarming numbers from the Battle of Wilson's Creek. On 10 August 1861, the day of the battle at Wilson's Creek, the wounded from Boonville began arriving from the railhead of the Pacific Railroad at Sedalia, Missouri. In the days ahead the number of wounded swelled to nearly 1,000 after the men injured at Wilson's Creek made their painful journey by wagon for more than 100 miles to the railhead of the southwest branch of the Pacific Railroad at Rolla, and then by train to St. Louis.[9] Adaline and John Couzins met the trains with wagonloads of bandages, lint for packing wounds, and clean undergarments. Adaline supervised the care of the wounded as they were carried to the unfinished New House of Refuge. But the sudden arrival of so many wounded overwhelmed the facility. The onslaught also overwhelmed the municipal City Hospital at Fifth and Chestnut and the St. Louis Hospital operated by the Catholic Sisters of Charity at the corner of Spruce and Fourth. Matters grew substantially worse after nearly 500 additional wounded arrived in the city following the federal evacuation of Springfield on 18 August. Three weeks after the Battle of Wilson's Creek, many men had not yet been treated. The wounded lay wherever space could be found for them, and they remained in the clothing they had worn in battle. They waited with bullets still lodged in their bodies.[10]

The appalling conditions that prevailed among the wounded after these first engagements added to the pressures bearing down on commanding general John C. Frémont. Jessie Frémont acted swiftly to deflect criticism from her husband. She invited the renowned social reformer, Dorothea Dix, to St. Louis. At Jessie Frémont's bidding, Dix met with William Greenleaf Eliot, who had drafted plans for a sanitary commission in the West. Dix gave Eliot's plan her blessing, and on 5 September 1861, General Frémont issued General

Orders, no. 159, establishing the Western Sanitary Commission. Frémont appointed Eliot a commissioner and filled the remaining three posts with members of Eliot's church: the banker James E. Yeatman (who became president of the commission), the wholesale grocers Carlos S. Greeley and George Partridge, and the physician John B. Johnson. With the exception of the Tennessee-born Yeatman, all the commissioners were New Englanders.[11]

In September and October the commission outfitted the New House of Refuge and contracted for the use of a number of beds at the St. Louis Hospital and the City Hospital, arrangements that provided for 1,730 patients. Additionally, military patients with measles were housed in separate quarters at the City Quarantine Grounds. Benton Barracks, which soon housed the largest military hospital in the city, provided 1,000 beds for convalescent patients.[12]

The Western Sanitary Commission functioned independently from the eastern U.S. Sanitary Commission, organized initially by the Unitarian minister Henry Whitney Bellows in Philadelphia (subsequently presided over by the prominent journalist and landscape architect Frederick Law Olmsted). There were several reasons for the separate organization. Yeatman and Eliot insisted that they had acted to meet urgent needs in the West at a time when Bellows's organization focused its attention on the East. Moreover, Jessie and John Frémont's penchant for independent activity led them to support a separate organization. Once they were established, Yeatman and Eliot did not want to subordinate their activities to the U.S. Sanitary Commission.

Yeatman rebuffed an early effort by Bellows to absorb the Western Sanitary Commission, and the battle of wills continued with Olmsted. Writing Bellows in October 1861, Yeatman insisted that it was the "deliberate and unanimous" decision of the Western Sanitary Commission to remain a separate organization. This was a decision, he added, that was "not likely to be changed." He explained that "whatever we could do as a sub-committee or branch of your Commission, we can do equally well, or better, retaining our present organization, and cooperating with you." He stressed that the Western Sanitary Commission would confine itself to "local work in our district."

Early in November 1861, after Frémont had been relieved of command, Dr. DeCamp (amid charges of mismanagement) was replaced by Dr. J. J. B. Wright as the department's medical director. Wright did not approve of army collaboration with the civilian Sanitary Commission, and he threatened to halt the commission's activities in army camps. Eliot appealed to General

Halleck, who recognized the political wisdom of cooperating with the commissioners and ordered Wright to do so as well.[13] But the battle with the U.S. Sanitary Commission continued. Olmsted hoped that by stressing cooperation the national organization could make the St. Louisans "virtually . . . an auxiliary society, granting them the distinctive name of the Western San. Com. which may be interpreted 'Western [branch of] San. Com.'" But the matter was not so easily resolved, and by spring 1862, as agents of the Western Sanitary Commission began raising money in New England (the principal location of support for the U.S. Sanitary Commission), the St. Louisans seemed to be in direct competition with Olmsted's organization. By early 1864 New Englanders had contributed over $500,000 to the Western Sanitary Commission. Boston merchants alone sent goods valued at $10,000 to the Grand Mississippi Valley Sanitary Fair in 1864.[14]

In mid-April 1862 Olmsted wrote to Yeatman to complain that there was no need for "these two machines." The U.S. Sanitary Commission had been established for the "purpose of sending the contributions of the benevolent— of Boston for instance—where they are most wanted." If Yeatman believed that the commission neglected St. Louis, "why not call on us?" If the St. Louisans continued to appeal for benevolent support in Boston and elsewhere in the East, the result would be "to create distrust and unnecessary expense." Early in May, Yeatman replied. The U.S. Sanitary Commission, he said, had initially neglected St. Louis and made the creation of a separate organization a necessity. Then, rather than accept the St. Louisans' offer of collaboration, it had sent salaried agents to St. Louis in an ineffectual effort to take control of sanitary operations in the West. As for raising money in the East, Yeatman saw no wrong in it. "We made the demand and nobly have the patriotic people of the North responded— they did not have to give unless they were willing to do so." Nor did he believe that the St. Louisans generated any "rivalry or jealousy" in their common benevolent endeavor with the U.S. Sanitary Commission:

> We felt that our work was a peculiar, and to some extent a local one, but still a mammoth one, and that it could be best done by us, and this I had supposed was fully understood by you, so . . . it is grating to have those engaged in the same good cause to come forward and object to what we are doing. . . . If you have supplies for the West and desire to send them to us we can make good use of them and will not object to receive them from any source from which they may come.

Olmsted passed the matter back to Bellows, urging him to write to Yeatman. Yeatman's letter "pains me," concluded Olmsted, evidently convinced of his own disinterestedness in the affair, "it so entirely misconceives the purpose and spirit of mine."[15]

The Western Sanitary Commission would not become a "branch" of the U.S. Sanitary Commission, and Bellows and Olmsted soon stopped pressing the issue. Their commission faced far more difficult problems with numerous state sanitary commissions that diverted energies and resources from the national organization. For the most part, Yeatman was correct that the regional focus of the Western Sanitary Commission augmented and did not duplicate the activities of the U.S. Sanitary Commission. Olmsted wisely chose to recognize Yeatman as a fellow laborer in the field of wartime benevolence.[16]

This wartime benevolence fundamentally altered the social life of St. Louis. As the loyal women of the city constructed a patriotic home front, they formed a new social elite. The conditional Unionism that had sustained the old elite in the early months of the sectional crisis lost all credibility after the fighting at Boonville and Wilson's Creek. Some friends of the Southern cause openly expressed their contempt for the federal government's coercive policy, and they were made to pay a significant price for their candor. Most of the old elite either quietly supported the conservative Unionism practiced by Governor Hamilton Gamble, or they bit their tongues and bided their time. For the unconditional Unionists, however, the war worked as a powerful stimulant. For the loyal women, a patriotic home front justified their entry into fields of labor for which they had previously been considered unfit. As Sarah Jane Hill noted amid the frenzied activity of the early days of the war, some of the barriers that limited the female sphere of activity were easily breached by those women who seized the opportunity to do so. As wounded federal soldiers and Confederate prisoners poured into St. Louis, the Ladies' Union Aid Society called on women to leave their parlors and to assume the burdens of hospital labor. "We were called on to assist the surgeons in their operations and to nurse the patients," recalled Sarah Hill. "There were no regular nurses then and volunteer nurses were scarce." Amid the confusion of war she and her sister left the sheltered environment of their father's household to tend to the needs of sick and wounded soldiers. The necessities of war as well as sentiments of patriotism quickly overcame what had seemed in peacetime an impregnable standard of decency. "My sister and I would visit the hospital three or four times a week," she reported. "We were not forbidden, and there was no protest against it."[17]

Ever larger fund-raising activities also provided the loyal women of St. Louis with ample opportunities for social display. Perhaps because the disciplined machinery of war was so brutally apparent, the pageantry and display of homefront activities elaborated a feminine iconography of classical order and beauty, themes of pastoral tranquillity, and the familiar activities of community life. Strikingly absent during the war were the masculine themes of power and progress that dominated the great exhibitions of the nineteenth century, beginning with the Crystal Palace Exhibition in London in 1851 and continuing with the world's fairs at the close of the century (including the Chicago World's Columbian Exposition in 1893 and the St. Louis Louisiana Purchase Exhibition in 1904).

During winter 1861–1862 the Ladies' Union Aid Society offered a series of tableaux to raise money for homefront causes. Sarah Hill recalled that "one evening they were all classic. Another evening they represented celebrated scenes and incidents in history." The tableaux were displayed in the Mercantile Library and employed "the most prominent women and girls, socially." Phoebe Couzins was one of the most poised and beautiful of the group. Her father had worked closely with the Committee of Safety during the secession crisis, and her mother labored dauntlessly in the field during the bloodiest engagements of 1862. The daughter of Congregationalist minister Truman M. Post also joined in the tableaux. A relatively new arrival to the city, Post added to the influence of the Northeast. A native of Middlebury, Vermont, and a graduate of Middlebury College, he had moved west in the 1830s to take a position as professor of ancient languages and ancient history at Illinois College. In 1847 he accepted a call to become pastor of the Third Presbyterian Church (later reorganized as a Congregationalist Church) in St. Louis. In 1851 his congregation began construction of First Trinity Congregational Church (at Tenth and Locust) and dedicated the new building in 1860. In the tableaux, presented to benefit the Western Sanitary Commission, Post's daughter offered "a perfect Grecian profile," which made her a stunning representation of the "Goddess of Liberty."[18]

Even more successful financially were readings offered to benefit the Aid Society and the Sanitary Commission. The women secured the services of Dr. E. F. Berkley, rector of St. George's Episcopal Church (then on Locust at the corner of Seventh). A popular elocutionist, Berkley offered his readings at the Mercantile Library and attracted large gatherings to hear his dramatic presentation of Alfred Tennyson's "Charge of the Light Brigade" and other popular pieces.[19] In March 1862, when Jefferson Barracks came under the supervision of the Army Medical Department for use as a hospital, the women organized a Sanitary Commission fair to raise money to improve the facility.[20]

A Sylvan Fete during three days in June 1863 raised funds for the Western Sanitary Commission. The women took four rooms of the recently completed Lindell Hotel on Washington Avenue and decorated them with a "feast of flowers" to represent the four seasons of the year. Phoebe Couzins was chosen as Queen of Flowers, and her "flower maidens" performed in the processions and dances "with great vivacity and ability." Tableaux and "fancy dances" filled the evenings with further elaborations of the theme of the seasons. Sarah Hill worked with other women to make bushels of paper flowers for the decorations that were rejuvenated each morning with a new shipment of fresh flowers.[21] Indeed, the women missed few opportunities to raise money for their work. On 4 July 1863, as James Eads presided over the launching of the gunboat *Winnebago*, the Ladies' Union Aid Society operated a concession stand.[22]

By March 1862 federal forces pressed south against Confederate armies in northwest Arkansas and against fortified positions at Fort Henry (near the confluence of the Cumberland and Ohio Rivers) and Fort Donelson (near the confluence of the Tennessee and Ohio Rivers). The federal offensive culminated in Arkansas at the Battle of Pea Ridge in March and in Tennessee at the Battle of Shiloh in April. These battles and General Grant's extended campaign against Vicksburg brought continuous waves of sick and wounded soldiers to St. Louis and confronted the women volunteers with the most horrific experiences of the war. During the Battle of Pea Ridge, the Western Sanitary Commission cared for more than 1,000 wounded Union and Confederate soldiers. Working as a nurse was Mary Whitney Phelps of southwest Missouri, who had accompanied her husband (a future Missouri governor), Colonel John S. Phelps, into the field.[23] By May 1862, a St. Louis resident reported that the streets were crowded with the ambulatory sick and wounded. They filled the streets "from the levy on Chestnut Street up [to] the Planters House on 4th street." The wounded continued to arrive by the hundreds. "Today there was 800," reported the observer, who thought that at least "160 died last week."[24] It was a ghastly scene but no longer an uncontrolled one.

For some of the women volunteers the realities of war proved to be overwhelming. Simon Pollak, a St. Louis physician of Czech birth, followed Grant's forces to Fort Henry. There, accompanied by a group of St. Louis women nurses, he tended to the wounded on a hospital ship provided by the Western Sanitary Commission. Dr. Pollak, a native of Prague, had taken a general degree in medicine there in 1835 and a surgical degree a year later. He then emigrated to the United States in 1838, staying briefly in New York City and later that year moving to New Orleans and then to central Tennessee. A trip back to New Orleans brought him into contact with a number of St. Louisans, and he removed to St. Louis in March 1845. He soon collaborated and socialized with the leading physicians of the city, including William M. McPheeters and M. Gratz Moses. A pioneer in the education of the blind in St. Louis, Pollak traveled in 1859 first to Boston (where he met the reformer and educator Dr. Samuel Gridley Howe) and then to England and to Europe to visit the leading facilities for the blind. Anticipating the outbreak of civil war, Pollak returned to St. Louis sometime after the Camp Jackson affair in May 1861 and before the Battle of Wilson's Creek in August. He immediately sensed the social tensions that the conflict generated. Pollak was firm in his commitment to the Union cause, and interaction with the pro-Southern doctors McPheeters and Moses must have been severely strained. Pollak recalled in general that "American families turned their backs on me, socially and professionally. Not so my German families." Discouraged by the hostility of so many old St. Louis friends, Pollak moved to New York and soon began working with the U.S. Sanitary Commission. At its direction he returned to St. Louis and received General Halleck's authorization to work with the surgeons of the Army Medical Corps.[25]

As Grant advanced against Forts Henry and Donelson, Pollak led a medical party supported by the Western Sanitary Commission. They traveled by rail to Cairo and then by steamboat to Fort Henry. Of the women nurses who accompanied him, Pollak found "only two—Mrs. Couzins and Mrs. Kershaw—who were worth anything." Adaline Couzins had taken a leading role in the formation of the Ladies' Union Aid Society. "Mrs. Kershaw" was, perhaps, Margaret E. Kershaw, the wife of the St. Louis engraver and printer James M. Kershaw.[26] Couzins and Kershaw took on the disagreeable but essential task of tending to the physical needs of the wounded soldiers. "They changed the bloody, torn and muddy garments of the wounded soldiers; bathed them; performed all kinds of menial work." Phoebe Couzins recalled boarding the hospital steamer with her sister when it returned to St. Louis with its cargo of wounded and dead soldiers. Looking for their mother, who had "for the first time . . . left her home charge," the Couzins girls witnessed briefly but vividly the horrors of war: "Maimed, bleeding, dying soldiers by the hundreds, were on cots on deck . . . and boxes—filled with amputated limbs, and dead were awaiting their last rites." Phoebe Couzins thought that her mother and her fellow female nurses moved through the carnage like "ministering angels."[27]

The other women, described by Pollak as "society imps," thought their role should be to fan the fevered brows of the men and read to them. When asked to clean the wounded, as Couzins and Kershaw were doing, these women "turned up their noses, pouted and flatly refused to do anything of the kind." The society women included Mrs. Chauncey I. Filley and the wife of General Clinton Bowen Fisk. A Methodist and a temperance man, Fisk was a native of western New York who had arrived in St. Louis in 1860.[28] He and his wife were strongly committed to the Union cause, but Pollak thought that Mrs. Fisk, like Mrs. Filley, was "a torment, not a relief, to the soldier." Often still "suffering from shock" and "writhing in pain," the wounded men shrank from their attentions, begging "for a moment's quiet and rest." In his report to the Western Sanitary Commission, Pollak was "not very complimentary." He offended the prominent women whose "names were heralded in the daily press for their loyalty and self-sacrificing devotion." Pollak's criticism of them undoubtedly contributed to the hostility that he and William Greenleaf Eliot felt toward each other. Pollak resented Eliot's influence over the other members of the Western Sanitary Commission, and Eliot disliked Pollak's haughty and independent manner.[29]

At Fort Donelson, Pollak worked on the hospital steamer *Continental* under the command of an army surgeon. Adaline Couzins and Mrs. Kershaw accompanied him, as did six Sisters of Mercy, whose intelligent work and valuable experience Pollak warmly welcomed. At Donelson the hospital boat took on board 1,300 wounded Union and Confederate soldiers and brought them all alive to St. Louis. The Union wounded went to the City Hospital, the Confederate wounded to the Sisters of Charity's St. Louis Hospital. Confederate prisoners who were not wounded went to the Gratiot Street prison.[30]

As the wounded arrived, Sarah Hill turned the care of her baby over to her mother and went to the City Hospital. There she worked closely with

Adaline Couzins and, within a few weeks, accompanied Couzins and Pollak to care for the wounded at the Battle of Shiloh. A dozen women accompanied him on this trip, which he made once again aboard the Western Sanitary Commission's hospital ship, the *Continental*. The women had been coworkers for months. They wore black dresses covered with "large white aprons while on duty, and that was most of the time." The ship left St. Louis about noon on Friday 5 April and reached Shiloh on Sunday, a few hours before the battle ended. On the way downriver the women outfitted the main salon of the ship with two rows of cots, "made ready with clean fresh bedding to receive our poor boys."[31]

St. Louisans had known that a major battle was shaping up near Shiloh, and the women nurses hoped to have an opportunity to see the contending armies grandly arrayed in the field of battle. What they found was "a scene of indescribable confusion and horror." Facing a horizon "dark with smoke," the ship landed, and the male nurses went ashore to begin bringing in wounded soldiers. The field was muddy from a previous night's rain, and "many of the living and dead were almost buried in the mud, and trampled upon by man and beast." With hospital tents overflowing, the wounded lay unattended on the wet and muddy ground. "Horses, mules, men, cannon, commissary stores, and ammunition seemed piled together," recalled Hill. Pollak inadvertently stood on the face of a wounded man who had been nearly buried in mud: "But for the groan elicited by my boot on his face he would have died in the mud." Affairs were more orderly aboard the hospital ship but no less grim; surgeons performed numerous amputations, and the room where these operations were performed "looked like a butcher's shamble." For the next forty-eight hours the *Continental* prepared to return to St. Louis. Surgeons and nurses aboard another Western Sanitary Commission hospital boat, the *City of Louisiana*, were similarly employed. In the weeks ahead it transported more than 3,000 wounded soldiers from Pittsburg Landing to St. Louis. By the end of the war, the Western Sanitary Commission had outfitted more than a dozen floating hospitals.[32]

Alongside the Western Sanitary Commission boats at Pittsburg Landing were hospital boats from Cincinnati that had been supplied by the U.S. Sanitary Commission. Long rows of fresh graves with crude wooden shingles marked the resting place of those who could be identified. Unidentified human remains were put in a large pit and covered with quicklime and dirt. Piles of dead horses and mules were surrounded by cordwood and set on fire.

As the *Continental* left Shiloh for the fifty-hour trip upstream to St. Louis, Sarah Hill lamented that mud, dead horses, mangled soldiers, and the blood-spattered operating room were "all we saw of the battlefield of Shiloh."[33]

When the *Continental* arrived at St. Louis, Pollak hired an omnibus to carry the Sisters of Mercy to their convent, paying for the transportation with the funds of the Western Sanitary Commission, and Eliot complained. Later, when General Curtis authorized Pollak to permit the Sisters to visit sick and dying Catholic soldiers in the city's hospitals and prisons, the antagonism between Pollak and Eliot grew worse. According to Pollak, guards at the Gratiot Street prison (privates of the Eleventh Iowa Infantry) "grossly insulted" the Sisters. Pollak protested to Curtis, who censured the officers responsible for the men. When the Eleventh Iowa fought with distinction at the Battle of Corinth, Curtis revoked the censure, and an angry Eliot obtained signatures from all the members of the Western Sanitary Commission (except Pollak), endorsing a letter to the War Department urging that nuns be excluded from the St. Louis hospitals and prisons. Although not himself a Catholic, Pollak took satisfaction that no such exclusion was imposed. Shunned thereafter by the Western Sanitary Commission, he formally withdrew from the organization. He continued his work in St. Louis under the auspices of the U.S. Sanitary Commission "with the approval of the Secretary of War!"[34]

Eliot undoubtedly questioned the loyalty of the Catholic nuns. Catholic religious orders contributed to the needs of sick and wounded soldiers, refugees, prisoners, and orphans, but many of those they aided were rebels or Southern sympathizers. The Sisters of Mercy operated an industrial school to provide housing for children orphaned by war. The school also sheltered children whose parents could not care for them. One woman, the wife of a Confederate soldier, placed her two children in the school for that reason. The Sisters of Mercy especially provided a means for families to communicate with Confederate prisoners, delivering to them pies and cakes and other foods that supplemented their prison rations. It was this Catholic charity for Confederates that Eliot evidently hoped to stop.

From spring 1862 through the surrender of Vicksburg in July 1863, St. Louis had the largest concentration of wartime medical activity in the West. John V. Lauderdale, a young physician from New York City, joined the medical staff at Jefferson Barracks in spring 1862 and soon shipped out on board an army hospital ship, the *D. A. January*, named for Derrick A. January, a

prominent wholesale grocer in St. Louis and a member of the board of directors of James Yeatman's bank. A Kentucky native, January had been a prominent figure at the conditional Unionist meeting presided over by Robert
Campbell early in 1861. January's loyalty had been questioned by Provost
Marshal Bernard Farrar in December 1861, and January sided with the pro-
Southern members of the chamber of commerce who struggled with unconditional Unionists for control of that organization early in 1862. He did
not play a conspicuous role in Yeatman's Sanitary Commission, but the
federal hospital ship bore his name presumably because he had paid for it
or donated it. The ship ensured that January's name would be firmly tied
to the Union cause.[35]

From April to December 1862, the *D. A. January* made twenty trips up
the Tennessee River or down the Mississippi River to carry sick and wounded
soldiers to hospitals farther north. It made six trips to Pittsburg Landing in
April, May, and June. It made other trips to Paducah and Columbus, Kentucky, and to Helena, Arkansas. With beds for 330 men, it made half its trips
badly overcrowded. On eleven trips, seven of them overcrowded, the sick and
wounded were brought to St. Louis or to Jefferson Barracks. On other trips
the men were carried farther north, to Keokuk, Iowa, or east on the Ohio River
to Mound City, Illinois, and Louisville, Kentucky. In 1863 the *D. A. January*
carried over 400 men from Arkansas Post to St. Louis. From March to June
it remained moored as a floating hospital at Milliken's Bend, on the west bank
of the Mississippi River near Vicksburg. It spent most of the month of July in
dry dock in St. Louis, where it received new boilers and a new name, the U.S.
hospital steamer *Charles McDougall,* in honor of the army's medical director. Early in August, the boat carried a load of nearly 400 men from Milliken's
Bend to St. Louis. Thereafter, the men brought out of Vicksburg in August
and September were taken to hospitals in Memphis. After the crisis at Vicksburg had passed, the burden on St. Louis substantially lifted.[36]

John Lauderdale's letters home (to Geneseo, New York) recorded his
experiences aboard the *D. A. January* and chronicled his frequent trips to
St. Louis (where his brother Willis ran the telegraph office at the Planters'
House Hotel). Lauderdale sent home a detailed account of a trip in June 1862.
The *D. A. January* gathered up 460 men at Pittsburg Landing and Savannah,
on the opposite bank of the Tennessee River. The badly overcrowded boat
made its way north and managed to leave 100 of the wounded at the Marine
Hospital in Paducah. At Jefferson Barracks only 30 of the wounded could be

accommodated. Upriver, at Keokuk, they delivered their full cargo of sick and wounded soldiers.

While in Keokuk, Lauderdale took note of "the contributions of the Sanitary people in different parts of the country." He noticed a blanket marked to indicate that it came from Muscatine, Iowa (a few miles north of Keokuk). The hospital used sheets that had been sent from Ohio. On a rack, one towel indicated that it came from "New Bedford," and the one next to it was marked "U.S. Hospital." Private benevolence substantially augmented the supplies provided through the War Department. A number of cornhusk mattresses in Keokuk were marked to indicate that they came from the "Ladies' Union Aid Society, St. Louis."[37]

The Western Sanitary Commission called on women to volunteer for a variety of war-related tasks. In addition to the nearly 300 nurses employed by the commission during the war, women sewed hospital garments, rolled bandages, and prepared meals. As Union lines extended down the Mississippi, the commission's efforts expanded as well. Early in 1862, it established a home in St. Louis for discharged soldiers on their way home, for those passing through the city on furlough, and for the recovering wounded who needed rest but not hospital care. The home also housed prisoners being exchanged— Confederates heading south and Federals heading north. After 1863 it also provided shelter to the families of freedmen who had enlisted in the army. Between 1862 and 1864 it cared for more than 20,000 soldiers. The commission opened similar homes in Memphis, Tennessee; Vicksburg, Mississippi; Helena, Arkansas; and Columbus, Kentucky. These five together sheltered and fed more than 150,000 soldiers during the war.[38] The commission also established seven hospitals in the lower Mississippi Valley and extended its benevolence to help meet the pressing needs of refugees, particularly the "contraband," the former slaves who made their way to Union lines by the thousands. A new organization, the Freedmen's Relief Association—with its Ladies' Freedmen's Relief auxiliary—emerged from the Sanitary Commission as an administrative structure through which benevolent energies could be applied to the needs of slaves freed by Lincoln's Emancipation Proclamation.

In 1862 and again in 1864 Anna Clapp obtained major contracts from the U.S. Surgeon General to supply garments for hospitals in the West. Although the government never hired female nurses, at Benton Barracks Hospital the head surgeon, Dr. Ira Russell, provided space for the women of the Ladies' Union Aid Society to store their donated materials, and he placed the women in charge of the kitchen. Miss Bettie Broadhead, daughter of the provost marshal, oversaw the society's cooking operations at the barracks. The women of the society established a work department that designed a system of manufacture, consisting of tightly organized piecework, that produced between 3,000 and 4,000 garments a week. Volunteer members combined packs of precut garments together with the buttons and thread needed for their assembly. The society then distributed these materials, "all counted and measured in the right proportions," to women who did the final sewing for a fixed price. Desire for this piecework among the poor women of St. Louis proved to be so great that the society limited the size of the packages to be distributed to three or four dollars' worth per week. Hundreds of women gathered at the society's city office on Thursday mornings to take their numbered tickets and wait their turn to receive a package of sewing material. A committee of the society's members examined the finished work and authorized payment from the cashier's office.[39]

Male nurses employed by the Western Sanitary Commission received fifteen dollars a month and one meal a day. The women were paid a daily rate of forty cents and also received one meal a day. The commission stipulated that each hospital bed be ventilated by at least 640 cubic feet of air and, except in emergencies, that a nurse be provided for every thirty beds.[40] The theory followed by Yeatman's Western Sanitary Commission and by Olmsted's U.S. Sanitary Commission rested primarily on the conviction that cleanliness in general and sufficient fresh air aided healing and recovery and diminished contagion. The U.S. Sanitary Commission surgeon Elisha Harris described the crowded conditions and the deleterious effects that he worked to correct: "In hospitals and transports the natural evacuations and bodily exertions, the suppurating wounds, the gangrenous parts, and uncleansed persons and clothing of vast numbers of soldiers in an unhealthy condition, are combined to vitiate the local atmosphere."[41] The solution seemed to lie in building well-ventilated wards and to ensure ample room for each of the patients.

Ventilation, of course, did not solve the problem of infection and putrefaction that plagued Civil War hospitals. A phenomenon known as "hospital gangrene" made some hospitals scenes of widespread infection requiring repeated amputations that led to high death rates. This infection—probably involving the staphylococcus bacteria—spread from patient to patient in infected hospitals, as surgeons probed wounds to extract bullets and as they amputated shattered limbs. Physicians used opium-based medicines to treat diarrhea and pain, and they used ether and chloroform to sedate patients before operations.[42] These procedures marked significant advances. Opium—sprinkled as a powder on open wounds or administered orally as laudanum (opium dissolved in alcohol) or paregoric (opium and camphor dissolved in alcohol)—made it possible for physicians to alleviate pain. The use of anesthesia greatly reduced the risk of death from shock during radical surgery like amputation. But Joseph Lister did not introduce antisepsis in the practice of surgery until 1865. Physicians during the Civil War took it for granted that wounds would swell with infection and discharge pus. Gangrene—infection producing putrefaction of the flesh—required amputation, but physicians viewed infection by itself as part of the healing process. Cleanliness in washing and dressing wounds did not prevent the infection caused by shot and shell and by the surgeon's instruments and hands, but it certainly helped to reduce its spread and duration.

As the Western Sanitary Commission's field of labor extended southward, it attracted the attention of women in the East who were eager to serve the Union cause as nurses to the soldiers and as relief workers and teachers among the freedmen. Maria R. Mann, a native of Massachusetts and a niece of Horace Mann, began work at the City Hospital as a nurse with the Western Sanitary Commission. In fall 1862 she became an agent for the commission at Helena, Arkansas. She arrived there in January 1863 and discovered appalling conditions. The freedmen—men, women, and children—came to the commission hospital in pitiful condition. Many had been exposed to the elements for months without adequate food or clothing. Her letters home expressed her shock. Diarrhea killed the weakest of her charges. All were covered with swellings and open sores. They died at a horrific rate. In one month more than half the black refugees in Helena died, although their places were quickly filled by new arrivals. The former slaves died in such large numbers that proper Christian burials were impossible. To Mann's horror, the corpses were piled on carts with dead horses and mules to be buried in common pits. Worst of all, thought Mann, the black women were frequently reduced to prostitution in their desperation to feed and clothe themselves. It was with great difficulty that she undertook the reformation of "this Sodom."[43] But with Western Sanitary Commission support, she supervised the construction of a new hospital, a new school, and new shelters to replace the squalid camp on the edge of town. By spring 1863, the able-bodied men had been enlisted as soldiers and the remaining refugees had been placed on plantations leased to Northern speculators. In fall 1863, Mann considered her work in Arkansas finished, and she returned to St. Louis.

In St. Louis Mann worked to provide relief to the black refugees gathered at "Camp Ethiopia." She found "utter misery and despair" there, in part because physical conditions were deplorable but also because the people's labor was coerced by "mounted orderlies" who acted like slave drivers, directing the labor of the black refugees on the city's fortifications and on the wharf, unloading steamboats and coal barges. At night, she observed, the refugees were "discharged . . . without compensation or a comfortable shelter." She located better grounds for the contraband camp and began supervising the erection of shelters. Soon she reported that the black refugees lived and labored in comparative comfort and happiness. Mann left St. Louis to take the position of director of the new Colored Orphanage in Washington, D.C.[44]

Emily Elizabeth Parsons, daughter of the prominent Harvard legal scholar Theophilus Parsons, reported experiences of self-liberation as she labored among wounded soldiers, first at St. Louis's Lawson Hospital and later in the field during the siege of Vicksburg. A single woman in her mid-thirties, Parsons had suffered significant hearing loss as a child from scarlet fever. Bad eyesight and lameness that had resulted from childhood accidents also hampered her activity. In the war, however, she found the means to overcome her handicaps and to secure a degree of independence that she had never imagined for herself. Inspired (as so many women of her generation had been) by Florence Nightingale's service in the Crimean War, Parsons gained admission to Massachusetts General Hospital at the beginning of the Civil War. With her father's blessing, she trained to be a nurse, and after a year-and-a-half of study, she was recommended by the hospital's surgeons for service in the army hospital at Fort Schuyler on Long Island. She began her nursing career in October 1862, but fearing that too much exposure to the sea would damage her health, she soon moved to New York City. There, Parsons met Jessie Frémont, who recommended her to James Yeatman. In January 1863 Parsons arrived in St. Louis and began work at the Lawson Hospital but soon relocated to the Benton Barracks Hospital. Under the supervision of the surgeon Ira Russell (of Natick, Massachusetts), Parsons took charge of the supply room and supervised the female nurses.[45]

Mann's and Parsons's arrival in St. Louis illustrates the continuing influence of the Northeast in the border city. In the Western Sanitary Commission, Parsons worked closely with William T. Hazard, the Rhode Island–born owner of the Albion and Empire Mills in St. Louis. Hazard and his wife Rebecca moved to St. Louis from Quincy, Illinois, in 1850 and took leading roles in the organization of the Western Sanitary Commission and the Ladies' Union Aid Society. Two women who befriended Parsons also illustrate the strong influence of northeasterners. One was the wife of William Chauvenet, a native of Pennsylvania who helped to found the U.S. Naval Academy before taking a chair in mathematics at Washington University (where he also served as chancellor from 1862 to 1869). Parsons's other close friend in St. Louis was Connecticut-born Cynthia King. She had married Washington King in 1836 and moved with him to St. Louis in 1844. He died suddenly of a stroke in August 1861 as he returned home from a visit with General Frémont. It was as a widow that Cynthia King welcomed fellow New Englander Emily Parsons into her home when the newly trained nurse arrived in St. Louis in January 1863.[46]

Although northeasterners dominated both the Ladies' Union Aid Society and the Western Sanitary Commission, the female nursing corps of 300 was a more heterogeneous lot. The Benton Barracks hospital drew women from Iowa, Illinois, and Nebraska as well as from the Northeast. It also drew local women. Miss Lucy J. Bissell, the descendant of an old St. Louis family, left her St. Louis County home to serve as a Western Sanitary Commission nurse throughout the war. She first volunteered in Cairo, Illinois, in July 1861 and later moved to Bird's Point, Missouri. For more than a year she lived in a tent and subsisted on soldiers' rations. After a brief furlough at home she took a nursing post in Paducah, Kentucky. In February 1864 she began work at Benton Barracks. She spent the last year of the war—from July 1864 to June 1865—at the military hospital at Jefferson Barracks.[47]

As the Western Sanitary Commission outfitted a new floating hospital, the *City of Alton,* to care for sick and wounded soldiers from the Vicksburg campaign, Hazard called on Parsons to take charge of the nurses and the supply room of the ship. "I am going to Dixie!" she exulted to her mother as she prepared for her month-long journey downriver. On 13 February 1863 Hazard joined Parsons on board, and she began the task of bringing order to what she viewed as the chaos around her. "Such a scene of confusion and dirt, and Soldiers!" she exclaimed to her mother. But the experience was an exhilarating one. "I feel now as if I had really entered into the inner spirit of the time," she wrote. She sensed in herself "the feeling which counts danger as

nothing, but works straight on as our Puritan forefathers worked before us."
She hastened to interject a declaration of modesty: "I do not mean that *I* am
anything heroic." But she knew that she had entered into a world she had
never before known: "I am understanding what it is to be in the army."[48]

Hazard recruited Parsons to work on the *City of Alton*, partly because he
had recently lost the services of another young female nurse, Margaret Elizabeth Breckinridge of Philadelphia. As her family name suggested, she had
prominent family ties in Kentucky. Her paternal grandfather was John
Breckinridge, attorney general in Thomas Jefferson's second administration.
In 1862 she journeyed to St. Louis, ostensibly to visit her brother, although
she soon found work as a nurse with the Western Sanitary Commission.
During winter 1862–1863 she made two trips down the Mississippi River on
the *City of Alton*. On her second trip, in January 1863, she returned to St. Louis
with a cargo of more than 160 wounded men. One-third of them lay on the
floor of the crowded hospital ship, and in the intense cold Breckinridge made
hot water bottles of the soldiers' canteens to help warm her freezing patients.
The suffering reminded her of an ironic verse in a song popular with the
troops: "So I've had a sight of drilling, / And I've roughed it many days; / Yes,
and death has nearly had me, / Yet, I think, the service pays." Breckinridge
had planned another trip down the river, but illness prevented it. She returned
to Philadelphia in June 1863 and died the next year.[49]

As the *City of Alton* made its way downriver, Parsons passed scenes of
previous battles. "We steam under the yellow flag," she reported, noting that
the Confederates "do not usually fire upon that." Nevertheless, they stopped
at federal outposts along the way to learn about conditions on the river and
to monitor the activity of guerrilla forces. At Island Number 10 they learned
that the federal garrison had recently fought off a guerrilla attack of several
thousand men. "How little I thought," she reflected as they continued their
voyage, "when reading the accounts of the battle there, that I should ever sail
by it!" At Helena, the scene of Maria Mann's labors, Parsons got her first view
of the squalid conditions of the freedmen. "Imagine living in the midst of what
the children call a 'dirt pie,'" she wrote, "and you will have an idea of the
condition of the people!" After another day's journey on the river she declared,
"We are in full sight of Vicksburg." The hard work for which she had prepared soon commenced.[50]

Parsons arrived above Vicksburg as Grant continued the ultimately fruitless attempt to bypass the Confederate batteries by creating a water route west

of the main channel of the Mississippi. "We look over at Vicksburg as you look at Boston from Brookline," Parsons wrote in a letter home, "and see it quite as well." She watched as one of the federal gunboats attempted to silence Confederate artillery that harassed federal troops cutting a canal on the other side of the Mississippi. She found the scene of battle strangely serene and the exploding artillery shells beautiful. "It's a curious sight to see a little cloud hover in the air, and know that it is such an engine; it looks very pretty if you can forget for a minute what it is."[51]

Parsons repeatedly noted the tenderness and affection that the soldiers displayed for her and for one another. "If those who object to women in hospitals could only hear the speeches that are made to us," she wrote to her mother, "I think their objections would be answered." As she passed among the soldiers, "hard hands were stretched out to clasp mine," and the words, "'Oh, it is so good to have a woman come,'" greeted her. A woman's presence reminded the soldiers of their wives or mothers, she thought, and in itself it helped to ease their suffering. "It is real cheery now," one soldier told her, "to have a woman come round one, it seems like home." She saw a healthy soldier, "a fine-looking man," watching over another man stricken by typhoid fever. "I was so struck by their feeling for each other that I asked if they were old friends." She learned that they had been comrades-in-arms for several years. They were more than old friends—"they were old soldiers."

As the hospital ship filled with sick and wounded men, Parsons reported that the Western Sanitary Commission nurses under her direction were fully engaged and that the six women volunteers who had sailed with them from St. Louis were much needed for cooking and other chores. As the *City of Alton* prepared for its return to St. Louis, Parsons contemplated the terrible struggle that lay ahead if the federal forces succeeded in taking Vicksburg. "They talk of the taking of Vicksburg," she wrote home, "but, Mother, if the talkers could see it!" Parsons spoke with the authority of a veteran. "I never realized in the East what a war was," she continued. "Now I have been down to it." She had cared for the wounded "just brought from the battle." They came with "such wounds as never come home to us at the East." She had seen the face of war straight on and knew "at what cost the work is done, and how nobly, too, that cost is borne." And "side by side with all this noble stirring is the Secesh spirit contrasting with it at every turn." Parsons regarded with disgust the sullen white civilians whose animosity she sensed in Memphis and other locations on the river. "Here," she concluded, "you really see the struggle between the two elements."[52]

The *City of Alton* made its way upstream to Memphis, where the wounded were transferred to a Western Sanitary Commission hospital and the ship cleaned for a return trip to Vicksburg. The women continued north to St. Louis by packet. When their vessel was pressed into federal service at Cairo, they completed their journey by railcar and arrived in St. Louis early in March. The grueling round-trip to Vicksburg had taken a month and had left Parsons seriously ill with malaria. As she recuperated, she reproached her mother for suggesting that she return home to rest. "Of course I am getting well," she insisted, "and you must not say I am 'worn out.'" There was nothing unusual about her illness; she had "got sick going down the river, as a great many do." She would not think of leaving her field of labor: "I am glad I went; it was an experience, every way, I would not have lost."[53]

When she recovered, Parsons returned to Benton Barracks, where she exercised "direct and complete control over the female nurses" and also directed the male nurses through their male supervisors, the "ward-masters." Parsons wrote to her mother, proudly emphasizing the broadened nature of her authority: "I tell these men what I wish to have done, how I wish to have it done and when they are to see that it is done." While the female nurses brought patients their food and medicine, the male nurses kept the wards clean and changed the patients' linen. Parsons supervised all of them, beginning her day in the kitchen before breakfast and ending, often late in the evening, with an inspection of the wards. She had become accustomed to military discipline and found strength in it. "You have no idea how our soldiers live," she wrote home. "I am so accustomed to living among them, that I do not know what I shall do when I return to civil life, if ever I do." And, she added, with as much seriousness as humor, "I am inclined to think I shall follow the army for a profession."[54]

During spring 1863, as Grant pressed his campaign against Vicksburg, activity at the military hospitals in St. Louis sharply increased. After the surrender of Vicksburg, the Western Sanitary Commission cared for 30,000 Confederate prisoners, many of whom were wounded, sick, or near starvation.[55] Parsons's duties increased proportionately. She expected that she would soon be responsible for thirty or forty female nurses. Increasingly, the wives of Union soldiers turned to nursing to contribute as directly as possible to the war effort. In May "a lady of about forty" came to Benton Barracks to be a nurse. "Her husband is off engineering, or something like it," explained Parsons, "and she wanted to do something for the soldiers; so she has turned nurse."[56] Another nurse, whose husband was at Vicksburg, had lost a young child. "It was brought to the hospital and she took care of it here," reported Parsons. The child died in the nurse's room at Benton Barracks. "The mother is still here," she noted; "she wished to remain." The devotion of the women nurses to the Union cause did not diminish the burden Parsons felt as their supervisor. "You have no idea of the difficulty of keeping discipline in this place with all these women," she complained. It was a lonely task since she needed to remain aloof from all cliques: "It is sometimes the most wearisome part of the work." Nevertheless, she knew that she would never return to her antebellum way of life. "I never expect to *live* at home again," she wrote her mother somewhat curtly in July 1863, following the fall of Vicksburg; "I shall always be working somewhere or other, I hope."[57]

Increasingly, Benton Barracks became a complex social entity. Patients included "refugees, contrabands, soldiers, both black and white." In March 1864 Parsons reported treating numerous cases of frostbite caused because "the negroes lay in the woods and fields in cold weather while escaping from their masters." One man had lost his entire foot to frostbite, but he seemed "bright and cheery; freedom seems to be the main thing." Black and white patients were separated by ward, and among the black refugees and soldiers Parsons and her nurses found ample opportunity to act as teachers as well. In the "colored wards the nurses are teaching their men to read, write, and, in some instances, to cipher." Parsons also attempted to train "colored women as nurses among the blacks." It was "a difficult task," she reported, "but one worth trying." By early April 1864 a separate hospital for blacks had been established at Benton Barracks. In St. Louis, a group of black women organized a Colored Ladies' Union Aid Society with the object of helping to care for sick and wounded black soldiers. Parsons noted that the Copperhead spirit in St. Louis permitted kind treatment of blacks if it was done without any implication of racial equality. When the black women took the street railway to Benton Barracks, they were obliged to stand outside the horse-drawn car on the exposed platform. A protest by leading white Unionists led to a compromise. Now, reported Parsons, these loyal black women were allowed to enter the cars and seat themselves on Saturdays. The blacks' hospital brought to the forefront the deep-seated racial prejudice that Parsons had once thought the abolitionists had exaggerated.[58]

The Western Sanitary Commission devoted about 10 percent of its resources to freedmen's relief. Mrs. Lucien Eaton served as president of the Ladies' Freedmen's Relief Association that linked the Ladies' Union Aid Society to the newly formed Freedmen's Relief Association. Her husband, a prominent St. Louis lawyer and an active figure in raising black troops in St. Louis, superintended the contraband camp in St. Louis.[59] Under Mrs. Eaton's direction, the Relief Association refitted the old Lawson Hospital into the Refugee and Freedmen's Home. In another major undertaking, the association established the St. Louis Freedmen's Orphanage (and established orphanages as well in Memphis and Vicksburg). These activities continued long after the war. In fact, the Western Sanitary Commission did not formally disband until William Greenleaf Eliot's death in 1886. Then, its remaining assets helped to establish a nursing school named in his memory.[60]

Some Confederate wives worked as nurses. Parsons recalled that the wife of a Confederate soldier learned of her husband's death while at work at the hospital at Benton Barracks. However, Julia Gratiot Chouteau, wife of Charles P. Chouteau, found the doors of the City Hospital closed to her when she presented herself as a volunteer. The hospital surgeon, Dr. John T. Hodgen, told her that he would not permit admission to anyone of her class. Hodgen had been a professor of anatomy and physiology at the McDowell Medical College before the army confiscated it for use as the Gratiot Street prison.[61] Julia Chouteau asked what Hodgen meant by referring to her class and learned that he meant "persons suspected of disloyalty to the government." Hodgen knew Charles P. Chouteau to be the heir to one of St. Louis's great fur trading and slave-owning families. Chouteau had entered the iron business in 1850, and he was one of many wealthy, prominent, and conservative men who had attended the conditional Unionist meeting presided over by Robert Campbell at the east front of the courthouse on 12 January 1861. Chouteau had supported General William Harney during the early weeks of the secession crisis. Although he took no part in the war, he supported the Union cause. In spring 1862, when wounded soldiers filled St. Louis hospitals, Chouteau led an expedition up the Missouri River taking supplies to his mines in Montana.[62] Julia Chouteau protested to Hodgen that she had never acted in a disloyal manner, and she probably had not. But the association of her family's name with slavery and with Southern culture was enough to bar her from the Union hospital.

As the scope of activities undertaken by the Western Sanitary Commission extended south to Vicksburg and east to Nashville and Chattanooga,

Frederick Law Olmsted planned a spring 1863 tour of the Mississippi Valley, including a brief but politic visit with Yeatman in St. Louis and concluding with a review of his commission's operations in Chicago. In Olmsted's journal of his western tour he drafted a portrait of St. Louis and its citizens that drew on the perspective he had earlier brought to the Deep South during the 1850s in his reports to the *New York Times*. He also brought to this portrait his newly heightened sense of urban design. Before taking on the duties of directing the U.S. Sanitary Commission, he had been the principal creator of New York City's Central Park. He believed in order and efficiency and in the creation of tranquil urban spaces. Slavery and the Slave Power stood squarely in the path of progress, and they were being swept away. Beyond the war against slavery, Olmsted looked for signs of grandeur in the nation's burgeoning cities.

In March 1863 Olmsted began his western tour. It brought him into direct contact with the living conditions of common soldiers (bedeviled during his visit by high water) and the freedmen refugees. He found the soldiers well supplied and on the way to becoming a reliably disciplined force. The freedmen seemed in good condition, and Olmsted noted that although they demonstrated no sentimental attachment to former masters, they exhibited a strong bond with their own families and with their locale. After meeting with Generals Sherman and Grant at Young's Point, Mississippi (near Vicksburg), and finding both men warmly supportive of the Sanitary Commission's work, Olmsted traveled north to St. Louis, with stops in Memphis and Cairo.

His St. Louis visit was hurried. He arrived on 4 April and departed two days later. On the evening of his arrival he dined at the Yeatman home, located on a hill at the northern end of Broadway.[63] The two men found that their earlier rivalry had largely disappeared. There remained more than enough work to occupy both Sanitary Commissions. No longer concerned with jurisdictional issues, Olmsted regarded Yeatman and St. Louis instead with the eye of a cultural critic. The city did not seem "particularly Western" to him. The masonry construction that dominated gave the city a substantial look, "more so than most eastern towns," he thought, "more so than New York on average." He observed "few buildings of notable character," but he found "many which are respectable." After his dinner with Yeatman he thought that his judgment regarding St. Louis's architecture could be applied as well to the city's society: respectable but not notable.

Olmsted noticed in the Yeatman household the muted mannerisms of the South. He found the family "well-bred" but "neither genteel nor stylish." He also discerned the family's pride in its Southern origins. Yeatman was the stepson of John Bell, a U.S. senator from Tennessee and the Constitutional Unionist Party presidential candidate in 1860. Olmsted found the Yeatmans "hot and strong Unionists." They hated the rebels, and (although they had recently owned slaves) they were "zealous" in what Olmsted described with mild sarcasm as their "newly emancipated repugnance to Slavery." In their home he found some good paintings "and an exquisite small statue by an Italian sculptor." But the grounds reminded him of the "plantation rudeness" that he had encountered during his antebellum tours of the South. He noted of the estate an "inequality of keeping and untidiness."

Olmsted thought that if he had prodded the Yeatmans on their "pride in being Southern," they might well have regarded that pride as a weakness. By contrast, "what they never thought of concealing or suppressing or re-straining from its utmost outpouring was their satisfaction in being St. Louisians." This was a trait that he discovered throughout the city: "No subject was talked of that did not give occasion for some new method, (always used confidently and with certainty that it was kindness to do so) for trumpeting St. Louis. It was the same with every man & woman we met in St. Louis. The devout dwellers in Mecca do not worship the holy city more than every child of St. Louis, his city." The "most notable thing" he learned of St. Louis was "the pleasure of the people to talk about it—what it had been, what it would be."

Olmsted toured the city's hospitals without comment and offered only a mild criticism of "poorly contrived" Benton Barracks. What attracted his attention were the city's cultural amenities, its potential for grandeur. He toured the Botanical Garden, built by the retired merchant Henry Shaw, that was to be given to the city when Shaw died. Olmsted commended Shaw for his hard work in rising from personal poverty to munificent wealth. But he found the existing garden "a dwarfish & paltry affair for a town like St. Louis."[64] The prospect of enlarging the garden with an additional gift of sev-eral hundred acres of adjacent lands (later to become Tower Grove Park) brightened Olmsted's perspective since it would make possible a "park of noble breadth and delicious repose of character." As order and efficiency gave way to grandeur, Olmsted had no doubt that the citizens of St. Louis would welcome a park as "a pleasure-ground . . . for rural-recreations."

St. Louisans would welcome the pleasures that city gardens and parks would provide, but it would probably be some time before these amenities would appear. Olmsted found that "the tide of commerce incessantly flows through every man's brain. . . . You perceive it as strongly in those of the quieter callings—the teachers, preachers, physicians, as in others." Everyone in St. Louis busied themselves with the "foundation-laying of civilization." To be sure, "Some stones for the superstructure are being set," but they were as yet too closely joined to the foundation, and "the sense of commercial speculation is never wholly lost."

Olmsted judged the Mercantile Library—the most venerable of the city's cultural institutions—as "the most respectable matter that I came into contact with in St. Louis." The large hall pleased his eye, and he noted that "a goodly number of men and women, boys and girls" used the library to read books as well as to admire the statues and paintings (he judged these works of art to be far from grand but believed that even mediocre art had the capacity to lift the human spirit). Nevertheless, as he noted, "the Mercantile Library . . . is mercantile." It was the product of philanthropy wedded to commerce. One gentleman told Olmsted that "people here live very much to associate all their benevolence with business." Civic improvements flourished as long as St. Louisans linked them to "a business advantage." In this regard he noted with pleasure that "the public schools were an object of pride with the citizens" and that the "buildings are large."

Olmsted never saw a policeman on the city's streets although he witnessed several episodes that warranted the presence of the police, which offended his sense of orderliness. John Lauderdale noted the same absence of police. Resting in his room aboard the *D. A. January* on the St. Louis levee, he heard "a prolonged cry of distress down on the lower deck." Investigating, he found a white deckhand "having a little battle" with a black soldier. "The white had the black by holding one of his fingers between his teeth." The soldier's blood flowed freely, and Lauderdale wondered, "Where are the Police?" The answer, he wrote to his family, "is they are a harmless body of men, who wear no uniform, and are only seen occasionally, & wear a pale silver star on their coats." John Couzin's police force left much to be desired in Yeatman's and Lauderdale's views. "When wanted, they are not to be found," concluded Lauderdale.

Olmsted also noted an absence of beggars in the city. Since there appeared to be no effective police force to suppress pauperism, he concluded that the absence of beggars reflected the general prosperity of the city, despite the economic liabilities connected with the war. In the German section of town he saw "new and smart furniture" and observed the women "nearly all smartly dressed." "I saw no squalid poverty," he concluded, "except among the negroes & fugitives from the seat of war."

It was the broad base of the city's prosperity that particularly impressed Olmsted. He believed that there were more men of moderate means in St. Louis (men of a social standing that the English had begun to call "middle class") than in any European city of the same size. This fact demonstrated a remarkable upward mobility in the city, he believed, and he discussed the subject at some length with an "old resident, distinguished for his interest in the poor & needy, and who had been a mayor of the city." He asked the former mayor how many members of this substantial middle class "came to St. Louis comparatively poor men." The St. Louisan answered, "There is scarcely one that did not begin here by sweeping out his employer's store or office. . . . We nearly all began here with nothing but our heads and hands." Olmsted concluded that this rapid rise to prosperity helped to explain why St. Louisans lived so well "within their own houses" while they continued to live "very poorly" in the public spaces "out of their own houses."

Olmsted left St. Louis on 6 April to take the train to Chicago. He encountered in the process the transportation bottleneck across the Mississippi that continued to plague St. Louis until the construction of James Eads's steel and iron railway bridge (completed in 1874). To reach the St. Louis, Alton and Chicago Railroad terminal on the east side of the river, Olmsted took passage on a steam ferryboat. He boarded at the appointed hour but waited impatiently for twenty minutes as several men struggled to herd swine on board. "Swine are hard to drive upon a ferry-boat," he observed dryly. No sooner had one group of pigs been driven on board than others in the rear turned their heads and plodded down the gangplank. By fits and starts the swine were loaded, although one maverick broke loose and trotted freely upriver on the levee. To Olmsted's surprise and relief, the ferryboat captain did not wait for this last pig to be captured and loaded. Instead he set out for Illinois, and Olmsted took his leave, with evident pleasure, of "the Mississippi and its steam boat business." He discovered that his delay in crossing the Mississippi had postponed the departure of his train to Chicago. He ended his visit to St. Louis with the disapproving observation that timetables took second place to swineherding in the city that aspired to wealth and grandeur.[65]

When Olmsted noted that St. Louisans loved to talk about their city, he touched on a theme of civic pride that played a central role in homefront activity. In the next year, St. Louisans organized the Grand Mississippi Valley Sanitary Fair, which they hoped would be the biggest and most successful event of its kind in the country. The Sanitary Fair of May and June 1864 marked the high point of homefront activity, and it offered to the loyal women of the city a public recognition of their efforts to defend the Union. As the Baptist minister Galusha Anderson observed, the fair proved to be a "mighty agency for curing us of our selfishness." For a time at least the fair "broke in upon our commercialism and led us to think of others and to do something for their welfare."[66] Sanitary fairs became major social events in New York and Philadelphia, and Chicago mounted its own fair in 1865. Planning for the St. Louis fair began late in January 1864, when the women associated with the Western Sanitary Commission called on the men to create an administrative structure for it. At a meeting on 1 February at the Mercantile Library, Major General William S. Rosecrans, commander of the Department of the West, was made honorary president of the event and named to an executive committee. A separate executive committee of women planned most of the activities. These were the same women who were the leading figures in the Ladies' Union Aid Society. Mrs. Chauncey I. Filley served as president of the executive committee, Mrs. General Van Antwerp and Miss Phoebe Couzins as secretaries, Mrs. Samuel Copp as treasurer, and Miss Anna Bracket edited the newspaper, the *Daily Countersign,* published during the fair.[67] Other members included Adaline Couzins and Anna Clapp as well as Minerva Blow (the wife of Congressman Henry T. Blow) and Apolline Blair.

The fair opened ceremoniously on 17 May 1864, declared a holiday by St. Louis's mayor, James S. Thomas. It opened to the public the evening of 18 May and continued through the evening of 18 June. The price of admission on opening day was two dollars, on the second and third day, one dollar. Thereafter, visitors were admitted for fifty cents. The buildings were located on Twelfth Street between Washington and Olive Streets, an area that was then on the western border of the city's business district. The main building was located on Twelfth Street between Olive and St. Charles. The Women's Department took responsibility for decorating this "Grand Fancy Court," which housed an art gallery and featured the "Delphic Oracle." General Grant had the Oracle tell his fortune when he visited. The Grand Court also featured a giant shoe, depicting the nursery rhyme "The Old Lady in the Shoe," and Grant's daughter Nellie represented the old lady.[68]

The purpose of the fair was to raise money to support the activities of the Sanitary Commission. After paying the price of admission, the visitor encountered rows of booths that offered for sale a wide variety of goods, including pillows with needlepoint covers commemorating famous battles, a wide assortment of food, and at the insistence of the German community, beer. Although the women tried to ban all alcoholic beverages from the fair, it was agreed to limit them to Missouri wines and beers. The Germans' fondness for beer made the work of temperance reform exceedingly difficult in St. Louis. John Lauderdale complained that "St. Louis has such a mixed population, that it is very difficult to control opinion on the side of right." He lamented that "the German people adhere so strongly to their merchaums & beer, and their miserable faith" (presumably a criticism of the fact that religious faith did not prevent Germans from drinking on Sundays). But Germans were not the only drinkers in St. Louis. "I never saw a city where there is as much drinking of liquor as here," noted Lauderdale. "*Everybody*—almost—drinks." In addition to the numerous beer shops and gardens frequented by the Germans were grog shops dispensing distilled spirits by the dram. Looking out on the levee from his room aboard the *D. A. January*, Lauderdale counted thirty grog shops, where the roustabouts, draymen, and sailors "get all the liquor they want." To discourage public drunkenness, the fair organizers prevailed on the mayor to close all taverns and grog shops within a six-block radius of the fairgrounds.[69]

Black soldiers from regiments stationed at Benton Barracks performed guard duty at the fair. High points in the festivities included a contest to select the most popular general, to be determined by votes purchased at a dollar each. More than half the votes were cast for General Winfield Scott Hancock, who had been severely wounded while repulsing General Pickett's charge at Gettysburg in 1863. His popularity evidently derived from his recent successes in Virginia, at the Battle of the Wilderness (5–6 May 1864), and at the Battle of Cold Harbor (1–3 June). But George B. McClellan, removed from command two years earlier, drew the second largest number of votes. Both William Tecumseh Sherman and Benjamin F. Butler garnered more votes than the war's most successful general and the man with the closest ties to St. Louis, Ulysses S. Grant.

Among the most popular activities, judged by the fair's receipts, were booths operated by the city's dry goods merchants and grocers. Also popular were the activities organized by the Drama and Public Amusements Committee and the Skating Park. A Children's Committee operated a Fishing Pond with considerable success. The largest revenues came from the sale of food and drink: the sale of beer and wine brought in $5,000. A New England Kitchen, a Holland Kitchen, the Laclede Cafe, and two soda fountains brought in $22,000. Daily raffles and several grand-prize raffles made a great deal of money as well.

In addition to the activities on the fairgrounds, entertainments offered at the Mercantile Library and at Washington University also benefited the Western Sanitary Commission. To celebrate the 300th anniversary of William Shakespeare's birth, Dr. C. W. Stevens offered dramatic readings at the Mercantile Library, and the young women of the Mary Institute performed a concert of vocal music at Washington University.

Another high point was a raffle on the closing night that offered three bars of Nevada silver, valued at a total of $12,000. On a more partisan note, St. Louis County donated the Smizer farm to the fair. With Mrs. Daniel Frost, Mrs. William Smizer had been banished from St. Louis in March 1863. The Smizer farm had been confiscated, evidently for failure to pay an assessment levied on rebel sympathizers. It provided the fair with one of its most popular raffles, bringing in about $40,000.[70] Total receipts for the Sanitary Fair reached nearly $620,000, with net profits exceeding $550,000. As Yeatman noted, the fair raised $3.50 per inhabitant, more on a per capita basis than the U.S. Sanitary Commission fairs in Philadelphia and New York had raised.[71] The fair directors allocated the largest portion of the profits ($345,000) for medical supplies but provided substantial sums to support the Ladies' Freedmen's Relief Association and other soldier and refugee relief activities.[72]

In the arena of race relations, the fair proved to be far from ennobling. The Reverend Henry A. Nelson, pastor of the First Presbyterian Church, created a stir when he invited two black ministers to join him for lunch at the fair's Laclede Cafe. Nelson was a native of Amherst, Massachusetts, who had served as pastor of the Auburn, New York, Presbyterian Church for a decade before accepting a call to St. Louis in 1856. As Nelson and his guests arrived and took their seats, some visitors expressed outrage, and several of the female attendants refused to serve the group. Nelson and his companions remained seated, and the tension mounted. Finally, one young woman came forward to wait on the group, and they managed to take their lunch in relative peace. The *Republican* lamented that such acts of fanaticism occurred with increasing frequency. In an attempt to ridicule the "exceedingly repulsive scene," the paper published a lithograph that caricatured the black ministers. In the background, the artist depicted a group of five attractive young white women looking at the seated men with disapproval. To the side, one homely white woman wearing spectacles appears willing to step forward to serve the ministers.[73]

The fair demonstrated the extent to which women in St. Louis had emerged from the domestic sphere to participate directly in relief activities and in the planning and operation of a major public event. Not surprisingly, the women who had been active in the Ladies' Union Aid Society and in the Sanitary Fair went on to champion women's rights, particularly woman suffrage, in the postwar years. Phoebe Couzins studied law at Washington University and became one of the first female attorneys in the United States. Rebecca Hazard won election as president of the American Woman's Suffrage Association in 1878. Hazard had already joined Phoebe Couzins, Anna Clapp, Virginia Minor, and others to launch the Woman Suffrage Association of Missouri in 1867. That organization counted among its members many of the men who had worked most closely with women in wartime relief activities, notably William Greenleaf Eliot and James E. Yeatman.[74]

For women as well as for men the Civil War tested physical strength and moral stamina. As the first weeks of service in the field stretched into months and years, the labor of nursing took a heavy toll. Couzins's compatriot, Margaret Breckinridge, died in 1864 of an illness thought to have been brought on by physical exhaustion. Parsons suffered several bouts of illness during the war and died in 1880 at the age of fifty-six. Adaline Couzins and fellow nurse Arethusa Forbes suffered frostbite while in the field with Frémont's forces during fall 1861; the ordeal forced Forbes to retire from the service. Couzins labored on, through the war and through a major cholera outbreak in St. Louis in 1866. The cholera epidemic reached its height during the summer months. Health authorities recorded more than 3,500 deaths from the disease in 1866 and nearly half that number died in the last two weeks of August. In October, when the epidemic subsided, Mayor James S. Thomas publicly thanked Adaline Couzins: "Would that we had many more such ladies as Mrs. J. E. D. Couzins."[75] But Couzins was not unscathed; she had suffered a minié ball wound during the siege of Vicksburg, which contributed to her disability in old age. Petitioning Congress for a pension for Couzins, Forbes drew a heroic picture of her now-bedridden friend: "That petticoat, with the rebel bullet-hole and the bent hoop skirt . . . ought to speak loudly for pension." It did; Congress awarded Couzins a disability pension in 1888.[76]

For women as well as for men, the Civil War had a transforming effect. Soldiers and civilians alike carried into the war shared concepts of patriotism, courage, and a common faith that divine providence guided their actions and determined their fate. These ideas and beliefs were not shattered by the war—in some respects they were strengthened—but they were rendered more somber and far less self-righteous. Early in the war Sarah Hill witnessed what she described as "a wonderful exhibition of courage." She worked as a nurse assisting in the treatment of a young soldier whose elbow had been shattered by a minié ball. The surgeon wanted to amputate the arm above the elbow, but the young man protested, insisting that he would rather have a rigid arm than half an arm. Finally, the surgeon agreed to treat the wound. Probably fearing that the doctor would amputate his limb if he lost consciousness, the soldier "refused to take a sedative" (ether or chloroform). For more than an hour he lay on the operating table "white and grim" as the surgeon "probed and extracted splinters and pieces of bone." As Hill watched, the soldier fainted twice, bathed in a cold sweat. But he bore his suffering quietly: "He never made a moan."[77]

Emily Parsons witnessed and described many deathbed scenes. Generally she found that the dying men took comfort when she read to them from the Bible. Clearly, she took comfort when, as she read, a soldier's suffering eased, and he passed peacefully into death. She never lost her sense that the war represented God's will. "I want you should understand," she instructed her sister in May 1863, "the many sides and inner life of this war." One read daily about heroism on the field of battle. But, "side by side" with it "is another heroism, grander, more courageous, working for eternity." God's grace awaited the fallen hero. "The men want to be told these things," insisted Parsons, "they care for them, ask for them."

For Sarah Hill, the horrors of war gradually hardened her romantic vision of the courageous soldier. At the close of the war a soldier's courage revealed to Hill not the sublimity of the human spirit but a mortal capacity to endure hardship with a heart-deadened resolve. At the beginning of the war she had thrilled to watch the Eighth Wisconsin Infantry march by her house in St. Louis. The young men were "clean and wholesome looking" as they passed by carrying Old Baldy, their war eagle, on a perch alongside the American flag. Hill saw the regiment again when she visited her husband after the fall of Vicksburg in July 1863. The Eighth Wisconsin marched in review through the streets of the surrendered city. Now, Hill noted, "they were stern lipped . . . their battle flag torn and bullet-riddled." Old Baldy was still on his perch, the living symbol of war's ferocity. She saw the Eighth Wisconsin for the last time as they were mustered out of service at Benton Barracks in 1865. The regiment had been reduced to "just a handful of men." Grim-faced, they carried Old Baldy on his perch, but Hill noticed that the bird's wings drooped and that "he had lost the fierce aggressive look of four years before."[78]

By war's end, suffering and death had become ordinary events for Emily Parsons. She never once questioned her faith in divine providence, but what had earlier seemed to her to be "wonderful" exhibitions of courage had been rendered by experience part of a predictable pattern. In one of her last letters home, she told of the arrival of a young man who had fought in eleven battles "and is now shot through the chest." It was better to be shot almost anywhere than in the chest, she noted. "These chest wounds are very dangerous things," she wrote, and she did not expect him to live long. From experience she knew that chest wounds were far more dangerous than they looked. She knew what to expect, even if the soldier did not: "Just a little hole, perhaps healed up and the hurt inside; a little more pain, a little harder breathing, and weaker and weaker day by day; so they go."[79]

8

"Terror . . . of Shot and Shell"

S OUTH OF ST. LOUIS, in the village of Carondelet (later annexed to the city), James Buchanan Eads oversaw the construction of ironclad gunboats for the War Department. From spring 1861 through spring 1864, he maintained a feverish pace of production. With each launching, Eads's boatyard added strength to the Union's river navy, which became the spearhead of General Winfield Scott's Anaconda Plan. Moreover, with each launching the merchants and manufacturers of St. Louis came a step closer to reestablishing their commercial ties to the cotton South. For artisans across the North, the material demands of the Civil War increased workloads. But the extraordinary pace of production at Carondelet placed a particularly heavy burden on St. Louis's ship carpenters and on the ironworkers of the city's foundries. Molders and forgemen turned out armor for Eads's gunboats at a number of locations in the city, for example, the Filley brothers' Excelsior Stove Works, Hudson Bridge's Stove Works, and the R. C. Totten and Company Foundry on Main Street and the Chouteau, Harrison and Valle Foundry and Rolling Mills on Broadway. Workers molded plates of iron for armor and rolled sheets of iron for the gunboat turrets.[1]

The challenge of war energized Eads. A self-taught mathematician and engineer (his personal motto was "Drive On"), he had always embraced challenge. Even in an era noted for its celebration of ambition and vigor, his capacity for work astonished his contemporaries. Named in honor of his successful cousin, James Buchanan, Eads overcame the adversity of an impoverished youth. He moved to St. Louis from his birthplace in Indiana as a lad of thirteen and went to work, first as a clerk and later in various capacities on steamboats.

Denied a formal education, Eads studied and pursued his passion for invention in his spare time. In his early twenties, he convinced two St. Louis boat builders to join him in the business of clearing snags from rivers and salvaging cargo from wrecked steamboats. He and his partners found no

shortage of work. Steamboat companies paid to have snags cleared, and shippers and insurance underwriters paid salvagers up to 75 percent of the value
of recovered cargoes. Goods lost for five years or more belonged to whoever
retrieved them. Eads designed a diving bell for his new line of work by knock-
ing out one end of an empty whiskey keg and weighting the open end with
lead. With the barrel secured to a boat by cable and fitted with an air hose
attached to pumps on the boat, he became a diver, walking on the river bottom with his head in the air chamber, feeling blindly for sunken treasure. He
and his partners also built a double-hulled snag boat, or "submarine," beneath which he worked. Derricks on deck enabled operators to hoist snags
and salvaged goods from the riverbottom. Eads became an experienced riverman with an unrivaled knowledge of the changing configuration of riverbeds
and currents. In time, the salvaging business provided him with a solid fortune, but it also probably contributed to the lung ailments that plagued him
from the 1850s until his death in 1887. As historian Howard Miller writes, "Eads
never understood the perils of too-rapid decompression." What his physicians diagnosed as tuberculosis "was probably aggravated by caisson disease,"
more commonly known as the bends.[2]

At the suggestion of his physicians, Eads retired from business in the 1850s.
For a time he lived quietly at his home on Compton Hill, south of the city's
business district. However, his interest in things mechanical and in the river
never dimmed. When the Civil War ended he took up the engineering challenge of constructing a railroad bridge across the Mississippi. He completed
his plans for the St. Louis bridge in 1868 and celebrated its opening in 1874. A
National Historical Landmark still in use, the Eads Bridge became its designer's most enduring work. During the Civil War, however, his knowledge
of western rivers was put to a different test.

An unconditional Unionist in the secession crisis, Eads instinctively
understood the strategic importance of the western rivers for both the Union
and Confederate causes. During the secession winter, he watched with mounting frustration as Confederate forces fortified the lower Mississippi at Columbus and at Island Number 10, a few miles upstream from New Madrid.
Farther east, Confederate engineers, with slave laborers brought north from
Alabama, constructed earthen forts on the Cumberland and Tennessee Rivers near their confluence with the Ohio. As Eads realized, the Union needed
a strong river navy to break through these defenses. Shortly after the fall of
Fort Sumter, he contacted his friend, Attorney General Edward Bates, and

alerted him to the need for prompt action on the western rivers. At Bates's urging, Eads soon traveled to the capital to present his plans to the War Department.

In Washington, Eads found that Secretary of War Simon Cameron and Secretary of Navy Gideon Wells shared his view that federal forces in the West needed a river navy, but he also discovered that the naval commander John Rodgers and the naval engineer Samuel Pook already had been given responsibility for raising it. Rodgers and Pook, in consultation with boat builders in Cincinnati, had settled on the design of the first ironclad gunboats and were not initially inclined to defer to the St. Louis salvager. Pook's general design plan gave the boats their nickname, "Pook's Turtles." He specified that the boats be one hundred seventy-five feet long, fifty-one and one-half feet wide at the beam, and seven feet in the hold. They were to draw no more than six feet of water, carry thirteen heavy guns, and be protected with two-and-one-half-inch iron plating. To shield the gundeck from enemy fire, Pook designed a rectangular housing of oak planks, the sides of which sloped inward at about thirty-five degrees. The housing extended over the gundeck, pilothouse, and the stern paddle wheel and was surrounded by shuttered gunports. A Cincinnati steam engineer proposed two six-foot stroke, twenty-two-inch bore engines that he located in the hold, forward of the wheel and on either side of a single driveshaft. Twin smokestacks rose above the craft in the manner of commercial steamboats. Rodgers detailed the method of constructing and attaching the iron plating. The plates were to be cast in one- to two-foot widths, with a lip on each side. The lip would be half the thickness of the plate so that the plates could overlap as they were bolted to the boat's planking. The plates were to be assembled vertically from one foot below the waterline and were to meet in an angled butt joint with the plates of the upper housing.

Of the thirteen guns the gunboats carried, three were located at the bow, four on each side, and two at the stern. The bow guns represented the vessels' greatest firepower. In the bow were rifled forty-two-pounders, converted from older smoothbore cannon. They fired an eighty-seven-pound explosive shell. The initial armament of the gunboats was far from ideal. The rifles fired projectiles that were twice the weight for which the guns, as smoothbore cannon, originally had been designed. In the heat of battle and with excessive powder charges, they could (and did) explode. The six thirty-two-pounders that each boat carried have been described by one historian as "obsolete relics of the three-decker battleship days." As soon as more modern weapons became available—notably the advanced weapons designed by John Dahlgren and Robert Parrott—gunboat commanders eagerly replaced the dangerous forty-two-pound rifles and the antiquated thirty-two-pounders.[3]

The positioning of armaments on the gunboats reflected their tactical functions. In naval artillery pieces, as in the infantryman's musket, rifling greatly increased a weapon's range. Commanders used the large rifles in the bow in long-range bombardment while the pilot worked to hold the vessel in position. Pilots quickly discovered that they enjoyed far greater control if they could power the vessel into the current rather than back against it. The difficulty they encountered when the bow guns were fired while the boat was heading downstream meant that commanders preferred to position their craft downstream from a target. If this proved to be impossible, they fired long range from fixed positions while tied to trees on the shore. The ease with which either maneuver could be accomplished depended on the configuration of the river and the enemy fortifications the gunboats faced. When they ventured close to shore, they steamed in circles, firing broadsides into their target.

In August 1861 the War Department announced that it would accept bids for the construction of seven ironclad gunboats meeting the specifications set out by Pook and Rodgers. The responsibility for reviewing and accepting bids and for procuring the finished boats, lay with the army's quartermaster general, Montgomery C. Meigs. For Eads, this proved to be fortuitous. In a letter from Meigs's brother-in-law, Congressman Frank Blair, the quartermaster general learned that the danger of low water on the Ohio River during the summer months made St. Louis a better location than Cincinnati for the construction of the western flotilla. Despite Pook's and Rodgers's familiarity with the Cincinnati boatyards, Eads (who submitted the lowest bid) won the War Department contract. He agreed to complete the boats by 10 October 1861, giving the artisans that he employed for the work three months to construct seven boats.

As construction at the Carondelet boatyard began, Commander Rodgers tested the effectiveness of the armor plating that Eads had begun to procure from St. Louis foundries. Rodgers set up a firing range on a sandy stretch of riverbank and he positioned a ten-pound Parrott rifled gun progressively closer to sheets of iron plate. He had the gun fired first from 800 yards, then from 500 yards, and finally from as close as 200 yards. The armor, and presumably Eads's credibility, passed Rodgers's tests.[4]

In September Commodore Andrew H. Foote replaced Rodgers as commander of the emerging gunboat fleet. A native of Connecticut and a strong temperance man, it was Foote, in the 1840s, who made his ship the *Cumberland* the navy's first temperance ship. In 1862, while commanding the western flotilla of gunboats, he succeeded in bringing an end to the navy's traditional alcohol ration. A man of stern bearing, Foote arrived in St. Louis on 6 September 1861 and quickly developed a high regard for Eads's organizational and engineering abilities. Eads and his men worked without stint to meet the terms of the War Department contract and with a will to confront the growing Confederate threat south of St. Louis. Eads pressed forward even as government delays in scheduled payments required him to carry the cost of production. On 12 October, just two days after the completion date specified in the contract, he launched the first of the gunboats, the *Carondelet.* Within days he launched three more: *St. Louis, Louisville,* and *Pittsburg.*[5] As the four gunboats steamed off to be armed and outfitted, Eads supervised the completion of the remaining three boats at a shipyard in Mound City, Illinois, on the Ohio River. In the fall, these boats—the *Cairo,* the *Mound City,* and the *Cincinnati*—made their way downstream to join the federal flotilla at nearby Cairo.

While work proceeded on the seven gunboats, Eads contracted separately with the War Department to convert one of his snag boats into what would be the largest, most powerful gunboat in the federal fleet. He had first acquired the 633-ton vessel as the retired U.S. snag boat *Benton* in 1857, when he expanded his river-salvage operations. For the next few years, the *Benton* became Eads's *Submarine Number Seven.* As a snag boat, the vessel featured two hulls between which divers descended to the riverbottom and snags or sunken cargo were hauled to the surface. Eads restored the name *Benton* to the boat and cleared from its deck the derricks and pumps of the salvaging trade. He joined the two hulls together at the deck level and below at the hold. By extending the boat's sides, the two hulls joined together with a single blunt bow and stern. To protect what became the gundeck, Eads fashioned a superstructure similar to what Pook had designed for the *Carondelet* and her sister vessels. The *Benton* measured two hundred feet long and seventy-five feet wide. A single smokestack rose from its center, above the boilers. A domed pilothouse roof protruded from the gun armor deck directly in front of the stack. Eads positioned the *Benton's* single paddle wheel somewhat forward from the stern. The gundeck carried sixteen cannon, two aft, four in the bow, and five on each side. He protected the gundeck and pilothouse with three-and-one-half-inch armor; the enclosed wheelhouse carried two-and-one-half-inch armor. He finished his work on the *Benton* in mid-November. At about the same time he converted a smaller snag boat, the 355-ton *Essex,* into an ironclad that carried five guns.[6] At Foote's request, Eads accompanied the *Benton* as it made its way from Carondelet to Cairo early in December 1861. About forty miles below St. Louis, near Cape Girardeau, the vessel ran aground in the shallow river. Perturbed that the captain and his executive officer did not seek his advice as a shipbuilder and an experienced riverman, Eads retired for the night as the crew struggled vainly to haul the *Benton* into deeper water. The next morning, he noted that the river had dropped another six inches, and he proposed to the frustrated captain that the crew deploy large ropes, or hawsers, ashore and pull the *Benton* in a direction "directly opposite" to that tried by the captain the night before. As he recalled the event, the captain gave him command of the boat. Eads directed that five or six hawsers be attached to stout trees on the shore and to three steam-powered capstans on the bow. The maneuver, with additional help from several steamboats, eventually freed the *Benton,* although in the process a link of chain, more than one inch thick, snapped into three pieces, one of which pierced the captain's arm. The *Benton* proceeded to Cairo. Foote wanted a more powerful vessel and ordered new engines installed. On 24 February 1862 he commissioned the *Benton,* and the boat served as his flagship until he took sick leave in May. [7]

On 15 January 1862 Commodore Foote officially accepted Eads's seven gunboats into service. They were the first warcraft—boat or ship—to be specifically built as ironclads, and they saw action at Forts Henry and Donelson in less than a month. The *Carondelet* and the other six gunboats carried crews of 159 sailors and several officers. A study of the crew of the *Cairo* revealed that 47 men came from the city of Cairo, 43 came from New York City, and 19 from Boston. St. Louis contributed 8 crewmen. More than one-third of the crew were foreign-born, with Irishmen making up the largest contingent, 17. As the gunboats pressed farther south, contraband slaves also joined the crews.[8]

Even on the more spacious *Benton,* quarters below deck were cramped. Foote's successor, Charles Henry Davis, described the captain's quarters; he found them small and "not well situated." Located amidships, he had the ship's pantry and galley on one side of him and a contingent of marines on the other. "I am exposed to all the noises, sights, and smells of the vessel," he complained. Worse, the captain had no privacy. If he "let down the blinds and opened the doors" the entire crew could look in on him. If he left the blinds and doors shut, the air was stifling. "Added to these inconveniences," reported the unhappy commander, "the cabin is dark."[9] Life on a river gunboat clearly differed from life aboard a seagoing vessel.

Captain and crew undoubtedly welcomed the opportunity to emerge from the dark confines of the gundeck and the hold. When not exposed to enemy fire, gunboat crews extended their living space to the armor-plated roof of the gundeck. Sailors attached laundry lines to the flagstaffs and erected canvas awnings to provide shelter from the sun.[10]

After the Battle of Belmont, Missouri, in November 1861 Grant prepared his force at Cairo for what he expected would be an advance against Confederate forces at Columbus, or farther east, at Forts Henry and Donelson. When Halleck replaced Frémont in January 1861, Grant had traveled to St. Louis to present his plan for an assault on the two forts. He returned disappointed; Halleck seemed as cautious as Frémont had been. Events soon took a positive turn, however. Acting under orders from General McClellan to support Don Carlos Buell, who commanded the Department of the Ohio from headquarters at Louisville, Grant took the opportunity to move on his own authority against Henry and Donelson. Foote's flotilla of gunboats proved to be essential in the campaign.

A few days before Foote officially took command of the gunboats, the *Essex* and the *St. Louis* engaged in a skirmish that illustrated the important role that they would play in the fight to control the Mississippi Valley. On 11 January 1862, the commander of the *Essex*, Captain W. D. Porter, learned that steamers were heading north from Columbus towing an artillery battery. The Confederates evidently intended to extend their defensive positions north toward Cairo, and the *Essex* and the *St. Louis* headed downstream to meet them. When the Confederate boats came into view, the largest of the group of three fired a heavy shell-gun and sent a projectile ricocheting off a sandbar to within 200 feet of the Union gunboats. As the Confederates came into closer range, the *St. Louis* fired on them with its rifle cannon and the *Essex*, too, opened fire with its bow guns. The Confederate steamers retreated, with the largest boat covering the withdrawal, "rounding to occasionally," in Porter's words, "and giving us broadsides." The *Essex* and the *St. Louis* continued their pursuit, however, until the Confederate gunboats reached the shelter of the Columbus batteries.[11]

On 2 February 1862, Grant sent half his force of 17,000 men aboard river steamers to a point about nine miles below Fort Henry on the east bank of the Tennessee River. Foote supported the operation with his flagship, the *Cincinnati,* and with the *Carondelet, Essex,* and *St. Louis.* Three timberclad gunboats also joined the federal flotilla as escorts for the troop transports. By 10:00 P.M. 5 February, all the troops had arrived at the rendezvous point, and Grant ordered an attack on Fort Henry to begin at 11:00 A.M. the next day. That night Grant positioned a brigade to the rear of Fort Heiman, a Confederate fortification on the west bank of the Tennessee. There the Union troops occupied ground that was higher than Fort Henry, directly across the river. At 11:00 A.M. 6 February federal troops and gunboats advanced in unison against the fort. The troops attempted to invest it from the east while the gunboats began an attack from the river. The brigade advancing on Fort Heiman found the place evacuated. Grant learned that the Confederates had also decided to evacuate Fort Henry, moving the bulk of their troops out of the range of the gunboats and placing them on the road to Fort Donelson. About 2:00 P.M., Confederate general Lloyd Tilghman boarded the *Cincinnati* and offered his surrender to Commodore Foote. Grant arrived an hour later to take command of Fort Henry.[12]

Although most of the Confederate soldiers at Fort Henry made their way to Donelson to continue the fight, its capture gave federal forces access to a river that remained navigable as far upstream as Muscle Shoals in northern Alabama. Grant reported that all the gunboats had been hit repeatedly in the attack on Fort Henry but that the damage generally had been slight. The exception was the converted snag boat *Essex,* which took a shell in its boiler and exploded, leaving forty-eight soldiers and sailors dead or wounded. Grant ordered the *Carondelet* to continue up the Tennessee to destroy the bridge of the Memphis and Ohio Railroad.

The fall of Fort Henry had been accomplished almost entirely by Foote's gunboats. The force that Grant had landed with the intent of investing the fort had been unable to advance due to the heavily wooded terrain and high water that flooded the shoreline. The bombardment by the gunboats disabled seven of Tilghman's big guns and convinced him that he could not continue to hold his position. One of the Confederate officers reported that the attack of the gunboats "exceeded in terror anything that the imagination had pictured of shot and shell, plowing roads through the earthworks and sandbags, dismantling guns . . . setting on fire and bringing down buildings within the fortification, and cutting in two, as with a scythe, large trees in the neighborhood."[13]

On 7 February Grant moved his force overland against Fort Donelson on the Cumberland River, about a dozen miles to the east. He led a reconnaissance party along the two roads that linked Fort Henry to the town of Dover and to Fort Donelson, two miles south of the town. He found Donelson a formidable fortification. It occupied about 100 acres, including a bluff high above the Cumberland River. The Confederate engineers protected the fort's guns well by cutting into the bluff that rose as high as 100 feet above the river. To the north and south of the fort were ravines fully flooded by the high water. To the west, Confederate rifle pits controlled a ridgeline running north and south. Abatis protected the two defiles that cut through the ridge.

Foote's flotilla moved on toward Donelson with several troop transports. Grant advanced overland from Fort Henry with 15,000 men and invested Fort Donelson from the west. He faced 21,000 Confederate soldiers well entrenched in the rifle pits and in the fort. On 13 February the *Carondelet* arrived in front of Donelson and fired its bow guns from long range. That night Foote arrived aboard the *St. Louis* (now his flagship), with the *Louisville* and the *Pittsburg*. The damage sustained by the *Essex* and *Cincinnati* at Fort Henry had not been repaired in time for them to participate in the fighting at Donelson.[14] Grant recalled his objectives as the battle at Fort Donelson unfolded:

> The plan was for the troops to hold the enemy within his lines while the gunboats should attack the water batteries at close quarters and silence his guns if possible. Some of the gunboats were to run the batteries, get above the fort and above the village of Dover. . . . That position attained by the gunboats it would have been but a question of time—and a very short time, too—when the garrison would have been compelled to surrender.[15]

As planned, Foote began his bombardment at 3:00 P.M. on 14 February. Grant had a clear view of the advancing boats and saw that they fell back under a withering fire that badly damaged several of them, including Foote's. The *St. Louis* sustained fifty-nine hits. One shell struck the pilothouse, killed a pilot, and injured Foote. As the commander descended to the gundeck to have his wound dressed, another shell struck the *St. Louis* below the waterline and wounded him in the left arm. The *St. Louis* drifted out of action, as did the *Louisville*. As the *Carondelet* fought on, a rifled gun exploded, scattering dead and wounded across the gundeck. The men could not work the guns without slipping in the blood of their fallen comrades. As the fighting died down at Donelson, Foote left for Cairo with the most badly damaged gunboats. The *St. Louis* and the *Carondelet* remained on the Cumberland to protect the troop transports.[16] Grant described the action as he and the Confederate defenders saw it unfold: "The leading boat got within a very short distance of the water battery, not further off I think than two hundred yards, and I soon saw one and then another of them dropping down the river, visibly disabled."[17]

The fighting at Donelson exposed a weakness of the gunboats. As Grant noted, he had planned for the boats to silence the water batteries and then move upstream to occupy Dover, thus cutting off the Confederate garrison from any line of supply. But the gunboats could elevate their cannon only slightly, a limitation that prevented them from menacing the Confederate artillery positioned high on the bluff. Moreover, shot fired from the bluff hit the gunboats on the top of the gundeck housing, where it could not be deflected, by its angled sides, as was shot fired from the water batteries. Rear Admiral Henry Walke, commander of the *Carondelet*, led the assault on Donelson and kept his boat in action despite heavy damage. He recalled that his crew were mostly Philadelphians, with a sizable contingent of Bostonians and "just enough men-o'-war's men to leaven the lump with naval discipline." The crew of the *Carondelet* fought well, as did the men on the *Pittsburg* and the *St. Louis*. All the gunboats sustained heavy damage. In Walke's description, the shot fired from the bluff "knocked the plating to pieces, and sent fragments of iron and splinters into the pilots." As the *Carondelet* circled and fired broadsides into the water batteries, shot from the bluff shattered flagstaffs and smokestacks and tore off the boat's side armor "as lightning tears the bark from a tree." Overall, eleven men in the flotilla died at Fort Donelson and fifty-three were wounded. Half the casualties had occurred on the hard-fighting *Carondelet*.[18] As night fell on 14 February the Confederates wired Richmond that they had won a great victory. Grant retired for the night, uncertain of the outcome of the engagement. With the gunboats out of action, and Dover unoccupied, he feared that Donelson could withstand a lengthy siege.

Early the next morning Grant received a note from Foote explaining that he was injured and asking that Grant meet with him on his flagship. There, Foote explained the necessity of returning his boats to Mound City for repairs. He would return, he said, within ten days. Grant prepared for siege. But the gunboats had had a greater effect on the Confederate defenders at Donelson than it first appeared. Fearing that they would be trapped between Grant's army to the west and Foote's gunboats to the east, the Confederates attempted to break through the federal lines. Grant witnessed the action as he returned from his meeting with Foote. Sensing that the Confederate thrust to the federal center exposed the defenses of the fort, Grant ordered an attack on the Confederate right. The federal advance proved to be decisive as the Confederate's attempt faltered and then failed. The advance on the Confederate right succeeded. By the evening of 15 February federal forces occupied the Confederate rifle pits on the federal left and prepared to take the fort itself the next morning. During the night Confederate generals John Floyd and Gideon Pillow escaped with about 3,000 men to Nashville. Cavalry commander Nathan Bedford Forrest also escaped with his mounted troop of about 1,000 men. General Simon Bolivar Buckner, whom Grant knew well, surrendered the fort on 16 February. The route to Nashville had been opened.[19]

The capture of Forts Henry and Donelson forced Confederate commander Albert S. Johnston to withdraw from central Tennessee. Their fall also forced Leonidas Polk to withdraw his outflanked garrison of 20,000 men from Columbus. Federal forces commanded by Buell advanced from Louisville to Nashville, and Grant moved his army of 40,000 men up the Tennessee River to Pittsburg Landing, about twenty miles north of the rail junction at Corinth, Mississippi. Eads's gunboats moved onto the Mississippi while a Tennessee River flotilla of 200 transports and 14 small gunboats supported Grant's army.[20]

Foote advanced with the *Pittsburg* and the *Carondelet*—and by 24 February the *Benton*—to the confluence of the Ohio and Mississippi. On 14 March his flotilla of eight gunboats, ten mortar boats, and several transports steamed down the Mississippi to Columbus, where 2,000 federal troops joined his expedition. The next day Foote arrived at Island Number 10. Polk reinforced the Confederate position at New Madrid and fortified the island (about fifty miles downstream from Columbus). Here the meandering Mississippi made a horseshoe bend to the north before doubling back again to the south. Island Number 10 lay at the bottom of the first bend. Confederate general John

P. McCowan had arrived on the island from Columbus on 26 February and begun the task of overseeing the construction of new defenses. Polk concentrated troops and heavy guns from Columbus on the island and sent additional reinforcements upstream from Fort Pillow. McCowan placed two artillery batteries on the island—a strip of land about 1 mile long and 450 yards wide—and five batteries across the river on the Tennessee shore. A floating battery of nine guns lay anchored on the north side of the island.[21]

While McCowan prepared his defenses, federal general John Pope landed an army by steamboat above Sikeston (about 150 miles south of St. Louis) to strike Confederate defenses at New Madrid, a location he described as "the weak point of the system of defense on and around Island No. 10." With New Madrid under federal control, the fortified island would be cut off from its downstream line of supply. From Sikeston, Pope marched "as fast as possible" to New Madrid, fighting a running battle over the distance of twenty miles. The Confederates at New Madrid fought determinedly, twice driving back federal attacks on 2 and 3 March. On 6 March Pope sent a force of 3,000 men around New Madrid to Point Pleasant, a river town further downstream, where he hoped to begin to cut the Confederate line of supply.

On 12 March after receiving heavy guns from Cairo, Pope began a determined daylong bombardment of Confederate positions at New Madrid. Convinced that the position could not be held, McCowan ordered its evacuation the next night. An elated General Pope occupied the town on 14 March and took possession of thirty-two pieces of artillery left behind by the hastily departing Confederates. The next day Foote deployed two of his mortar boats and began his attack on Island Number 10. On 16 March he began long-range shelling, although his pilots struggled against the current. The next day Foote attempted to increase the stability of the gunboats by lashing the more powerful *Benton* between the *Cincinnati* and *St. Louis*. In this configuration they advanced to within 200 yards of the closest Confederate battery. In the ensuing fight, the *Benton* took five hits, the *Cincinnati* one, and a rifled gun exploded on the *St. Louis*, leaving fifteen men dead or wounded. Several of the Confederate guns were disabled in the federal attack, but the rebel batteries were far from being silenced. As evening fell, Foote withdrew. He later reported to Halleck that "this place is stronger and even better adapted for defense than Columbus was."

Once in control of New Madrid, Pope wanted to move his army of 25,000 men across the Mississippi and attack the Confederate batteries on the Tennessee shore from the rear. On 17 March he asked Foote to run the Confederate battery with two or three gunboats to help protect the crossing; Foote declined the request. Three days later, however, he asked his gunboat commanders their advice and found that only Walke of the *Carondelet* thought the maneuver possible. In frustration, Pope ordered the construction of a canal to bypass the fortified island.

By 1 April Pope's engineers had completed a six-mile canal fifty feet wide but only four feet deep. The troop transports could use it, but not the gunboats. The next day, after the transports and supply barges had been brought though the canal, Pope prepared to cross the Mississippi without the aid of the gunboats. That decision forced Foote into action, and he directed Walke to "avail yourself of the first foggy or rainy night" and run the battery. On 4 April at 10:00 P.M., with all vulnerable points protected with sacks of coal, stacks of cordwood, bailed hay, and chain cable (to strengthen the armor of the pilothouse), the *Carondelet* set out with the veteran riverman, William B. Hoel, as the new pilot. A fire in one of the smokestacks illuminated the vessel and threatened to give it away. Walke closed the flue caps and extinguished the blaze. But the flames shot out again as soon as the flue caps were opened, and Confederate gunners soon opened fire.

The Confederate batteries succeeded in hitting the *Carondelet* twice as it passed around the bend, but the boat sustained no damage. As Walke rounded the second bend in the river and approached New Madrid, he fired his guns in a prearranged pattern to announce his arrival as a federal gunboat. By 1:00 A.M. the *Carondelet* had been secured at the New Madrid landing. Pope immediately asked Foote to send more gunboats. The "lives of thousands of men" and the success of the federal campaign "hang upon your decision." Reluctantly, Foote ordered the *Pittsburg* to join the *Carondelet* below Island Number 10. The *Pittsburg* left Foote's flotilla at 2:00 A.M. on 7 April in a heavy thunderstorm and arrived at New Madrid three hours later. The same day, the *Carondelet* and *Pittsburg* silenced the Confederate batteries opposite New Madrid, and the federal crossing began. On 8 April, as Pope advanced against the rear of the shore batteries, the Confederate defense of Island Number 10 collapsed. He took 5,000 prisoners as Confederates attempted to escape around the advancing federals on the Tennessee side of the river and through the swamps and shallows on the Missouri side.

Although Foote had doubted its effectiveness, the bombardment by the gunboats had badly demoralized the Confederate garrison on the island. On

17 March, a week after the gunboat attack began, the regimental surgeon with the Forty-sixth Tennessee wrote to his wife that "our officers tell the men openly that we are whipped and that we will be taken prisoners." After four more days of shelling, the doctor reported that he was overwhelmed with requests for medical discharges and sick leave. At least one of the one hundred fifty requests came from a man whom he and his wife knew: "Jimmy Coney has been after me for two or three days, but I have positively refused and I recon [sic] that he will be an enemy forever—But he is in better health than I ever saw him and looks as stout as anybody."[22]

After the Battle of Shiloh and the subsequent Confederate withdrawal from Corinth, Grant moved his headquarters to Memphis. Foote received a promotion to rear admiral in recognition of his successes at Forts Henry and Donelson and at Island Number 10, but he continued to suffer from the wounds he had received at Donelson. The fifty-six-year-old commander took sick leave early in May. Captain Charles H. Davis took command of the gunboats until David D. Porter became commander of the Mississippi Squadron five months later. When Davis arrived on board the *Benton* on 9 May, he found Foote bedridden and very ill. His wounded foot in particular caused him great pain. He appeared "thin and worn," and he suffered from digestive disorders brought on, as Davis thought, by the fetid atmosphere of the lower Mississippi Valley. Foote returned home in the vain hope of recuperating. He died on 26 June 1863.[23]

The federal campaign at Island Number 10 demonstrated that on the lower Mississippi the greater power of the *Benton* produced superior maneuverability in comparison with the seven original gunboats. With federal forces advancing toward Vicksburg, the War Department contracted with Eads to convert two large side-wheelers, the *Lafayette* and the *Choctaw,* into ironclad gunboats at the Carondelet shipyard. Both were commissioned at Cairo in fall 1862. Walke took command of the *Lafayette.* Also that fall, the War Department transferred the river navy from the Department of the Army to the Department of the Navy. Because the navy already had a ship commissioned as the *St. Louis,* Eads's gunboat of the same name became the *Baron Dekalb.* Two of Eads's original seven gunboats, the *Cairo* and the *Dekalb,* were sunk by Confederate torpedoes on the Yazoo River above Vicksburg.[24]

In the spring campaigns of 1862, when the effectiveness of the gunboats became apparent, the War Department contracted with Eads to build a lighter class of ironclad, capable of ascending the Tennessee and Cumberland Rivers to escort federal troop and supply boats. For this purpose, Eads built the *Osage* and the *Neosho*. With gunwales only six inches above the waterline to minimize the need for heavy plating, the boats presented a very low profile in the water. The superstructure protecting the gundeck curved above the gunwales about four feet in height and carried one-inch iron armor. The sides carried two-and-one-half-inch armor from the top of the gunwales to a depth of two-and-one-half-feet below the waterline. In place of the gunports that adorned the larger gunboats, the *Osage* and *Neosho* carried a revolving turret that contained two eleven-inch guns protected by six inches of iron plate. The turrets rose only a few feet above the deck cover. Fully armed and loaded, these boats drew only three-and-one-half feet of water.[25]

When he contracted to build these smaller boats, Eads had hoped to install steam turrets of his own design. But the relative success of the ironclad *Monitor* in Hampton Roads in March convinced the War Department that the turret designed by its builder, Swedish-born inventor John Ericsson, should be installed in the new gunboats. Eads continued to advocate his turret design, however, and the War Department eventually agreed to allow its limited use. As Eads undertook to build the *Osage* and *Neosho*, he also contracted with the War Department to build larger versions with two gun turrets. These propeller-driven gunboats were intended for service on the lower Mississippi. The *Chickasaw, Milwaukee, Winnebago,* and *Kickapoo* each had one turret of Ericsson's design and one of Eads's design.

Eads designed his turret to overcome operational difficulties inherent in Ericsson's design. Ericsson constructed his turrets with one-inch sheets of rolled wrought iron bolted together to a thickness of from eight to fifteen inches. A central shaft ran from the roof of the turret to the keel. Tie rods transferred the weight on the turret to the central shaft, and gears located below the gundeck allowed the turret to rotate. It soon became evident, however, that the interface between the turret and the deck produced problems.

Beneath the deck armor, the turret met a bronze ring that was cut into the wooden deck and milled flush with it. Turnbuckles enabled the turret engineer to adjust the weight of the turret on the ring. When the gunboat was under way, the engineer kept the full weight of the turret on the ring to prevent water, washing over the boat's low gunwales, from flooding the gun deck. In action, the weight of the turret on the bronze ring would be reduced to facilitate rotation. In practice, however, the turret frequently jammed. Applications of hot tallow inside and out sometimes provided sufficient lubrication, but friction between the turret and the bronze track produced problems that could not be fully solved.[26]

Other problems with the Ericsson design also became apparent as gunboats fitted with his turrets came under enemy fire. To keep the turret's bolts from being shot away, Ericsson positioned them with the nuts on the inside. When hit by enemy shot, the nuts often broke loose and shot across the gundeck like musket balls; to protect themselves, sailors fashioned interior wood sheathing. Moreover, when the boat was in action, the gunports on the turret remained open, exposing the gunners to musketfire as they cleaned and reloaded the cannon.

Eads offered solutions to each of these problems. He used eight sheets of one-inch rolled iron and had the two inner layers riveted together. The six outer layers were then drilled with tapered holes and screwed into threaded holes that had been drilled into the rivets of the inner layer. The tapered holes in the outer layers helped to prevent the screws from being hammered by enemy shot into the inner layers. The inner layer of riveted armor provided added protection. Eads also fashioned trip levers for the gunport stoppers in his turrets. The levers automatically opened the stoppers as the cannon were run into position, and they automatically closed the stoppers when the cannon recoiled after being fired.

Eads solved the problem of friction by positioning the base of the turret on a track of ball bearings located just above the keep on the flat-bottomed boat. This configuration did away with the awkward central shaft and tie rods in Ericsson's design. It also increased the vertical dimension of the turret while maintaining a two-foot lower profile than Ericsson's. The added vertical size of Eads's turret permitted him to install a steam-powered hydraulic cylinder to raise and lower the gundeck. The hydraulic lift raised the guns to their firing position and lowered them to the hold. In the hold, two stationary galleries on either side of the movable turret allowed sailors to clean and load the cannon without being exposed to enemy fire. Steam-powered gun carriages ran the cannon into position and controlled their recoil; steam power also rotated the turret. To reduce the boat's overall weight, Eads's turret carried eight inches of armor only where it rose above the deck armor. Below it, he reduced the thickness of the turret wall to one inch. The turret also required one-third of the crew needed to operate the *Monitor.* Six men operated Eads's turret—three men on the gundeck and three men below deck. It also fired much faster than Ericsson's model. As the guns in Eads's turrets attacked fortified positions, they appeared to produce a continuous stream of fire.

The launching of gunboats at Carondelet became occasions for popular celebrations. Crowds of St. Louisans gathered for the events, probably at the invitation of Eads, and they undoubtedly enjoyed the opportunity to examine these powerful new machines of war. The launching of the *Chickasaw* on 12 February 1864 offered one such opportunity, although it ended in unexpected disarray and death. About 200 men and women boarded it as workers prepared to knock out the stays that held it in dry dock. As the boat slipped into the Mississippi River, sailors put out the anchor. The anchor rope, coiled at the bow, played out quickly, and a portion of it swept across the deck at the bow as it pulled tight. Seeing the danger, the commander called for the visitors at the bow to move aft. Several people did so too slowly. The anchor rope pulled many people into the river, including Jennie Eads, the daughter of the boat's builder, and O. B. Filley, the son of the former mayor O. D. Filley. Sailors plucked most of the victims from the water, but one woman drowned in the accident.[27]

With the fall of Vicksburg on 4 July 1863, federal forces had cleared the last major obstacle to Union control of the lower Mississippi Valley. On 23 July, after several commercial vessels made the journey from St. Louis to New Orleans without encountering enemy attack, Treasury Secretary Salmon P. Chase authorized the Customs House in St. Louis to "clear boats and cargoes, except on prohibited articles, for New Orleans." Although the government continued to require shippers to post bonds to secure their promises not to land without authorization at "intermediate points," St. Louisans rejoiced that the Mississippi had been reopened to commerce.[28]

The ironclads had been indispensable in securing this outcome. Eads and St. Louis artisans had been indispensable as well. Federal forces deployed one hundred twenty gunboats on western waters during the Civil War; twenty-two of these carried sufficient armor to be considered ironclads. Fourteen of the ironclads had been built at Eads's Carondelet shipyard, and he shared in the design of four others at Mound City. His ability to meet the exacting production schedule he set for himself owed a great deal to the willingness of the artisans he employed to work long hours. The enthusiasm that characterized the early years of the war also aided the enterprise. Even so, Eads offered substantial cash bonuses to the men who stayed with the work, reportedly thus paying out several thousands of dollars.[29]

A visitor to the shipyard in 1862 noted the intense pace of work. Dr. John Lauderdale of the army's Medical Department toured the shipyard in August. Since that spring, he had been stationed on the army hospital boat the *D. A. January*. He remained in his cabin as his ship was drawn into dry dock at Carondelet for caulking and other repairs. Before making his way back into the city, Lauderdale walked through the yard that covered more than twenty acres and included engine shops, sawmills, a gas works, and machinery for shaping the iron plates used to armor the gunboats.[30] Lauderdale saw the *Osage* and *Neosho* in production and "pretty near ship shape." The *Milwaukee* and the *Choctaw* remained in the early stages of construction, with "hulls . . . not much more than laid." It was a hot day, with the mercury rising to 100 degrees in the shade. Nevertheless, Lauderdale found the boats "alive with men who are working away in the hot sun." The scene of nine men hauling a large section of iron plate into position to be riveted particularly impressed him. The "business of riveting," he observed, employed a great many men and a surprising number of boys. He thought that boys were employed because they could run faster than adults as they brought the hot rivets to the workers who drove them home. He found it an amusing sight to see the blacksmiths pull white-hot rivets from the forge and "pitch them over among the boys." As he watched the boys scamper about, Lauderdale "wondered that they did not get hit with them."[31]

Although Lauderdale found the behavior of the blacksmiths toward the boys curious but amusing, what he saw may have reflected an underlying tension at the boatyard that he did not recognize. Less than two years later, by the time of the *Chickasaw*'s launching accident in February 1864, major outbreaks of labor unrest disrupted manufacturing enterprises in St. Louis and across the North. As labor leader William Sylvis later noted, "The nationalism which maintained class peace behind Union lines, had worn thin by the mid-point of the Civil War."[32] Early in 1864 that sense of nationalism disappeared. Wartime inflation represented an underlying problem, and labor shortages, over time, created unprecedented antagonisms between workers and employers. Indexed to 1860, prices rose 56 percent by 1864 and 68 percent by 1865. Wages also rose, but not nearly as fast. Indexed to 1860, wages rose 30 percent by 1864 and 50 percent by 1865. In late winter and early spring 1864, strikes swept across the North. A clerk at the McCormick plant in Chicago reported that April, "Our molders are going on their fourth strike for an advance in wages since last fall." When strikes seemed to threaten the federal war effort, Lincoln's administration did not hesitate to deploy soldiers as strikebreakers. In March 1864, workers at the West Point Foundry in Cold Springs, New York, went on strike for higher wages. The lessee and manager of the plant was Robert P. Parrott, an 1824 graduate of West Point who began managing the foundry in 1839. There he had developed a reinforced cast-iron rifled cannon and an expanding projectile to take the rifling. During the Civil War the War Department ordered thousands of Parrott guns of various caliber and Parrott projectiles ranging from 10 to 300 pounds. The threatened disruption in the production of these weapons brought a quick end to the strike. Two companies of federal troops occupied Cold Springs. The commander declared martial law and jailed the strike leaders. The workers returned to the foundry at their old wages.[33]

Labor discontent in St. Louis also led to military intervention in spring 1864. Perhaps because the editors feared military censorship, the English-language newspapers reported the problem through third parties. The *Democrat* reprinted a story from the *Belleville [Illinois] Miner,* to report that "the machinists and blacksmiths of St. Louis, as well as the tailors and shoemakers of the same city are now out on strike." The workers had begun "uniting for complete recognition of their individual and collective rights."[34] The tailors and shoemakers demanded higher wages, but the machinists and blacksmiths also complained that there were "too many boys in their workshops." These complaints struck a positive chord among journeymen in all the trades. A Mass Meeting of Mechanics at the rotunda of the courthouse included stove- and hollowware molders, machine molders, brass finishers and molders, carpenters and joiners, ship carpenters and caulkers, brick molders, steam- and gas-pipe fitters, paper hangers, horseshoers, plasterers, painters, tinners, and members of the typographical union.[35]

The journeymen tailors had been the first to stop work. They demanded increased wages, a recognition of their union, and an end to the wartime practice of hiring girls as apprentices. The merchant tailors rejected the workers' demands and responded to the strike by organizing the Merchant Tailors Association, through which they collectively resolved not to negotiate with the journeymen. The journeymen should not dictate the terms of their employment, said the merchant tailors, and they had no right to bar women from the shops. The journeymen responded that they would continue to demand recognition of their union. As for a rise in the rate of pay, they explained that they wanted, for example, $1.50 more than the current rate of $8.50 for a fine dress coat. It took about four ten-hour days to make such a coat, they said, and the increased rate they demanded would allow them to earn $2.50 a day. As for the female apprentices, the journeymen insisted that they did not object to the presence of women in the shops, only to the fact that the merchants paid the female apprentices less than male apprentices. If the merchants insisted on employing women, they should be paid the same rate as men.[36]

As the strike progressed, the journeymen struggled to maintain their unity. At a mass meeting, held four weeks after the strike began, journeymen listened to speeches in English, German, and French. The president of the journeymen tailors' union told the gathering that the merchants were willing to increase the rate of pay but that they were unwilling to recognize the union and would not stop hiring women at low pay. The merchants, said the labor leader, thought that they could break the union because the journeymen were divided by national origin. He reminded the strikers that they had succeeded in uniting and that by continuing to stand together they could "hold firm until all of their demands were met."[37]

Late in March, journeymen shoemakers joined the growing strike. The Boss Shoemakers denounced the journeymen and insisted that they would not be dictated to and that they would "pay such wages as the journeymen may deserve." Having been journeymen themselves, the Boss Shoemakers explained, they knew "that each laborer is worth his wages—a superior one high wages, and an inferior one in proportion." By mid-April, however, the *Republican* reported that in the shoemakers' strike, most of the shops "acceded to the demand of the strikers, for an advance of 25 percent."[38]

The molders' strike against Giles and Oliver Filley's Excelsior Stove Works became a particularly bitter episode in the wider unrest. The Filleys stood at the forefront of the city's Republican leadership. Eads must have relied on their large shop to produce much of the iron armor for the federal gunboats. The strikers complained that the Filley brothers hired far too many boys as apprentices. With more boys in the shop than the journeymen could possibly train as molders, the practice degraded the trade. The Filleys hired the surplus apprentices only to perform simple tasks and not to learn the trade. J. S. Fincher, secretary of the National Union of Machinists and Blacksmiths, addressed a rally of St. Louis strikers on 7 April. Members of his union were on strike, he said, to keep their trade "perfect."[39]

In addition to the problem with the boys, the striking molders complained that the Filley brothers imported German molders and paid them a substandard wage. Giles and Oliver Filley responded to their workers' complaints by firing the leaders of the strike. Richard L. Parker, one of the striking molders, vented his anger at the strikers' rally. If he could, he said, he would ride the "scab covered Filley" like a broken-down nag. "That name Filley," continued Parker, "how it grates upon my feelings!" The Filleys had driven workmen from their shop "because they dared to exercise the right of freemen!" The Filleys had imported twenty-five German sand-molders and paid them two dollars a day. Parker rejoiced that eighteen of this group had found better employment, and he praised the immigrants who left the Filleys' shop as "an honor to the German population of St. Louis."[40]

On 18 April, Giles Filley published "Card-to-the-Public" in the *Republican* and the *Democrat*. He began by explaining the patriotic reasons for importing skilled workers in his St. Louis shop. The journeymen, he complained, had interfered with the freedom of the imported workers. When the German molders arrived at the Stove Company, a group of journeymen molders took "possession" of them and forced them to leave the boardinghouse that Filley had provided for them. The Germans had then been forced to join the journeymen's association. Fear of violence, he said, prevented the German workers from fulfilling their contract with him. He praised the men who continued to work in his shop (the men denounced as scabs by the striking journeymen) as "respectable and good men."[41]

For the people who sympathized with the employers, it seemed clear that the strikers took advantage of the fact that skilled workers were greatly in demand. George H. Frost, a railroad surveyor working in St. Louis at the time of the strike, believed that high wages made workers self-indulgent. "They are earning so much," he wrote his brother in June, "that they will not work half the time." He predicted that "as soon as the times change," the workers would suffer because "the bosses will show them no mercy."[42]

As it happened, the strikers felt the effects of their employers' wrath while demand for their labor remained strong. On 29 April 1864, General William Rosecrans, commander of the Department of the Missouri, issued General Orders, no. 65, and placed the workingmen of St. Louis under martial law. Speaking at a national labor convention in Chicago the following January, William H. Sylvis described Rosecrans's order as the product of a "combined effort on the part of the employers of the city." The bosses had persuaded Rosecrans, Sylvis believed, that "those engaged in the strike and in the union movement" were "disloyal men."[43]

Whether or not Rosecrans had acted at the direct behest of employers, Sylvis and the St. Louis strikers correctly concluded that nothing in the general's order favored the workers. Rosecrans attacked the unions as "organizations led by bad men," and he blamed these "combinations" for attacking "private rights and the military power of the nation." These men prevented "journeymen mechanics, apprentices, and laborers from working" unless the employers accepted the rates of pay and the rules for "internal management" dictated to them by the unions. The strikes interrupted the production of articles "required for use in the navigation of the Western waters, and in the military, naval and transport service of the United States." Therefore, Rosecrans directed, "No person shall directly or indirectly" try to stop a person from working "on such terms as he may agree upon" in any "manufacturing establishment" where "any article is ordinarily made" that the U.S. military required for navigation or transportation. In addition, he directed that "no person shall watch around or hang about any such establishment for the purpose of annoying the employees there or learning who are employed there." He went further, to proscribe the unions themselves, ordering that "no association or combination shall be formed or continued, or meeting be held, having for its object to prescribe to the proprietors . . . whom they shall employ" or how to manage the operation of their shops. All workers would be provided with military protection against harassment or intimidation by union men. Finally, Rosecrans directed all employers in the city to supply him with a list of the names and addresses of the men who had gone on strike and of "all who have taken an active part in any combination." The commanding general placed Colonel J. H. Baker of the Eighteenth Minnesota Volunteers in charge of executing his edict.[44]

Neither the *Republican* nor the *Democrat* expressed an opinion in the matter, although both published translations of the harsh criticisms of Rosecrans's action that appeared in the German press. The *Neue Zeit* denounced the "military arbitrariness" of the order. The *Westliche Post* decried "an attack on the freedom of labor and the right of association." The *Anzeiger des Westens* warned that the order's "elastic nature" gave free reign to the "individual motives of the authorities." The order stunned the workingmen who responded, in evident trepidation, with a petition to Rosecrans asking that he include in his order a requirement that the employers hire no more than five apprentices for each journeyman. The German press, fearing military despotism more than the degradation of the trades, criticized the workingmen for acquiescing in martial law. The *Anzeiger* complained that the workers, in their narrow concern with conditions in the shops, "recognize the controlling power of the military authorities over peaceable citizens in a peaceable State: nay, they even request interference with civil liberty." The *Neue Zeit* similarly complained that the workingmen's petition tacitly accepted Rosecrans's authority in civil matters. The *Westliche Post* warned that the widespread use and acceptance of martial law threatened the United States with despotism.[45]

The strongest individual protest came from Carl Bernays, editor of the *Anzeiger*. He sent a copy of Rosecrans's order, together with a lengthy letter of protest, to President Lincoln. Bernays protested that Rosecrans had wrongly characterized the striking workers as disloyal men. It was true that the members of the iron-molders association persuaded their fellow workers to join the union and "strike for higher wages and for the adoption of their charter and rules by the manufacturers." But Bernays insisted that no evidence existed that the strikers acted "for disloyal purposes or to prevent work to be done which was ordered by the Government." Moreover, strikes elsewhere in the country had not resulted in military intervention. He mentioned New York City, Philadelphia, Cincinnati, Pittsburgh, and Troy and Albany, New York, where he thought the disruption of war-related production had been much greater than in St. Louis. He did not mention the military intervention that had ended the strike in the West Point Foundry in Cold Springs, New York, or the fact that General Stephen G. Burbridge in Louisville issued orders very similar to Rosecrans's. Bernays feared that federal authorities had come to regard St. Louis as conquered territory.

Bernays insisted that he had not taken sides in the labor dispute. He believed that the issues should be worked out by the parties involved, "and not by the sword of a military commander." He further explained that he "cheerfully" accepted the suspension of the writ of habeas corpus "to reach treason." Moreover, he accepted the "paramount right of the President to take extraordinary measures to put down this rebellion." But Rosecrans's order constituted an attack on the fundamental rights of loyal citizens. "We are not half through with the destruction of slavery," wrote Bernays, "and we already begin to attack free labor." He reminded the president that earlier in the war he had expressed his opinion to Oliver Filley that the federal government did not intend to "run churches." At that early point in the struggle, Bernays thought the president could not have imagined "that one of your military commanders might undertake to decide with the sword the greatest social question of the century." Running churches, in his view, paled in comparison to "running workshops or, rather, changing the entire character of the industrial life of the American nation." In the United States, he concluded, "slave and free labor have created all the capital." It would be disastrous if slavery and free labor "have to be destroyed totally or partially in order to maintain capital alone."[46] The social crisis of the late nineteenth century had become apparent in the last year of the Civil War.

9

"Slavery Dies Hard"

IN A FAMOUS PUBLIC LETTER to Horace Greeley, Abraham Lincoln on 22 August 1862 offered a succinct statement of his border state policy. Greeley had urged the president to enforce vigorously the Second Confiscation Act (passed by Congress that July) and to make emancipation the great moral foundation of the Northern war effort. Lincoln replied that his paramount purpose remained what it had been since the start of the war: "I would save the Union. . . . I would save it the shortest way under the Constitution. . . . If I could save the Union without freeing *any* slave, I would do it, and if I could save it by freeing *all* the slaves I would do it; and if I could save it by freeing some and leaving others alone I would also do that."[1]

When Lincoln wrote these words, he had already decided on an emancipation policy that abolished slavery in most of the Confederacy and that left it alone in the border states. He announced this policy on 22 September 1862, after the Union army had thwarted Lee's invasion of the North at the Battle of Antietam. He issued the Emancipation Proclamation on 1 January 1863. He had decided against freeing all the slaves, but the proclamation promised federal aid and protection for emancipated slaves. Moreover, the president committed his administration to an emancipation course that would soon embrace the recruitment of black troops. In an awkward but telling sentence that Lincoln had crossed out of his draft letter to Greeley, he warned that "broken eggs can never be mended, and the longer the breaking proceeds the more will be broken."[2] By summer 1863, the Union army actively recruited black troops in the North, in the border states, and in the occupied regions of the Confederacy. These developments created complex administrative problems in Missouri, where the interests of loyal slaveholders frequently came into conflict with the federal government's evolving emancipation course.

To the people who emerged as Radical Republicans in Missouri it seemed inevitable that slavery would be a casualty of the Civil War. But to those who formed the conservative wing of the party, the slavery issue raised difficult questions of equity for slave owners and of stability in a postemancipation society. St. Louis's leading conservatives—Attorney General Edward Bates and Postmaster General Montgomery Blair—exerted a powerful influence in Washington, D.C., over affairs at home. Of the two men, Bates followed the more conservative course. He fully supported the Harney-Price agreement, and he strongly resisted emancipation as a Union war aim. But by December 1861, he had lined up in support of Lincoln's proposal for compensated emancipation in the border states. In Bates's mind, however, emancipation remained firmly linked to colonization—that is, to the removal of African Americans from the United States. Bates feared that the alternative, emancipation without colonization, would lead to citizenship for blacks, an outcome that he found loathsome. Lincoln rejected Bates's recommendation that colonization be made a condition of the Emancipation Proclamation, heeding instead the recommendation of Secretary of War Edwin Stanton, who pointed out that freed slaves would provide an eager pool of recruits for the Union army. Nevertheless, Bates continued to believe that Lincoln sided with conservatives on the colonization issue, and he urged Missouri's governor, Hamilton Gamble, to cooperate with the administration to secure compensated emancipation and what Bates hoped would be a postwar program of colonization.[3]

The Blairs had differed with Bates on the issue of the Harney-Price agreement; they and their supporters had worked earnestly to have General Harney removed from command. The Blairs shared Bates's view that federal authorities in Missouri should protect the property rights of loyal slaveholders; indeed, it was Frank Blair who had pioneered the idea that compensated emancipation should be tied to a plan for colonization. It was in this spirit that his political ally, Thomas T. Gantt, lavishly commended Harney in May 1861 for his firm declaration that he would hold Missouri for the Union while protecting private property. Gantt's family traced its ancestry to Maryland though he himself had been born in Georgetown, in the District of Columbia. After a severe leg injury ended his West Point career in 1832, he turned his attention to the law. He entered the Maryland bar in 1838 and the next year moved to St. Louis. From 1839 to 1844 he practiced law in partnership with Montgomery Blair; in 1845, he succeeded Blair as U.S. district attorney. Gantt married Mary Carroll Tabbs of Maryland that same year (her grandfather, Charles Carroll of Carrollton, was one of the signers of the Declaration of Independence). He served as an unconditional Unionist delegate in the Missouri State Convention in 1861 and later held a staff position with General McClellan. Gantt returned to St. Louis in July 1862 and served (until November) as provost marshal general for the Department of the Missouri under the conservative command of General John M. Schofield.[4]

After thanking General Harney for his proclamation, Gantt had asked (on behalf of a slave-owning friend from Greene County) a more explicit question: did the U.S. government intend "to interfere with the institution of negro slavery in Missouri?" Harney replied that though he had no specific directions from the War Department on the matter, he did not expect his government to make any distinction between slave property and other forms of property. Harney cited the policy adopted by General Benjamin F. Butler in Maryland. "Already," he noted, "since the commencement of these unhappy disturbances slaves have escaped from their owners, and have sought refuge in the camps of United States troops from Northern states and commanded by a Northern General." When that happened General Butler saw to it that the slaves "were carefully sent back to their owners." Moreover, Butler promised the protection of federal troops in the event of any slave insurrection. "I repeat it," Harney concluded in his reply to Gantt, "I have no special means of knowledge on this subject, but what I have cited." Yet the commander felt certain that it was Lincoln's intention to protect slavery where it existed in the loyal states.[5]

Missouri slaveholders (comprising less than 10 percent of the white families in the state) were reassured as well by Hamilton Gamble's first official act as governor. In a proclamation issued on 3 August 1861, he promised to maintain peace and stability in the state and full protection of slave property: "No countenance will be afforded to any scheme or to any conduct calculated in any degree to interfere with the institution of Slavery existing in the State. To the very utmost extent of Executive power, that institution will be protected."[6]

In September, General Frémont's emancipation order briefly excited a radical opposition (particularly among the St. Louis Germans) to the conservative policy outlined by Harney, supported by Bates and Blair, and vigorously enforced by Gamble. However, the conservatives' sweeping victory over Frémont ensured that his successor, General Henry W. Halleck, would restore the conservative policy favored by most Missouri Unionists and, for the time being, by President Lincoln. After taking command of the new Department of the Missouri, Halleck issued General Orders, no. 3 (20 November 1861), in which he excluded from Union camps all persons not explicitly authorized to be there. Foremost on Halleck's list were fugitive slaves from loyal masters. Like his fellow commanders in Kentucky, Virginia, and Maryland, Halleck intended his order to separate the Union army from any involvement with slavery in the loyal state of Missouri.[7] But neutrality proved to be elusive. Wherever Union troops entered slave territory, slaves left their masters (whether they were Unionist or not) and offered their services to the federal forces. At Fortress Monroe, Virginia, General Butler admitted a growing number of slaves into his lines, proclaiming them to be "contraband of war"—that is, property useful to the enemy and legitimately confiscated by military authority. He drew a distinction between returning slaves to owners in the nominally loyal state of Maryland and confiscating slaves from openly disloyal Virginians. His policy, jokingly referred to by Lincoln as "Butler's Fugitive Slave Law," received the support of Secretary of War Simon Cameron and was soon codified by Congress in the First Confiscation Act in July 1861.

The Confiscation Act proved to be the entering wedge of federal emancipation policy, but its effects in Missouri were not immediately evident. Because Frémont had been chastised by Lincoln for exceeding the terms of the act, Halleck hoped to steer a neutral course by excluding blacks from military encampments. His exclusion order warned that "important information respecting the number and condition of our forces is conveyed to the enemy by means of fugitive slaves who are admitted within our lines." The commander therefore directed "that no such persons be hereafter permitted to enter the lines of any camp, or of any forces on the march, and that any now within such lines be immediately excluded therefrom." Halleck further directed the exclusion of "unauthorized persons of every description" and urged caution in the "employment of agents and clerks in confidential positions."[8]

Congressional responses to Halleck's exclusion policy revealed the division in Republican ranks that delineated the party's radical and conservative camps. The Pennsylvania ironmaster, Thaddeus Stevens, sharply criticized Halleck's effort to exclude fugitive slaves from federal lines. The Illinois congressman Owen Lovejoy joined in the criticism. However, rising to Halleck's defense was Frank Blair.[9]

In St. Louis, as in Congress, political factions began to take shape around the issues of emancipation and the rights of loyal slave owners. The radical faction, led by Frank Blair's cousin, B. Gratz Brown, and by another native Kentuckian, the St. Louis attorney Charles D. Drake, organized the General Emancipation Society of Missouri as a vehicle to criticize Lincoln's border state cautiousness and to press for immediate emancipation in Missouri. One member of the Emancipation Society, the St. Louis physician Rudolf Doehn, wrote to Frank Blair seeking clarification concerning the congressman's views on slavery. Aware that he risked losing significant support in the German community, Blair drafted a lengthy but familiar reply. He announced himself as "a friend" of emancipation who had always warmly embraced Thomas Jefferson's belief that the American Republic had no room for slaves. For emancipation to be successful, however, Blair believed that it must be "gradual in its operation" and accompanied by "compensation to loyal owners of slaves." Moreover, "Provision should be made for separation of the white and black races." He believed that "the people of Missouri will require the removal of the blacks as a condition precedent to their liberation."[10]

The St. Louis lawyer Lucien Eaton also joined the Emancipation Society and demonstrated the social impact of the northeastern elite, which had been enlarged in St. Louis during the 1850s. Eaton's parents were natives of Massachusetts who had migrated westward to New York and then to Iowa. He returned East to study law at Harvard and then moved to St. Louis in 1858. A member of William Greenleaf Eliot's Church of the Messiah, Eaton married Emily F. Partridge, daughter of the Western Sanitary Commission leader George Partridge. Eaton was quick to enlist as a volunteer under Nathaniel Lyon, and he participated in the capture of Camp Jackson. As the anniversary of that event approached, he joined the Emancipation Society. The proportion of Germans (like Doehn) at the first meeting worried him. Displaying the nativism of his Protestant New England roots, he feared that the society might "merge into a German ('Dutch') affair." But the level of German participation did not concern him at the second meeting, and for three days in mid-June he attended an Emancipation Convention in Jefferson City as a proud delegate of the Federal Emancipation Society of Missouri. This activity placed him in the radical camp, but he and the society avoided taking extreme positions. He noted in his diary that "the Convention in its proceedings was harmonious, [and] unanimous in its support of the immediate initiation of gradual emancipation." By supporting gradual abolition immediately begun, Eaton and the Emancipation Society distanced themselves from William Lloyd Garrison and the radical abolitionists who denounced slavery

and slaveholding as sin and demanded its immediate, uncompensated abolition. At the convention, observed Eaton, there had been "no ultra doctrines
broached."[11]

Although moderate in tone, the radical initiative on emancipation represented a significant challenge to Frank Blair's political leadership. He faced
reelection in fall 1862. With the *Westliche Post* and the *Missouri Democrat*
generally favorable toward emancipation and hostile to Blair's conservative
course, the congressman and his supporters took steps to generate a more
favorable press environment. Henry Boernstein, who had been rewarded for
his loyalty to the Republican Party with a consulship in Bremen, Germany,
returned to St. Louis at the urging of Blair's supporter Henry T. Blow. Blow,
too, had been rewarded for his support of Lincoln with an appointment as
U.S. minister to Venezuela. (Blow quickly decided that he did not want to
watch the momentous events taking place in Missouri and the United States
from such a distance; he returned to St. Louis early in 1862.)[12] Boernstein
joined his friend Carl Bernays (also recalled from a diplomatic post in Zurich)
to edit the *Anzeiger des Westens* as a counterweight in the German community to the radical *Westliche Post*. In August Frank Blair sold his one-sixth
interest in the *Missouri Democrat* and used the proceeds to launch a new
English-language newspaper, the *St. Louis Union*. Joining Blair in this new
venture were John How, Oliver D. Filley, and Peter Foy who took the position of editor. Earlier, Foy had been Gratz Brown's successor as editor of the
Missouri Democrat but had left that position to become (with Blair family
support) postmaster of St. Louis. Foy kept that job as he took on the new task
of editing the *Union*. Blair's efforts paid off. Population growth in the city
had produced two congressional seats in St. Louis County; Blow ran unopposed in the southern district and Blair squeaked out a narrow victory (by
153 contested votes) in the northern district.[13]

For the time being, Blair and his conservative allies prevailed over their
radical opponents. But Halleck's restrictive policy toward fugitive slaves soon
proved to be difficult to administer and gave the radicals fresh opportunities
to protest. Complications arose because some slaves had been admitted to
Union lines during Frémont's pursuit of Confederates in southwestern Missouri. They were said to have provided valuable information to federal forces,
and they required protection from vengeful masters. Early in October 1861
Colonel John C. Kelton in Boonville had sent several slaves by riverboat to
Jefferson City. The colonel informed the assistant adjutant general there that

they had given to an officer in his command "important information" that saved Union troops "from surprise." The slaves "now seek protection from their masters who threaten to kill them." The colonel believed that they could be usefully employed in Jefferson City "where they can work on the fortification." Later the Boonville slaves were sent to St. Louis, where they evidently were spared the effects of Halleck's subsequent exclusion order.[14]

Other fugitive slaves were not so fortunate. Lieutenant Colonel John S. Phelps, a slaveholding Douglas Democrat from Springfield (and later a Democratic governor of Missouri) commanded federal troops guarding the railhead at Rolla. A native of Connecticut, he entered the bar in 1835 and two years later moved to Springfield, where he bought land and slaves. In 1844 he won election to Congress and served in the House for the next eighteen years. The Phelps's home in Springfield served as a hospital following the Battle of Wilson's Creek; it was to his home that Nathaniel Lyon's body was carried.[15] Phelps enforced with conviction and alacrity Halleck's exclusion order. At his direction, citizens in the Rolla area brought in "four fugitive slaves, belonging to citizens in Southwest Missouri." He held them in his camp "for safe keeping, in order to be restored to their owners." Phelps's actions did not go unopposed. One of the slaves, a man named Kelly, had been employed as a servant by a soldier who believed the master, James Vaughn of Christian County, to be disloyal. The soldier's term of service expired, and he continued to employ Kelly as a servant in his home near Rolla. When Phelps had the black man seized, the former soldier protested to Secretary of War Cameron. "It is strange," he wrote, that "any part of the United States army here at Rolla is engaged hunting up & guarding the slaves of traitors while the secessionists are robbing & plundering loyal men in the western part of the state." On the other hand, from Phelps's point of view, Kelly and the other slaves had been stolen by Frémont's troops. Phelps had feared losing his own slaves as well and held "a portion" of them at the Rolla camp. "They feared," he insisted, "they might be stolen by persons in the Army," and they "fled to me for protection." He kept his slaves in his camp until he could "provide for their comfort and safety" elsewhere. As for the four "fugitive slaves," he awaited orders. Governor Gamble wanted them returned immediately to their owners, but Secretary Cameron, responding to the former soldier's complaint, telegraphed Phelps to hold them until the owners' loyalty could be determined.[16]

The complexities of the fugitive slave issue bedeviled Halleck, despite his best efforts to avoid controversy. On 18 December 1861, somewhat surprisingly, he invoked the exclusion order to direct the release of sixteen black men held in jail in St. Louis and advertised for sale under state law. This situation confronted Halleck with a conflict between the slave laws of Missouri and the First Confiscation Act. The slaves had been brought to St. Louis from southwestern Missouri by Frémont's troops. Following state law they had been placed in jail and their descriptions advertised. If they were not claimed by their masters within three months, Missouri law authorized the city sheriff to sell them to pay the cost of their incarceration. Because the City of St. Louis had been placed under martial law and the sheriff acted under the direction of the U.S. Army, Halleck concluded that the Confiscation Act "over-rules" Missouri's slave statutes and that the slaves were being "held in custody without the authority of law and contrary to General Order no. 3." Halleck directed that the prisoners be released. Thereafter, their status would be determined by the civil authorities of the state—state courts would decide whether or not they had been properly confiscated by the Union army. Halleck had carefully refrained from violating the rights of loyal slave owners: they could appeal to the "local civil tribunals of this State" for the return of their slave property. The "mandates" of the state courts, he concluded, "will always be duly respected by the Military authorities of this Department." Except where federal legislation required an officer to act—that is, to confiscate slaves employed to further the rebellion against the United States—"military officers . . . will avoid all interference with such questions."[17]

Halleck made every effort to maintain a neutral stance regarding slavery in Missouri, but a clear distinction between state and federal areas of responsibility proved to be impossible to define. His exclusion order directed officers not to harbor fugitive slaves, but they were not authorized to determine a black person's status. In an effort to comply with General Orders, no. 3, a commander near Rolla directed his subordinates to report to him that "having expelled all fugitive slaves there are none within their camps,—either male or female." Eight of the responses stated simply that there were no fugitives in their camps. The commander of the Second Ohio Battery took the opportunity to express his hostility toward blacks: "I am not a Nigger man [and] have had no fugitives in my Battery nor have none now and dont intend to have." However, another officer explained a more complex situation, one that once again required Halleck to elaborate upon his order. The officer reported that he had responded to the exclusion order by having all black persons in his camp examined. One woman, employed as a cook, had been claimed by an officer as the fugitive slave of his father-in-law. "In compliance with your order . . . she was given up to him." All the rest (who were valued servants) "claim and insist that they are *free*." The reporting officer found it impossible to determine otherwise. "Some of them, I have no question, are so; others I have as little doubt have been slaves—but no one is here to prove it." "In the absence of any direct evidence" that they were slaves, the officer hesitated "to conclude that they were slaves" and turn them out of his camp.[18]

The return of the female fugitive slave embarrassed Halleck's efforts to maintain neutrality regarding slavery, and he again attempted to bring clarity to his order. It was emphatically not the duty of an officer to deliver an alleged fugitive to "masters or pretended masters," he insisted. Congress had recently made this point explicit, and Halleck had fashioned his General Orders, no. 3, to comply with the congressional directive. "The object of these orders," he continued, "is to prevent any person in the Army from acting in the capacity of negro catcher, or negro stealer. . . . The relation between slave and his master, or pretended master is not a matter to be determined by military officers." It was for this reason that he had ordered that all fugitives be excluded from military camps, "to keep clear of such questions." Determinations concerning a person's status as a slave rested entirely with the civil authority in the state: "Masters or pretended masters, must establish the rights of property to the negroes as best they may, without our assistance or interference." At the same time, he judged it to be entirely proper for officers to employ blacks in their camps. "Orders no. 3," he concluded, "do not apply to the authorized private servants of officers, nor to negroes employed by proper authority in camps."[19]

The exclusion order, as Halleck explained it, prevented federal troops in Missouri from removing slaves from the control of masters, and it required officers to exclude from their camps blacks who sought protection from masters. Blacks who presented themselves as free persons could be admitted, however, particularly if they could provide useful labor. Once slaves entered federal camps, owners found that it was difficult to get them back. From his headquarters at Cairo, Illinois, General Ulysses S. Grant faced a largely hostile white civilian population in nearby Kentucky and Missouri. He acknowledged that General Orders, no. 3, required that he neither "ignore" nor "in any manner interfere with the constitutional rights of loyal citizens." But when he judged citizens not to be loyal, he did not feel it to be his duty to "in any manner contribute to their comfort." This policy extended to slavery. Masters and their agents, when any question of their loyalty existed, could not enter Union lines to search for their slaves, "much less . . . invoke our aid and assistance for any purpose whatever."[20] Grant had no intention of enmeshing himself in the fine points of what distinguished passive loyalty from active disloyalty, and he would not accommodate his command to civilian needs. He would not use his army actively to liberate slaves, but otherwise the exclusion order meant little to him.

The order could not override the emancipation implications of the First Confiscation Act, however. Early in 1862, Provost Marshal General Bernard G. Farrar and U.S. District Attorney James O. Broadhead acted jointly to free a group of slaves. Their action marked the first instance of wartime emancipation in Missouri and represented the first tentative step toward the wartime destruction of slavery throughout the state. Both Farrar and Broadhead were men with old Virginia ties. Although Farrar was a native St. Louisan himself, his father had been born in the Old Dominion and later settled in St. Louis as a physician. Farrar aligned himself politically with Frank Blair during the secession crisis and served as an aide to General Lyon during the capture of Camp Jackson. When Halleck took command, he appointed Farrar provost marshal general for the Department of the Missouri.[21] A generation older than Farrar, Broadhead was Virginia-born. The practice of law brought him into St. Louis in 1859.[22] During the secession crisis, he joined with Frank Blair to form the Committee of Safety; early in 1862 he accepted the appointment as U.S. district attorney.[23]

The objects of Farrar's and Broadhead's concern were a number of slaves held at the Gratiot Street prison after they had been captured with a group of Confederate soldiers. Farrar asked Broadhead for his opinion concerning the applicability of the Confiscation Act to the imprisoned slaves. In his February 1862 opinion, Broadhead noted that the act made no mention of emancipation. It stated only that masters who used their slaves' labor (or allowed it to be used) in the service of the rebellion, "shall *forfeit* his claim to such labor." Although the Confiscation Act provided for proceedings by tribunals of loyal citizens to dispose of property forfeited under its terms, Broadhead found "no provision for the case of slaves." Therefore, he reasoned, "It needs no argument to show that the evident intention of the act was to make the slave *eo instanti* free." No reason existed for "the military authorities to hold slaves thus seized." The willingness of a slave owner to allow his property to participate in "hostile service" became the slave's "deed of emancipation."[24]

A vigorous enforcement of the Confiscation Act might have significantly weakened slavery in Missouri. But the solicitude that Lincoln displayed toward loyal slaveholders ensured a cautious application of the law. Moreover, a concerted proslavery interest, composed of men who were conditional Unionists at best, gained power in the state as Governor Gamble sought a broad base of political support and as most of the federal troops from the neighboring free states left Missouri for battlefields farther south. In March 1862 the War Department briefly combined the Department of the Missouri with the larger Department of the Mississippi. In mid-April, Halleck assumed a field command, and on 1 June he created the Military District of the Missouri, placing General John M. Schofield in command. With Halleck's departure most of the free state troops stationed in Missouri departed as well. Schofield, a close ally of Governor Gamble, also commanded the Missouri State Militia. The two men urged Lincoln to permit the state militia to take sole charge of maintaining order in the state. Deeply worried by the prospect of losing federal military protection, a delegation of St. Louisans, led by Henry T. Blow, went to Washington, D.C., seeking a commander for Missouri who would work independently of the governor. Frank Blair supported the Blow delegation, having already expressed his opinion that "the State military organization should be disbanded as soon as practicable, and a military commander in the State authorized without respect to Gov. Gamble." Blair also had personal reasons for wishing to see an expanded federal military role in Missouri. As his wife, Apolline, noted in an August 1862 letter to her husband, they both hoped "to get rid of Schofield & Gamble" so that Lincoln "would make you military governor."[25]

Eventually, the effort to replace Schofield succeeded. However, from June through September 1862 Schofield, like Halleck before him, worked closely with Gamble to halt the erosion of slavery in Missouri. The Second Confiscation Act (passed in July 1862) confirmed what Broadhead had inferred concerning the First Confiscation Act—that slaves owned by enemies of the United States were free. But the issue of loyalty in Missouri was seldom clearcut. In October 1862, when an official of the St. Louis Customs House attempted to secure free papers for four slaves owned by Joseph Wright (the son of Confederate major Uriel Wright), he was told by Schofield's recently appointed provost marshal general, Colonel Thomas T. Gantt, that slaves could be freed under the terms of the new Confiscation Act only through the decree of a federal court "of competent jurisdiction."[26] Gantt, together with

Frank Blair, Samuel Glover, and James Broadhead, had begun to follow a conservative course on the issue of emancipation. They stood with Gamble, determined to protect the slave property of loyal masters. Without a positive finding of a master's disloyalty, Gantt insisted, slaves in Missouri would not be freed.

Largely due to complaints about the state militia and the continuing plague of guerrilla attacks across the state, Lincoln in September 1862 replaced Schofield with General Samuel R. Curtis, the victorious commander at the Battle of Pea Ridge in Arkansas the previous March. For the next eight months (until Lincoln restored Schofield to command in May 1863), the balance of power shifted to the proponents of emancipation. Curtis, a former Iowa congressman, left no doubt that he would enforce the emancipation provisions of the Confiscation Acts. He appointed Franklin A. Dick provost marshal general. In December 1862 Curtis issued orders summarizing the terms of the Second Confiscation Act and the War Department's directives concerning it. He then issued specific directions of his own to the district provost marshals throughout the state. The commander instructed them to protect the freedom of persons emancipated by the acts of Congress "against all persons interfering with or molesting them; and they will arrest all persons guilty of such conduct." When emancipated slaves were confined without criminal charges, it was the duty of provost marshals "to examine into all such cases, and report the facts to the Provost Marshal General." In an effort to protect the property rights of loyal slave owners, Curtis also required provost marshals to "take evidence as to the facts" and to fill out a form for each slave liberated under the terms of the Second Confiscation Act. An incident in central Missouri made the need for specific directions and firm enforcement clear. After the local provost marshal issued papers emancipating "a Negro who belongs to a Rebel," local authorities jailed the freed slave for sale to satisfy a debt of his former master. The commander at Jefferson City responded sternly. "You will order the release of the said negro *immediately,*" he directed the district provost marshal, "and see that your order is *promptly obeyed.*"[27]

As federal authorities enforced the emancipation provisions of the new act, the efforts of loyal slave owners to control their slave property became increasingly difficult. Lincoln's earlier offer, made in March 1862, to "cooperate with any State which may adopt gradual abolishment of slavery," began to gain political strength in Missouri, particularly if gradual emancipation could be supported by federally funded compensation for slaveholders. In

December 1862 Congressman John W. Noell and Senator John B. Henderson each introduced legislation to provide compensation for loyal Missouri slave owners if the state adopted a program of emancipation. The House bill designated $10 million for this purpose and required the state to pass an act of immediate emancipation by 1 January 1864. Noell's bill passed in January 1863. Meanwhile, Henderson's Senate bill designated $20 million for compensation and allowed for gradual emancipation, to be completed by 4 July 1876. The Senate bill passed in February 1863; the House considered but did not pass the Senate's version of the bill. These activities coincided with Governor Gamble's effort to secure gradual, compensated emancipation in the state legislature. Late in December 1862, the governor presented his plan to the general assembly. Proslavery legislators joined with radicals (who opposed compensation) to defeat Gamble's proposal. The legislature adjourned late in March 1863 without having acted on the slavery issue.[28]

Meanwhile, General Curtis's vigorous enforcement of the Confiscation Acts infuriated slaveholders, and Samuel Glover and the conservative St. Louisans protested his proemancipation policies. In April 1863 Glover complained to Lincoln that under Curtis's authority, provost marshals freed slaves "on the mere statements of the slaves."[29] Charles Jones, of Franklin County (some miles west of the city, but in the St. Louis Military District), had appealed to Lincoln in March 1863, informing him that many of his slaves had gone off to the federal garrison at Washington, Missouri "& took what they call free or Protection papers." No one, Jones believed, would question his loyalty. Yet the loss of his slaves threatened his livelihood. "Even the nurse, that assisted in attending to my smallest child went off," Jones lamented. With no one to work his farm and no one to tend his stock, his land became useless for the support of his "helpless little children." Jones had visited the federal garrison at Washington and had seen his slaves staying there. They showed him their freedom papers, and the captain commanding told Jones that "I could not get them, & that he would resist any & every effort to retake them." Jones also lodged a similar complaint with the St. Louis Military District commander, Brigadier General J. W. Davidson, informing him that twelve of his slaves had gone to Washington. Whether or not Jones got his slaves back is not known. What is known is that a month later two St. Louisans (James Huey and John Newcum) were arrested by federal authorities in Louisville, Kentucky, with a group of seven blacks in their possession. Huey and Newcum said that they were the property of "A. Weiseman" of St. Louis, who had purchased them from Charles Jones of Franklin County. The federal authorities believed that Huey and Newcum intended to sell the blacks in Kentucky and asked Provost Marshal Dick to inquire into the loyalty of all the parties concerned. Dick provided the requested information, asserting that "Charles Jones is a loyal man—his sale to Wiseman was in good faith—his title to the negroes in question was good—Wiseman is also believed by me . . . to be loyal." With this report, Huey and Newcum were discharged, "and the negroes turned out."[30] This action evidently permitted the intended sale to proceed. Whether or not Charles Jones regained control of his departed slaves at Washington, Missouri, he probably succeeded in cutting his losses where he could by selling slaves in Kentucky.

The impasse over slavery in Missouri frustrated Lincoln. The president had crafted the Emancipation Proclamation to continue to allow Missouri to deal with slavery as its citizens saw fit. But the state's failure to adopt a policy of gradual emancipation placed it increasingly at odds with the federal government's evolving policy. On New Year's Day 1863, when Lincoln declared free most of the slaves in the Confederacy, he also directed that federal military forces assist and protect the freed population. This directive dramatically altered the dynamic of the federal government's involvement with slavery in the states. As General Grant pressed his campaign against Vicksburg, thousands of slaves made their way to Union posts on the Mississippi River—in Arkansas, Mississippi, and Louisiana—and these people immediately became the charges of the federal government.

St. Louisans first saw these newly freed persons in March 1863 when Chaplain Samuel W. Sawyer, the superintendent of contrabands in Helena, Arkansas, brought a group of 500 black refugees to St. Louis.[31] Under orders from General Benjamin M. Prentiss, commanding the Eastern District of Arkansas, Sawyer established the first contraband camp in St. Louis, to the surprise and chagrin of General Curtis. The contrabands arrived aboard the steamer *Jesse K. Bell*, which had been seized at Helena by Sawyer over the angry protestations of its captain, pilot, watchman, clerk, and bartender. The ship's crew told the chaplain that they had no intention of making either their vessel or their services available to a band of ragged black refugees. When persuasion failed, Sawyer found that a direct order in General Prentiss's name worked. Although one child died during the trip north, another child had been born. "In the main," Sawyer reported, "we had a pleasant trip." Sawyer reached St. Louis in the middle of the night and presented himself to General Curtis the next morning. Prentiss had sent a letter of explanation with Sawyer, but the Arkansas commander (although inferior in rank) had given Curtis no advance warning. Sawyer reported that the arrival of the contrabands startled Curtis and initially angered him. "*Five hundred contrabands!*" he shouted when Sawyer made their presence known, "what in the world shall I do with them!"

A chaplain in an Indiana volunteer regiment, Sawyer had worked for some time among the Arkansas contrabands. When Maria R. Mann arrived in Helena in January 1863 as an agent of the Western Sanitary Commission, she thought that Sawyer had utterly failed to carry out a successful program of relief.[32] In all likelihood, however, he had done the best he could as federal resources were overwhelmed by the flood of black refugees. As aid began arriving from the commission, and as Prentiss transferred more than 1,000 refugees to St. Louis, conditions in Helena improved, and Maria Mann supervised the construction of dwellings, a hospital, and a school.

Curtis immediately wrote to Prentiss expressing his outrage at the unheralded arrival of the Arkansas contrabands. "The State of Missouri must not be made the depot for the paupers of Arkansas," he insisted. Curtis understood that Prentiss faced a "troublesome and perplexing" problem, but he argued that "you only transfer it by sending the negroes to my command." He closed his letter sternly: "I will have to send [them] back if you repeat the shipment."[33] Some "prominent citizens," as Sawyer described them, advised Curtis not to accept the contrabands, arguing that because Missouri remained a slave state their liberty might be endangered. Perhaps, these citizens suggested, the contrabands could be sent on to Cincinnati, or to Keokuk. But Curtis, as his anger subsided, decided otherwise. The commander saw an opportunity to make the effects of the Emancipation Proclamation felt in a state that continued to cling tenaciously to the institution of slavery. Slaves freed in Arkansas were not subject in any way to Missouri's slave laws. It was Curtis's wish, as Sawyer reported, to establish "a precedent of shipping & unloading contrabands . . . where we had an armed force to prevent disturbance."[34]

Curtis's quartermaster housed the contrabands at the empty Missouri Hotel, located near the river on the corner of Main and Morgan. The building was large enough to accommodate 1,000 people. As the freedmen disembarked on the levee, it seemed to Sawyer that "the whole city nearly" watched them walk with their baggage to the hotel. Curtis assigned a few men from the Thirty-seventh Iowa Volunteers to guard the building. He also assigned Sawyer a quartermaster, a surgeon, and some men from an Illinois regiment who had been captured and paroled by the Confederates to work in the hotel as clerks. Curtis recognized the St. Louis Ladies' Contraband Relief Society and provided them with an office at the hotel and with another building that the society outfitted as a hospital. With the contrabands settled, Sawyer thought that his work in St. Louis had ended. Curtis thought otherwise. When Sawyer applied for a furlough to visit his family in Indiana, he found that the general "was peremptory & said I must remain here to organize a plan of distributing contrabands to applicants for them." As Sawyer focused on the task of finding work for the refugees, he noted thankfully that "not a murmur has been heard from the press." He found work for them on fortifications around St. Louis and on the levee, where they loaded and unloaded government stores. Within a week he reported that he had found employment for 150 and that he expected to "send off" another group of 150 that day. The system of hiring out the contrabands ensured that few remained at the hotel for any length of time. With transportation paid for by the Contraband Relief Society, many of the refugees were sent to the free states. Those who were employed locally did not leave St. Louis County, and their employers had to satisfy a committee of the Contraband Relief Society of their "loyalty & responsibility."[35] "We are ready for another load," Sawyer wrote to Prentiss on 16 March. Sawyer thought that "Gen. Curtis will not object to their coming." In fact, "He expects them . . . he looks for you to send the contrabands at your discretion."[36]

Shortly after Sawyer settled the refugees in the Missouri Hotel, J. L. Richardson of the American Missionary Association (AMA) arrived in St. Louis to open a school for the freedmen. An abolitionist benevolent society based in New York, the AMA became the leading organization in the field of freedmen education during the Civil War and Reconstruction. In April Richardson gained the assistance of a second teacher, Lydia A. Hess. Sawyer, who later wrote to the AMA to praise the work of these teachers had probably played a role in securing their services.

Richardson opened his first classroom in a vacant section of the kitchen at the hotel. But within two weeks the women of the Contraband Relief Society had fitted out a proper classroom elsewhere in the hotel. On 18 May, as the number of pupils grew to fifty, Richardson moved the school to a nearby church on Washington Street. On the third day of its operation, however, the wooden structure was burned by a "few wicked boys," in Richardson's description, "most likely backed by secesh men." He moved the school back to the Missouri Hotel and soon reported to the AMA that under his tutelage and Miss Hess's the students were "generally quick to learn."[37]

As more contrabands arrived in St. Louis, Sawyer found ample demand for their services. "We have had applications for over *two thousand* hands," he reported. Most of the requests for laborers came from Illinois, but "the calls from Iowa increase." He also reported that "the contrabands are rather pleased with the idea of the negroes running a big Hotel in St. Louis." In mid-April, Curtis assigned Sawyer to duty as superintendent of "contraband persons of African descent" in St. Louis.[38] Among the tasks facing him was that of providing the emancipated slaves with free papers to protect them from Missouri's slave laws. A few days after his appointment he reported to Curtis that he had drawn up free papers for more than 1,100 of the Arkansas refugees. He also reported the attempted kidnapping of two of his charges by slave traders who intended to sell their captives in Kentucky. A soldier drove off the attackers. Overall, Sawyer concluded that the contraband transfers had gone well. "We have had applications for thousands of hands beyond our supply," he reported to General Curtis, "& the demand instead of abating is on the increase."[39]

Conservative Unionists complained frequently about Curtis's vigorous enforcement of the Confiscation Acts and about his stern policy of assessing and banishing "friends of the enemy." Supported by Bates and Montgomery Blair, Glover and Broadhead successfully pressed the president for Curtis's removal. In March 1863 Lincoln ordered him replaced by Major General Edwin V. Sumner. But Sumner's sudden death on his way to St. Louis left a thoroughly dispirited Curtis in command until May. Lincoln then turned once more to Governor Gamble's old ally, John Schofield.[40] The president cited no wrongdoing on Curtis's part when he announced the change. He had acted, he told Schofield, because he was convinced that the vast majority of loyal Missourians supported an emancipation policy and that their view could not take hold because of factional divisions in which "General Curtis, perhaps not of choice, [was] the head of one faction, and Governor Gamble that of the other." Because "I could not remove Governor Gamble," observed Lincoln, "I had to remove General Curtis." The president then offered Schofield a few words of advice: "Let your military measures be strong enough to repel the invader and keep the peace, and not so strong as to unnecessarily harass and persecute the people." It would not be easy to strike a proper balance. "It is a difficult role," Lincoln acknowledged. "If both factions, or neither, shall abuse you, you will, probably, be about right." "Beware," cautioned the president, "of being assailed by one and praised by the other."[41]

A few days after taking command, Schofield learned of a confrontation between slave owners and federal troops at Benton Barracks that immediately presented him with the issues of slavery and freedom that had bedeviled all federal commanders in Missouri. Although he intended to restore the army's official stance of neutrality toward slavery in Missouri, he found that when masters tried to extract their slaves from federal encampments, their actions threatened outbreaks of physical violence that inevitably involved the military authorities. The commander at Benton Barracks, Colonel Benjamin L. E. Bonneville, reported to Schofield late in May 1863 that, citing the official policy of neutrality, he had refused to help several white men who presented themselves to him as masters seeking to retrieve fugitive slaves. The two men then joined a group of "six or eight others" and went to the corral "saying that *they knew what to do*." As the slave catchers approached the black men they claimed as their slaves, a group of civilian laborers intervened, saying that "the negroes could go if willing but must not be maltreated." When the slave catchers violently seized the black men and knocked them to the ground, a general melee ensued during which one of the slave catchers drew a knife. At that point the provost guard arrested the slave catchers and escorted them outside the barracks. Bonneville acknowledged that the slave catchers had been "somewhat injured" during the fight and the arrest. To guard against a recurrence of such an "annoyance," he dismissed from camp all "persons of color" employed by the quartermaster. In the future he vowed to "rigidly exclude them from the Post."[42]

The episode at Benton Barracks presented Schofield with a conflict between the rights of Missouri slaveholders and the responsibility of military authorities in Missouri to remain neutral toward those rights. He called on the St. Louis lawyer Lucien Eaton to advise him on the issue of slavery and freedom in Missouri.[43] Schofield sought his advice undoubtedly aware that as early as February 1863 Eaton had begun work as an agent for George L. Stearns of Massachusetts to recruit soldiers from the "refugees . . . liberated by Grant's campaign at Vicksburg." With Emily Eaton (Lucien's wife) leading the activities of the Ladies' Contraband Relief Society it is likely that a number of the Arkansas refugees sent by Superintendent Sawyer to free states became soldiers in the Massachusetts black regiments raised by Stearns at the direction of Governor John A. Andrew.[44] By asking for Eaton's views, Schofield seemed to be taking Lincoln's advice to find the middle ground. Schofield knew the conservative position on the question of slaveholder rights; from Eaton he learned the radical view.

Eaton distinguished among "Contrabands," "Freedmen," "Men entitled to freedom (owned in Missouri)," and "Negroes from Kentucky and Tennessee." These categories overlapped considerably, but they underscored the growing complexity of the issue of slavery and freedom in Missouri after the issuance of the Emancipation Proclamation. Although the term "contraband" had come to refer to all black refugees, Eaton reminded Schofield that it properly applied to those persons "employed by the rebels & captured by our forces." These were the persons effectively freed by the First Confiscation Act. There were few of this class in Missouri, reported Eaton, but those who could provide evidence that they had been employed by rebel forces were issued "certificates of freedom" by the provost marshal general. "Freedmen" referred to those who had been freed by the Emancipation Proclamation. Since Missouri had been exempted from the proclamation, people in this group needed to offer evidence that their owners resided in a state that was included in it. If they did so, they received from the provost marshal general a certificate indicating that they were free.

The third group were persons owned in Missouri who were entitled to freedom under the terms of the Second Confiscation Act. "This class has been the most difficult to deal with," reported Eaton. But "on due proofs of disloyal ownership," the provost marshal general issued certificates of freedom. Negroes from Kentucky and Tennessee (states, like Missouri, that were excluded from the Emancipation Proclamation) were "presumptively free," said Eaton, because they came into the state as refugees from masters presumed to be disloyal. They were not issued certificates of freedom, however; instead, they were issued passes to leave Missouri and enter one of the free states.[45]

As Eaton's categories suggested, the only persons who remained identifiably slaves in Missouri were those without the provost marshal's certificates of freedom or military passes authorizing them to leave the state. This system, Eaton continued, had been put in place after Samuel Sawyer arrived in St. Louis with the first shipment of 500 contrabands from Arkansas. The positive requirement of military assistance and protection for the persons freed by the Emancipation Proclamation had been the impetus for a systematic distinction between free persons and slaves in Missouri.

Eaton noted the continuing problem of kidnapping. Franklin A. Dick, under Curtis's command, had attempted to solve it by establishing a system of certification to prevent "negroes who are free from being run off by Traders." But the variety of slave employments in St. Louis soon required Dick to modify his order, which, he explained, "will not be construed to interfere with the ordinary use of slaves actually employed in this City or County— nor with negroes being taken upon Steamboats as hired servants or deck hands—nor will it prevent free negroes from voluntarily leaving the City." These exclusions left ample room to maneuver for clandestine slave traders.[46]

Schofield's effort to follow Lincoln's advice and define a middle ground between conservatives and radicals could not disguise the fact that his reappointment strengthened Governor Gamble's hand. In June 1863, Gamble called the state convention into session to consider gradual emancipation as a provision of the Missouri Constitution. Attorney General Bates returned to St. Louis to urge the convention forward, and the delegates approved Gamble's plan on 1 July. According to the plan, gradual emancipation would begin in 1870. In that year, slaves between the ages of twelve and forty would be freed with the stipulation that they would remain as servants, "subject to the authority of their late owners," until 1876. Slaves under the age of twelve in 1870 would remain under their master's control as servants until their twenty-third year. Slaves older than forty would remain servants for the rest of their lives.[47] It was an astonishing measure, resting on an expectation that the slaves in Missouri would patiently bear the cost of their own emancipation over the next generation. If Gamble's plan worked, Missouri slave owners would continue to control the labor power of their "servants" for another twenty years. His plan deviated widely from Lincoln's expectations, and it remained to be seen whether the radicals would acquiesce in its ratification.

The conservatives' adoption of Gamble's emancipation plan prompted Schofield to try to limit the effectiveness of the Confiscation Acts. Early in July 1863 he directed district provost marshals to report to the provost marshal general each incidence of slaves claiming freedom due to the disloyalty of their masters. Schofield stipulated that each report must contain the names of witnesses "so that the matter may be turned over to the civil authorities." He prohibited provost marshals from themselves confiscating "the property of any individual." They were simply to gather evidence of disloyal activity and forward it to the provost marshal general.[48]

Schofield also did his best to restore Halleck's exclusion order. He made it clear to his subordinates that federal aid and protection did not, as a general rule, extend to blacks in Missouri. On 14 July an officer commanding a federal detachment guarding the railhead at Sedalia telegraphed his commander in Jefferson City: "Two hundred and Seventy Negroes, arrived here last night mostly women and children suffering for something to eat what shall I do with them[?]" The answer came back blunt and cold: "Subsistence will be issued only to persons in the service. We have nothing to do with feeding any other parties."[49]

In mid-July Schofield wrote to the secretary of war requesting clarification concerning fugitive slaves and the rights of loyal slave owners: "It is very clear to my mind that persons declared free" by the First and Second Confiscation Acts "are free by the operation of the law and the disloyal acts of their owners." But he questioned the policy instituted by General Curtis of issuing certificates of freedom to such persons: "Is it any part of the duty of the Military authorities to furnish evidence of such freedom or must they be left to plead the acts either in suit for freedom, or in defense against the person claiming their services or labor?" Schofield acknowledged that the Emancipation Proclamation "expressly required" military authorities "to enforce its provisions and to give protection to the persons liberated by it." Although Congress had passed an Article of War in March 1862 forbidding the use of military force to capture or return fugitive slaves (on pain of being dismissed from the service), Schofield wondered (evidently recalling Colonel Bonneville's actions at Benton Barracks) if military authorities in Missouri were obliged to protect a civil officer from violence "if he undertakes to arrest a fugitive from labor, when found in a military camp."[50]

Secretary Stanton sought the opinion of Judge Advocate General Joseph Holt who, differing in some details from Lucien Eaton in his report, identified three classes of slaves and former slaves in Missouri. Composing the first class were those effectively freed by the First Confiscation Act. They were not directly under the protection of the U.S. military, however, and contrary to Eaton's opinion they should not be issued certificates of freedom. They were left to protect their freedom in the civil courts through the writ of habeas corpus. A second class of persons had been freed by the Second Confiscation Act; they should carry certificates from the military declaring their freedom and, like slaves freed by the Emancipation Proclamation, they "are necessarily under the military control and protection of the government of the United States." A third class constituted slaves who were fugitives from loyal masters. In the opinion of the War Department, "The duty of the military authorities in reference to this class of fugitives from labor, is that of absolute non intervention." If an owner "shall attempt to arrest one of these fugitives from labor, in the presence of the military authorities, he must do so on his own responsibility, and cannot claim from such authorities, nor can they extend to him, any support or protection whatever."[51]

As the struggle over slavery continued, divisions between radicals and conservatives deepened. Schofield had the editor of the *Missouri Democrat* arrested for publishing a confidential letter to him from Lincoln. An angry radical committee of seventy people led by Charles Drake arrived in Washington on 27 September 1863 to meet with Lincoln in an effort to secure Schofield's removal. The president kept them waiting for three days as conservatives urgently lobbied Bates and Montgomery Blair. In St. Louis, one of Frank Blair's former allies, Henry T. Blow, joined the radical attack. In a speech delivered at the Mercantile Library, he embraced emancipation and defended the radical treasury secretary, Salmon P. Chase, who was locked in battle with the Blairs on the issue. Blair responded with a letter to the *Union* in which he contrasted his own military service with Blow's civilian status: "Did it ever occur to Mr. Blow that there are tens of thousands of conservative men 'in the field of conflict' shedding their heart's blood for the cause, while he remains safely at home to malign them with doubts as to their loyalty to the Union?"[52] To Lincoln, who had seen far more of Missouri's contentious politics than he could possibly have wished, the conflict between radicals and conservatives must have seemed interminable.

Schofield could slow but not stop the erosion of slavery in Missouri. Indeed, what proved to be the institution's deathblow was about to be delivered. During the first two years of the war, Lincoln opposed the enlistment of black men in the Union army. After issuing the Emancipation Proclamation, however, he gradually relented. First he lifted his ban on the recruitment of black men in the free states. By spring 1863, he had authorized the recruitment of black soldiers in the border states and in the occupied regions of the Confederacy. In the North and the South the rights of citizenship had traditionally been associated with the obligation to serve in the militia. The decision to raise black troops—and, most pointedly, to make soldiers of men who had been slaves—breached a long-standing racial barrier. The Missouri radicals, led by B. Gratz Brown in Congress and by Charles D. Drake in the Missouri General Assembly, strongly supported Lincoln's decision to raise black troops. As Drake declared in September 1863, "No traitor is too good to be killed by a Negro, nor has any traitor a right to insist on being killed by a white man."[53] But conservatives resisted federal recruitment efforts and their implications. The object of conservative resistance remained the defense of the rights of loyal slave owners.

On 22 May 1863 the War Department announced the establishment of a bureau to oversee the recruitment of black troops. Shortly thereafter, Adjutant General Lorenzo Thomas authorized Colonel William A. Pile of the Thirty-third Missouri Volunteers to extend recruitment activities into Missouri. Thomas also gave Pile verbal instructions to preface his activities by persuading Governor Gamble to endorse the policy. As the War Department grew impatient with the slow pace of recruitment in Missouri, Schofield reported to Thomas that although Gamble had "unhesitatingly" consented to recruitment, he had insisted on "qualifications" necessary to prevent any "interference with the slaves of loyal masters and avoid any violation of the laws of the State." Schofield did not mention that Gamble had also insisted that the new black regiment not be credited to Missouri. Pile accommodated the governor by restricting his recruitment to the southwestern corner of the state and by calling the troops "Arkansas Volunteers (colored)," to be stationed at Helena. Schofield reminded Thomas that in Missouri recruitment must proceed cautiously since "this is a matter of no little delicacy" that "might give rise to great difficulty."[54]

The delicacy of the matter became evident when the War Department authorized Colonel Pile to raise a second regiment of black troops, this one to rendezvous at Keokuk. In September 1863 Schofield complained to the department that recruiting officers, "with armed parties of negroes," swept across the northern counties of the state "enlisting all who would go with them" and making no distinction between loyal and disloyal masters. The "intense excitement" that this produced "compelled" Schofield to suspend all recruitment activity in the state.[55] There were few blacks in these counties, and Schofield believed that the first regiment raised by Pile "absorbed all the negroes fit for military duty" who were "*unquestionably* entitled to their freedom under the Confiscation Act." Those that remained were slaves of loyal men or slaves of men who "cannot be proven" to be disloyal by the terms of the Second Confiscation Act. Schofield sensed that the Lincoln administration had concluded that all able-bodied black men should be recruited, regardless of the loyalty of their masters. To maintain his credibility, and to protect the interests of loyal slaveholders, he assured the War Department that this view was shared by the loyal slave owners of the state. He suggested that loyal masters receive "receipts" for enlisted slaves with which they could lay "claim upon the Government for the value of the services lost."[56]

Waiting until after the fall harvest, Schofield ordered a resumption of recruitment on 14 November 1863. The new orders stipulated that "all able-bodied colored men, whether free or slaves, will be received into the service" and that "all persons enlisted into the service shall forever thereafter be free." Loyal owners would be compensated at the rate of $300 for each slave recruited when they filed an oath of allegiance in their own behalf and a deed of manumission for the enlisted slave. Under the new rules, "The State and county in which the enlistments are made shall be credited with the recruits enlisted," and all recruits would be sent to St. Louis. There, the black troops would be mustered in by Colonel Pile at Benton Barracks, to be known as Missouri regiments of U.S. Colored Troops. A board of examiners in St. Louis immediately began selecting officers for the new regiments from white applicants "accompanied by satisfactory certificates of loyalty and good character."[57]

Because Schofield's orders placed all powers of enlistment under the control of local provost marshals, he effectively left much of the recruiting in the hands of slave owners. Black men who made the decision on their own faced a difficult and dangerous journey to the nearest army outpost. One man who succeeded in getting to Jefferson City from an outlying plantation reported that he had hidden during the day and traveled at night to avoid bushwhackers. The new recruit reported seeing three black men killed by bushwhackers on his way to the state capital.[58] Slave patrols—although they had been made technically illegal under martial law by the federal prohibition against the assembly of bands of armed civilians—continued to operate where local provost marshals sympathized with slave owners. Near Mexico, Missouri, a Unionist protested to a St. Louis friend in December 1863 that slave patrols prevented blacks from entering the town to enlist. His complaint to the local provost marshal fell on unsympathetic ears: "Loyal men are daily humiliated by the acts of these imposters who grin deridingly when our government issues an Edict . . . [knowing they] will not obey the orders if possible to avoid them."[59]

When black men succeeded in enlisting on their own initiative, they often left behind families that were vulnerable to abuse by angry masters. Richard Glover, a slave near Mexico, successfully enlisted in December 1863. When he wrote to his wife, Martha, from his post at Benton Barracks, he received a prompt but distraught reply. "I have had nothing but trouble since you left," she lamented. "You recollect what I told you how they would do after you was gone." Her fears had proven to be well founded. Her master, George W. Cardwell, threatened not to feed her children. He had beaten her, "scandalously," as she put it. She concluded by begging her soldier husband to return: "You ought not to left me in the fix I am in & all these little helpless children to take care of."[60]

By December 1863, radicals in St. Louis had reason to believe that their views on emancipation accorded with the dominant opinion in the North and in the Republican Party. Lincoln's decision to extend federal aid and protection to the people freed by the Emancipation Proclamation fundamentally changed the discussion concerning slavery and freedom in the states. A new federal sphere of interest had been defined, within which it soon seemed proper and necessary to recruit black soldiers. Moreover, in a nation that had always equated citizen and soldier it became obvious that African Americans as a class would acquire new rights and privileges in the postemancipation United States. An old discussion, regarding the propriety of emancipation, was coming to an end; a new one, considering the status and destiny of African Americans, had just begun.

In March 1863, as the new federal involvement in emancipation began, Secretary of War Stanton appointed three members to the newly created American Freedmen's Inquiry Commission. The fact that the commissioners— Dr. Samuel Gridley Howe, Robert Dale Owen, and James McKaye—were well-known abolitionists and social reformers suggested that the discussion that was about to begin would be more pleasing to B. Gratz Brown and Charles D. Drake than to Frank Blair, Edward Bates, or Hamilton Gamble. Charged with reporting to the War Department on the condition of the freedmen and on the policies and programs needed to provide for their security and future progress, the commissioners went into the field to examine encampments and to interview those persons whom they deemed most knowledgeable about conditions and future prospects.

In late November and early December the commissioners conducted interviews in St. Louis. First on the list to be interviewed were B. Gratz Brown and Franklin A. Dick, both strong critics of Governor Gamble. Asked about the treatment of fugitive slaves, Brown informed the commission that there had been a time when fugitives sought refuge in St. Louis only to be arrested, imprisoned, and "sold for jail fees." That practice had been "entirely broken up," however. Since General Schofield had issued orders forbidding the involuntary removal of blacks from Missouri, Brown thought that the practice of selling slaves in Kentucky had also been ended. As for any government support, he believed that African Americans in Missouri needed no special help. As a group, they were "more intelligent and self-reliant than the slaves of the cotton States." Once free they "can take good care of themselves." Some temporary supervision of black refugees from the Southern states would be necessary but would not be needed for Missouri slaves. Brown also reminded the commission that in St. Louis many leaders of the black community "are wealthy and respectable," and the black community "in a general way . . . manage very well for themselves." He suggested as an "impression" rather than a "mature thought" that it might be wise to have county commissions empowered to hire out blacks who did not find work on their own. But in general, he thought that black people would understand the necessity of labor: "They are actuated by the same motives as . . . other laboring men." He also testified that he believed the prospects for emancipation were good. A small majority in the legislature favored convening anew the state convention for the purpose of making "arrangements for immediate emancipation." Governor Gamble's reluctance to pursue such a course remained the final obstacle to be overcome. Swift progress seemed certain. At one time, he recalled, "the opponents of the system of enlistment" went so far as to "prevent the negro regiments from having any arms put into their hands until they left the State."[61] That practice had been ended, and as recruitment continued Brown felt certain that the day of total emancipation could not be far off.

Dick explained to the commission the problem posed by the conservative provost marshal general, James O. Broadhead. Enlistment of black troops under General Schofield's orders should be carried out by strong antislavery men, Dick argued. Preferably these men should be from outside Missouri and thus unlikely to be drawn into the fratricidal political warfare that had become so deeply personal and vindictive in the state. Schofield's decision to rely on local provost marshals for recruitment seemed to Dick almost "vicious, so far as the interests of this State are concerned." He regarded Gamble as an honest man, but the governor's hostility toward antislavery men and measures ran so deep "that he cannot see straight or feel right" on the subject. Furthermore, "Gen. Schofield is greatly under his influence." In practice, Dick regarded "the General as one hand of the Governor." A commissioner asked Dick if Governor Gamble was "pro-slavery in his feeling." "Indeed he is," he replied, explaining that Gamble's concessions to antislavery men had been won by political coercion. "If a fellow stops you in the highway, and says, 'Give me your money, or I will blow out your brains,' you surrender your purse, but not out of kindness." So it was with Gamble. For that reason, only anti-slavery men should administer the program.

As he completed his testimony, Dick assured the commissioners that the able-bodied black men in the state would eagerly join the army once they were protected from the "terrorism" resorted to by slave owners. He almost feared a swift end to the war because slavery in Missouri might survive. "The Northern people know nothing of the iniquities of slavery, nor of its effects," he said. At a distance, the institution "is dark," but viewed closely "it is intensely black." "I have lived in this State twenty-one years," he concluded. "I regard it as absolutely indispensable that we should eradicate [slavery], in order that we may have a country such as we should have." He did not fear the conse-quences of immediate emancipation, and he vehemently opposed the idea of compensation for slaveholders. It might be just to provide single women and the elderly with some compensation for the loss of their slave property, but no money should go to young men. He had no patience with them: "They have brought ruin on our State." He viewed immediate, uncompensated emancipation as an act of public justice: "I would not have them compen-sated, because . . . they hold property which has become a public injury, that a necessity for its destruction has arisen, & the general welfare requires that it should be destroyed. . . . What I dread is, to have the slave element con-tinue in this State. It is just fighting the devil all the time."[62]

A leader of the antebellum free black community, the Reverend Edward L. Woodson, testified that the poor blacks in St. Louis would not become a burden on public charity. He told the commissioners that there were six black churches in the city—three Baptist congregations with 1,400 members and three Methodist with 600 members—and each congregation maintained a poor fund to be used to help needy members. "When a man dies without leaving any property, we bury him," Woodson said; "we have always done that because we don't like to have the white people think we can't take care of ourselves."[63]

Several of the "leading members" of the Ladies' Contraband Relief Society also met with the commission.[64] They reported that they had raised $5,000 in money and supplies of clothing from friends in New York, Boston, and other locations in the East. The women considered their field of labor to extend from St. Louis to Vicksburg. Along that stretch of the Mississippi they believed that there were at least 100,000 contrabands clustered at various points. In St. Louis, the women reported, General Schofield had relocated the contraband camp from the Missouri Hotel to Benton Barracks on the northern edge of the city. The commission visited the new camp, where the superintendent reported that the only people to remain there for long were the very young, the aged, and the infirm. The women of the society found the contrabands from the South "very degraded" and "much more helpless than the Missouri slaves." At Benton Barracks the commission saw a group of contrabands from Mississippi clustered around one stove and a group from Missouri clustered around another. The superintendent explained that "the Missouri negroes disdained to associate with those from Mississippi, considering themselves far above them."[65]

The commission also visited a school established in 1862 by the American Missionary Association and another operated by free blacks (funded by tuition payments of twenty-five cents a week per student). They found forty students at the first school who varied in age from five to twenty and seemed well ordered, attentive, and "eager to learn." At the other one they found eighty students and a wide range of ages, but they were disappointed to discover that the school lacked "that degree of discipline which is essential to the attainment of the full advantages of the instruction furnished."[66]

The American Freedmen's Inquiry Commission reminded St. Louis radicals that their views were in the ascendancy in Lincoln's administration. But when the commissioners left town, Schofield remained in command, and outrages continued against black men attempting to enlist and against their families when they succeeded. A slave woman from Paris, Missouri (Monroe County), wrote to her husband at Benton Barracks in January 1864 that she was being treated "worse and worse every day." Her owners would not allow her to receive letters from her husband, so the couple corresponded through a sympathetic neighbor. "Do the best you can," she urged her husband, "and do not fret too much for me for it wont be long before I will be free and then all we make will be ours." An officer at Benton Barracks reported to Pile similar mistreatment of the families of two "good Soldiers" in his company. The owners "refused to let [the wives] go to the Post Office to get their letters, and if any one comes to them and brings them letters and reads them to them he is shure to whip them for it." The officer hoped that the army could do something "to relieve their families . . . and relieve them from a good deal of anxiety."[67]

Schofield's efforts to accommodate the War Department's demands for blacks troops with the traditional prerogatives of slave owners produced painful and irreconcilable contradictions. When three Pike County slaves tried to make their way to Hannibal to become soldiers, they were captured near Frankford and returned to their owners near Prairieville. The men were severely whipped for their transgression. The owner of one of them, a widow, offered five dollars to any man who would kill her slave. One of the men who had administered the whipping stepped forward, drew his pistol, and shot the would-be Union soldier dead.[68] As recruitment of black troops in Missouri continued to falter, Lincoln removed Schofield from command in January 1864.

On 20 January, Schofield's last day as commander in Missouri, the *Democrat* published a lengthy account, "The Colored Recruits at Benton Barracks." The paper praised Pile and commented favorably on the eagerness of the new recruits to learn to be good soldiers. But it also noted that "the soldiers frequently receive intelligence that their wives and children, left behind, are subjected to severe maltreatment." The situation demanded the attention of the military authorities.[69] Indeed, Schofield's removal gave Pile, now a brigadier general, reason to hope that the War Department would embark on a more aggressive recruitment policy and provide protection for black soldiers and their families. Schofield's replacement, General William S. Rosecrans, took command in St. Louis at the end of January. About the same time, Pile became aware of Richard Glover's plight at Benton Barracks. Angered by the information contained in the letter from Glover's wife, Pile identified her owner and inquired about the children. He clearly hoped to find that Cardwell had a son of military age not living at home. Such information would sustain a presumption of disloyalty, which in turn would make it possible for Pile to free Martha Glover and her children. Instead, the general learned that all of Cardwell's seven children were living at home and that the oldest one was a fourteen-year-old girl. He could do no more than direct his adjutant general to write Cardwell "remonstrating against his treatment" of the soldier's wife and warning that if it continued "the military authorities would have to interfere." In response to Pile's threat, Cardwell applied to his local provost marshal for a pass to take Martha and her three youngest children to Kentucky. Thoroughly incensed, Pile intervened. An interview with Martha revealed that the frightened mother had agreed to go with Cardwell to Kentucky because he had threatened to sell her young children without her if she refused. Pile seized the mother and children and reported to his new commander, Rosecrans, that Cardwell "pretends to be Loyal but associates constantly with the worst rebels in the country."[70] Pile recognized that the only sure way to end this sort of intimidation was to end slavery. In letters to Missouri congressmen Henry T. Blow and B. Gratz Brown, he urged swift action to secure "*emancipation immediate* and *unconditional*." He explained to the lawmakers that "having been instrumental in causing the enlistment" of black troops, he could not sit idly by and "see their families threatened."[71]

Slavery lived on in Missouri, but Congress brought its demise a step closer in February 1864 by making slaves liable for the draft. A gathering of African Americans in St. Louis celebrated the event and noted that as more black men became federal soldiers, the last vestiges of slavery would necessarily disappear.[72] Rosecrans seized on the new federal legislation to forbid any movement of African Americans from Missouri to Kentucky. On 1 March 1864 the commander ordered that since black men were needed "to fill up the quota of the various Districts required by the draft," no further movement of them from Missouri would be tolerated.[73]

Black soldiers, too, sensed that conditions had fundamentally changed and acted accordingly. Sam Bowman, stationed at Benton Barracks Hospital, wrote to his wife near Tipton, Missouri, in May 1864, promising to protect her. At the same time, he warned his wife's master of dire consequences if he mistreated her. He told his wife that he had orders from General Pile to bring her to St. Louis if she wished to come. "So it lays to your own choice to stay or come," he wrote. "If You donot want to stay tell Mr Wilson in a decent manner, that You do not." He then addressed his comments to his wife's owner: "General Pile says if You Mr. Wilson is as good a Union man as Sam Hannah recommends you to be you will let her come on good terms and give her a piece of writing to shew that You are what you profess to be." He then warned Wilson about the consequences of any mistreatment:

If you do not . . . we will shew You what we intend to do.—We are not expecting that this will insult a Union man. You know that a

Soldiers wife is free.[74] Read this letter to her and let her return her own answer. I will find out whether this has been read to her in afull understanding with her or not, and if I should find out that she has never heard her deliverance I will undoubtedly punish you. . . . You can See I have power. . . . I write You with this determination that by the 20th day of May this matter must & will be closed so you can rest till Then or doit sooner as it will be better for You. . . . I want you to understand that we hav labord in the field to Subdue Slavery and now we mean to protect them.[75]

Private Spotswood Rice wrote similarly from Benton Barracks Hospital to his daughters and their owner in Glasgow, Missouri. "Dear Children, be assured that I will have you if it cost me my life. . . . Your Miss Kaitty said that I tried to steal you," he continued, "but I'll let her know that god never intended for man to steal his own flesh and blood. . . . Oh! My Dear children how I do want to see you." To his daughters' owner, Kitty Diggs, Spotswood had this to say:

I want you to remember this one thing that the longor you keep my Child from me the longor you will have to burn in hell and the qwicer youll get their for we are now makeing up a bout one thoughsand blacke troops to Come up tharough and wont to come through Glasgow and when we come wo be to Copperhood rabbels and to Slaveholding rebbels for we don expect to leave them there root neor branch. . . . I want you to understand kittey diggs that where ever you and I meets we are enmays to each orthere I offered once to pay you forty dollars for my own Child but I am glad now that you did not accept it. . . . I have no fears about geting mary out of your hands this whole Government gives chear to me and you cannot help your self

Spotswood Rice[76]

Pile filled the draft quota and reported to the War Department in May 1864 that he had recruited about all of the black troops he could in Missouri. He estimated that 4,000 able-bodied men remained outside the army, but he noted that slave owners had adopted a new tactic to keep their laborers on the land: "Their masters have made contract with them for the summer giving them part of the crop to be raised." Sharecropping concessions, combined with the old pattern of intimidation and with lurid new stories of the recent massacre of black soldiers by Nathan Bedford Forrest's troops at Fort Pillow, succeeded in "over-coming their disposition to enlist."[77] Evidently hoping to reach some of these 4,000 potential soldiers, Rosecrans in early August authorized General Thomas Ewing Jr., commanding federal forces in eastern Kansas, to send recruitment detachments into Missouri. The action produced a howl of protest from Governor Willard P. Hall, and before the end of the month Rosecrans issued new orders that once again placed recruitment in the hands of Provost Marshal General Broadhead and the district provost marshals.[78] Nevertheless, by the end of the war more than 8,300 black men from Missouri had joined the Union army, amounting to nearly 40 percent of the state's black male population of military age.[79]

As the work of recruitment continued in Missouri, so too did the work of freedmen relief in St. Louis. Benton Barracks continued to process large numbers of contrabands during winter and spring 1863–1864. Chaplain W. H. Corkhill assumed the responsibilities of superintendent in January and reported at the end of March that nearly 1,000 names had been entered into his books. More than 200 of that group had been "hired out under contract to *loyal* responsible parties." More than 300 had taken responsibility for finding their own employment locally and in neighboring states. Some of his charges were dead or dying from smallpox; they had been "left upon the Levee by steamboats in the advanced stages of the disease and forthwith have been sent to these Quarters." About 100 had died, including 18 small children and 30 of the adults who had arrived sick.[80]

Corkhill reported that once at the Benton Barracks camp, the people fared as well as could be expected. But the poor condition of the black refugees provided ample evidence that they had suffered greatly as they struggled to make their way to safety and to freedom. The effort of federal authorities to remain neutral on the issue of slavery and freedom in Missouri had contributed substantially to the plight of the black refugees. Not only had these people not been inoculated against smallpox, but they also had often been denied food.

The disruptive conditions of war and radical victories at the polls in fall 1864 ensured that the gradual emancipation plan would fail. Radicals in Missouri controlled the general assembly and the state convention. All that remained to be done was to remove the slavery statutes from the state's legal code and to adopt a constitutional prohibition against their reintroduction. On 11 January 1865 the delegates to the state convention passed an emancipation ordinance that brought an immediate and uncompensated end to slavery in Missouri. On the same day, the new radical governor, Thomas C. Fletcher, proclaimed the convention's ordinance the law of the state. In February the general assembly passed a concurrent resolution ratifying the Thirteenth Amendment to the Constitution (passed by Congress late in January and ratified by the required two-thirds of the states in December).[81] In the end, the legal death of slavery in Missouri came swiftly. However, its legacy could not be eradicated with a legislative pen stroke, and the death throes of the peculiar institution continued long after its legal demise. Brigadier General Clinton B. Fisk, later to be assigned as an assistant commissioner of the Freedmen's Bureau for Kentucky and Tennessee, wrote James E. Yeatman in St. Louis in March 1865 describing conditions in the interior of the state. Fisk, a native of western New York, moved first to the Michigan Territory and then, in 1860, to St. Louis. He joined the Thirty-second Missouri Volunteers and rose to the rank of brevet Major General by the end of the war. He had fought guerrillas in the state throughout the conflict. "Slavery dies hard," he wrote. "I hear its expiring agonies & witness its contortions in death in every quarter of my Dist[rict]." In Boone, Howard, Randolph, and Callaway Counties he reported that the convention's emancipation ordinance caused social upheavals equal to any he had seen in Arkansas and Mississippi following the issuance of the Emancipation Proclamation in January 1863. Some former masters employed bushwhackers to threaten "to hang or shoot every negro he can find absent from the old plantation." A few masters "have driven their black people away from them with nothing to eat or scarcely wear." The result was a new outpouring of black refugees. Fisk appealed to Yeatman, president of the Western Sanitary Commission, for aid.[82]

Beyond the suffering, African Americans in St. Louis envisioned a new era and celebrated its birth. Later in 1865, blacks there established a state branch of the National Equal Rights League, begun by John Mercer Langston in 1864. In St. Louis on 3 October 1865, the league elected the Reverend G. P. Wells chairman of the organization and Blanche K. Bruce, soon famous as Reconstruction senator from Mississippi, secretary. Ohio-born Enos Clarke, a representative in the Missouri General Assembly, addressed the crowd and endorsed black suffrage. The league vowed to "demand those rights and privileges which rightfully and logically belong to us as freedmen, and as those who have never deserted the flag of our common country in the hour of its darkest peril." Among those rights sought was "the universal right to the ballot box." After appointing a committee of seven to arrange future meetings and speakers, the St. Louis League issued its *Address to the Friends of Equal Rights:* "We ask not for social equality with the white man, as is often claimed by the shallow demagogue; for a higher law than human must forever govern social relations. We ask only that privilege which is now given to the very poorest and meanest of white men who come to the ballot-box." The address emphasized the military service of black men, thousands of whom had "bared their breasts to the remorseless storm of treason, and by hundreds went down to death in the conflict." While loyal black men laid down their lives to save the Union, the "bitterest enemy of our right to suffrage remained . . . at home, safe, and fattened on the fruits of our sacrifice[,] toil and blood."[83] Military service had provided black men and their families with a gateway to freedom. It might yet, as Edward Bates had feared, open a door to the basic rights of citizenship.

Ladies' Union Aid Society memorial (engraving by Major and Knapp, 1865)

Missouri Historical Society, St. Louis

Anna Lansing Clapp, ca. 1870
Missouri Historical Society, St. Louis

Grand Mississippi Valley Sanitary Fair (stereo photograph by J. A. Scholten, 1864)
Missouri Historical Society, St. Louis

James E. Yeatman, ca. 1860 (carte de visite)
Missouri Historical Society, St. Louis

Adaline Couzins (carte de visite by R. Goebel)
Missouri Historical Society, St. Louis

Samuel R. Curtis
Library of Congress

John M. Schofield
Library of Congress

Gunboats under construction at Carondelet (*Harper's Weekly*, 5 October 1861, wood engraving by Alexander Simplot)

St. Louis Mercantile Library Association at the University of Missouri–St. Louis

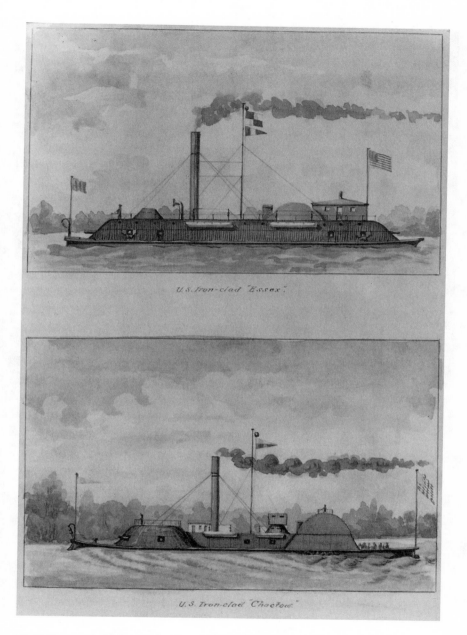

Civil War ironclads *Essex* and *Choctaw* (watercolors by Ensign D. M. N. Stouffer, ca. 1864–1865)
  Library of Congress

Gratiot Street Prison, 8th and Gratiot (stereo photograph by Emile Boehl, ca. 1868)
Missouri Historical Society, St. Louis

St. Louis in 1876 (*Harper's Weekly*, 8 July 1876, wood engraving by Schell and Hagen, after C. A. Vanderhoof)
St. Louis Mercantile Library Association at the University of Missouri–St. Louis

10

"A Foundation of Loyalty"

T HE LOYAL WHITE MEN of Missouri went to the polls in November 1864 to elect a president of the United States, state and federal representatives, a governor, and delegates to a new constitutional convention. The event marked the return to elected government in the state. Provisional governor Hamilton Gamble had died in January 1864, and the lieutenant governor, Willard P. Hall, completed his term. In February, at Governor Hall's urging, the state legislature authorized voters to call a new constitutional convention. The legislature then directed the convention to deliberate two matters that would require amendments to the state constitution: emancipation and a new standard of loyalty for the exercise of the electoral franchise. The era of provisional government gave way to the era of the test oath.

Voters went to the polls in Missouri under rules established by the old state convention in October 1861. Eligible to vote were men willing to swear allegiance to the Constitution of the United States and of Missouri and to promise not to take up arms against the governments of either. In June 1862 the state convention extended this test oath to jury members, officers of corporations, teachers, and ministers. The new constitutional convention reconsidered the wording of the test oath and made it a fixture of the state constitution.[1]

Missourians voted under extremely unsettled conditions. Sterling Price's raid in October 1864 left St. Louis untouched, but much of the state remained in anxious and uncertain circumstances. Adding to this climate were prominent political leaders who openly rebelled against the conservative remnants of Gamble's provisional government and Lincoln's border state policy. Charles D. Drake, a St. Louis attorney and a rising leader of the Radical Republicans, joined with U.S. senator B. Gratz Brown and with Radicals across the North to oppose the renomination of President Lincoln and to support the rival candidacy of the quixotic John C. Frémont. Frémont's withdrawal from the race in October restored a degree of unity to Republican ranks in

Missouri, but in a state ravaged by guerrilla war and with a test oath restricting the suffrage, 52,000 fewer citizens voted in 1864 than in 1860.[2]

In the Missouri governor's race, Thomas C. Fletcher, a prominent St. Louis Republican and a respected military leader, easily defeated his Democratic rival. Voters also approved the new constitutional convention and elected a sizable majority of Radicals as delegates to that body. Two of St. Louis's delegates, the prosperous merchant Isidor Bush and the physician Moses L. Linton, had also been members of the 1861–1863 state convention. But with one additional exception, the other delegates were new. Conservatives were quick to attack the quality of the delegates. Edward Bates, who had resigned as Lincoln's attorney general in 1864 and returned to St. Louis, judged the convention to be "composed of inferior materials." He focused his criticism on Drake and a few others but insisted that "there is not a man in it, of high and general reputation for talents or learning or virtue." Bates published a series of letters in the *Missouri Democrat* explaining in detail his view that "the Convention now sitting in St. Louis is revolutionary—in its origin, in its composition and character." In his last letter, dated 31 May 1865, he reminded readers that he had "enlisted for the war" and that the struggle had not ended as long as "arbitrary power" continued to endanger the fundamental principle of the Founding Fathers, "*Liberty according to law.*"[3]

Because the test oath in Missouri became a national emblem of Radical Republican excess and corruption, even those who originally supported the measure felt compelled in their later commentary to cast a critical eye on the quality of the delegates elected to the convention. The Baptist minister Galusha Anderson supported its work before leaving St. Louis in 1866. But he recalled in a 1908 account of his Civil War experiences in the border city that Missouri voters had been anxious to elect delegates who were "uncompromisingly in favor of immediate emancipation," and they had not been "sufficiently careful in demanding that they should also be men qualified to do their part intelligently in reconstructing the organic law of the commonwealth."[4] Charles Drake judged his fellow delegates to be "sensible, upright and worthy" but added that "only a very small number of them had ever had experience in lawmaking." In a more detached frame of mind, the historian Thomas Barclay compared the membership of the two bodies and found more lawyers, editors, and bankers in the earlier state convention and more farmers and small town merchants in the constitutional convention. Drake forged a Radical majority from the rural delegates. Although St. Louis sent several men of prominence, the city's delegation quickly found itself in the minority on the test oath and other issues.[5]

The St. Louis delegation consisted of Drake and four men from the German community: H. J. Stierlin, William D'Oench, Isidor Bush, and Ferdinand Meyer. With the exception of Kentucky-born Moses Linton, the rest—George K. Budd, Henry A. Clover, Chauncey I. Filley, Wyllys King, and George P. Strong—were natives of northeastern states.[6]

Four days before the convention convened in St. Louis, at the Mercantile Library, Fletcher took office in Jefferson City as Missouri's first elected governor since the beginning of the war. Republicans enjoyed overwhelming power in the state. In addition to the governorship and the constitutional convention, they controlled both houses of the state legislature, both of the state's U.S. senators, and all but one of the state's federal congressmen. Although full civilian rule was soon restored in Missouri, the hegemony of the Republican Party and the military background and bearing of Governor Fletcher suggested that the boisterous democracy of the antebellum era would not soon be revived.

Fletcher moved directly from a field command to the governor's mansion. Born in Jefferson County, southwest of St. Louis, he moved to the city in 1856 as a land agent for the Pacific Railroad. He quickly rose to prominence in politics, joining Frank Blair and Gratz Brown to build the city's Republican Party. He served as a delegate to the 1860 Republican National Convention. During the secession crisis, Nathaniel Lyon appointed him assistant provost marshal general for St. Louis. The following year, he recruited the Thirty-first Missouri Volunteers and led that regiment into battle as a colonel in Frank Blair's brigade. Wounded and captured north of Vicksburg in December 1862, he languished for five months in Richmond's notorious Libby Prison before being exchanged in May 1863. He rejoined his regiment in time to witness the surrender of Vicksburg. Later, at Chattanooga, he led his regiment in the legendary fight at Lookout Mountain. Promoted to brigade commander, he joined William Tecumseh Sherman's Atlanta campaign. In 1864 illness brought him back to St. Louis. While he recuperated, the state's new military commander, William Rosecrans, called on him to take command of two volunteer regiments and to engage Sterling Price's invading army. Fletcher inflicted heavy damage on the Confederates at the Battle of Pilot Knob in September 1864. Promoted to brigadier general, he rejoined Sherman and participated in the destructive federal March to the Sea. While still in the field, Fletcher learned that Missouri Republicans had nominated him for governor.[7]

The constitutional convention began its deliberations in St. Louis on 6 July, and the delegates met their first objective quickly by overwhelmingly voting to amend the constitution to end slavery. Only four delegates voted against the measure. The convention paused in its deliberations as William Greenleaf Eliot led the delegates in prayer: "Thanks be to God for this day that light has now come out of darkness."[8] Although a deep divide soon separated St. Louisans from the Drake majority, the triumphant moment of emancipation occasioned widespread celebration. On Saturday, 14 January 1865, the St. Louis delegate George K. Budd read Governor Fletcher's emancipation proclamation to an assembled throng. Missouri's federal commander, General Grenville M. Dodge, ordered a sixty-gun salute. "The sonorous voices of the great guns," reported the *Democrat*, "sent their reverberations far and near, telling the people for miles around that Missouri was free." For men like Budd, a celebration of emancipation seemed long overdue. A native of Philadelphia, he represented the new elite that had risen to economic power in the 1850s and secured political power through the Republican Party during the Civil War. A frequent writer on matters of currency and finance in the antebellum years, he had held the office of city comptroller. He was also a prominent member of Henry A. Nelson's First Presbyterian Church. He maintained close ties with the city's merchant elite as well as with eastern capitalists. During the war, he became a leader in the sale of U.S. bonds in St. Louis.[9]

The day of festivities ended with a display of fireworks and with the friends of emancipation illuminating public and private buildings throughout the city. According to the *Democrat*, Fourth Street was "the center of attraction." Rockets were fired from the cupola of the courthouse and all the windows of the Planters' House Hotel were illuminated and decorated with transparencies. All along Fourth Street businesses were "handsomely lit up" with "illuminated mottoes." For more than two hours, the length of Fourth Street—from Franklin Avenue to Walnut Street—was filled "with people of both sexes and all colors, and other streets were also full of people looking at the sight." Throughout the city, groups of blacks celebrated; "their rejoicings were unbounded." Many citizens, of course, did not join in the celebration. The *Democrat* noted, perhaps with relief, that "the whole affair passed off with the utmost harmony and good order."[10]

Beyond emancipation, the constitutional convention struggled with the vexing issue of suffrage. A few days after Eliot offered his prayerful thanks for emancipation, the Unitarian minister complied with a request by the convention to speak on the subject of attaching an education test to the exercise of the electoral franchise. Eliot had given a good deal of thought to the subject, and he urged the delegates to make the ability to read and write (in any language) a requirement for voting. Such a requirement, when augmented by a strong system of state-funded public schools, would help to protect Missouri from future disorder. Moreover, because he believed that Negro suffrage would soon be the law of the land, he argued that an "educational test is exactly what we want, to make it safe." On the day that Eliot spoke, the convention received a petition from the Fifty-sixth Missouri Volunteers, a black regiment, "praying the Convention to extend to colored soldiers the right of suffrage." "I am opposed to negro suffrage," declared Eliot, "until those who are to enjoy it are better prepared for its exercise, not because of their color, but because of their ignorance." He believed that without an education requirement, black suffrage would add "to the present mass of ignorant voters" a burden that "would be almost more than our free institutions could bear."[11]

After the emancipation decision had been made, the unity of the convention quickly dissolved. St. Louisans, led by the Germans, turned against the Radical leader, Charles Drake. A former supporter of the nativist Know-Nothing movement, Drake continued to display his distrust of the foreign-born. Although Arnold Krekel, the German leader in St. Charles County (west of St. Louis), chaired the convention and generally supported Drake, most Germans resisted his influence and favored a swift end to the convention after the work of emancipation had been done.[12] The beginnings of a political opposition took shape around this anti-Radical faction, but Drake continued to command a solid majority. Under his leadership, the convention broadened the existing definition of disloyalty to include everyone who had expressed sympathy for, or in any way had aided, the rebellion. To a degree, the constitutional convention built on the work of the earlier state convention and continued to bar men from voting or holding office if they had engaged in armed hostility against the state or the United States. But the new proscription also included men who had lent "aid, comfort, countenance or support to persons engaged in any such hostility." The constitution now barred from political participation men who had provided

money or information to rebels or had communicated with them. It disenfranchised men if they had advised anyone to enter the Confederate army
or if they had shown sympathy for or celebrated the triumph of Confederate arms. As in the earlier proscription, men deemed disloyal were not only
barred from voting but also from jury service and the practice of law, from
serving as officers of corporations or as professors or teachers, and from
preaching or performing marriages.[13]

Among the St. Louis delegates, the staunch Unionist Chauncey I. Filley
supported Drake and the logic of the sweeping proscriptions. However, Isidor
Bush spoke for most of the St. Louis delegation as he led the minority opposition to the Radicals' disenfranchisement provisions. Born in Prague and
raised in Vienna, he had fled political repression in Europe after the failed
liberal revolutions of 1848. He had published a Jewish religious newspaper in
New York City before moving to St. Louis, where he became a leading wholesale merchant in wines and liquors. He was one of the original members of
the B'nai El Congregation in St. Louis (formed in 1852), the second permanent Jewish congregation in the city. Early in the war, Frémont included him
in his circle of advisers. With the war over, Bush recoiled from the Radicals'
proposals for political repression.[14]

As Drake's German opponents observed, the Radicals eagerly sought to
exclude from political participation men they deemed disloyal, but they did
not press to extend political participation to all men of undisputed loyalty.
George Husmann, a native of Prussia and a leading American wine maker
(first at Hermann, Missouri, and later in California's Napa Valley), drafted a
minority report for the convention's Committee on the Executive to protest
the use of the word "white" in the majority report concerning qualifications
for holding elective office. "We believe all men . . . are equal," he wrote. He
expressed the views of his German constituents, "by protesting against any
distinction . . . between white, black, red or brown." Husmann lodged the
minority's "solemn protest against the inserting of the word 'white' in any
article of the new Constitution of our State." Repeated efforts to strike the
word from the document failed.[15]

In the developing fight with Drake, Isidor Bush reminded St. Louisans
that the Radical leader had a solid record of antiblack as well as antiforeign
prejudice. As a member of the Missouri House in 1860, Drake had joined a
small group of legislators to support a measure intended to drive free blacks
from St. Louis. A state law passed in 1845 and revised in 1847 already required

that free persons of color possess licenses from the county in which they re-sided. The proposed legislation declared that all free blacks and mulattoes who had moved to Missouri since 1847 "shall be reduced to slavery" if they re-mained in the state after the first Monday of September 1860.[16] Drake, for his part, did not disavow his past, and he did not hesitate to acknowledge that it was his primary goal to maintain the political hegemony of the Republican Party. As he explained, he wanted to "erect a wall and a barrier in the shape of the constitution" to keep the enemies of the party of Lincoln, the party of the Union, and the party of emancipation forever out of political power.[17]

As Drake and his supporters crafted their constitutional barrier, Gover-nor Fletcher initiated the restoration of civil law. On 7 March 1865, at the behest of General John Pope, the military commander of Missouri, Fletcher declared that no organized enemy force existed in the state. This declaration enabled Pope to end martial law. The return to civil law, in turn, alarmed a number of delegates to the convention. Henry A. Clover, a St. Louis County judge and chairman of the Committee on the Judiciary, pointed out in his report to the full convention the problems that he expected to encounter. The delegates had just passed an ordinance of emancipation, Clover noted, and yet, there were numerous judges in the state who would welcome an oppor-tunity to challenge the "right or authority" of the convention to "deprive a citizen of property without compensation." Similarly, he warned, the convention's effort to preserve the elective franchise "in purity" might be "frittered away" by unfavorable and hostile judicial interpretations of law. Finally, he cautioned, any judge hostile to the Union cause could entertain civil actions to counter the confiscation measures, banishments, fines, and imprisonments executed under martial law in the state. A native of New York City, Clover had moved to St. Louis in 1844 and sided with the Free-Soil fac-tion of the Democratic Party. With martial law ended, he feared the conse-quences of the restoration of civil law. To meet the crisis, he urged the convention "to vacate . . . all the judicial offices of the state." The conven-tion added sheriffs to Clover's list of offices to be vacated and passed the "oust-ing ordinance," as it came to be called, with only five dissenting votes. The ordinance set 1 May as the date by which all designated offices would be va-cated and filled with appointees of the governor until elections under the new constitution filled the posts in a regular manner.[18]

The constitutional convention adjourned on 10 April after having set 6 June as the date for the ratification vote on the new constitution. Drake had been careful to impose the new ironclad loyalty oath on the electorate that would vote on ratification. As a further precaution against the possibility of defeat, the secretary of state appointed Drake to administer the registration of the soldiers' vote. Drake had 10,000 ballots printed and distributed to Missouri soldiers stationed at Jefferson Barracks, at Camp Douglas in Illinois, and at Little Rock, Arkansas. As the ratification vote approached, he declared that the new constitution would secure Missouri "firmly on a foundation of Loyalty." Lincoln's assassination on 14 April provided an ominous backdrop for the Missouri referendum on the Radicals' new constitutional restraints.

Opponents of the new constitution lacked unity of purpose, but their criticism of the document revealed the shape of the conflicts that soon restructured political life in the state. Edward Bates took a dim view of political developments in Missouri and in the nation. He regarded the emancipation ordinance as an unnecessary, emotionally charged deception that enabled Radicals, under the "false pretense" of acting to erase "the blot of slavery," to seize power. He viewed the act of gradual emancipation, passed by the state convention two years earlier, to be entirely sufficient (despite the fact that under its provisions slavery in Missouri would continue until 1876). He took some pleasure in learning that Clover "made a speech in the Convention against negro suffrage," but generally he looked on in despair. He began to reread a history of the French Revolution as he contemplated "with painful doubts and fears, the present critical condition of our own country." He campaigned vigorously against ratification, although he advised those who could take the test oath in good conscience to do so and thereby qualify themselves to vote against the new constitution. He had been correct to regard Clover as an emerging ally. Although Clover had crafted the ousting ordinance, he opposed the loyalty oath and refused to sign the redrafted constitution. In 1865 he also declined an appointment by Governor Fletcher to the state supreme court as a replacement for one of the justices removed under the ousting ordinance.[19]

Governor Fletcher offered only guarded support for what opponents called the Drake constitution. Fletcher would have preferred a legislative approach to the franchise issue. By placing the ironclad oath in the constitution, the Radicals made it unnecessarily difficult, in Fletcher's view, to modify the terms of proscription as conditions might permit. Senator Gratz Brown expressed similar views. Moses Linton, a Catholic, emerged as the leading critic of the new constitution's provision limiting a church's ownership of tax-exempt property to the church itself. In St. Louis, opposition to the new constitution ran wide and deep.[20]

Awaiting the voters' decision on ratification, Governor Fletcher enforced the ousting ordinance in a piecemeal fashion, at times acting with determination. When two judges in western Missouri (Lafayette County), known to Fletcher to be disloyal men, refused to vacate their offices, he dispatched a company of black troops to install his appointees. On that occasion, the soldiers locked the offending judges in a former slave pen until they agreed to turn over the court records to the men appointed to replace them. Elsewhere, when Fletcher deemed judges to be loyal, he did not necessarily require that they be reappointed. Moreover, in some localities, where judges followed the ordinance and vacated their posts, he did not make new appointments.[21]

The biggest test of Fletcher's authority in the enforcement of the ousting ordinance came from the justices of the state supreme court. Justices John D. S. Dryden (who had recently moved to St. Louis from Palmyra, in northeast Missouri) and the prominent St. Louis attorney William V. N. Bay remained on the bench determined to serve out the six-year terms to which they had been elected in 1864. The court's third justice, Barton Bates (the eldest son of former Attorney General Edward Bates) had resigned in February 1865, before the passage of the ousting ordinance, to focus his energies on his and his father's financial affairs.[22] When the 1 May deadline set by the ordinance arrived, the supreme court stood in recess, scheduled to reconvene on 5 May. When Dryden and Bay did not appear in court that day, Governor Fletcher assumed that they had acquiesced in the ordinance, and he appointed three new justices to take their place. They announced that the high court would begin a new session in St. Louis on 12 June, a week after the ratification vote. To Fletcher's surprise and dismay, Dryden and Bay issued an identical call.

As the fight over the supreme court took shape, eligible voters went to the polls on 6 June to pass judgment on the work of the constitutional convention. In St. Louis, opponents of the constitution won an overwhelming victory, carrying 80 percent of the vote. As Drake had expected, the soldiers' vote proved critical for ratification. Civilian voters across the state opposed the constitution by a margin of about 1,000 votes; with the soldiers' votes, it carried by nearly 2,000.[23]

On 12 June Justices Dryden and Bay arrived at the courthouse an hour earlier than the usual starting time of ten o'clock and occupied a courtroom before the new judges arrived. Fletcher's men went to work in another room, but they soon discovered that the court's clerk sided with Dryden and Bay and refused to deliver court records to them. Two days into this impasse, Fletcher directed the commander of the state militia to remove Dryden and Bay from their posts. Declaring the ousting ordinance an unconstitutional abridgment of the old constitution, the two men refused to step down. The militia commander ordered the St. Louis police chief physically to remove the judges. As a police force moved against them, the militia commander stationed 600 soldiers on the streets near the courthouse and held another 100 in reserve in the militia armory on the corner of Walnut and Twelfth Streets. Finally, the police seized the court records from the protesting court clerk, and the tenure of the new justices began.[24]

Although Radicals were more firmly entrenched in power than before, Frank Blair's return to St. Louis on 20 June 1865 signaled the beginning of an organized political opposition in the state. He returned as the victorious commander of Sherman's Seventeenth Corps in the Atlanta campaign and in the subsequent long march through Georgia and the Carolinas. His admirers held a banquet in his honor at the Lindell Hotel on 22 June and heard him express his intention to challenge Radical control. He led the call for a statewide meeting on 26 October at Verandah Hall in St. Louis. About 1,000 delegates attended the three-day affair, and Blair found himself working closely again with old allies, including Committee of Safety men Samuel T. Glover and James O. Broadhead.[25]

As Blair lashed out against the Radicals, the test oath issue took shape as a legal cause around which an effective opposition emerged. Blair and others in the opposition realized that the oath was most vulnerable to legal challenge as it applied to lawyers and ministers. The rights of the states to determine the eligibility of voters had yet to be challenged by the Fourteenth Amendment or constrained by the Fifteenth Amendment. The application of the test oath to lawyers and ministers, however, opened constitutional challenges on the grounds that the oath represented ex post facto legislation and a bill of attainder and thereby violated the federal Constitution. In late October 1865 the state supreme court convened in St. Louis for its fall term and heard two cases, *State v. Garesché* (1865) and *Cummings v. Missouri* (1866), which marked the beginning of the fight against the test oath in Missouri.

The first case involved Alexander J. P. Garesché, a practicing attorney in St. Louis who refused to take the test oath. As a young man, he had studied law in St. Louis with Thomas T. Gantt, but he parted company with his mentor during the secession crisis. Garesché joined the state militia muster at Camp Jackson. Although he took no further part in the Civil War after his capture and parole, the issue of loyalty badly divided the Garesché family. In December 1861 General Henry W. Halleck included the wife of Garesché's cousin, his sister (Mary), and his wife (Laura) in a list of disloyal persons to be assessed. The cousin, Peter Bauduy Garesché, left St. Louis for Columbia, South Carolina, at the beginning of the war and served in the Confederate army as inspector of the Columbia powder magazine. His wife, Juliette McLane Garesché, remained in St. Louis and was among those assessed. She later joined her husband in South Carolina with their four children and served as a nurse to wounded Confederate soldiers (and to a number of black workers badly injured in an explosion at her husband's powder magazine). When the Missouri Supreme Court overturned the test oath for lawyers, Bauduy Garesché returned to St. Louis with his family and reestablished a successful law practice. On the other side of the sectional fight, Garesché's oldest brother, the West Point graduate Colonel Julius P. Garesché, served with General William Rosecrans and died at Murfreesboro.[26] In the Garesché case, not surprisingly, the Radical appointees to the state supreme court ruled in favor of the test oath. In a significant victory for the Missouri Radicals, moreover, the U.S. Supreme Court declined to review the state decision. Garesché joined the legal team that argued against the test oath in the *Cummings* case.[27]

The *Cummings* case developed from a protest by the Catholic archbishop of St. Louis, Peter Richard Kenrick, against the test oath for clergy. Kenrick, an Irishman by birth, remained neutral during the Civil War. After the ratification of the new constitution, he drafted a public letter in which he avoided an open defiance of the law but left little doubt that he would direct his priests to defy it. In his letter of 28 July 1865, Kenrick expressed his hope that "the civil power" of the state would "abstain from extracting such an oath" from priests. But if the state did require the oath, Kenrick instructed the Catholic clergy to inform him "of the particular circumstances of your position" so that he could offer his "counsel and assistance." Kenrick's statement confirmed Bates's conviction that the Catholic Church would fight against the oath.[28]

Protestant clerics also responded negatively to the test oath. Episcopal bishop Cicero Stephens Hawks, a native of North Carolina, took a somewhat less confrontational position than Kenrick. Hawks became rector of Christ Church in St. Louis in 1844 and subsequently became the first Episcopal bishop of Missouri.[29] He instructed his priests to take the oath if they could do so in good conscience. If they could not take it, he advised them to remain in their pulpits and await developments. Henry A. Nelson, a Radical on most issues and pastor of the First Presbyterian Church in St. Louis, joined the protest. Nelson agreed with Senator Gratz Brown that the test oath for lawyers and clergymen violated civil and religious liberty. He himself had taken the oath when he became a curator of the University of Missouri, but he insisted that an oath imposed on clergymen overstepped the bounds of state authority.[30] Galusha Anderson defended the intentions of the Radicals even after he left St. Louis. In the July 1867 edition of the *Baptist Quarterly,* he reminded readers that the Baptists in Missouri who denounced the loyalty oath as an assault of their religious liberties were the same Baptists who had found slavery entirely consistent with their Christian faith. "The Convention intended sacredly to guard religious liberty," he wrote, although he admitted that the delegates had gone too far. Nevertheless, he insisted that harsh measures had not been intended or practiced. Across the state, grand juries returned thirty-six indictments against ministers in twenty-eight counties. Few of the indicted were arrested, and all who were arrested were released within a few days.[31]

Radicals responded to their critics by insisting that the regulation of individual pursuits by the state violated no constitutional rights when the regulations were necessary for the common good. "Religious liberty is a political right," declared a petulant Governor Fletcher. As for the protesters, he predicted that "when these outraged gentlemen go to the Supreme Court of the United States with their complaint, they will be told that there is not a sentence or a word in the Constitution of the United States which gives them the right to preach at all." "I deny," he concluded, that the test oath "is an infringement of religious liberty secured to any person by the Constitution of the United States." He promised to enlarge the state penitentiary, if necessary, to accommodate the protesting clergymen.[32]

On Sunday 3 September 1865, in the Mississippi River town of Louisiana, north of St. Louis, a Catholic priest, John Cummings, preached to his small Irish congregation. Following the instructions he had received from Bishop Kenrick, he had refused to take the test oath. The Radical leadership in the town responded swiftly. On the Tuesday following Cummings's sermon, a grand jury indicted the priest. That Friday he was arrested and held in jail for a week before being tried, convicted, and fined for his offense.[33] In late October 1865 the Missouri Supreme Court convened in St. Louis to hear his appeal. Without dissent, it upheld the oath for the clergy. On appeal, the U.S. Supreme Court agreed to review the state court's decision.[34]

Protests against the test oath mounted on other fronts as well. Despite the outcome of the *Garesché* case, a number of prominent St. Louis attorneys failed to take the oath before the passage of the 2 September 1866 deadline. Standing firm with the Radicals in this confrontation was Charles Drake's old law partner, Judge Wilson Primm. When Blair's supporter, Samuel T. Glover, refused to take the oath for lawyers, a St. Louis County grand jury indicted him, and Judge Primm promptly found him guilty and fined him the $500 prescribed by the constitution. Primm also vowed to bar from his courtroom any attorney who did not take the oath. Glover pressed an appeal and joined with Blair to advance a legal assault against the oath.

During the fall elections in 1866, Blair refused to take the oath. He argued that he could not take it because he had taken up arms against the state of Missouri when he joined Lyon in the capture of Camp Jackson and helped to drive Governor Jackson from the state capital. "I would not take the oath," said Blair, "and they would not let me vote."[35] He went to court, where Drake served as defense attorney for the two election officers named in Blair's suit. The circuit court decision went against Blair, as did the decision of the state supreme court. He appealed to the U.S. Supreme Court, which agreed to review his case.[36]

As these new challenges to the test oath in Missouri made their way to the Supreme Court, many lawyers, reluctantly and offering mild protests, took the oath. Included in this group was the leading conservative, William Napton, who managed to convince the clerk administering the oath to attach a disclaimer to the signed document. Napton took the oath, he said, without "denying or disavowing any opinions or sympathies expressed or entertained" in reference to any past actions of the state or federal governments. He did not view these opinions or sympathies as "having anything to do with one's allegiance or loyalty." He protested "the validity of all that part of the oath which related to past acts" as being fundamentally in conflict with the Constitution and with the "fundamental principles of all our state govts."[37]

As the *Cummings* case went to the Supreme Court, Montgomery Blair joined Garesché to prepare the priest's argument. His old adversary in the *Dred Scott* case, Reverdy Johnson, joined the former postmaster general in this task. David Dudley Field of New York, whose brother was Supreme Court justice Stephen J. Field, also joined in the appeal. Johnson and Field had recently won a major victory over congressional Radicals in *Ex parte Milligan* (1866), and they hoped to strike another blow in the *Cummings* case. Governor Fletcher appointed U.S. senator John Henderson to present the state's argument. The high court's decision in the *Cummings* case, delivered by Justice Field and concurred in by Justices Wayne, Grier, Nelson, and Clifford, overturned the test oath for clergy, finding that it constituted a bill of attainder and an ex post facto law in violation of the Constitution. Justice Miller filed a strong dissent, and Justices Chase, Swayne, and Davis joined him. The dissenting justices viewed the test oath as a reasonable qualification for professional practice, and they denied that the Missouri constitution's provision violated the federal Constitution. The *Milligan* and *Cummings* decisions made the ideological division on the high court clear. Lincoln had appointed all the dissenting justices; those forming the majority had been appointed before his election.

Taken together, *Cummings* and two related decisions handed down in December and January 1866–1867 fundamentally altered the course of Reconstruction. The Court paired *Cummings* with *Ex parte Garland* (1866), in which the justices found unconstitutional, on the same grounds as *Cummings*, a congressional law that required a test oath for lawyers practicing before federal courts. The Court's decision in the third case, *Ex parte Milligan*, came first and struck the heaviest blow against congressional plans to use military law during Reconstruction in the former Confederate states. In *Milligan*, the Court overturned a wartime conviction in Indiana of a disloyal civilian by a military tribunal, insisting that military law could be applied to civilians only under immediate conditions of war.[38] Although the Supreme Court refused to review the Missouri court's decision upholding the test oath for lawyers, the federal decisions in *Cummings* and *Garland* prompted the state supreme court—in the case *In re Murphy and Glover* (1867)—to reverse its decision in the *Garesché* case and to overturn the test oath for lawyers.[39]

During spring 1866, conflicts between the Radicals and their opponents focused on Blair's old friend and ally, Peter L. Foy, the St. Louis postmaster since 1864. The Radicals wanted him out, and they pressed their candidate, William McKee, for the job. McKee was the principal owner of the *Missouri Democrat*, and a decade later he was a central figure in the Whiskey Ring scandal. Both of Missouri's senators (Henderson and Gratz Brown) supported McKee, but the Blair faction prevailed with President Andrew Johnson, who reappointed Foy. Foy promptly appointed Blair collector of internal revenue for Missouri, although with Brown and Henderson opposed, the U.S. Senate refused to confirm the appointment of either Blair or Foy. In the absence of a new presidential appointment for St. Louis postmaster, however, Foy stayed in office.[40]

Blair seemed to welcome a return to political battle, and a true battle it became. During a speech in Warrensburg, Missouri, he carried a concealed pistol and calmly held his ground as an enraged knife-wielding young man rushed the speaker's stand. A Blair supporter intervened and stabbed the would-be assailant to death.[41] The danger of widespread violence increased as Radicals rallied their supporters around emotionally patriotic themes. On 10 May 1866, as Radicals organized a rally in St. Louis to celebrate the fifth anniversary of the capture of Camp Jackson, speakers occupied the rotunda of the courthouse and the east and west fronts of the building. The speeches continued until midnight. The *Democrat* reported that "the celebration of the first victory of loyal men over traitors in Missouri has been splendidly successful." A few attempts by Copperheads to disrupt the proceedings only demonstrated that the spirit of 1861 lived on. Illuminated transparencies decorated the spaces between the pillars on the east front of the courthouse. "Loyal men shall rule, not rebels," proclaimed one panel. "Union and liberty forever" and "All honor to Gen. Lyon and the patriots of 1861," proclaimed the second and third. Henry A. Clover greeted the gathering at the east portico and introduced the principal speakers, the first of whom was Governor Fletcher. He took the opportunity to castigate Congressman John Hogan, a Democrat, for his opposition to the Radical regime. Governor Richard Oglesby of Illinois, who focused his wrath on President Johnson, followed Fletcher. Drake spoke next and again attacked Hogan. A letter from Carl Schurz in Detroit expressed his "sympathy with the objects you strive to attain." A Committee on Resolutions, including the lawyer Lucien Eaton, the journalists John F. Hume and Emil Preetorius, and Charles Drake, recommended a series of declarations that the crowd overwhelmingly endorsed. One resolution commended Congress for passing the Civil Rights Act over Johnson's veto. Henry Shaw, a former slaveholder but never an ideologue, and always comfortable among the city's leading men, earlier provided the rally's dignitaries with refreshments at his Tower Grove estate.[42]

By late June 1866, tensions within the wartime Republican coalition in Missouri had reached the bursting point. In an open letter to the people of the state, Gratz Brown announced that considerations of health prevented him from seeking reelection to the Senate by the general assembly after the fall elections. In fact, he had decided not to seek favor any longer with Drake and the Radicals. He took the opportunity to denounce the Missouri Constitution of 1865 as "unworthy of a free people." He went on to say that disenfranchisement, even for treason, could be justified only as a temporary measure. "Universal suffrage will triumph in the end," he predicted; "the capacity of voting is the protection against . . . all those antagonisms which threaten to wreck and engulf liberty."[43]

Building on the momentum provided by Brown's defection, Blair's political faction held its nominating convention at the Mercantile Library in July. Frank Blair, Lewis Bogy, James O. Broadhead, Thomas T. Gantt, and Samuel T. Glover formed the group's steering committee. Bogy later had the distinction of being Missouri's first native-born U.S. senator. Having been a conditional Unionist during the war, he joined Blair's faction as a conservative supporter of President Johnson.[44]

Johnson's conservative and conciliatory policy toward the former Confederate states and their rebel leaders strengthened Blair's anti-Radical campaign in Missouri. But with congressional hostility toward Johnson mounting, the president's course also meant that federal authority divided sharply on the volatile issue of race and civil rights. The debate over the legitimacy of restricting the vote among white men had lent credence to a wider consideration of extending voting rights across the barrier of race. The drive for Negro suffrage began in 1864 with the formation of the National Equal Rights League, and John M. Langston, its president, soon brought the fight to Missouri. Langston, a free person of color, moved from Virginia to Ohio after the death of his parents in 1834. He graduated from Oberlin College and worked as a civilian during the war to raise black troops, including the famed Fifty-fourth Massachusetts regiment that fought with distinction at Fort Wagner.[45]

In October 1865 a gathering of black men and women in St. Louis formed the Missouri Equal Rights League and chose as their president the Reverend G. P. Wells, pastor of the Second Colored Baptist Church of St. Louis. He had been closely associated with the Reverend John Richard Anderson, recently deceased, who had been pastor of the Second Colored Baptist Church and Harriet Scott's pastor. Anderson's mother had been the slave of Sarah Bates, the sister of Edward Bates. Anderson had won his freedom, however, and worked as a typesetter for Elijah P. Lovejoy before becoming pastor of the St. Louis black Baptist congregation. Early in 1864 Anderson died suddenly at the age of forty-five. Wells, with two associates, prevailed on Galusha Anderson to preach a memorial service; more than a year later, he delivered the sermon after gathering his information from the pastor's friends and associates. The black minister had never openly challenged slavery, Galusha Anderson observed, but John Richard Anderson would certainly have celebrated the day of emancipation, had he lived to see it. Wells and others raised the funds necessary to have Galusha Anderson's sermon printed and circulated. The memory of the Reverend J. Richard Anderson clearly aided the cause of equal rights in Missouri.[46]

The St. Louis black educator, James Milton Turner, also became active in the Missouri League. Like Langston, Turner had studied at Oberlin College. The Missouri League also elected Blanche K. Bruce secretary. He had been born a slave in Virginia in 1841 and moved, presumably with his master, to Missouri sometime before the Civil War. Highly literate (like the Reverend John Richard Anderson, he may have served an apprenticeship as a printer), Bruce opened a school for blacks in Hannibal, Missouri, during the war. The work of the Equal Rights League brought him into contact with Turner, and it was probably through his influence that Bruce left Missouri to study at Oberlin College. In 1868 he moved to Mississippi and became active in Republican politics; in 1874 he was elected to the U.S. Senate.[47]

A leading white participant in the Missouri League was Enos Clarke, a member of the state legislature. Clarke, a lawyer, moved to St. Louis from Utica, New York, in 1862. The Radical leadership appointed him as curator of the University of Missouri (he served from 1865 to 1868), but he soon followed the Liberal Republican path being blazed by Gratz Brown and Carl Schurz and broke with the Radicals. He delivered an address at the organizational meeting of the Missouri Equal Rights League, after which the league passed a series of resolutions demanding "the universal right to the ballot box" and the "rights and privileges due free men" who have never deserted the flag of our common country in the hour of its darkest peril."[48]

In November 1865 Langston arrived in St. Louis to launch a six-week campaign around the state for Negro suffrage. He spoke first at Turner Hall and returned to St. Louis to deliver the last speech of his Missouri tour. He spoke again in January 1866 as the Missouri League celebrated the first anniversary of emancipation in the state and reviewed a parade of black troops before delivering an address at Washington Hall. In March Enos Clarke took the floor of the Missouri House to advocate Negro suffrage and to present the legislature with a petition submitted by the Missouri Equal Rights League.[49]

In Missouri, and throughout the former slave states, black men who had served as Union soldiers became a formidable presence in the fight for equal rights. Not since the Camp Jackson affair had the potential for violence in St. Louis been so great. Major outbreaks of violence in Memphis and New Orleans seemed to foreshadow dangerous times ahead for St. Louis. In Memphis, on 1 May 1866, an altercation between a black man and a white man quickly escalated when a group of black soldiers prevented the police from arresting the black man. Soon, a white mob, led by Irish policemen and firemen, attacked blacks throughout the city. When the violence ended, hundreds of black schools, churches, and homes lay in ruins. Forty-six black men and two white men died in the fighting.

More troubling still for St. Louisans were the unstable conditions in New Orleans. There, Radicals attempted to reconvene an 1864 constitutional convention for the purpose of extending suffrage to loyal black men and denying the vote to whites who had been disloyal. As a small contingent of delegates gathered, a force of 200 former black soldiers approached the hall to lend support. City police then intervened and carried out what the military district's commander, General Philip Sheridan, later described as "an absolute massacre." The police killed thirty-four black men and two white Radical delegates.[50]

Obviously worried that St. Louis could become the scene of similar butchery, General William Tecumseh Sherman met in St. Louis on 9 August with Governor Fletcher and two members of Blair's faction, Gantt and Glover. Sherman commanded the Division of the Mississippi, which included Missouri, and he sought assurances that political rivalry in the city would not turn violent. At the meeting, Gantt and Glover protested that Fletcher had organized and armed two regiments of Negro militia in St. Louis. This provocation, said the governor's critics, could easily lead to violence. At Sherman's urging, Fletcher agreed to disband it and did so early in September.[51]

As the fall elections approached, General Winfield Scott Hancock became military commander in Missouri and urged Fletcher to call on him for troops to maintain the peace. But Hancock had only three companies available to him, and soon he could not meet all of Fletcher's requests. In the week before the elections, Sherman sent two additional companies from Kansas to western Missouri. An outbreak of cholera in August probably served to dissipate political passions somewhat in St. Louis, but it would have been foolish to ignore the potential for violence. On the night of 10 August, 10,000 St. Louisans were said to have gathered at Union Park to commemorate the Battle of Wilson's Creek. "Glorious Demonstration" read the headlines in the *Democrat*: "Congress Sustained. Johnson Thoroughly Ventilated. His Policy Repudiated. Great Enthusiasm. Radicals United and in Earnest."[52]

Early in September President Johnson arrived in St. Louis as he completed his "Swing Around the Circle" campaign against his Republican opponents in Congress. By the time he delivered his St. Louis speech on 8 September, it had become commonplace for hecklers to interrupt the president's rambling orations. St. Louis proved to be the low point of a politically disastrous presidential tour. With the violence in New Orleans still fresh in everyone's mind, Johnson applied his anti-Radical invective to the city's political passions. Without referring to the role played by the police in the New Orleans massacre, he blamed the bloodshed on the agitations of the Radicals in that city. In his fight with Republicans in Congress, he compared himself with Moses and Jesus Christ. As president, he had pardoned leading Confederates "when they repented," and now the Radicals wanted to crucify him:

> I have been maligned; I have been called Judas Iscariot, and all that . . . Judas Iscariot! Judas! There was a Judas once, one of the twelve apostles. Oh yes; the twelve apostles had a Christ. (A Voice, "And a Moses, too!") (Great laughter). . . . [The president rambled on and the heckling continued:] Yes, yes, they are ready to impeach [me]— (Voice—"Let them try it") . . . they would vacate the Executive department of the United States, (A Voice—"Too bad they don't impeach him"). . . . So far as offenses are concerned—upon this question of offenses, let me ask you what offenses I have committed? (A Voice—"Plenty, here, to-night").

When Johnson left St. Louis for Washington, D.C., he invited Democratic Congressman John Hogan to join the presidential entourage that included Secretary of State William H. Seward and General of the Army Ulysses S. Grant. Hogan, an Irishman by birth and a shoemaker by trade, had moved to St. Louis from Illinois and established himself as a wholesale grocer in the early 1850s. Loyal to the Southern Rights wing of the Democratic Party, he served as postmaster in St. Louis during James Buchanan's presidency. He gladly accepted Johnson's offer to join the anti-Radical campaign, and much to Grant's annoyance, took it upon himself to introduce the president and his party at every stop. Johnson seemed to enjoy Hogan's bellicose style. Grant regarded the St. Louis congressman as a Copperhead and resented his rhetorical embrace.[53]

Two weeks after the election, Missouri Republicans held a statewide meeting at the Planters' House Hotel in St. Louis. Despite the Radical victory, the signs of division were plain. Gratz Brown urged universal manhood suffrage—that is, Negro suffrage and an end to the disenfranchisement of whites. The senator also recommended the removal of the test oath for the professions. Ten Radicals promptly walked out of the meeting. Of the nineteen who remained, all but three of them—including Drake and John F. Hume (until 1866 the editor of the *Missouri Democrat*)—voted in favor of Brown's resolutions. William M. Grosvenor, the new editor of the *Missouri Democrat,* soon supported Brown as well. A native of Massachusetts, Grosvenor joined a Connecticut volunteer regiment at the beginning of the war and rose to the rank of captain. After being wounded at Port Hudson in October 1863, he accepted a commission as colonel of a Louisiana black regiment. He returned to New Haven and to his career in journalism in 1864 but moved to St. Louis in 1866 to serve as one of the editors of the *Democrat.* He soon championed the political career of Carl Schurz and took a leading role in the organization of the Liberal Republican movement. His journalistic investigations uncovered the Whiskey Ring scandal.[54]

In January 1867 the heavily Radical Missouri state legislature met to select Brown's replacement in the Senate. From the outset, Drake seemed the favored candidate, although Brown opposed him, as did the St. Louis Germans. A movement to replace Drake with Fletcher collapsed, however, and Drake easily defeated Blair for the open Senate seat. The legislature then began impeachment proceedings against Judge James C. Moodey, a conservative, who had been appointed to the St. Louis County Circuit Court by Governor Fletcher in October 1865. A friend of Bates, Glover, and Broadhead, Moodey had hoped to secure from President Johnson an appointment to the U.S. Supreme Court in 1866. Instead, he became an object lesson in Radical enforcement of the test oath. Early in February 1867 Moodey impaneled a jury without applying the test oath required by the constitution. Quickly, the house impeached and the senate convicted, and the Radicals removed him from office.[55]

In January 1867, with Radicals at the height of their power, Sterling Price returned to Missouri. An old friend, William B. Napton, encouraged him to settle in St. Louis, where admirers purchased a house for him. He had returned to Missouri in precarious health. The 1864 raid into the state had broken his army and, to a considerable extent, his spirit. Weakened at Pilot Knob in southeast Missouri and defeated at Westport, near the Kansas border, he had struggled southward with a disintegrating army into Arkansas. Plagued by desertion and mutiny, he formally surrendered his Confederate command to federal authorities in New Orleans in May 1865. With a number of former Confederate leaders, Price left the United States for Mexico, where he hoped to rebuild his antebellum life as a landed aristocrat. Within a year, however, his health began to fail. With his central Missouri estate deeded to his paroled son, Price had hoped to establish himself as a merchant in St. Louis, but he died there on 29 September 1867, shortly before his fifty-ninth birthday. On 3 October his body lay at rest at the First Methodist Episcopal Church on the corner of Eighth and Washington Streets. That afternoon, a large funeral procession accompanied the general's casket to Bellefontaine Cemetery.[56]

The outpouring of sympathy for Price in St. Louis underscored the central dilemma that the Radicals faced. They could continue to rally their supporters around themes of patriotism and retribution, but magnanimous sentiments gained a widening appeal. Shortly before Price's death, Philip Sheridan visited St. Louis on his way to the Indian wars in the West. President Johnson had removed him from his Southern command following the general's critical report concerning the New Orleans riot. Radicals in St. Louis honored him with a torchlight procession of more than 4,000 veterans, who carried a banner that read: "The Phil of Radicalism a tough cure for rebels."[57] But for Frank Blair and other opponents, including Blair's formerly estranged cousin Gratz Brown, the Radicals' drive to insulate the Republic from disloyalty threatened oligarchy. Drake's heavy-handed political approach also alienated a new leader of the St. Louis Germans, Carl Schurz, who quickly emerged as the Radicals' leading opponent.

The high tide of Radicalism began to ebb in Missouri in spring 1867, when the proprietors of the *Westliche Post,* including Emil Preetorius, urged Schurz, then in Detroit, to join them as an owner and editor of the influential St. Louis newspaper. The opportunity to work with Preetorius appealed strongly to Schurz, who had known the older man as a leading figure in the liberal revolution of 1848 in Germany. During the Civil War, Schurz had raised and led

German troops, although Confederate forces overran his Eleventh Corps at Chancellorsville and again on the first day of fighting at Gettysburg. After the war, Schurz toured the South at the request of President Johnson. His report, describing the former rebels as beaten but unbowed, displeased Johnson, who initially suppressed it. The congressional fight to publish Schurz's report became the first major fight between Johnson and his Radical enemies. Once in St. Louis, Schurz quickly rose to prominence in Missouri's Republican Party. He served as a delegate to the Republican National Convention in 1868, and during the presidential campaign of that year, he canvassed Missouri for Grant. In a carriage ride from Springfield to Sedalia, Schurz took the advice of Radicals and passed through the "somewhat lonesome region" with a revolver in his lap, "ready for action." The precaution "proved unnecessary," however, and he soon judged the political repression perpetuated by Drake and his supporters to be unnecessary for maintaining peace in the state.

Senator Drake also stumped the state for the Radical cause in September 1868. "This then is the one solitary and vivid issue," he declared. "*Shall the people that saved the country rule it, or shall rebels and traitors?*" It was a simple message, and it allowed him to place his opponents on the side of rebellion and treason, regardless of their war record. In his partisan attacks, he linked Frank Blair with the treason of "Jeff Davis," with the "Butcher" Nathan Bedford Forrest (a reference to the massacre of black troops at Fort Pillow in April 1864), and with the Irish draft rioters in New York City (who had lynched nearly a dozen blacks in July 1863). Expanding on his anti-Irish theme, and giving fresh expression to his old nativist biases, he denounced the Democratic Party for dancing to "the music of the brogue . . . over the graves of 300,000 dead." What he did not say, of course, was that many Irishmen were among the 300,000 Union dead and that it was Blair who had fought against Forrest and the Confederacy while Drake had remained at home.

Across the country, the 1868 elections marked the high tide of Radicalism. The Radicals rode to victory on Grant's long coattails and swept aside the Democratic challenge mounted by Horatio Seymour of New York and vice presidential candidate Frank Blair.[58] For the time being, Republicans maintained their wartime coalition and successfully portrayed the Democrats as the party of treason. Blair provided a particularly easy target for Republican scorn. In a public letter addressed to James O. Broadhead (who nominated him for vice president at the Democratic National Convention), Blair made his views plain. "There is but one way to restore the Government and the Constitution," he declared. The next president should declare the congressional Reconstruction acts "null and void" and command the army "to undo its usurpations at the South." A Democratic administration, he said, would "disperse the carpetbag Southern governments" and "allow white people" to regain control of the state governments.[59]

In New York, the German-born illustrator for *Harper's Weekly,* Thomas Nast, seized on the Broadhead letter to caricature Blair as an ally of unreformed rebels and the brutal Ku Klux Klan. In a cartoon published shortly before the election, Nast depicted Blair—together with Confederate leader Wade Hampton of South Carolina and a stereotypical Irishman—as one of three witches tending a brew labeled "C. S. A." and "K. K. K." Nast drew Blair holding his letter to Broadhead. Beneath the drawing appeared a parody of the incantation of Shakespeare's witches in "Macbeth": "Hand of treason, reeking red, / Poison fang of Copperhead, / Hampton's torch, Fred Douglass's fetter, / Booth's revolver, Blair's letter." A drawing of Blair appeared again after the election. It showed "October Gales" blowing away a diminutive Blair (again clutching his Broadhead letter) and a bemused Seymour, as the shattered planks of the Democratic Party platform—labeled "Repudiation," "Slavery," "Rebellion," and "Secession"—flew over their heads.[60] Nast's vivid imagery proved to be somewhat misleading, however. The defeat of Seymour and Blair in 1868 marked the end of a political era, not the beginning of one. By 1874 Nast had refocused his attention on political corruption, and it was the Radicals, together with their black allies, who became the subjects of his scorn.[61]

As Schurz looked back on the fight against Radicalism in Missouri, he judged Drake to have been an honest man but obsessed with holding the state in his rigid control. Drake wanted to be the "Republican boss of the State," wrote Schurz, who soon had an opportunity to challenge Drake's control. Senator John Henderson had effectively ended his political career when he broke with the Republicans to vote against conviction in the impeachment trial of Andrew Johnson. His term expired in March 1869, and Drake and the Radicals intended to replace him when the state legislature met in January. Schurz feared that if Drake succeeded in selecting the replacement, he would be "fully duplicated" in the Senate. Schurz himself became a candidate and won election to the Senate, despite Drake's opposition. A disgruntled Drake hastily returned to Washington, D.C., as Schurz celebrated the "annihilation" of Drake's "party-dictatorship in Missouri."[62]

As Radicalism receded in Missouri and in the nation, its legacy came more sharply into view. Missouri Radicals let the issue of Negro suffrage languish for two and a half years after Enos Clarke lay the petition of the Missouri Equal Rights League before them. But in the fall election of 1868, the legislature put before the electorate a Negro suffrage amendment to the state constitution. The voters decisively defeated the measure; in St. Louis, it lost by a two-to-one margin. However, when Congress passed the Fifteenth Amendment in February 1869, the Missouri legislature quickly ratified it. The Equal Rights League leader, James Milton Turner, then joined Radical leader Charles Drake to bring out nearly 20,000 new black voters in 1870.[63]

For women as well as for African Americans, the Civil War shattered some barriers and called many more into question. In St. Louis, on 8 May 1867, several of the women who had organized and supervised the work of the Ladies' Union Aid Society (LUAS) and the Western Sanitary Commission met at the Mercantile Library to organize the Woman Suffrage Association of Missouri. The LUAS president, Anna Clapp, attended the meeting. Her close wartime associates in the LUAS, Rebecca Hazard and Lucretia Hall, also attended. Penelope Allen, the sister of General John Pope, joined the association. Born in Kaskaskia, Illinois, she had married Beverly Allen, a successful St. Louis attorney, whose untimely death in 1845 left her a thirty-one-year-old widow and mother of two children. She did not remarry and remained an active member of the woman suffrage movement until 1902. She was remembered as "one of the most brilliant" of the "broad-minded, liberal women and men" who began the long struggle for woman suffrage in Missouri.[64]

The founders of the Missouri Woman Suffrage Association elected Virginia Minor as their first president and joined a national movement that considered the extension of the franchise to women a cause equal in importance to Negro suffrage. In December 1866, during a congressional discussion of suffrage in the District of Columbia, Senator Gratz Brown explicitly embraced this argument. "As a matter of fundamental principle," he declared, he did not "recognize the right of society to limit [suffrage] on any ground of race, color, or sex."[65] However, woman suffrage proved to be too radical to win easy acceptance. Radicalism in Missouri could not breach the barriers of race and sex. When Missouri voted down the black suffrage proposal in 1868, it became clear that the associated fight for woman suffrage would be a difficult one. For Minor, who had moved to St. Louis from Virginia by way of Mississippi, the association of women's rights with Negro rights was at once uncomfortable and unavoidable. "Can a woman or a negro vote in Missouri?" she asked rhetorically after the 1868 vote. She drew the troubling but obvious conclusion that the white men of Missouri had "placed us on the same level" with blacks. Minor insisted that women should no longer "submit to occupy so degraded a position."[66]

When Congress passed the Fifteenth Amendment in 1869, a similar sense of outrage spread through the ranks of woman suffrage advocates across the country and led to the formation of two national organizations, the National Woman Suffrage Association (NWSA), led by Susan B. Anthony, and the American Woman Suffrage Association (AWSA), led by Lucy Stone. Anthony's organization pressed for a federal constitutional amendment; Stone's worked to secure woman suffrage in the states. The St. Louis advocates of woman suffrage favored Anthony's approach. When the NWSA met in St. Louis in October 1869, Minor and her compatriots joined in the national organization's opposition to the ratification of the Fifteenth Amendment. Minor pressed the constitutional argument for women's rights from another direction as well. Working with her husband, the St. Louis lawyer Francis Minor, she developed an interpretation of the Thirteenth and Fourteenth Amendments to argue that when a state denied women the right to vote they denied them the equal protection of the law (guaranteed in the Fourteenth Amendment) and consigned them to a state of involuntary servitude (prohibited in the Thirteenth Amendment). Speaking to the meeting of the NWSA in St. Louis, she insisted that "the Constitution of the United States gives me every right and privilege to which every other citizen is entitled." The federal Constitution did not give the states the "power to prevent" a class of citizens from voting.[67]

By 1871 the suffrage movement in St. Louis showed signs of internal strain. Rebecca Hazard convinced the officers of the Missouri Suffrage Association to merge their organization with Lucy Stone's AWSA. Virginia Minor—joined by the vivacious Phoebe Couzins, who had recently graduated from Washington University with a degree in law—declared her continued loyalty to Susan B. Anthony's NWSA. Minor continued to press her constitutional arguments for woman suffrage. On 15 October 1872 she attempted to register to vote in St. Louis. Turned away, she and her husband filed a suit (women could not yet sue on their own behalf in Missouri). The state supreme court ruled against the Minors, arguing that the Fourteenth Amendment had been passed to protect former slaves, not women. On appeal, the U.S. Supreme Court issued a unanimous decision on 29 March 1875. The justices agreed with the Minors that women were citizens by the terms of the Fourteenth Amendment, but they insisted that suffrage was not an automatic right of citizenship. The states could deny the vote to women on the same principle that they denied it to children and to convicted felons.[68]

The passage of the Fifteenth Amendment disappointed the supporters of woman suffrage, but it hastened the demise of the test oath. Blair, vehemently opposed to black suffrage, harnessed racial animosity to his anti-Radical cause. The prospect of black men voting on an equal basis with white men—or worse, black men voting while white men were disenfranchised—represented his greatest fear regarding the effects of emancipation without colonization. Nevertheless, he found that his arguments against the test oath gained strength as black men won the right to vote. Even Charles Drake, who had fathered the oath but who had never fully embraced equal rights, acknowledged that with black men voting, white men should no longer be disenfranchised. This shift in political perspective accomplished what Blair's suit could not: there would be no constitutional judgment against the test oath for voting. To no one's surprise, the state supreme court ruled against Blair in March 1867. After many delays, the U. S. Supreme Court handed down its decision in *Blair v. Ridgley* late in January 1870. Reduced to eight justices, the Court divided evenly on the matter.[69]

It became clear after *Blair v. Ridgley* (1870) that a judicial nullification of the test oath for voting could not be expected soon. That realization, combined with the ratification of the Fifteenth Amendment early in February 1870, greatly strengthened the Liberal effort in Missouri to amend the 1865 constitution to get rid of the most objectionable features of the test oath. Late in February the legislature submitted three constitutional amendments to the voters. One eliminated the ex post facto features of the test oath, requiring from voters only a statement of current support for the constitutions of Missouri and the United States. The second amendment eliminated the test oath entirely for jurors. The third removed it as a requirement for holding office.[70]

Signs of the erosion of Radical power multiplied as Gratz Brown began his bid for the governorship in spring 1870. By September Brown and Senator Schurz formally launched the Liberal Republican movement in St. Louis. There and across the North, Liberals broke ranks with the "Stalwart" Republicans and organized to oppose Grant's reelection in 1872. In Missouri, Radical hegemony collapsed, and the constitutional amendments easily passed in the November election. A number of Radicals joined with Liberal Republicans and Democrats to end the era of the test oath. Even the black leader, James Milton Turner, urged newly enfranchised black men (representing 12.4 percent of registered voters in the state and 8 percent of registered voters in St. Louis County) to vote in favor of the new amendments. The Liberal Republicans, in coalition with Democrats, also won a decisive victory. Gratz Brown was elected governor, and Frank Blair won election to the legislature. When Drake, seeing the handwriting on the wall, resigned his Senate seat on 19 December 1870 to accept an appointment as chief justice of the U.S. Court of Claims, Blair was chosen by the legislature to complete Drake's unfinished term.[71]

Although the objectionable test oath had been removed from the state constitution, hostility toward the Drake constitution of 1865 remained. In his 1871 inaugural message, Governor Brown urged the general assembly to pass enabling legislation to call a new constitutional convention. After considerable debate and delay, the legislature acted in March 1874, a year after Brown had left office. Voters passed the proposition in November 1874 by a slim majority. Elections for delegates occurred in January 1875 and the constitutional convention met in Jefferson City from May to August of that year. In a light turnout, voters ratified the new constitution in October 1875. Although it imposed significant fiscal restraints on the legislature, of greater immediate importance to the future of St. Louis was a provision permitting the city to separate from St. Louis County. The move gave the city the home rule it had long sought. But the provision also defined a boundary between city and county that thereafter prevented the city's expansion.[72]

As the era of the test oath ended in Missouri, the federal government also lifted postwar disabilities on former Confederates. In 1872 Congress removed the proscriptions imposed by the Fourteenth Amendment.[73] In the new climate of political toleration, many of the men whom Drake had intended to bar forever from public life returned to positions of prominence and power.

Three Confederate comrades in arms—Thomas C. Reynolds, Joseph O. Shelby, and Trusten W. Polk—successfully made the transition from rebel to respected citizen. An anti-Benton Democrat, Reynolds had dueled with Gratz Brown (and left him wounded) in 1856 and had been elected lieutenant governor in 1860. Following the collapse of the Harney-Price agreement, Reynolds joined Governor Claiborne Jackson in exile. When Jackson died in 1862, Reynolds became the chief executive of the Confederate State of Missouri. He spent much of the war in the field with Sterling Price and with Gratz

Brown's cousin, the Confederate cavalry commander "Jo" Shelby. Reynolds, Price, and Shelby fled to Mexico at the end of the war.

Price and Shelby returned to Missouri in 1867. Shelby turned from his failed hemp business in western Missouri to railroad building and mining and settled in St. Louis. A Gold Democrat, he supported Grant and McKinley over their Democratic rivals (including Horatio Seymour and Frank Blair in 1868) and publicly repented his role as one of the Missouri Border Ruffians in the antebellum struggle over Kansas. (On that subject, Shelby said that he should have been shot.) With the support of former governor Thomas C. Fletcher, now a successful lawyer in St. Louis, President Cleveland appointed Shelby U.S. marshal for the Western District of Missouri in 1892. In that post, he suppressed rebellious railroad workers during the Pullman strike of 1894.

Reynolds returned to St. Louis from Mexico in 1868 and was elected to the state legislature in 1874. By the mid-1880s, however, he suffered declining physical and mental health. Plagued by "persistent melancholy" and "hallucinations," he died in 1887 from a fall down an elevator shaft, a presumed suicide.[74] The St. Louis lawyer Trusten Polk had served briefly as an antebellum governor of Missouri before being elected to the U.S. Senate in 1857, leaving that post to join the Confederacy. He was captured and imprisoned at the Johnson's Island prison camp near Sandusky, Ohio, although federal authorities soon paroled him for reasons of health. He promptly returned to the field, however, and joined Price's raid into Missouri in 1864. After a brief exile in Mexico, he returned to St. Louis and resumed his law practice as soon as the state supreme court overturned the test oath for lawyers in 1867.

Several prominent Missouri Confederates settled in St. Louis for the first time after the war. West Point–trained John Sappington Marmaduke had been captured at the end of Price's 1864 raid and was imprisoned at Fort Warren, Massachusetts. Released in August 1865, he first traveled to Europe and then in May 1866 settled in St. Louis, where he launched the *Journal of Agriculture* in 1868. It failed after four years, but it provided Marmaduke with a sufficient reputation as a modern agriculturist to justify his appointment in 1874 as secretary of the Missouri State Board of Agriculture. In 1875 he became a member of the state's railroad commission, and in 1884 he followed in the footsteps of his father, Meredith Marmaduke, and was elected governor.[75]

At the close of the war, Thomas W. Freeman moved to St. Louis. A Kentucky native who settled in Missouri in the early 1850s, he served two terms in the Confederacy Congress, representing Missouri. He settled in St. Louis, evidently with the goal of reestablishing his law career; however, he died of a fever in October 1865. Confederate Missouri's adjutant general and secretary of state, Warwick Hunter enjoyed a more substantial postwar career in St. Louis. He returned to the state after the war, practiced law in Jackson County for some time, and was elected to the state supreme court in 1874. Thereafter, he resided in St. Louis for thirty years, serving for a time as a circuit court judge.

Other old Confederates moved away. Thomas L. Snead, who had served as Price's aide-de-camp and as a Confederate congressman during the war, did not return to St. Louis, where he had edited the *Bulletin* before the war. He moved to New York City and became editor of the *Daily News*. Nevertheless, his history of the secession movement in St. Louis became a standard account for future historians. Basil Duke, who also wrote a history of the Confederate cause in St. Louis, returned briefly to the city after the war and then moved to Kentucky, where he pursued a successful legal career.[76]

The postwar years carried old Unionists in new directions as well. Galusha Anderson left St. Louis in 1866 to begin an academic career. He served as president of Denison University in Ohio for a number of years and died at his home in Massachusetts in 1918.[77] Henry T. Blow served two terms as a Republican congressman during the Civil War. Deciding not to seek a third term, he returned to his Carondelet home, south of St. Louis, early in 1867. In that year, his brother, the pro-Southern Taylor Blow, had Dred Scott's remains moved from the abandoned Methodist cemetery, which was being claimed by the growing city, to the new Catholic Calvary Cemetery. (Taylor Blow had become a Catholic in 1865.) Like the Protestant Bellefontaine Cemetery adjacent to it, Calvary did not allow the burial of African Americans except as servants of the whites to be interred there. In 1957, a granddaughter of Taylor Blow placed a stone on the previously unmarked grave. A bronze plaque donated by the St. Louis African American community also marks the burial site.[78]

John E. D. Couzins, whose wife Adaline and daughter Phoebe helped launch the woman suffrage movement in St. Louis, remained a loyal Republican after the war. He resigned from the St. Louis Police Board in 1865 and thereafter held a number of minor U.S. government posts. In 1881 President Chester Arthur appointed the sixty-eight-year-old Couzins U.S. marshal for the Eastern District of Missouri. During the Great Southwest Strike of 1886, he vigorously defended the property of the Wabash Railroad from the fury of the strikers and their supporters. In that fight he sustained severe injuries after falling from a moving train; he never fully recovered and died at his home on 1 September 1887. A member of Galusha Anderson's Second Baptist Church during the Civil War, Couzins was remembered for his physical courage and strength as well as for his stern adherence to the Union cause.[79]

James O. Broadhead returned to the Democratic Party after the war and won election to the conservative state constitutional convention of 1875. The next year, he was appointed a special U.S. counsel in the prosecution of the Whiskey Ring cases. The investigation soon focused on the internal revenue inspector John McDonald and on the Radical editor William McKee. Broadhead's investigation revealed that McDonald and McKee, working with President Grant's personal secretary, controlled federal patronage in St. Louis and manipulated the federal whiskey tax to finance the Radical fight against Carl Schurz and Gratz Brown. In 1872 McKee (with whiskey tax revenue) broke with the increasingly reform-minded *Missouri Democrat* and founded the pro-Grant *St. Louis Globe*. Three years later, again with funds skimmed from the whiskey tax, he bought out the rival *Democrat* and launched the *St. Louis Globe-Democrat*. By this time, he and others in the Whiskey Ring were profiting personally from the diverted tax funds. Broadhead's work contributed to more than 200 indictments and led to more than 100 convictions, including those of McDonald and McKee. In 1878, in recognition of Broadhead's national prominence, the members of the newly formed American Bar Association elected him as their organization's first president. In the early 1880s he served two terms in Congress. President Grover Cleveland appointed him U.S. minister to Switzerland in 1895. He resigned that post in 1897 and died in St. Louis the following year.[80]

The memory of the Union cause in St. Louis proved to be easier to maintain than the political cohesion of the wartime Republican Party. A statue of Thomas Hart Benton had been unveiled in May 1868. Schools and businesses closed for the event, and a crowd of 40,000 gathered at Lafayette Park to witness the celebration. Thirty cannon were fired to commemorate Benton's thirty years in the senate. Frank Blair delivered an oration for the occasion, and John C. Frémont, perhaps uncomfortable in such close proximity to his old foe, attended as an honored guest. Jessie Frémont pulled the cord to uncover the bronze image of her father, clad in Roman toga and sandals, facing West. Carved on the pedestal were the words, "There Is the East. There Lies the Road to India." The opening of Forest Park on the western edge of the city in 1876 provided the occasion for the unveiling of a statue of Edward Bates.

Each side of the red granite pedestal displayed bronze medallion reliefs of Bates's close friends and supporters: James B. Eads, Hamilton R. Gamble, Charles Gibson, and Henry S. Geyer. A statue of Frank Blair in Forest Park followed in 1885. Ulysses S. Grant's statue was unveiled in front of City Hall in 1888. An equestrian statue of General Franz Sigel was dedicated in Forest Park in 1906. In 1913 the St. Louis German-American Alliance dedicated a nude female statue near the Compton Heights Reservoir, "The Naked Truth," to memorialize the German journalists Carl Schurz, Emil Preetorius, and Carl Daenzer. In 1914, after considerable debate, the city authorized the erection of a Confederate memorial in Forest Park. Designed in part by the architect Wilbur Tyson Trueblood, the thirty-foot granite pillar features on its south face a bronze relief depicting a young man striding purposely southward. An older woman stands behind him expressing concern and resolve. A younger woman also falls behind him, displaying a greater sense of anxiety as she releases him from her embrace. A young boy looks up to the man in admiration. On the north face of the pillar, protected by a cannon pointing north, an inscription quotes Robert E. Lee in praise of the men who fought for the "Southern Confederacy." They had been "activated by the purest patriotism" and had fought to preserve the "independence of the states" and to "perpetuate the constitutional government" established by the Founding Fathers.[81]

The monuments erected in honor of Nathaniel Lyon tell a more complex story of philanthropy and historical memory. The first one, a thirty-foot red granite obelisk, was dedicated on 13 September 1874 at Lyon Park, a location that had previously been a part of the U.S. Arsenal grounds. (The parcel of land that became Lyon Park had been given to St. Louis by an act of Congress in 1871.) For many years, Lyon Park served as a public gathering place for celebrations of the capture of Camp Jackson and for commemorations of Lyon's death.

In the 1920s, members of a group called the Camp Jackson Union Soldiers Monument Association raised money to erect a second monument to the general. In 1929 the new equestrian statue was unveiled at the location of Camp Jackson. Thirty years later, it was relocated to the northwest corner of Lyon Park; memories of the Civil War lived on among Lyon's enemies as well as his champions. In 1959, Harriet Frost Fordyce, the daughter of General Daniel M. Frost, commander of the state militia at Camp Jackson, donated more than $1 million to St. Louis University. The purpose of the gift was to enable the university to purchase more than twenty acres of land then being

redeveloped by the city. As a condition of the gift, the school named the entire campus after General Frost, who had lived in St. Louis until his death in
1900. The land purchased by the university included the site of the equestrian statue of Lyon; with the cooperation of city officials it was removed to
Lyon Park.[82]

The creation of the Frost Campus of St. Louis University on the site of
Camp Jackson provided a lesson in the longevity of historical memory. But
there were plenty of memories to go around. When Galusha Anderson recalled the Camp Jackson affair, he attached particular significance to an event
he had witnessed on the morning after the state militia had been removed
from the encampment. Anderson joined a crowd that included supporters
and opponents of the federal troops, who were busy gathering up the equipment left behind by Frost's men. Near Anderson stood two black girls whom
he knew to be slaves from a nearby house. They were "grinning with delight"
as the federal soldiers loaded wagons with the militiamen's gear. Also nearby
stood a white girl whom Anderson knew to be from a Southern family with
strong secessionist views. "We'll whip you yet," exclaimed the white girl,
shaking her fist at the soldiers. The soldiers did not respond. But the black
girls, still smiling, replied, "They've got all your tents."[83] Frost's surrender at
Camp Jackson had been a defining moment for St. Louisans, including slaves,
who supported the Union cause.

Notes

Introduction

1. Allan Nevins, *The Emergence of Lincoln*, vol. 2, *Prologue to Civil War, 1859–1861* (New York: Charles Scribner's Sons, 1950), 440.

2. Richard H. Sewell, *Ballots for Freedom: Antislavery Politics in the United States, 1837–1860* (New York: Oxford University Press, 1976), 316–20; Allan Nevins, *Frémont: Pathmarker of the West* (1939; reprint, Lincoln: University of Nebraska Press, 1992), 421–38, 473–81; James M. McPherson, *Battle Cry of Freedom: The Civil War Era* (New York: Ballantine Books, 1988), 350–51.

3. There is no doubt that such opinions existed, but their influence is not self-evident. A one-sided use of this evidence is offered in Jeffrey S. Adler, *Yankee Merchants and the Making of the Urban West: The Rise and Fall of Antebellum St. Louis* (New York: Cambridge University Press, 1991).

4. Wendell Phillips, *Speeches, Lectures, and Letters* (New York: Negro Universities Press, 1968), 369.

5. Born in France in 1758, the elder Lucas immigrated to the United States in 1784 with a letter of introduction from Benjamin Franklin, then U.S. minister to France. On the recommendation of Albert Gallatin, President Jefferson appointed Lucas justice of the territorial superior court in the newly acquired Louisiana Territory. See Lawrence O. Christensen et al., eds., *Dictionary of Missouri Biography* (Columbia: University of Missouri Press, 1999), 505–7 (hereafter cited as *DMB*).

6. *DMB*, 505; William Nisbet Chambers, *Old Bullion Benton, Senator from the New West: Thomas Hart Benton, 1782–1856* (Boston: Little, Brown and Company, 1956), 66, 72.

7. Chambers, *Benton*, 74–76; Charles van Ravenswaay, "Bloody Island: Honor and Violence in Early Nineteenth Century St. Louis," *Gateway Heritage* 10 (spring 1990): 4–21.

8. [Thomas Hart Benton], *Thirty Years' View; or a History of the Working of the American Government for Thirty Years, from 1820 to 1850*, 2 vols. (1856; reprint, New York: Greenwood Press, 1968), 1: i–vi.

9. On southern dueling, see Bertram Wyatt-Brown, *Southern Honor: Ethics and Behavior in the Old South* (New York: Oxford University Press, 1982), especially 349–61.

10. Benton, *Thirty Years' View*, 1: 70–77.

1. "A Citizen of the United States"

1. Ray Allen Billington, *Westward Expansion: A History of the American Frontier*, 3d ed. (New York: Macmillan Company, 1967), 332; Lewis Atherton, *The Frontier Merchant in Mid-America* (Columbia: University of Missouri Press, 1971), 59–114.

2. Paul E. Johnson, *A Shopkeepers' Millennium: Society and Revivals in Rochester, New York, 1815–1837* (New York: Hill and Wang, 1978), 66–71; Charles G. Sellers, *The Market Revolution: Jacksonian America, 1815–1846* (New York: Oxford University Press, 1991), 3–33.

3. The earliest description of the event appeared in the *Missouri Republican,* 30 April 1836. It is quoted at length in Janet S. Hermann, "The McIntosh Affair," *Missouri Historical Society Bulletin* 26 (January 1970): 125–26. The fullest account from memory is in John F. Darby, *Personal Recollections* (St. Louis: G. I. Jones and Company, 1880), 237–41.

4. Theodore Dwight Weld, *American Slavery As It Is: Testimony of a Thousand Witnesses* (1839; reprint, New York: Arno Press, 1969), 156–57; Henry Boernstein, *Memoirs of a Nobody: The Missouri Years of an Austrian Radical, 1849–1866,* trans. Steven Rowan (St. Louis: Missouri Historical Society Press, 1987), 189–90. Mid-twentieth-century treatments of Lovejoy perpetuated the antislavery version of the McIntosh lynching. McIntosh, writes one historian "had been roasted alive over a slow fire of green wood." See Leonard L. Richards, *"Gentlemen of Property and Standing": Anti-Abolition Mobs in Jacksonian America* (New York: Oxford University Press, 1970), 101.

5. Florence Doll Cornet, ed., "The Experiences of a Midwest Salesman in 1836," *Missouri Historical Society Bulletin* 29 (July 1973): 234–35; Hermann, "The McIntosh Affair," 126–27; Weld, *American Slavery As It Is,* 156–57; J. Thomas Scharf, *History of St. Louis City and County,* 4 vols. (Philadelphia: Louis H. Everts, 1883), 2: 1825; Darby, *Personal Recollections,* 237–41; *DMB,* 229–30.

6. Richards, *"Gentlemen of Property and Standing,"* 101–11.

7. *St. Louis Observer,* 5 May 1836; Hermann, "The McIntosh Affair," 132–33; on the subject of mobism generally, with brief accounts of the McIntosh affair, see Paul A. Gilje, *Rioting in America* (Bloomington: Indiana University Press, 1996), and David Grimsted, *American Mobbing, 1828–1861: Toward Civil War* (New York: Oxford University Press, 1998).

8. *DMB,* 474–75. Lawless had been appointed circuit court judge in 1834. He served three years and died in St. Louis in 1846.

9. Mary Ellen Rowe, "'A Respectable Independence': The Early Career of John O'Fallon," *Missouri Historical Review* 90 (July 1996): 393–409; *DMB,* 579–80.

10. James Neal Primm, *Lion of the Valley: St. Louis Missouri* (Boulder, Colo.: Pruett Publishing Company, 1981), 182–85; Louis Filler, *The Crusade Against Slavery, 1830–1860* (New York: Harper and Row, 1960), 80–81.

11. Merton L. Dillon, *Elijah P. Lovejoy, Abolitionist Editor* (Urbana: University of Illinois Press, 1961), 122–23, 147, 157–59, 161–68.

12. Paul C. Nagel, *John Quincy Adams: A Public Life, a Private Life* (Cambridge: Harvard University Press, 1997), 364–65.

13. Stephen B. Oates, *To Purge This Land with Blood: A Biography of John Brown* (Amherst: University of Massachusetts Press, 1984), 41–42.

14. Merton L. Dillon, *Benjamin Lundy and the Struggle for Negro Freedom* (Urbana: University of Illinois Press, 1966), 258.

15. Quoted in Kenneth C. Kaufman, *Dred Scott's Advocate: A Biography of Roswell M. Field* (Columbia: University of Missouri Press, 1996), 53.

16. Paul Finkelman, *An Imperfect Union: Slavery, Federalism, and Comity* (Chapel Hill: University of North Carolina Press, 1981), 217–28.

17. The widely cited state cases were *Harry et al. v. Decker and Hopkins* (1818) and *Rankin v. Lydia* (1820). See Helen Tunnicliff Catterall, *Judicial Cases Concerning American Slavery and the Negro*, 5 vols. (1926; reprint, New York: Negro Universities Press, 1968), 1: 294–95; 3: 283.

18. Kaufman, *Roswell Field*, 102–9. Examining all of the St. Louis Circuit Court records for the period 1806 to 1865, historian Robert Moore found over two hundred suits initiated, with seventy-eight individuals (some of them children of freed mothers) winning their freedom. Most occurred after *Winny* and before the state supreme court decision in the *Dred Scott* case. See Robert Moore Jr., "A Ray of Hope, Extinguished: St. Louis Slave Suits for Freedom," *Gateway Heritage* 14 (winter 1993–1994): 4–15.

19. Kaufman, *Roswell Field*, 102–9.

20. William Hyde and Howard L. Conard, *Encyclopedia of the History of St. Louis: A Compendium of History and Biography for Ready Reference*, 4 vols. (New York: Southern History Company, 1899), 2: 1195–96; Necrology Collection, Missouri Historical Society (hereafter MHS), St. Louis; "The Story of an Old Clerk," MHS, *Glimpses of the Past* 1 (July 1934): 67. Krum and Field were both Democrats who supported the Republican Party during the Civil War. When Krum died in St. Louis in 1883, William Greenleaf Eliot led the funeral service.

21. Kaufman, *Roswell Field*, 63, 102–9.

22. Petition of Dred Scott to Hon. John M. Krum, Judge of the St. Louis Circuit Court, 6 April 1846, *Dred Scott v. Emerson*, Missouri State Archives, Jefferson City. The original manuscript of this petition, long hidden in the unprocessed records of the St. Louis Circuit Court, has recently been discovered and preserved through the efforts of Dr. Kenneth Winn and his staff at the Missouri State Archives.

23. In the summary of the *Dred Scott* case I have cited sources for quotations. Otherwise, the summary is drawn from Walter Ehrlich, *They Have No Rights: Dred Scott's Struggle for Freedom* (Westport, Conn.: Greenwood Press, 1979), 7–81; Don E. Fehrenbacher, *Slavery, Law and Politics: The Dred Scott Case in Historical Perspective* (New York: Oxford University Press, 1981), 121–50; and Kaufman, *Roswell Field*, 94–120, 135–48, 180–90.

24. Kaufman, *Roswell Field*, 136.

25. Ibid., 146.

26. For population figures, see Leonard P. Curry, *The Free Black in Urban America, 1800–1850: The Shadow of the Dream* (Chicago: University of Chicago Press, 1981), 245–50.

27. On the broader Jacksonian expression of these views, see Harry L. Watson, *Liberty and Power: The Politics of Jacksonian America* (New York: Farrar, Straus and Giroux, 1990), 242–43.

28. Kaufman, *Roswell Field*, 146.

29. James H. Lucas was the brother of Charles Lucas, the young man killed by Benton in the 1817 duel. In 1851 James H. Lucas founded the private place that bore his

name and provided many of the city's leading citizens with comfortable residential space. In 1866 he became the first president of the Missouri Historical Society in St. Louis. See Charles Van Ravenswaay, "Years of Turmoil, Years of Growth: St. Louis in the 1850s," *Missouri Historical Society Bulletin* 22 (July 1967): 318, and "In Memoriam. J. B. C. Lucas," *Missouri Historical Society Collections* 3 (1910): 320–21.

30. Charless was assassinated on a city street in 1859; he had testified against his assailant in a recent court proceeding. See Frances Hurd Stadler, *St. Louis Day by Day* (St. Louis: Patrice Press, 1989), 104–5.

31. Quoted in William Nisbet Chambers, *Old Bullion Benton, Senator from the New West: Thomas Hart Benton, 1782–1858* (Boston: Little, Brown, 1956), 340–41.

32. Benton traditionally had supported the principle that the Missouri General Assembly, because it elected the state's U.S. senators, had the right to instruct them on political matters. However, he responded to the Jackson Resolutions by insisting that he would take instructions only from the electorate.

33. Kaufman, *Roswell Field*, 174.

34. Judge Scott is quoted in John A. Bryan, "The Blow Family and Their Slave Dred Scott," *Missouri Historical Society Bulletin* 5 (October 1948): 20–21.

35. Quoted in Kaufman, *Roswell Field*, 177.

36. See, for example, Salmon P. Chase, *Union and Freedom, Without Compromise: Speech of Mr. Chase, of Ohio, on Mr. Clay's Compromise Resolutions* (Washington, D.C. [1850]).

37. Kaufman, *Roswell Field*, 186; Hyde and Conard, *Encyclopedia of the History of St. Louis*, 2: 869. Garland published *The Life of John Randolph of Roanoke* (New York: D. Appleton and Company, 1854) shortly before he died.

38. In 1857, when congress divided Missouri into two federal judicial districts, Wells became the first judge of the U.S. District Court for the Western District of Missouri. An unconditional Unionist and an advocate of wartime emancipation in Missouri, Wells died in St. Louis in 1864. See Roy T. King, "Robert William Wells: Jurist, Public Servant, and Designer of the Missouri State Seal," *Missouri Historical Review* 30 (January 1936): 107–31; *DMB*, 785.

39. Quoted in Kaufman, *Roswell Field*, 189.

40. Ibid., 202.

41. The hand-drawn firemen's map of St. Louis is in the MHS collection.

42. Edward Edwards, *History of the Volunteer Fire Department of St. Louis* (St. Louis: Edward Edwards, 1906), 62–65.

43. *Missouri Republican*, 10 July 1841. The printed "Confessions" of Madison, Warrick, Seward, and Brown, together with lithographic portraits of the men, are in a bound volume of court records in the Missouri Historical Society, St. Louis. Although stylized in certain respects (Brown's confession is particularly suspect regarding his involvement with abolitionists), there is no reason to doubt that the men traveled freely and widely on the western waters.

44. Edwards, *History of the Volunteer Fire Department*, xvii, 169–78, 204.

2. "A High Wall and a Deep Ditch"

1. James Neal Primm, *Economic Policy in the Development of a Western State: Missouri, 1820–1860* (Cambridge: Harvard University Press, 1954), especially 18–31.

2. Robert E. Shalhope, *Sterling Price: Portrait of a Southerner* (Columbia: University of Missouri Press, 1971), 15–17; Albert Castel, *General Sterling Price and the Civil War in the West* (Baton Rouge: Louisiana State University Press, 1968), 3; John Vollmer Mering, *The Whig Party in Missouri* (Columbia: University of Missouri Press, 1967), 66–67.

3. J. Mills Thornton, *Politics and Power in a Slave Society: Alabama, 1800–1860* (-Baton Rouge: Louisiana State University Press, 1978); Harry L. Watson, *Liberty and Power: The Politics of Jacksonian America* (New York: Hill and Wang, 1990).

4. Jeffrey S. Adler, *Yankee Merchants and the Making of the Urban West: The Rise and Fall of Antebellum St. Louis* (New York: Cambridge University Press, 1991), 29.

5. *Missouri Republican,* 12 April 1841.

6. Benton is quoted in William Nisbet Chambers, *Old Bullion Benton, Senator from the New West: Thomas Hart Benton, 1782–1856* (Boston: Little, Brown and Company, 1956), 172–74.

7. *Missouri Republican,* 2 November 1841.

8. James Neal Primm, *Lion of the Valley: St. Louis, Missouri* (Boulder, Colo.: Pruett Publishing Company, 1981), 144.

9. Adler, *Yankee Merchants,* 36.

10. "Remarks of Charles P. Johnson on the Occasion of the Presentation of the Portrait of Oliver D. Filley to the Missouri Historical Society, Thursday, May 21, 1903," *Missouri Historical Society Collections* 2 (July 1906): 1–12; William C. Winter, *The Civil War in St. Louis* (St. Louis: Missouri Historical Society Press, 1994), 118–19, 125; Steven Rowan, trans., ed., *Germans for a Free Missouri: Translations from the St. Louis Radical Press, 1857–1862* (Columbia: University of Missouri Press, 1983), 9, 10, 13, 15, 78n, 172n.

11. William Hyde and Howard L. Conard, *Encyclopedia of the History of St. Louis* (St. Louis: Southern History Company, 1899), 1: 225–27; *DMB,* 220–21.

12. Adler, *Yankee Merchants,* 85, 111, 130–36, argues on limited evidence that northeastern capitalists abandoned St. Louis for Chicago.

13. Primm, *Lion of the Valley,* 229; Sarah Forbes Hughes, ed., *Letters and Recollections of John Murray Forbes,* 2 vols. (Boston: Houghton, Mifflin and Company, 1900), 1: 177.

14. *DMB,* 179, 580; John Neal Hoover, *Cultural Cornerstone, 1846–1998* (St. Louis: Mercantile Library, 1998), 282–340; Primm, *Lion of the Valley,* 236.

15. [Thomas Hart Benton], *Thirty Years' View: A History of the Working of the American Government for Thirty Years, from 1820 to 1850,* 2 vols. (1856; reprint, New York: Greenwood Press, 1968), 2: 694–96.

16. Quoted in Chambers, *Old Bullion Benton,* 314.

17. Ibid., 316–18.

18. Allan Nevins, ed., 2 vols. *The Diary of Philip Hone, 1818–1851* (New York: Dodd, Mead and Company, 1927), 2: 809–10.

19. Quoted in Chambers, *Old Bullion Benton*, 322–23.

20. Quoted in Benton, *Thirty Years' View*, 2: 719.

21. Ibid., 2: 723.

22. Charles E. Rosenberg, *The Cholera Years: The United States in 1832, 1849, and 1866* (Chicago: University of Chicago Press, 1962), 2–3, 101–20.

23. William M. McPheeters, "History of Epidemic Cholera in St. Louis in 1849," in *One Hundred Years of Medicine and Surgery in Missouri* (St. Louis: St. Louis Star, 1900), 63–79. McPheeters worked amid a great deal of uncertainty and confusion regarding the disease. It was not until 1866 that English investigators identified contaminated drinking water as the medium through which the disease spread. In 1883 a German bacteriologist identified *Vibrio cholerae* as the germ that caused it. In retrospect it becomes clear that in the crowded poorer sections of St. Louis, located near the river and the stagnant ponds described by McPheeters, wells providing drinking water were easily contaminated from privies with the human fecal matter that bears the cholera bacteria.

24. Katharine T. Corbett, "Draining the Metropolis: The Politics of Sewers in Nineteenth-Century St. Louis," in *Common Fields: An Environmental History of St. Louis,* ed. Andrew Hurley (St. Louis: Missouri Historical Society Press, 1997), 111–13. Curtis came to St. Louis with considerable experience in river-drainage projects. A native of New York and a graduate of West Point, he left the army and eventually settled in Keokuk, Iowa, as chief engineer. He worked in St. Louis as chief engineer for three years before returning to Keokuk, where he was elected to three terms in Congress as a Republican. During the Civil War, he returned to St. Louis, notably as commander of the Department of the Missouri from September 1862 to May 1863. See, *Dictionary of American Biography,* 4: 619–20.

25. McPheeters, "Epidemic Cholera," 79.

26. William B. Napton diary, 101–2, n.d. (1854), William Barclay Napton Papers, MHS, St. Louis.

27. It was Napton who drafted the Jackson Resolutions for state senator Claiborne Jackson. During the Civil War, a son, Thomas L. Napton, served with Nathan Bedford Forrest. Napton's sympathies lay with the South, but he moved his family and law practice to the security of St. Louis in 1863 and avoided any difficulties with the federal authorities. Voters returned Napton to the state supreme court in 1872, and he remained on the bench until 1880 (see *DMB*, 568–69).

28. Adler, *Yankee Merchants*, 120–21.

29. Benton, *Thirty Years' View*, 2: 735.

30. Chandler, *Old Bullion Benton*, 348, 361–62.

31. *Union*, 9 May 1849.

32. Henry Boernstein, *Memoirs of a Nobody: The Missouri Years of an Austrian Radical, 1849–1866*, trans. Steven Rowan (St. Louis: Missouri Historical Society Press, 1997), 187–88.

33. Salmon P. Chase to Edwin M. Stanton, 2 July 1849, Edwin M. Stanton Papers, Library of Congress, Washington, D.C.

34. Quoted in William E. Parrish, *Frank Blair: Lincoln's Conservative* (Columbia: University of Missouri Press, 1998), 44.

35. [Thomas Hart Benton], *Mr. Benton's Anti-Compromise Speech. Speech of Mr. Benton, of Missouri, in the Senate of the United States, June 10, 1850* (Washington, D.C., 1850).

36. Benton, *Thirty Years' View,* 2: 749–80.

37. Ibid., 2: 788.

38. After the speech, Benton left St. Louis for Washington. In December the Missouri legislature convened, and the struggle for Benton's Senate seat entered its final phase. See Chandler, *Old Bullion Benton,* 369–72.

39. Parrish, *Frank Blair,* 46, 48, 53. St. Louisans named one of the city streets after Kossuth.

40. The popular Whig mayor of St. Louis, Luther Kennett, defeated Benton. See Chandler, *Old Bullion Benton,* 406–10.

41. Marvin R. Cain, *Lincoln's Attorney General: Edward Bates of Missouri* (Columbia: University of Missouri Press, 1965), 59, 69, 71, 73; *DMB,* 116–17.

42. Parrish, *Frank Blair,* 54–60.

43. Polk had moved to St. Louis from Delaware in 1836. In the 1854 congressional race, in which Kennett defeated Benton, Polk (denounced by Benton as a "nullifier") ran a very poor third. During most of the Civil War, Polk served with Confederate general Sterling Price. See *DMB,* 618–19; Chandler, *Old Bullion Benton,* 406–8, 422; and Walter H. Ryle, "Slavery and Party Realignment in Missouri in the State Election of 1856," *Missouri Historical Review* 34 (April 1945): 331.

44. In the new election for governor, James S. Rollins, a Boone County slave owner who had been endorsed by Benton, Blair, and the *Democrat,* lost in a close race with proslavery Democrat Robert M. Stewart. Geyer successfully represented John Sanford before the U.S. Supreme Court in the *Dred Scott* case.

45. Parrish, *Frank Blair,* 64–65.

46. Geyer's term ended on 3 March 1857, three days before the Supreme Court delivered its decision in the *Dred Scott* case.

47. Curtis argued for Dred Scott's freedom, but he (like the Blairs) opposed the abolitionists' moral condemnation of slavery. In Boston, Curtis served as the U.S. commissioner charged with enforcing the federal fugitive slave law (passed with the Compromise of 1850), and he facilitated amid great controversy the return to slavery of Thomas Sims and Anthony Burns. See Albert J. Von Frank, *The Trials of Anthony Burns: Freedom and Slavery in Emerson's Boston* (Cambridge: Harvard University Press, 1998), 28, 266–76.

48. The court reporter misspelled the name Sanford. The discussion of the *Dred Scott* case relies on Walter Ehrlich, *They Have No Rights: Dred Scott's Struggle for Freedom* (Westport, Conn.: Greenwood Press, 1979); Don E. Fehrenbacher, *The Dred Scott Case: Its Significance in American Law and Politics* (New York: Oxford University Press, 1978); and Kenneth C. Kaufman, *Dred Scott's Advocate: A Biography of Roswell M. Field* (Columbia: University of Missouri Press, 1996).

49. Thomas Hart Benton, *Historical and Legal Examination of That Part of the Decision of the Supreme Court of the United States, in the Dred Scott Case, Which Declares the Unconstitutionality of the Missouri Compromise Act . . . By the Author of the Thirty Years' View* (New York: D. Appleton, 1857).

50. Chaffee did not stand for reelection in 1858. See *Biographical Directory of the United States Congress, 1774–1996* (Alexandria, Va.: CQ Staff Directories, 1997), 787.

51. Walter B. Stevens, *St. Louis, History of the Fourth City, 1763–1909* (St. Louis: S. J. Clarke Publishing, 1909), 320–22.

52. Quoted in Chambers, *Old Bullion Benton,* 428–34.

53. Ibid., 434–39.

54. A Virginian by birth, Wimer died in 1863, fighting for the Confederacy.

55. Parrish, *Frank Blair,* 73, 83, 85; *Biographical Directory of the United States Congress,* 669.

56. E. L. Pierce to Charles Sumner, 3 June 1853, and F. P. Blair to Charles Sumner, 25 October 1863, Sumner Papers, Houghton Library, Harvard University, Cambridge, Massachusetts; Joshua Leavitt to S. P. Chase, 7 November 1860, Chase Papers, Library of Congress, Washington, D.C.; Parrish, *Frank Blair,* 138–39; Norma L. Peterson, *Freedom and Franchise: The Political Career of B. Gratz Brown* (Columbia: University of Missouri Press, 1965), 113–14.

57. Parrish, *Frank Blair,* 81.

58. Ibid., 87.

3. "The Union, Without an *If*"

1. *Charles Sumner: His Complete Works* (1900; reprint, New York: Negro Universities Press edition, 1969), 5: 125–26.

2. Henry Boernstein, *Memoirs of a Nobody: The Missouri Years of an Austrian Radical, 1849–1866,* trans. Steven Rowan (St. Louis: Missouri Historical Society Press, 1987), 186n, 266.

3. *Washington, D.C. Globe,* 7 January 1841.

4. Francis P. Blair Jr., *The Destiny of the Races of This Continent. An Address Delivered Before the Mercantile Library Association of Boston, Massachusetts, on the 26th of January, 1859* (Washington, D.C., 1859).

5. The Campbell Minstrels were a popular touring group in the 1840s and 1850s, and like other blackface performers in theaters across the country, they incorporated into their acts topics of local interest. See Louis S. Gerteis, "St. Louis Theatre in the Age of the Original Jim Crow," *Gateway Heritage* 15 (spring 1995): 32–41.

6. See the correspondence and clippings in the Brown-Reynolds Duel Collection, MHS. Brown's wound caused him to limp for the rest of his life.

7. How had previously been elected mayor in 1853 and had led the police into the streets to help quell violence during the nativist riot of 1854. *Missouri Historical Society Bulletin* 23 (July 1967): 311–12.

8. [B. Gratz Brown], *Speech of the Hon. B. Gratz Brown, of St. Louis, on the Subject of Gradual Emancipation in Missouri. Delivered in the House of Representatives, February 12, 1857* (Jefferson City, Mo., 1857), 6–31.

9. William Nisbet Chambers, *Old Bullion Benton, Senator from the New West: Thomas Hart Benton, 1782–1858* (Boston: Little, Brown and Company, 1956), 442–43.

10. Camille N. Dry and Richard J. Compton, *Pictorial St. Louis: The Great Metropolis of the Mississippi Valley: A Topographical Survey Drawn in Perspective* (St. Louis: Compton and Company, 1876), 39; obituary of Barton Able, *St. Louis Republican*, 7 May 1877.

11. William C. Winter, *The Civil War in St. Louis* (St. Louis: Missouri Historical Society Press, 1994), 31.

12. James Neal Primm, "Missouri, St. Louis, and the Secession Crisis," in *Germans for a Free Missouri: Translations from the St. Louis Radical Press, 1857–1862*, trans., ed. Steven Rowan (Columbia: University of Missouri Press, 1983), 14.

13. On the Know-Nothings and the rise of the Republican Party, see Tyler Anbinder, *Nativism and Slavery: The Northern Know-Nothings and the Politics of the 1850s* (New York: Oxford University Press, 1992), 246–78.

14. Rowan, trans., ed., *Germans for a Free Missouri*, 118, 120.

15. Ibid., 119; also, 107n and 119n.

16. Two Missouri counties—St. Louis and Gasconade—voted for Abraham Lincoln in 1860. Gasconade County, west of St. Louis on the Missouri River, was the site of the German town of Hermann.

17. Rowan, trans., ed., *Germans for a Free Missouri*, 126.

18. Ibid., 124–26.

19. A participant in the failed liberal revolution of 1848, Schurz was widely regarded as the leading spokesman for German immigrants. After the Civil War he moved to St. Louis, where he was part owner and editor of the *Westliche Post*.

20. Rowan, trans., ed., *Germans for a Free Missouri*, 107–8.

21. Virginia Laas, *Wartime Washington: The Civil War Letters of Elizabeth Blair Lee* (Urbana: University of Illinois Press, 1991), 20, 21n, 23, 24n.

22. Rowan, trans., ed., *Germans for a Free Missouri*, 155.

23. James Neal Primm, *Lion of the Valley: St. Louis, Missouri* (Boulder, Colo.: Pruett Publishing Company, 1981), 244–46.

24. Ibid., 246.

25. Quoted in Robert E. Shalhope, *Sterling Price: Portrait of a Southerner* (Columbia: University of Missouri Press, 1971), 147.

26. [Basil W. Duke], *Reminiscences of General Basil W. Duke, C.S.A.* (New York: Doubleday, Page and Company, 1911), 37–38; *DMB*, 264–65.

27. Duke's *Reminiscences*, 36–37.

28. Laas, *Wartime Washington*, 28, 31n.

29. James O. Broadhead, "St. Louis During the War," in the Broadhead Papers.

30. Ibid.

31. Ibid.

32. Ibid.

33. Ibid.

34. Thomas L. Snead, *The Fight for Missouri: From the Election of Lincoln to the Death of Lyon* (New York: Charles Scribner's Sons, 1886), 44.

35. William E. Parrish, *Turbulent Partnership: Missouri and the Union, 1861–1865* (Columbia: University of Missouri Press, 1963), 7–8.

36. Broadhead, "St. Louis During the War."

37. Frost is quoted in William E. Parrish, *Frank Blair: Lincoln's Conservative* (Columbia: University of Missouri Press, 1998), 93. See also Snead, *The Fight for Missouri*, 114, and Winter, *Civil War in St. Louis*, 39.

38. Rowan, trans., ed., *Germans for a Free Missouri*, 155–56; Boernstein, *Memoirs of a Nobody*, 275–76.

39. Broadhead, "St. Louis During the War."

40. Ibid. Rather than accept reassignment, Bell retired to his farm in St. Charles (see Winter, *Civil War in St. Louis*, 39).

41. Broadhead, "St. Louis During the War."

42. Ibid.

43. Snead, *The Fight for Missouri*, 130.

44. Ray W. Irwin, ed., "Missouri in Crisis: The Journal of Captain Albert Tracy, 1861," *Missouri Historical Review* 51 (October 1956): 11.

45. Winter, *Civil War in St. Louis*, 39–40; Snead, *The Fight for Missouri*, 117, 118.

46. Irwin, ed., "Journal of Captain Albert Tracy," 13.

47. Ibid.

48. Shalhope, *Price*, 149, 151–53.

49. Snead, *The Fight for Missouri*, 77–78.

50. Ibid., 79–81, 88.

51. *DMB*, 329–30.

52. "Fragments of Broadhead Collection," MHS, *Glimpses of the Past* 2, 4 (March 1935): 43n.

53. Snead, *The Fight for Missouri*, 91, 101–4. The House passed the measure on 2 March; the Senate passed it on 23 March.

54. Irwin, ed., "Journal of Captain Albert Tracy," 13–15. Pecksniff is the unctuous hypocrite in Charles Dickens's *Martin Chuzzelwit*.

55. Snead, *The Fight for Missouri*, 132–35.

56. Ibid., 95–96, 136; Winter, *Civil War in St. Louis*, 138.

57. Irwin, ed., "Journal of Captain Albert Tracy," 15–16; Rowan, trans., ed., *Germans for a Free Missouri*, 200.

58. Rowan, trans., ed., *Germans for a Free Missouri*, 166.

59. Irwin, ed., "Journal of Captain Albert Tracy," 17–18.

60. Rowan, trans., ed., *Germans for a Free Missouri*, 179.

61. Snead, *The Fight for Missouri*, 147–50.

62. C. F. Jackson to Hon L. P. Walker, 5 May 1861, *The War of the Rebellion: A Compilation of the Official Records of the Union and Confederate Armies* (Washington, D.C., 1881), 1, i, 690 (hereafter cited as *OR*). Jackson closed his letter "with prayers for your success."

63. Broadhead, "St. Louis During the War."

64. Ibid.; Winter, *Civil War in St. Louis*, 120, 146. After the war, Cavender founded the Grand Army of the Republic in Missouri.

65. Snead, *The Fight for Missouri*, 151–57.

66. Winter, *Civil War in St. Louis,* 31–32; Broadhead, "St. Louis During the War."

67. Claiborne Jackson to J. W. Tucker, 28 April 1861, in "Fragments of Broadhead Collection," MHS, *Glimpses of the Past,* 2, 4 (March 1935): 53. Broadhead, then provost marshal general, found this letter in a search of Tucker's office after he had been arrested on charges of treason. The *Anzeiger des Westens,* 11 December 1861, reported: "That ill-favored clergyman *J. W. Tucker* of the old *State Journal* has taken up his quill and fires away ad nauseam in the new Price organ called the *Missouri Army Argus.* He adds, 'Who can read these words and hold in his heart that it is possible for anyone to desert General Price in the field before he receives the reinforcements that he must quickly have. Soldiers! Brave men! Stand by your *glorious* old leader but a little longer!'—Then he carries on about the many Confederate victories and a recognition of the Confederacy by England." Rowan, trans., ed., *Germans for a Free Missouri,* 294.

68. Snead, *The Fight for Missouri,* 162–64; Broadhead, "St. Louis During the War."

69. Broadhead, "St. Louis During the War"; Winter, *Civil War in St. Louis,* 131–32, 114.

4. "This Means War"

1. Steven Rowan, trans., ed., *Germans for a Free Missouri: Translations from the St. Louis Radical Press, 1857–1862* (Columbia: University of Missouri Press, 1983), 188–89.

2. Ibid., 189.

3. Ibid.

4. Ray W. Irwin, ed., "Missouri in Crisis: The Journal of Captain Albert Tracy," *Missouri Historical Review* 51 (October 1956): 20–21.

5. Thomas L. Snead, *The Fight for Missouri: From the Election of Lincoln to the Death of Lyon* (New York: Charles Scribner's Sons, 1886), 163.

6. William Tecumseh Sherman, *Memoirs of General W. T. Sherman,* 2 vols., Library of America edition (New York, 1990), 1: 184–90.

7. Henry Boernstein, *Memoirs of a Nobody: The Missouri Years of an Austrian Radical, 1849–1866,* trans. Steven Rowan (St. Louis: Missouri Historical Society Press, 1987), 294, 294n.

8. Snead, *The Fight for Missouri,* 170.

9. James O. Broadhead, "St. Louis During the War," Broadhead Papers.

10. [Ulysses S. Grant], *Personal Memoirs of U. S. Grant,* 2 vols. (New York: Charles L. Webster and Company, 1885), 1: 234–35.

11. Daniel M. Frost to N. Lyon, 11 May 1861, *OR,* 1, iii, 7.

12. N. Lyon to L. Thomas, 11 May 1861, *OR,* 1, iii, 4.

13. William C. Winter, *The Civil War in St. Louis* (St. Louis: Missouri Historical Society Press, 1994), 39–40.

14. Ibid., 40–42.

15. Unless otherwise noted, the description of the federal advance on Camp Jackson is adapted from the detailed accounts provided in ibid., 40–47, and Boernstein, *Memoirs,* 285–309.

16. Rowan, trans., ed., *Germans for a Free Missouri,* 207.

17. Lyon left Charles Salomon's Fifth U.S. Volunteers in charge of the Arsenal; he also deployed elements of the First and Second Reserves to guard streets around it. The Fifth Reserves, commanded by Charles Stifel, had not yet been armed, and it remained at its barracks at Stifel's Brewery.

18. William C. Winter, ed., "'Like Sheep in a Slaughter Pen': A St. Louisan Remembers the Camp Jackson Massacre, May 10, 1861," *Gateway Heritage* 15 (spring 1995): 56–71.

19. Sherman, *Memoirs,* 1: 190–91.

20. Protest of Brig. Gen. Daniel M. Frost, Missouri State Militia, to Capt. N. Lyon, Comdg. U.S. Troops in and about St. Louis Arsenal, 10 May 1861, *OR,* 1, iii, 5–6.

21. N. Lyon, Captain, Second Infantry, Comdg. Troops, to General D. M. Frost, Commanding Camp Jackson, 10 May 1861, *OR,* 1, iii, 6–7.

22. D. M. Frost, Brig. Gen. Comdg. Camp Jackson, M.V.M. to Capt. N. Lyon, Commanding U.S. Troops, 10 May 1861, *OR,* 1, iii, 7.

23. Sherman, *Memoirs,* 1: 190–91.

24. Mark M. Krug, ed., *Mrs. [Sarah Jane Full] Hill's Journal—Civil War Reminiscences,* Lakeside Press edition (Chicago: R. R. Donnelley and Sons Company, 1980), 13–14.

25. The *Republican,* 12 May 1861, reported "twenty or thirty innocent people killed or wounded." Winter, *Civil War in St. Louis,* 52, has noted that this and other contemporary casualty lists often conflicted. Winter's casualty list of twenty-eight civilians killed at Camp Jackson included two women, a boy aged twelve, two boys aged fourteen, and an unidentified boy judged to be about fourteen.

26. The *Republican,* the city's Democratic newspaper, insisted that Blandowski died from a leg wound caused by a minié rifle ball, with which only federal troops had been supplied. This cause of death was attested to by Dr. T. Griswold Comstock, a respected figure in the St. Louis medical community and a physician at the Good Samaritan Hospital (Winter, *The Civil War in St. Louis,* 66).

27. Sherman, *Memoirs,* 1: 190–91.

28. Lucien Carr, *Missouri, a Bone of Contention* (Boston: Houghton, Mifflin and Company, 1888), 306.

29. Boernstein, *Memoirs,* 310.

30. *Republican,* 12 May 1861.

31. Rowan, trans., ed., *Germans for a Free Missouri,* 210–11; Winter, *Civil War in St. Louis,* 53.

32. Sherman wrote that "the regulars had passed and the head of Osterhaus's regiment of Home Guards had come up." Peter Joseph Osterhaus had been a Prussian militia officer before immigrating to the United States in 1849. He moved to St. Louis from Illinois in 1851. In 1861 he joined Boernstein's Second Regiment, U.S. Volunteers, as a private but was soon elected major. He served under Grant at Fort Donelson and then under Sherman during most of the Civil War, rising to the rank of major general. If Sherman's memory concerning Osterhaus's presence was correct, the troops then passing along Olive Street were not Home Guards but U.S. Volunteers. In any case, they were

inexperienced Germans. See Sherman, *Memoirs*, 1: 190–91. On Osterhaus, see Rowan, trans., ed., *Germans for a Free Missouri*, 230n.

33. Sherman, *Memoirs*, 1: 191–92.

34. Carr, *Missouri*, 307. Carr wrote his history of Missouri as assistant curator of the Peabody Museum of Archaeology and Ethnology at Harvard College.

35. William E. Parrish, *Frank Blair: Lincoln's Conservative* (Columbia: University of Missouri Press, 1998), 102. See also Christopher Phillips, *Damned Yankee: The Life of Nathaniel Lyon* (Columbia: University of Missouri Press, 1990), 263. Phillips judged the role of Lyon and Blair in the sectional crisis a great "tragedy" because they contributed to "the ascendancy of radicalism in the nation as a whole." Interestingly, in his more recent biography of Claiborne Jackson, Phillips argues that the governor's defiance of Lincoln's call for troops "buoyed" proslavery partisans in St. Louis and throughout the state. See Christopher Phillips, *Missouri's Confederate: Claiborne Fox Jackson and the Creation of Southern Identity in the Border West* (Columbia: University of Missouri Press, 2000), 246.

36. Thomas L. Snead, *The Fight for Missouri: From the Election of Lincoln to the Death of Lyon* (New York: Charles Scribner's Sons, 1886), 95–96.

37. Grant, *Memoirs*, 1: 231–38.

38. Report of Capt. Nathaniel Lyon to Col. L. Thomas, 11 May 1861, *OR*, 1, iii, 4–5.

39. Lyon to Thomas, 11 May 1861, *OR*, 1, iii, 4–5; Hyde and Conard, *Encyclopedia of the History of St. Louis*, 2: 859.

40. Lyon to Thomas, 11 May 1861, *OR*, 1, iii, 5.

41. D. M. Frost, Brigadier General, Missouri Volunteer Militia, to General William S. Harney, U.S.A., Commanding the Department of the West, 11 May 1861; Wm. S. Harney to Lieut. Col. E. D. Townsend, Asst. Adt. Gen., Hdqrs. of the Army, Washington, D.C., 18 May 1861; N. Lyon to Col. L. Thomas, 12 May 1861, *OR*, 1, iii, 7–9.

42. Broadhead, "St. Louis During the War."

43. Snead, *The Fight for Missouri*, 170.

44. Winter, *Civil War in St. Louis*, 55.

45. Quoted in Parrish, *Blair*, 103.

46. Rowan, trans., ed., *Germans for a Free Missouri*, 253; William E. Parrish, *Turbulent Partnership: Missouri and the Union, 1861–1865* (Columbia: University of Missouri Press, 1963), 26–27.

47. Snead, *The Fight for Missouri*, 170; Rowan, trans., ed., *Germans for a Free Missouri*, 218–19.

48. Wm. S. Harney, Proclamation, 12 May 1861, *OR*, 1, iii, 370.

49. N. Lyon to L. Thomas, 12 May 1861, *OR*, 1, iii, 9; Parrish, *Blair*, 104–5; Rowan, trans., ed., *Germans for a Free Missouri*, 253.

50. Snead, *The Fight for Missouri*, 187.

51. Wm. S. Harney to Simon Cameron, 15 May 1861, *OR*, 1, iii, 373.

52. Rowan, trans., ed., *Germans for a Free Missouri*, 232.

53. Winter, *The Civil War in St. Louis*, 115–16.

54. Wm. S. Harney to the People of the State of Missouri, 14 May 1861, *OR*, 1, iii, 371–72.

55. Parrish, *Turbulent Partnership*, 27–28.

56. Quoted in Parrish, *Blair*, 105.

57. Sterling Price and Wm. S. Harney to the People of the State of Missouri, 21 May 1861, *OR*, 1, iii, 374–75.

58. Albert Castel, *General Sterling Price and the Civil War in the West* (Baton Rouge: Louisiana State University Press, 1968), 16–22, concluded that neither Jackson nor Price was sincere in their claims of neutrality. They simply wanted to prevent "a premature showdown." Christopher Phillips, in his recent biography of Claiborne Jackson, concurs. Phillips argues that Jackson expected Lyon and Blair to attack Camp Jackson and that such a provocation would push Missouri toward secession. See Phillips, *Missouri's Confederate*, 242–59.

59. Parrish, *Blair*, 106.

60. Rowan, trans., ed., *Germans for a Free Missouri*, 230, 230n.

61. N. Lyon to Capt. S. Williams, Asst. Adjt. Gen., Hdqrs., Dept. West, Saint Louis, Mo., 16 May 1861; N. Cole to General Lyon, Commanding, 16 May 1861, *OR*, 1, iii, 9–11.

62. Snead, *The Fight for Missouri*, 187–92.

63. Wm. S. Harney to Sterling Price, 24 May 1861, and Sterling Price to W. S. Harney, 24 May 1861, *OR*, 1, iii, 378–79.

64. L. Thomas to W. S. Harney, 27 May 1861, and Wm. S. Harney to E. D. Townsend, 29 May 1861, *OR*, 1, iii, 376, 377.

65. Sterling Price to W. S. Harney, 29 May 1861, *OR*, 1, iii, 380–81.

66. Parrish, *Blair*, 107; N. Lyon, Genl. Orders, no. 5, 31 May 1861, *OR*, 1, iii, 381. Harney sought reassignment to California but remained on inactive duty throughout the war.

67. Quoted in Rowan, trans., ed., *Germans for a Free Missouri*, 246–48.

68. James W. Goodrich, ed., "The Civil War Letters of Bethiah Pyalt McKown," *Missouri Historical Review* 67 (January 1973): 237.

69. Snead, *The Fight for Missouri*, 197–200.

70. Snead, *The Fight for Missouri*, 197–200.

71. Bates and Gibson resigned their federal offices in 1864 when Lincoln chose anti-slavery radical Salmon P. Chase to be Roger B. Taney's replacement as chief justice of the United States. Bates had requested the appointment himself. Both men returned to St. Louis, where Bates died in 1869. Gibson remained active in city affairs until his death in 1899. See Marvin R. Cain, *Lincoln's Attorney General: Edward Bates of Missouri* (Columbia: University of Missouri Press, 1965), 163, 311–14, 333; Winter, *The Civil War in St. Louis*, 116.

72. Grant, *Memoirs*, 1: 267–68.

5. "A Passion for Seeming"

1. Benjamin F. Butler, *Butler's Book* (Boston: A. M. Thayer, 1892), 179–80; James M. McPherson, *Battle Cry of Freedom: The Civil War Era* (New York: Ballantine Books, 1988), 285.

2. Mark E. Neely Jr., *The Fate of Liberty: Abraham Lincoln and Civil Liberties* (New York: Oxford University Press, 1991), 4.

3. Quoted in Neely, *Fate of Liberty,* 9.

4. Article 1 enumerates the powers of Congress and Section 9 specifies limits to these powers, including the prohibition, "The Privilege of the Writ of Habeas Corpus shall not be suspended, unless when in Cases of Rebellion or Invasion the public Safety may require it."

5. Marshall D. Hier, "The Able and Upright Judge Samuel Treat," *St. Louis Bar Journal* (winter 1995): 42–44; Hyde and Conard, *Encyclopedia of the History of St. Louis,* 4: 2295–98; Neely, *Fate of Liberty,* 32–33; R. B. Taney to Hon. Samuel Treat, 5 June 1861, Treat Family Papers, MHS. See also William C. Winter, *The Civil War in St. Louis* (St. Louis: Missouri Historical Society Press, 1994), 55. The *McDonald* habeas corpus case raised difficult issues that would continue to plague commanders in St. Louis, but McDonald himself soon proved troublesome for other reasons as well. After being released from imprisonment, he joined Sterling Price's Missouri State Militia and fought against Lyon at the Battle of Wilson's Creek (August 1861). There, he was said to have taken charge of Lyon's body as federal troops retreated, and it was McDonald who delivered Lyon's body to federal authorities in Springfield.

6. *Dictionary of American Biography,* 1: 594–96.

7. Hyde and Conard, *Encyclopedia of the History of St. Louis,* 2553; Marshall D. Hier, "The Spellbinding Voice of Uriel Wright," *St. Louis Bar Journal* (summer 1990): 34ff.

8. Hyde and Conard, *Encyclopedia of the History of St. Louis,* 4: 2553; M. Heinrichsmeyer, "Carondelet Formerly and Now," trans. Gustav Heinrichs, *Missouri Historical Society Bulletin* (October 1960): 78.

9. Quoted in William E. Parrish, *Turbulent Partnership: Missouri and the Union, 1861–1865* (Columbia: University of Missouri Press, 1963), 24.

10. *Missouri Daily State Journal,* [19?] June 1861.

11. Quoted in Parrish, *Turbulent Partnership,* 47.

12. In June 1862, the state convention formally recognized Wright's departure and ordered a special election in St. Louis to choose his replacement. He briefly returned to St. Louis after the war, but he no longer felt at home. He soon moved to Winchester, Virginia, where he died in 1869 at the age of sixty-four. See Hyde and Conard, *Encyclopedia of the History of St. Louis,* 4: 2553.

13. William M. Smith, "Old Broadway, a Forgotten Street, and Its Park of Mounds," *Bulletin of the Missouri Historical Society* (April 1948): 162; Hyde and Conard, *Encyclopedia of the History of St. Louis,* 4: 2512.

14. James W. Goodrich, ed., "The Civil War Letters of Bethiah Pyalt McKown," *Missouri Historical Review* 67 (January 1973): 239.

15. William F. Swindler, "The Southern Press in Missouri, 1861–1864," *Missouri Historical Review* 35 (April 1941): 394–400; Goodrich, ed., "Civil War Letters," 241–43.

16. Frederick J. Blue, *Salmon P. Chase: A Life in Politics* (Kent, Ohio: Kent State University Press, 1987), 269.

17. William Parrish argued that only impeachment could remove duly elected officials from office. It followed, therefore, that the reconvened state convention usurped the legislature's power of impeachment. Parrish judged the "legality" of the convention's

actions after the flight of Governor Jackson to be "highly questionable." Michael Fellman began his treatment of Missouri guerrillas during the Civil War by characterizing the Camp Jackson affair as a "coup d'etat" and the subsequent actions of the state convention as "quite Illegal." See Parrish, *Turbulent Partnership*, 47, and Michael Fellman, *Inside War: The Guerrilla Conflict in Missouri During the American Civil War* (New York: Oxford University Press, 1989), 10–11.

18. Quoted in Parrish, *Turbulent Partnership*, 7–8, 33.

19. Ibid., 10, 33–36.

20. Ibid., 37.

21. S. T. Glover to J. O. Broadhead, 29 July 1861, in "Fragments of Broadhead Collection," MHS, *Glimpses of the Past*, 2: 4 (March 1935): 65.

22. Quoted in William E. Parrish, *Frank Blair: Lincoln's Conservative* (Columbia: University of Missouri Press, 1998), 118.

23. Quoted in Pamela Herr, *Jessie Benton Frémont: A Biography* (New York: F. Watts, 1987), 65.

24. Herr, *Jessie Benton Frémont*, 71–72.

25. Quoted in A. Hunter Dupree, *Asa Gray, 1810–1888* (Cambridge: Harvard University Press, 1959), 157.

26. Herr, *Jessie Benton Frémont*, 151–52; Emerson is quoted at 122.

27. Allan Nevins, *Frémont: Pathmarker of the West* (1939; reprint, Lincoln: University of Nebraska Press, 1992), 343–44, 349, 351, 366; Hyde and Conard, *Encyclopedia of the History of St. Louis*, 2: 948–49. Grimsley's dragoon saddle became popular with army officers, and he grew wealthy with large government orders. He died in St. Louis in December 1861.

28. Nevins, *Frémont*, 388; Herr, *Jessie Benton Frémont*, 231.

29. Nevins, *Frémont*, 418; Benton is quoted at 448.

30. Ibid., 461; Herr, *Jessie Benton Frémont*, 294.

31. Nevins, *Frémont*, 473; Winter, *The Civil War in St. Louis*, 31–33, 69–70.

32. Winter, *Civil War in St. Louis*, 69–70.

33. Henry Boernstein, *Memoirs of a Nobody: The Missouri Years of an Austrian Radical, 1849–1866*, trans. Steven Rowan (St. Louis: Missouri Historical Society Press, 1987), 338.

34. Mark M. Krug, ed., *Mrs. [Sarah Jane Full] Hill's Journal—Civil War Reminiscences*, Lakeside Press edition (Chicago: R. R. Donnelley and Sons Company, 1980), 31.

35. Herr, *Jessie Benton Frémont*, 327.

36. Quoted in Parrish, *Turbulent Partnership*, 39.

37. Bates and Wright are quoted in ibid., 45–46.

38. Parrish, *Frank Blair*, 119–20.

39. Ibid., 120.

40. L. Polk to Hon. L. P. Walker, 28 July 1861, *OR*, 1, iii, 617–18.

41. Gid. J. Pillow to Major-General Polk, 28 July 1861, *OR*, 1, iii, 619.

42. Nevins, *Frémont*, 482.

43. Jared C. Lobdell, "Nathaniel Lyon and the Battle of Wilson's Creek," *Missouri Historical Society Bulletin* 17 (October 1960): 3–15; Albert Castel, *General Sterling Price and*

the Civil War in the West (Baton Rouge: Louisiana State University Press, 1968), 25–47; Robert E. Shalhope, *Sterling Price: Portrait of a Southerner* (Columbia: University of Missouri Press, 1971), 174–78.

44. Parrish, *Turbulent Partnership,* 67.

45. Robert E. Miller, "Zagonyi," *Missouri Historical Review* 76 (January 1982): 174–92.

46. Herr, *Jessie Benton Frémont,* 330; Blair is quoted at 332.

47. Nevins, *Frémont,* 494.

48. Robert L. Turkoly-Joczik, "Frémont and the Western Department," *Missouri Historical Review* 82 (July 1988): 371–72. Asboth later commanded a division at the Battle of Pea Ridge.

49. The *Democrat,* which Blair had helped establish in 1852, supported Frémont; the *Republican,* the city's proslavery Democratic paper, vehemently opposed him.

50. Parrish, *Frank Blair,* 123, 151; Steven Rowan, trans., ed., *Germans for a Free Missouri: Translations from the St. Louis Radical Press, 1857–1862* (Columbia: University of Missouri Press, 1983), 285n; and Nevins, *Frémont,* 495.

51. Orders, no. 3, Headquarters, District of North Missouri, 2 August 1861; Brigadier General John Pope to Colonel J. D. Stevenson, 2 August 1861; Pope to Commanding Officer, Iowa Forces, Keokuk, Iowa, 2 August 1862; Pope to Colonel Worthington, 2 August 1861; and Pope to J. H. Sturgeon, 3 August 1861, *OR,* 1, iii, 420–24.

52. Parrish, *Turbulent Partnership,* 54.

53. J. C. Frémont, Proclamation, Headquarters, Western Department, 30 August 1861, *OR,* 1, iii, 466–67. The first slaves freed by Frémont's orders were Hiram Reed and Frank Lewis. Both had been owned by Thomas Snead. See Vernon L. Volpe, "The Frémonts and Emancipation in Missouri," *Historian* 56 (winter 1994): 339–54.

54. A. Lincoln to Major-General Frémont, 2 September 1861, *OR,* 1, iii, 469–70.

55. J. C. Frémont to the President, 8 September 1861, *OR,* 1, iii, 477–78.

56. A. Lincoln to Maj. Gen. John C. Frémont, 11 September 1861, *OR,* 1, iii, 485–86. According to Lincoln's secretary, John Hay, the president feared that after issuing the emancipation order Frémont had "set up a bureau of abolition, giving free papers, and occupying his time apparently with little else" (see Volpe, "The Frémonts," 342).

57. Quoted in Nevins, *Frémont,* 517.

58. Quoted in Herr, *Jessie Benton Frémont,* 340–41.

59. Quoted in ibid., 341.

60. Parrish, *Turbulent Partnership,* 54–55.

61. Ibid., 56.

62. Ibid., 58.

63. Ibid., 65. A Kentucky native who had moved to St. Louis in 1839, McPherson was president of the Missouri Pacific Railroad. See William B. Stevens, *St. Louis. History of the Fourth City, 1763–1909* (St. Louis: S. J. Clarke Publishing Company, 1909), 229.

64. Parrish, *Turbulent Partnership,* 62. Snead's slaves clearly met the criteria set forth in the first Confiscation Act to justify their confiscation by federal authorities. Frémont's proclamation went further and emancipated them.

Civil War St. Louis

65. J. C. Frémont to the President, 8 September 1861, *OR*, 1, iii, 428–79.

66. Parrish, *Frank Blair*, 125; Frémont and Montgomery Blair are quoted in Nevins, *Frémont*, 520.

67. Quoted in Herr, *Jessie Benton Frémont*, 342.

68. Quoted in Nevins, *Frémont*, 530n.

69. Quoted in Parrish, *Turbulent Partnership*, 73.

70. Quoted in Nevins, *Frémont*, 532.

71. Quoted in ibid., 529.

72. Parrish, *Turbulent Partnership*, 77–80.

73. General Orders, no. 96, War Dept., Adjt. Gen.'s Office, 7 November 1861, *OR*, 1, iii, 565–66.

74. Quoted in Nevins, *Frémont*, 531.

75. Quoted in ibid., 535.

76. For Zagonyi's account of the attack, see Chas. Zagonyi to Col. J. H. Eaton, 28 October 1861, *OR*, 1, iii, 251–52.

77. Quoted in Nevins, *Frémont*, 536.

78. Quoted in ibid., 538.

79. L. Thomas to Hon. Simon Cameron, 21 October 1861, *OR*, 1, iii, 540–49.

80. Quoted in Parrish, *Frank Blair*, 128.

81. Quoted in Nevins, *Frémont*, 535.

82. Parrish, *Frank Blair*, 129.

83. Quoted in Nevins, *Frémont*, 496.

84. Eliot to Chase, 1 November 1861, Chase Papers; Nevins, *Frémont*, 543–45.

85. A. Lincoln to the Commander of the Department of the West, 24 October 1861, *OR*, 1, iii, 553–54.

86. Quoted in Herr, *Jessie Benton Frémont*, 351.

87. Nevins, *Frémont*, 569. The Frémonts undoubtedly savored a bitter vindication when Pope sustained one of the most stunning defeats of the war at the Second Battle of Bull Run in August 1862.

6. "A Friend of the Enemy"

1. M. Jeff. Thompson to Joseph Tucker, 16 July 1961, *OR*, 1, iii, 608–9.

2. J. C. Frémont, Proclamation, 14 August 1861, *OR*, 1, iii, 442; see also James O. Broadhead, "St. Louis During the War," Broadhead Papers.

3. William B. Hesseltine, "Military Prisons of St. Louis, 1861–1865," *Missouri Historical Review* 23 (April 1929): 381–82; William C. Winter, *The Civil War in St. Louis* (St. Louis: Missouri Historical Society), 84.

4. William G. B. Carson, "Secesh," *Missouri Historical Society Bulletin* 23 (January 1967): 123.

5. The succession of commanders in Missouri brought a succession of provost marshals. During Frémont's command (July–October 1861), Major Justus McKinstry served as provost marshal and quartermaster; in December 1861 he was arrested for sell-

ing war contracts. George E. Leighton and Bernard G. Farrar served as provost marshals during Henry Halleck's command (November 1861–March 1862), with Farrar continuing under John Schofield (January–September 1862). Thomas T. Gantt and Franklin A. Dick served under Samuel Curtis (September 1862–May 1863). When Schofield resumed command in Missouri (May 1863–January 1864), he appointed James O. Broadhead provost marshal. J. P. Sanderson served under William Rosecrans (January–December 1864). Sanderson's investigation of the clandestine Order of American Knights marked the end of military efforts to uncover disloyal persons in St. Louis. See Broadhead, "St. Louis During the War."

6. Schuyler Hamilton to Col. J. M. Tuttle, 7 February 1862, and Chas. C. Smith to Lieutenant-Colonel Burbank, 12 February 1862, *OR*, 2, iii, 245–46, 257–58.

7. Hesseltine, "Military Prisons," 383.

8. Schuyler Hamilton to Colonel Tuttle, 9 January 1862, *OR*, 2, iii, 185–86.

9. Quoted in Hesseltine, "Military Prisons," 384–85.

10. Major Genl. H. W. Halleck to Col. B. G. Farrar, 18 December 1861, in Ira Berlin et al., eds., *Freedom: A Documentary History of Emancipation, 1861–1867*, Series 1, vol. 1, *The Destruction of Slavery* (Cambridge: Cambridge University Press, 1985), 419–20 (hereafter cited as *Freedom*, 1, 1).

11. Schuyler Hamilton to Colonel Tuttle, 9 January 1862, *OR*, 2, iii, 185–86.

12. H. W. Halleck to General McClellan (for the President of the United States), 20 November 1861, *OR*, 1, viii, 817; A. Lincoln, 21 November 1861, endorsement of H. W. Halleck to General McClellan, 20 November 1861, *OR*, 2, i, 230.

13. H. W. Halleck to Brig. Gen. Lorenzo Thomas, 25 November 1861, *OR*, 1, viii, 817–18. Mark E. Neely Jr., *The Fate of Liberty: Abraham Lincoln and Civil Liberties* (New York: Oxford University Press, 1991), 36–37.

14. L. Thomas to Maj. Gen. H. W. Halleck, 25 November 1861 ("In reply to your telegram of the 20th instant the general-in-chief desires you to give your views more fully"); and H. W. Halleck to Maj. Gen. George B. McClellan, 30 November 1861, *OR*, 2, i, 231–33.

15. William Hyde and Howard L. Conard, *Encyclopedia of the History of St. Louis: A Compendium of History and Biography for Ready Reference* (New York: Southern History Company, 1899), 1: 259. Farrar remained close to Frank Blair and served as a pallbearer at his funeral. See William E. Parrish, *Frank Blair: Lincoln's Conservative* (Columbia: University of Missouri Press, 1998), 131, 288.

16. Hdqrs., Department of the Missouri, General Orders, no. 13, 4 December 1861; Abraham Lincoln and Wm. H. Seward to Maj. Gen. Henry W. Halleck, 2 December 1861; Hdqrs., Department of the Missouri, General Orders, no. 34, 26 December 1861, *OR*, 2, i, 155, 233–36; Neely, *Fate of Liberty*, 37.

17. W. Wayne Smith, "An Experiment in Counterinsurgency: The Assessment of Confederate Sympathizers in Missouri," *Journal of Southern History* 35 (August 1969): 362–64.

18. *Republican*, 28 December 1861; *OR*, 1, viii, 823–24, 490; Smith, "Counterinsurgency," 365–66.

19. Carson, "Secesh," 127–30. Charles C. Miller was the antebellum business partner of John Bowen, a Confederate army officer. See Winter, *The Civil War in St. Louis*, 22.

20. Carson, "Secesh," 127–30; James W. Goodrich, ed., "The Civil War Letters of Bethiah Pyalt McKown," *Missouri Historical Review* 67 (January 1973): 246.

21. W. G. Eliot to Gov. H. R. Gamble, 1 December 1862, *OR*, 1, xxii, pt. 1, 801–2. On 10 December 1862, Lincoln asked General Curtis to suspend General Schofield's order regarding assessments and to inform him of his views on the matter. Curtis replied that only military necessity could justify assessments and that such a necessity did not then exist. See Roy P. Basler, ed., *The Collected Works of Abraham Lincoln*, 8 vols. (New Brunswick, N.J.: Rutgers University Press, 1953), 5: 548.

22. War Dept., Adjt. General's Office, General Orders, no. 100, 24 April 1863, *OR*, 3, iii, 148–64.

23. Bernard G. Farrar, Special Orders, no. 61, 3 September 1862, *OR*, 2, iv, 486.

24. It was not incidental to their fate that three of the daughters of the wealthy slaveholder, Dr. John Sappington of Saline County, were the wives of the twice-widowed Claiborne Jackson. See Winter, *The Civil War in St. Louis*, 86; Charles van Ravenswaay, "Arrow Rock, Missouri," *Missouri Historical Society Bulletin* 15 (April 1959): 211n; *DMB*, 423.

25. Winter, *Civil War in St. Louis*, 85–86.

26. Hannah Isabella Stagg, "Local Incidents of the Civil War," *Missouri Historical Society Collections* 4 (1912): 68.

27. McAnally's account is in John A. Marshall, *American Bastile: A History of Arrests and Imprisonments of American Citizens During the Late Civil War* (1869; reprint, New York: Da Capo Press, 1970), 487–500. Marshall's title reveals his prejudice, but there is no reason to doubt the accuracy of McAnally's account.

28. Winter, *The Civil War in St. Louis*, 23.

29. Robert E. Miller, "Daniel Marsh Frost, C.S.A." *Missouri Historical Review* 85 (July 1991): 381–401; Winter, *The Civil War in St. Louis*, 138–39.

30. Miller, "Frost," 381–401; F. A. Dick to Col. W. Hoffman [commissary general of prisoners], 5 March 1863, *OR*, 2, v, 319–20. After the banishment, Frost moved his family to Matamoros, Mexico, and soon resigned his commission in the Confederate army, moving with his family to Cuba and then to Montreal. With his family safely settled in Canada, Frost sought a new Confederate command. He did not receive one, however, in part due to charges of desertion leveled against him by opponents in Arkansas. President Andrew Johnson pardoned Frost in October 1865, and he returned with his family to St. Louis, where he remained active in Democratic politics. He died in 1900 on his Hazelwood estate.

31. St. Louis Directory, 1860; Necrology Collection, MHS; Walter Ehrlich, *Zion in the Valley: The Jewish Community of St. Louis* (Columbia: University of Missouri Press, 1997), 42.

32. Parrish, *Frank Blair*, 172.

33. Hyde and Conard, *Encyclopedia of the History of St. Louis*, 1: 2512; Winter, *The Civil War in St. Louis*, 119.

34. Hyde and Conard, *Encyclopedia of the History of St. Louis,* 3: 1404–10.

35. Cynthia Dehaven Pitcock and Bill J. Gurley, "'I Acted from Principle': William Marcellus McPheeters, Confederate Surgeon," *Missouri Historical Review* 89 (July 1995): 384–405; MHS, Civil War Scrapbooks, vol. 1.

36. In January 1865 federal authorities banished McPheeters's wife Sallie to Arkansas, where she joined her husband for the final months of the war. On their return to St. Louis on 16 July 1865, federal authorities required the doctor and his wife to sign the loyalty oath they had for so long rejected. McPheeters resumed his medical career and prospered in St. Louis until his death in 1905 (Pitcock and Gurley, "McPheeters," 384–405).

37. Quoted in Milan James Kedro, "The Civil War's Effect upon an Urban Church: The St. Louis Presbytery Under Martial Law," *Missouri Historical Society Bulletin* 27 (April 1971): 179.

38. Quoted in ibid., 180.

39. Quoted in ibid., 181.

40. Major General Saml. R. Curtis to Abraham Lincoln, 30 December 1862, *OR,* 1, xxii, pt. 1, 884.

41. Basler, ed., *Works of Lincoln,* 6: 33–34.

42. George M. Apperson, "Presbyterians and Radical Republicans: President Lincoln, Dr. McPheeters, and Civil War in Missouri," *American Presbyterians* 73 (winter 1995): 239–49; William E. Parrish, *Turbulent Partnership: Missouri and the Union, 1861–1865* (Columbia: University of Missouri Press, 1963), 110–13; Hyde and Conard, *Encyclopedia of the History of St. Louis,* 3: 1404–8.

43. Bernard G. Farrar to Major Hunt, 8 March 1862, *OR,* 2, i, 173–74; Neely, *The Fate of Liberty,* 39.

44. Quoted in Neely, *The Fate of Liberty,* 39.

45. Quoted in ibid., 46.

46. Ibid.

47. M. M. Quaife, ed., *Absalom Grimes, Confederate Mail Runner* (New Haven: Yale University Press, 1926), 1–3, 43–44.

48. Ibid., 45, 159–62, 165, 175, 187.

49. Ibid., 163–65, 175.

50. Geo. E. Leighton to Lieut. Col. C. W. Marsh, 22 May 1862, *OR,* 2, iii, 574–75; Hesseltine, "Military Prisons," 386, 399.

51. Hesseltine, "Military Prisons," 387–88.

52. Samuel A. Rice and Louis D. Hubbard, Report Pursuant to Special Orders, no. 16, 12 December 1862, with an endorsement by James E. Yeatman of the Western Sanitary Commission, *OR,* 2, v, 75–76; Hesseltine, "Military Prisons," 388.

53. Wm. H. Van Buren, M.D., to Hon. E. M. Stanton, 10 May 1863, enclosing the report of Doctors Thomas Hun and Mason F. Gogswell of the United States Sanitary Commission, *OR,* 2, v, 587–89; Hesseltine, "Military Prisons," 391–93.

54. A. M. Clark, Surgeon and Acting Medical Inspector of Prisoners of War, to Col. W. Hoffman, Commissary General of Prisoners, Washington, D.C., 18 February 1864, *OR,* 2, vi, 967–69.

55. A. M. Clark, Surgeon and Acting Medical Inspector of Prisoners of War to Col. W. Hoffman, Commissary General of Prisoners, Washington, D.C., 22 February 1864, *OR*, 2, vi, 981–83.

56. Quoted in Hesseltine, "Military Prisons," 394.

57. Hesseltine, "Military Prisons," 389–90, 396; Griffin Frost, *Camp and Prison Journal, Embracing Scenes in Camp, on the March, and in Prisons* (1867; reprint, Iowa City: Camp Pope Bookshop, 1994), 27–35.

58. William J. Wooden to R. E. Wooden (his sister), 10 June 1863, and William J. Wooden to Nancy M. Wooden, 2 July 1863, Letters of William J. Wooden, Missouri State Archives, Jefferson City (hereafter cited as MSA).

59. William J. Wooden to Nancy M. Wooden, 13 July 1863, and William J. Wooden to Nancy M. Wooden, 23 July 1863, Wooden Letters.

60. William J. Wooden to A. E. Wooden, 3 August 1863; William J. Wooden to Nancy M. Wooden, 2 September 1863; William J. Wooden to A. E. Wooden, 17 September 1863; William J. Wooden to Nancy M. Wooden, 23 November 1863; William J. Wooden to Nancy M. Wooden, 26 January 1864; William J. Wooden to Isaac Wooden (his father), 4 March 1864, Wooden Letters. For biographical data on William J. Wooden, see George M. Cowan Jr. to Missouri State Archives, 8 August 1999, MSA.

61. Basler, ed., *Works of Lincoln*, 6: 326, 492.

62. Frank L. Klement, *Dark Lanterns: Secret Political Societies, Conspiracies, and Treason Trials in the Civil War* (Baton Rouge: Louisiana State University Press, 1984), 760.

63. Ibid., 136–50.

64. Frank L. Klement, *The Copperheads in the Middle West* (Chicago: University of Chicago Press, 1960), 183; Klement, *Dark Lanterns*, 76. Klement's critique of the Sanderson investigation is substantially the same in both studies; compare *Copperheads*, 170–205, and *Dark Lanterns*, 64–90. In *Dark Lanterns*, he added fresh details to the story and corrected minor errors that appeared in *Copperheads*.

65. Klement, *Dark Lanterns*, 64–65.

66. "Statement of William Taylor," *OR*, 2, vii, 251–54. "Edward F. Hoffman" submitted a less detailed report. He had attended meetings at Montgomery House on Broadway and named John Taylor as the leader. See "Report of Edward F. Hoffman," *OR*, 2, vii, 254–56. Klement described Hoffman as one of Sanderson's "most competent detectives," evidently because Hoffman reported no overt conspiracy. Klement described the meetings where Taylor met Hunt as gatherings of "Democratic Associations," where Hunt talked to Taylor "freely about the Order of American Knights, its objectives, internal organization, and its future." Taylor reported infiltrating well-attended meetings of the OAK itself (see Klement, *Dark Lanterns*, 79, 82).

67. J. P. Sanderson to [General W. S. Rosecrans], 20 August 1864, *OR*, 2, vii, 626–60. Hunt had been interrogated on 23 July 1864. See *DMB*, 413–14.

68. "To justify his generalizations about the American Knights," wrote Klement, Sanderson ordered the arrest of five alleged members: Charles L. Hunt, Charles E. Dunn, E. H. A. Habicht, Dr. John Shore, and Dr. James Barret. Secretary Stanton later ordered

the release of Hunt and (at General Grant's request) Dr. Barret. See Klement, *Dark Lanterns*, 85, 87. Klement (*Copperheads*, 193) mentioned Green B. Smith as a shadowy and untrustworthy character involved in allegations of disloyal activity in Indiana but made no mention of him in St. Louis. In *Dark Lanterns*, Klement does not mention Smith. In neither volume did Klement cite Sanderson's interview with Smith, published in *OR*, 2, vii, 626–60. Klement wrote that "Sanderson interrogated" the five OAK prisoners he listed, "promising each his freedom if he would confess to involvement in OAK activities and implicate bigger game." "Each of the five," wrote Klement, without mentioning Smith or Dunn's refusal to answer incriminating questions, "denied implication in any conspiracy" (*Dark Lanterns*, 82).

69. Joseph Darr Jr. to Captain Allen, Comdg. Gratiot Street Military Prison, 21 October 1864, *OR*, 2, vii, 1019; T. J. Churchill to Brig. Gen. B. McCulloch, 10 August 1861, *OR*, 1, iii, 110. Mrs. Hardesty was perhaps related to T. A. Hardesty, listed among the severely wounded Confederate soldiers at the Battle of Wilson's Creek three years earlier.

70. Hesseltine, "Military Prisons," 397–98.

71. Smith, "Counterinsurgency," 368–69, 372–74, 378–79.

72. Hesseltine, "Military Prisons," 398.

7. "Curing Us of Our Selfishness"

1. Hanna Isabella Stagg, "Local Incidents of the Civil War," *Missouri Historical Society Collections* 4 (1912): 65.

2. "Memorial, St. Louis Missouri Ladies' Union Aid Society," lithograph by Major and Knapp, 1870, MHS.

3. Camille N. Dry and Richard J. Compton, *Pictorial St. Louis, the Great Metropolis of the Mississippi Valley: A Topographical Survey Drawn in Perspective* (St. Louis: Compton and Company, 1876), 131; St. Louis Directory, 1860; Necrology Collection, MHS.

4. St. Louis Directory, 1860; William C. Winter, *The Civil War in St. Louis* (St. Louis: Missouri Historical Society Press, 1994), 125; "Remarks of Charles P. Johnson on the Occasion of the Presentation of the Portrait of Oliver D. Filley to the Missouri Historical Society, Thursday, May 21, 1903," *MHS Collections* 2 (July 1906): 1–12; *DMB*, 296–97.

5. L. P. Brockett and Mary C. Vaughan, *Woman's Work in the Civil War: A Record of Heroism, Patriotism and Patience* (Philadelphia: Zeigler, McCurdy and Company, 1867), 636–39.

6. Brockett and Vaughan, *Woman's Work*, 639–42.

7. William E. Parrish, "The Western Sanitary Commission," *Civil War History* 36 (March 1990): 18.

8. A concise discussion of this issue can be found in Gerald F. Linderman, *Embattled Courage: The Experience of Combat in the American Civil War* (New York: Free Press, 1987), 134–36.

9. Parrish, "The Western Sanitary Commission," 18.

10. "Missouriana," *Missouri Historical Review* 37 (April 1943): 321.

11. Parrish, "The Western Sanitary Commission," 19.

12. "Missouriana," 324; Robert Archibald, "Yeatman, Eliot Led Medical Effort During the Civil War," *St. Louis Business Journal,* 10–16 August 1992, 12.

13. Parrish, "The Western Sanitary Commission," 23.

14. Jane Turner Censer, *The Papers of Frederick Law Olmsted,* vol. 4, *Defending the Union: The Civil War and the U.S. Sanitary Commission, 1861–1863* (Baltimore: Johns Hopkins University Press, 1986), 34, 228, 229n.; George Winston Smith, "New England Business Interests in Missouri During the Civil War," *Missouri Historical Review* 41 (October 1946): 1–18.

15. Censer, *The Papers of Frederick Law Olmsted,* 4: 334, 336–37n.

16. The standard treatment of the U.S. Sanitary Commission is William Quentin Maxwell's *Lincoln's Fifth Wheel: The Political History of the United States Sanitary Commission* (New York: Longmans, Green, 1956). On the interaction between the U.S. Sanitary Commission and the Western Sanitary Commission, see 97–98 and 131–32.

17. Mark M. Krug, ed., *Mrs. [Sarah Jane Full] Hill's Journal—Civil War Reminiscences* (Chicago: R. R. Donnelley and Sons Company, 1980), 49.

18. William Hyde and Howard L. Conard, *Encyclopedia of the History of St. Louis: A Compilation of History and Biography for Ready Reference* (New York: Southern History Company, 1899), 3: 1786–91; Krug, ed., *Hill's Journal,* 59–60.

19. Krug, ed., *Hill's Journal,* 63.

20. Winter, *The Civil War in St. Louis,* 7.

21. Krug, ed., *Hill's Journal,* 153–54.

22. Paula Coalier, "Beyond Sympathy: The St. Louis Ladies' Union Aid Society and the Civil War," *Gateway Heritage* (summer 1990): 39–51; Forbes is quoted on 47.

23. After the Battle of Wilson's Creek, Mary and John Phelps cared for the body of Nathaniel Lyon in their Springfield home. In 1865 Congress recognized this service and Mary Phelps's work as a nurse. In 1870, she presided as vice president over the annual meeting of the National Woman Suffrage Association. See *DMB,* 614–15.

24. James W. Goodrich, ed., "The Civil War Letters of Bethiah Pyatt McKown," *Missouri Historical Review* 67 (January 1973): 245.

25. Frank J. Lutz, ed., *The Autobiography and Reminiscences of S. Pollak, M.D., St. Louis, Mo.* (St. Louis: St. Louis Medical Review, 1904), 85, 257–61.

26. [John Devoy], *A History of the City of St. Louis and Vicinity* (St. Louis: John Devoy, 1898), 369; "The Seal of the Missouri Historical Society," *Missouri Historical Society Bulletin* 13 (October 1956): 5. The Mrs. Kershaw mentioned by Pollak could also have been the wife of one of the Kershaw brothers, William L. or Andrew J., who operated a brass foundry in St. Louis. See the St. Louis Directory, 1860.

27. Coalier, "Beyond Sympathy," 44.

28. At the end of the war, Fisk was appointed assistant commissioner of the Freedmen's Bureau for Kentucky and Tennessee. In 1866 he opened a school for Negroes in an abandoned army barracks in Nashville; the next year the school was chartered as Fisk University. See *Dictionary of American Biography,* 6: 413–14.

29. Lutz, ed., *Autobiography of Pollak,* 269–71.

30. Ibid., 272–73.

31. Krug, ed., *Hill's Journal,* 77, 94–97.

32. "Missouriana," 323.

33. Krug, ed., *Hill's Journal,* 97; Lutz, ed., *Autobiography of Pollak,* 280–84.

34. Lutz, ed., *Autobiography of Pollak,* 285–91.

35. Hyde and Conard, *Encyclopedia of St. Louis,* 2: 1119; Dry and Compton, *Pictorial St. Louis,* 131; Devoy, *History of St. Louis,* 49; Winter, *The Civil War in St. Louis,* 81.

36. The 1862 and 1863 schedules for the *D. A. January* are reproduced in Frank R. Freemon, *Gangrene and Glory: Medical Care During the American Civil War* (Madison, N.J.: Fairleigh Dickinson University Press, 1958), 66, 143. McDougall is identified in Winter, *The Civil War in St. Louis,* 146.

37. Peter Josyph, ed., *The Wounded River: The Civil War Letters of John Vance Lauderdale, M.D.* (East Lansing: Michigan State University Press, 1993), 81, 83.

38. "Missouriana," 323.

39. Coalier, "Beyond Sympathy," 48.

40. Parrish, "The Western Sanitary Commission," 19.

41. Quoted in Maxwell, *Lincoln's Fifth Wheel,* 70.

42. Freemon, *Gangrene and Glory,* 210–12.

43. Louis S. Gerteis, *From Contraband to Freedman: Federal Policy Toward Southern Blacks, 1861–1865* (Westport, Conn.: Greenwood Press, 1973), 121.

44. Brockett and Vaughan, *Woman's Work,* 697–703; Ira Berlin et al., eds., *Freedom: A Documentary History of Emancipation, 1861–1867,* series 1, vol. 2, *The Wartime Genesis of Free Labor: The Upper South* (Cambridge: Cambridge University Press, 1993), 2: 571–73 (hereafter cited as *Freedom,* 1, 2).

45. [Emily Elizabeth Parsons], *Memoir of Emily Elizabeth Parsons* (Boston: Little, Brown and Company, 1880), 1–12; Brockett and Vaughan, *Woman's Work,* 273–78. Parsons suffered repeatedly from malaria during her labors in the Mississippi Valley. After she returned home, she regained her health long enough to establish the Cambridge Hospital before her death in 1880 at the age of fifty-six. Her father edited her wartime correspondence and privately published it as her memoir. He sent three copies to James Yeatman, asking that he keep one for himself and give copies to Emily Parsons's St. Louis friends, Mrs. William Chauvenet and Mrs. Cynthia King. See Theophilus Parsons to James Yeatman, 17 December 1880, enclosed in the copy of Parsons's *Memoir,* located in MHS.

46. Hyde and Conard, *Encyclopedia of St. Louis,* 1: 354, and 2: 1178; Lucy M. Schwienher, "The St. Louis Schools at the Outbreak of the Civil War," *Missouri Historical Society Bulletin* 13 (October 1956): 18.

47. Brockett and Vaughan, *Woman's Work,* 788.

48. Parsons, *Memoir,* 53–60.

49. Brockett and Vaughan, *Woman's Work,* 187–99.

50. Parsons, *Memoir,* 54–55, 61.

51. Ibid., 55.

52. Ibid., 57–67.

53. Ibid., 69.

54. Ibid., 75–76, 92.

55. "Missouriana," *Missouri Historical Review* 37 (April 1943): 324.

56. Parsons is perhaps referring to Sarah Hill, whose husband joined the army as an engineer.

57. Parsons, *Memoir,* 93, 105, 126, 129.

58. Ibid., 132–33, 138–40.

59. Frank Preston Stearns, *The Life and Public Service of George Luther Stearns* (1907; reprint, New York: Arno Press, 1969), 289; *Freedom,* 1, 2: 571–73.

60. Parrish, "The Western Sanitary Commission," 32, 35; Alvin Robert Kantor and Majorie Sered Kantor, *Sanitary Fairs: A Philatelic and Historical Study of Civil War Benevolence* (Glencoe, Ill.: SF Publishing, 1992), 168; Brockett and Vaughan, *Woman's Work,* 715.

61. St. Louis Directory, 1860.

62. Hyde and Conard, *Encyclopedia of St. Louis,* 1: 361–62; John E. Sunder, "Up the Missouri to the Montana Mines: John O'Fallon Delany's 'Pocket Diary for 1862,'" *Missouri Historical Society Bulletin* 19 (October 1962): 7, 7n.

63. Josyph, ed., *The Wounded River,* 69. Yeatman similarly welcomed Dr. John Lauderdale to St. Louis with a dinner at his home in May 1862.

64. Dr. John Lauderdale and his brother Willis, native New Yorkers, visited Shaw's garden at his Tower Grove home and were greatly impressed, particularly with Shaw's collection of tropical plants and fruit trees (Josyph, ed., *The Wounded River,* 71).

65. Censer, *The Papers of Frederick Law Olmsted,* 4: 585–602.

66. Quoted in Winter, *The Civil War in St. Louis,* 93.

67. Stagg, "Local Incidents," 68.

68. Ibid.

69. Josyph, ed., *The Wounded River,* 85.

70. Winter, *The Civil War in St. Louis,* 86; J. Thomas Scharf, *History of St. Louis City and County* (Philadelphia: Louis H. Everts and Company, 1883), 3: 546.

71. Jasper W. Cross, "The Mississippi Valley Sanitary Fair, St. Louis, 1864," *Missouri Historical Review* 46 (April 1952): 245.

72 Winter, *The Civil War in St. Louis,* 91–93.

73. Necrology Collection, MHS; Stagg, "Local Incidents," 68–69; *Missouri Republican,* 26 June 1864. Nelson left St. Louis in 1868 to take a chair at Lane Theological Seminary in Cincinnati. He died while visiting a son in St. Louis and was buried in Auburn, New York.

74. Hyde and Conard, *Encyclopedia of St. Louis,* 2: 1006–8.

75. "Cholera Epidemics in St. Louis," MHS, *Glimpses of the Past* 3 (March 1936): 72–74.

76. Coalier, "Beyond Sympathy," 39–51; Forbes is quoted on 47.

77. Krug, ed., *Hill's Journal,* 55.

78. Ibid., 331.

79. Parsons, *Memoir,* 95, 130.

8. "Terror . . . of Shot and Shell"

1. St. Louis City Directory, 1860. Eads's exact sources of supply are unknown, but he certainly relied on these major iron producers.

2. Quinta Scott and Howard S. Miller, *The Eads Bridge* (Columbia: University of Missouri Press, 1979), 68–74.

3. William D. Huffstot, "The *Carondelet,*" *Civil War Times Illustrated* 6 (August 1967): 7–8. John D. Milligan, "The First American Ironclads: The Evolution of a Design," *Missouri Historical Society Bulletin* (October 1965): 3–13.

4. William C. Winter, *The Civil War in St. Louis* (St. Louis: Missouri Historical Society Press, 1994), 78.

5. The city of Pittsburgh, for which the gunboat was named, did not acquire its modern spelling until after the Civil War. The fact that the *St. Louis* was the first gunboat to be commissioned has led some historians to conclude, wrongly, that it was the first one built. See, for example, Charles B. Boynton, *History of the Navy During the Rebellion* (New York: D. Appleton and Company, 1868), 1: 501–2, and Elmer L. Gaden Jr., "Eads and the Navy of the Mississippi," *American Heritage of Invention and Technology* 9 (spring 1994): 26. The *Carondelet* held the distinction of being the first gunboat launched at the Carondelet boatyard. See Winter, *The Civil War in St. Louis,* 78.

6. I am indebted to Professor Howard S. Miller for drawing my attention to Eads's drawn plans for the *Benton,* published in Donald L. Cannery, *The Old Steam Navy* (Annapolis, Md.: Naval Institute Press, 1990), 42.

7. James B. Eads, "Recollections," in *Battles and Leaders of the Civil War,* ed. Robert Underwood Johnson and Clarence Clough Buel, 4 vols. Castle Books edition (New York, 1956), 1: 340–41; Huffstot, "The *Carondelet,*" 10.

8. David F. Riggs, "Sailors of the *U.S.S. Cairo:* Anatomy of a Gunboat Crew," *Civil War History* 28 (September 1982): 266–73. The fullest account of living conditions aboard the gunboats is provided in Michael J. Bennett's forthcoming doctoral dissertation, St. Louis University, St. Louis.

9. Quoted in Spencer C. Tucker, *Andrew Foote: Civil War Admiral on Western Waters* (Annapolis, Md.: Naval Institute Press, 2000), 170.

10. See, for example, photographs of the *Carondelet* and *Cincinnati* in H. Allen Goswell, *Guns on the Western Waters: The Story of River Gunboats in the Civil War* (Baton Rouge: Louisiana State University Press, 1949), frontispiece and facing page 88.

11. Quoted in Boynton, *History of the Navy,* 1: 523–24.

12. Henry Walke, "The Gun-Boats at Belmont and Fort Henry," in Johnson and Buel, eds., *Battles and Leaders of the Civil War,* 1: 366; Tucker, *Foote,* 138.

13. Quoted in Florence L. Dorsey, *Road to the Sea: The Story of James B. Eads and the Mississippi* (New York: Rinehart, 1947), 67.

14. Tucker, *Foote,* 152.

15. [Ulysses S. Grant], *Personal Memoirs of U. S. Grant* (New York: Charles L. Webster and Company, 1885), 1: 302.

16. Tucker, *Foote,* 156, 160.

17. Grant, *Memoirs,* 1: 302.

18. Tucker, *Foote,* 155–56; Huffstot, "The *Carondelet,*" 8; Walke, "Gun-Boats," 359.

19. Dorsy, *Road to the Sea,* 73–76; Grant, *Memoirs,* 1: 293.

20. Kenneth R. Johnson, "Confederate Defenses and Union Gunboats on the Tennessee River: A Federal Raid into Northwest Alabama," *Alabama Historical Quarterly* 30 (summer 1968): 60.

21. The description of the federal campaign against Island Number Ten is derived from Lonnie J. White, "Federal Operations at New Madrid and Island Number Ten," *West Tennessee Historical Society Papers* 17 (1963): 47–67, John Carlton Mullen, "Pope's New Madrid and Island Number Ten Campaign," *Missouri Historical Review* 59 (April 1965): 325–43, and Huffstot, "The *Carondelet,*" 9–10.

22. Quoted in H. Blair Bentley, "Morale as a Factor in the Confederate Failure at Island Number Ten," *West Tennessee Historical Society Papers* 31 (1977): 124, 127.

23. Huffstot, "The *Carondelet,*" 11; Tucker, *Foote,* 195, 203. Foote died of Bright's disease, a chronic inflammation of the kidney that in his case led to kidney failure. Bright's disease is now thought to be an allergic response to an infection—especially a streptococcal infection—elsewhere in the body. See "Nephritis," in *The New Columbia Encyclopedia,* ed. William H. Harris and Judith S. Levey (New York: Columbia University Press, 1975), 1909.

24. Huffstot, "The *Carondelet,*" 11, 48. Torpedoes were anchored on the riverbottom with rods, wire detonators extending upward. They were intended to explode on contact, but water damage frequently made them ineffective. Also, they were easily swept away in high water or exposed in low water. See Johnson, "Confederate Defenses and Union Gunboats on the Tennessee River," 41.

25. Eads, "Recollections," 343.

26. This description of the Eads turret is derived from Dana Wegner, "Mr. Eads' Turret," *Civil War Times Illustrated* 12 (October 1973): 24–31.

27. *Democrat,* 11 February 1864.

28. James O. Broadhead, "St. Louis During the War," Broadhead Papers.

29. Huffstot, "The *Carondelet,*" 5; Eads, "Recollections," 338–39n.

30. Boynton, *History of the Navy,* 501–2.

31. Peter Josyph, ed., *The Wounded River: The Civil War Letters of John Vance Lauderdale, M.D.* (East Lansing: Michigan State University Press, 1993), 138.

32. Quoted in Mary R. Beard, *Short History of the American Labor Movement* (1920; reprint, New York: Arno Press, 1969), 67.

33. David Montgomery, *Beyond Equality: Labor and the Radical Republicans, 1862–1872* (New York: Vintage Books, 1967), 96–100; *Dictionary of American Biography,* 14: 260–61.

34. *Democrat,* 15 April 1864. I am indebted to the research of Theodore L. Listerman for the discussion of the labor movement and military intervention in St. Louis.

35. *Democrat,* 16 April 1864.

36. *Republican,* 3 April 1864; *Democrat,* 3 April 1864.

37. *Democrat,* 26 April 1864.

38. *Republican,* 3 April and 14 April 1864; *Democrat,* 3 April 1864.

39. *Democrat,* 8 April 1864.

40. Ibid., 16 April 1864.

41. *Republican,* 18 April 1864; *Democrat,* 18 April 1864.

42. George H. Frost to Frank Frost, 25 June 1864, St. Louis History Collection, MHS.

43. James C. Sylvis, *The Life, Speeches, Labors and Essays of William H. Sylvis* (1872; reprint, New York: Augustus M. Kelley, 1968), 135.

44. Major General Rosecrans, General Orders, no. 65, 29 April 1864, *OR,* 1: 34, iii, 345.

45. The reactions of the German press were published in English translation in the *Democrat,* 3 May 1864 and in the *Republican,* 5 May 1864.

46. Charles L. Bernays to Abraham Lincoln, 2 May 1864, printed in Bertram W. Korn, "The Jews of the Union," *American Jewish Archives* 13 (1961): 217.

9. "Slavery Dies Hard"

1. Roy P. Basler, ed., *The Collected Works of Abraham Lincoln,* 8 vols. (New Brunswick, N.J.: Rutgers University Press, 1953), 5: 388.

2. Ibid., 5: 389n.

3. Marvin R. Cain, *Lincoln's Attorney General: Edward Bates of Missouri* (Columbia: University of Missouri Press, 1965), 163, 213–22.

4. William Hyde and Howard L. Conard, *Encyclopedia of the History of St. Louis: A Compilation of History and Biography for Ready Reference* (New York: Southern History Company, 1899), 4: 2048.

5. Thomas T. Gantt to Brig. Genl. W. S. Harney, 14 May 1861, and Harney to Gantt, 14 May 1861, in *Freedom,* 1, 1.

6. Quoted in William E. Parrish, *Turbulent Partnership: Missouri and the Union, 1861–1865* (Columbia: University of Missouri Press, 1963), 123.

7. This policy, which conformed with Lincoln's border state policy, had already been enacted in Maryland by General John A. Dix, in Virginia by General George B. McClellan, and in Kentucky by General Don Carlos Buell. See Berlin et al., eds., introductory essay in *Freedom,* 1, 1: 399.

8. General Orders, no. 3, Headquarters, Department of the Missouri, 20 November 1861, *Freedom,* 1, 1: 417.

9. William E. Parrish, *Frank Blair: Lincoln's Conservative* (Columbia: University of Missouri Press, 1998), 137.

10. *Missouri Democrat,* 10 May 1862.

11. "Major Lucien Eaton," in *The Bench and Bar in St. Louis* (St. Louis, 1884); diary entries for 6 and 13 May and 15 and 17 June, Lucien Eaton Papers, MHS.

12. Hyde and Conard, *Encyclopedia of the History of St. Louis,* 1: 183–84.

13. Parrish, *Frank Blair,* 146–51. These election results were challenged by Blair's opponent, Samuel Knox; in spring 1864, the House assigned the congressional seat to

Knox. See Parrish, *Frank Blair,* 195–96, and Hyde and Conard, *Encyclopedia of the History of St. Louis,* 2: 1191.

14. Colonel John C. Kelton to Assistant Adjutant General, 6 October 1861, *Freedom,* 1, 1: 416.

15. Thelma P. Goodwin, ed., *State of Missouri Official Manual for the Year 1963–1964* (Jefferson City: Von Hoffman Press, n.d.), 19–20.

16. Lt. Col. John S. Phelps to Col. G. W. Dodge, 2 December 1861; John M. Richardson to Hon. Simon Cameron, 1 December 1861; H. R. Gamble to Majr. Genl. Halleck, 10 December 1861, *Freedom,* 1, 1: 417–18, 419n. In July 1862 Lincoln appointed Phelps military governor of Arkansas. He ran as the Democratic candidate for governor in 1868 and lost due to the disenfranchisement of many Democratic voters. He won election easily in 1876 after the new constitution of 1875 ended the test oath. As governor (1877–1881) Phelps vigorously suppressed the remnants of the railroad strike of 1877. See Goodwin, ed., *Missouri Official Manual,* 19–20.

17. Major General H. W. Halleck to Colonel B. G. Farrar, 18 December 1861, *Freedom,* 1, 1: 419–29.

18. Major General Asboth, Circular no. 2, Headquarters 4th Division, 18 December 1861, and Major General E. Waring Jr. to Acting Major General Asboth, 19 December 1861, *Freedom,* 1, 1: 420–22.

19. Major General H. W. Halleck to General Asboth, 26 December 1861, *Freedom,* 1, 1: 423.

20. Aide de Camp W. S. Hillyer to Colonel L. F. Ross, 5 January 1862, *Freedom,* 1, 1: 424.

21. Farrar later led a brigade in the campaign against Vicksburg and commanded the Military District of Natchez before returning to St. Louis, where he assisted in raising a regiment of black troops (the Sixth U.S. Colored Heavy Artillery). William C. Winter, *The Civil War in St. Louis* (St. Louis: Missouri Historical Society Press, 1994), 119.

22. Hyde and Conard, *Encyclopedia of the History of St. Louis,* 4: 2048.

23. Ibid., 1: 239–43; "Fragments of the Broadhead Collection," MHS, *Glimpses of the Past* 2 (March 1935): 43n.; Winter, *The Civil War in St. Louis,* 119.

24. Provost Marshal General Bernard G. Farrar to Major General Halleck, 4 February 1862, enclosing James O. Broadhead to Colonel B. G. Farrar, 2 February 1862, *Freedom,* 1, 1: 425–26. The passage from the First Confiscation Act is quoted by Broadhead and the emphasis added is his.

25. Frank Blair is quoted in Parrish, *Frank Blair,* 155; for Apolline Blair's comments, see 155n.

26. J. Howard to Major General Curtis, 10 October 1862, and Colonel John F. Tyler to Captain Griffing, 20 September 1862, bearing the endorsement of Colonel Thomas T. Gantt, 20 September 1862, *Freedom,* 1, 1: 437–38.

27. General Orders, no. 35, Headquarters, Department of the Missouri, 24 December 1862; Lieut. Green to Captain Minnick, 29 January 1863, *Freedom,* 1, 1: 441–45.

28. Lincoln is quoted in Parrish, *Turbulent Partnership,* 124; for a discussion of the emancipation debate in the Missouri legislature, see 130–48.

29. Glover is quoted in Parrish, *Frank Blair*, 178.

30. Charles Jones to Abraham Lincoln, 24 March 1863; Captain Stephen E. Jones [for the provost marshal general of the Department of the Missouri] to Colonel F. A. Dick, 15 April 1863, *Freedom*, 1, 1: 453–54. "A. Wiseman," the middleman in the deal, was probably businessman Antoine Wiseman, one of the original incorporators—together with Hudson Bridge, D. A. January, John Howe, and James H. Lucas, among others—of the St. Louis Railway Company. This was the company that hired William Tecumseh Sherman as president just before the Civil War. See Camille N. Dry and Richard J. Compton, *Pictorial St. Louis, the Great Metropolis of the Mississippi Valley: A Topographical Survey Drawn in Perspective* (St. Louis: Compton and Company, 1876), 42.

31. The term contraband had been applied to confiscated slaves by General Benjamin Butler in Virginia in 1861; it became the popular term used during the war to refer to all black refugees.

32. Maria R. Mann to "Elisa," 10 February 1863; Mann to unknown, fragment of letter, n.d., Maria R. Mann Papers, Library of Congress, Washington, D.C.

33. Saml. R. Curtis to Brig. Gen. B. M. Prentiss, 9 March 1863, *OR*, 1, 22, ii, 147.

34. Samuel Sawyer to Brig. Gen. Prentiss, 16 March 1863, in *Freedom*, 1, 2.

35. Lucien Eaton to Major Genl. Schofield, 30 May 1863, *Freedom*, 1, 2: 572.

36. Samuel Sawyer to Brig. Gen. Prentiss, 16 March 1863, *Freedom*, 1, 2: 565–67.

37. Joe M. Richardson, "The American Missionary Association and Black Education in Civil War Missouri," *Missouri Historical Review* 69 (July 1971): 433–48.

38. Samuel Sawyer to Maj. Gen. Curtis, 18 April 1863, *Freedom*, 1, 2: 568–69.

39. Ibid.

40. Parrish, *Turbulent Partnership*, 119–21.

41. A. Lincoln to General John M. Schofield, 27 May 1863, *OR*, 1, 22, 2: 293.

42. Col. B. L. E. Bonneville to Capt. H. C. Fillebrow[n], 28 May 1863, and Col. B. L. E. Bonneville to Col. C. W. Marsh, 20 July 1863, *Freedom*, 1, 2: 570, 571n.

43. Bonneville reported the incident at Benton Barracks on 28 May; Eaton, responding to Schofield's request, dated his report 30 May.

44. Frank Preston Stearns, *The Life and Public Service of George Luther Stearns* (1907; reprint, New York: Arno Press, 1969), 289.

45. Lucien Eaton to Major Genl. Schofield, 30 May 1863, *Freedom*, 1, 2: 571–73.

46. Special Orders no. 61 and 66, Headquarters, Department of the Missouri, Office of the Provost Marshal General, *Freedom*, 1, 2: 574n.

47. Parrish, *Turbulent Partnership*, 223–24.

48. Department of the Missouri, General Orders, no. 64, 8 July 1863, *OR*, 1, 22, ii: 359–60.

49. [Egbert B. Brown] to Major Genl. J. M. Schofield, 14 July 1863, *Freedom*, 1, ii: 576.

50. Maj. Genl. J. M. Schofield to Hon. E. M. Stanton, 17 July 1861, *Freedom*, 1, 1: 461–62.

51. Judge Advocate Genl. J. Holt to Hon. E. M. Stanton, 17 August 1863, *Freedom*, 1, 1: 462–64.

52. Quoted in Parrish, *Frank Blair,* 184.

53. Quoted in John W. Blassingame, "The Recruitment of Negro Troops in Missouri During the Civil War," *Missouri Historical Review* 58 (April 1964): 334.

54. War Department, General Orders, no. 143, 22 May 1863; J. M. Schofield to Brig. Gen. L. Thomas, 10 June 1863, *OR,* 3, 3: 215, 328–29. See also Blassingame, "Recruitment," 329, 331.

55. Endorsement by Hamilton Gamble in E. P. Cayce to M. P. Cayce, 19 June 1863, and J. M. Schofield to Col. E. D. Townsend, 29 September 1863, in *Freedom: A Documentary History of Emancipation,* ed. Ira Berlin et al., series 2, *The Black Military Experience* (Cambridge: Cambridge University Press, 1982), 227–28, 230–31 (hereafter cited as *Freedom,* 2).

56. Major General J. M. Schofield to Col. E. D. Townsend, 29 September 1863, *Freedom,* 2: 230–31.

57. Department of the Missouri, General Orders, no. 135, 14 November 1863, *OR,* 3, 3: 1034–36. See also Blassingame, "Recruitment," 331–32, and Michael Fellman, "Emancipation in Missouri," *Missouri Historical Review* 83 (July 1988): 47.

58. Testimony of R. A. Watt to the American Freedman Inquiry Commission, *Freedom,* 2: 235–36.

59. W. A. Poillon to Dr. Martine, 28 December 1863, enclosed in Surgeon Ira Russell to Assistant Adjutant General O. D. Greene, 13 January 1864, *Freedom,* 1, 1: 476–79.

60. Martha to My Dear Husband [Richard Glover], 30 December 1863, enclosed in Brig. Genl. Wm. A. Pile to Maj. O. D. Greene, 11 February 1864, *Freedom,* 2: 244–45.

61. Testimony of B. Gratz Brown before the American Freedmen's Inquiry Commission in St. Louis, 30 November 1862, *Freedom,* 1, 1: 471–72.

62. Testimony of Franklin A. Dick before the American Freedmen's Inquiry Commission, 1 December 1863, *Freedom,* 1, 1: 472–76.

63. Testimony of the Reverend Edward L. Woodson before the American Freedmen's Inquiry Commission, *Freedom,* 1, 2: 580–81. Woodson is listed in the 1860 St. Louis Directory with a residence on east Seventh Street, between Market and Walnut; in the 1865 directory he is listed at 120 Clark Avenue.

64. The women are not identified by name.

65. Testimony of Ladies' Contraband Relief Society before the American Freedmen's Inquiry Commission, and account of visits to contraband camp and hospital and color'd schools in St. Louis by the American Freedmen's Inquiry Commission, *Freedom,* 1, 2: 581–85.

66. Account of visits to contraband camp and hospital and color'd schools in St. Louis by the American Freedmen's Inquiry Commission, *Freedom,* 1, 2: 584–85.

67. Ann to My Dear Husband [Andrew Valentine, Company E, Second Missouri Colored Infantry] 19 January 1864; Capt. A. J. Hubbard to Brig. Genl. Pile, 6 February 1864, *Freedom,* 2: 686–88.

68. Affidavit of Aaron Mitchell, 4 January 1864, *Freedom,* 1, 2: 237–38; Jeff. A. Mayhill to Col. C. W. Marsh, 9 January 1864, *Freedom,* 2: 238n.

69. *Missouri Democrat,* 20 January 1864.

70. Brig. Genl. Wm. A. Pile to Maj. Genl. Rosecrans, 23 February 1864, *Freedom,* 2: 245–46.

71. Brig. Genl. Wm. A. Pile to Hon. Henry T. Blow, 26 February 1864; Brig. Genl. Wm. A. Pile to B. Gratz [Brown], 9 February 1864, *Freedom,* 1, 2: 248–49, 249n.

72. Blassingame, "Recruitment," 337.

73. Quoted in ibid., 333.

74. Bowman anticipated Congress on this point. In 1862 Congress freed the mothers, wives, and children of black men in federal service, but only if their owners were disloyal. It was not until March 1865 that Congress freed the families of all black soldiers. See the introductory material in *Freedom,* 1, 1: 513.

75. Sam Bowman to Dear Wife, 10 May 1864, *Freedom,* 1, 1: 483–85.

76. [Private Spotswood Rice] to My Children, [3 September 1864]; Spotswood Rice to Kittey Diggs, [3 September 1864], *Freedom,* 2: 689–90.

77. Brig. Genl. Wm. A. Pile to Brig. Genl. L. Thomas, 21 May 1864, *Freedom,* 1, 2: 607.

78. Blassingame, "Recruitment," 333.

79. The highest rates of enlistment by black men came from the states exempted from the Emancipation Proclamation: Delaware, 25 percent; Maryland, 28 percent; Missouri, 39 percent; Kentucky, 57 percent; Tennessee, 39 percent. See the introductory material in *Freedom,* 2: 12.

80. Hospital Chaplain W. H. Corkhill to A. A. A. Genl. J. H. Clendening, 28 March 1864, *Freedom,* 1, 2: 597–98.

81. Parrish, *Turbulent Partnership,* 201.

82. Brigadier General Clinton B. Fisk to James E. Yeatman, 25 March 1865, *Freedom,* 1, 1: 489; *Dictionary of American Biography,* 6: 413–14. Fisk shared Yeatman's philanthropic concerns. He founded Fisk University in Nashville, Tennessee, as a college to educate freedmen.

83. Quoted in Gary R. Kremer, *James Milton Turner and the Promise of America: The Public Life of a Post–Civil War Black Leader* (Columbia: University of Missouri Press, 1991), 18–21.

10. "A Foundation of Loyalty"

1. See Thomas S. Barclay, "The Test Oath for the Clergy in Missouri," *Missouri Historical Review* 18 (April 1924): 345–50.

2. Norma L. Peterson, *Freedom and Franchise: The Political Career of B. Gratz Brown* (Columbia: University of Missouri Press, 1965), 137; William E. Parrish, *Missouri Under Radical Rule* (Columbia: University of Missouri Press, 1965), 13.

3. Howard K. Beale, ed., *The Diary of Edward Bates, 1859–1866* (Washington, D.C.: U.S. Government Printing Office, 1933), 453, 571–612.

4. Galusha Anderson, *The Story of a Border City During the Civil War* (Boston: Little, Brown and Company, 1908), 344.

5. Anderson and Drake are quoted in Parrish, *Radical Rule,* 11–14.

6. *Journal of the Missouri State Convention, Held at the City of St. Louis, January 6–April 10, 1865* (St. Louis: Missouri Democrat, 1865), 3–4.

7. *DMB*, 302–4.

8. *Journal of the Convention*, 27. Eliot's prayer is quoted in Anderson, *Border City*, 345–46.

9. *Missouri Democrat*, 16 January 1865. Indicative of his standing in the community, Budd named one of his sons Wyman Crow in honor of the St. Louis merchant and civic leader. A daughter married George Pullman, of Pullman sleeping-car fame. Budd died in St. Louis in 1875. See *Missouri Historical Society Collections*, 1, 12 (1896): 12; MHS, *Glimpses of the Past*, 4 (1937): 162, and 9 (1942): 115; and William Hyde and Howard L. Conard, *Encyclopedia of the History of St. Louis: A Compilation of History and Biography for Ready Reference* (New York: Southern History Company, 1899), 1: 265.

10. *Missouri Democrat*, 16 January 1865.

11. *Journal of the Convention*, 53; W. G. Eliot, *Education as Connected with the Right of Suffrage. An Address Delivered Before the Constitutional Convention of the State of Missouri Jan. 24th, 1865* (n.p., n.d.). The convention did not adopt an educational test, in part because doing so would have disenfranchised many men who had served in the Union army.

12. In 1865 President Lincoln appointed Krekel U.S. judge for the Western District of Missouri, a post he held until his death in 1888 (*DMB*, 463–64).

13. Barclay, "Test Oath for the Clergy," 345–50; the language of the test oath is quoted in Martha Kohl, "Enforcing a Vision of Community: The Role of the Test Oath in Missouri's Reconstruction," *Civil War History* 40 (December 1994): 292.

14. Jacob Furth, "Sketch of Isidor Bush," *Missouri Historical Society Collections* 4 (1912): 303–9; *DMB*, 138–40.

15. Thomas S. Barclay, "The Liberal Republican Movement in Missouri," *Missouri Historical Review* 20 (October 1925): 18–19, 19n.

16. *Missouri Republican*, 3 May 1865.

17. Drake is quoted in Parrish, *Radical Rule*, 25–26.

18. Drake initially opposed the ousting order because he viewed it as an unnecessary distraction from the primary business of redrafting the constitution; in the end, however, he supported the measure. See Parrish, *Radical Rule*, 32–33. Clover's committee report is quoted in Thomas K. Skinker, "The Removal of the Judges of the Supreme Court of Missouri, in 1865," *Missouri Historical Society Collections* 4 (1914): 254–55. See also Hyde and Conard, *Encyclopedia of the History of St. Louis*, 1: 412–13, and Barclay, "Liberal Republican Movement," 21n.

19. Frederick W. Lehmann, "Edward Bates and the Test Oath," *Missouri Historical Society Collections* 4 (1914): 399; Beale, ed., *Diary of Edward Bates*, 439, 445, 451; Hyde and Conard, *Encyclopedia of the History of St. Louis*, 1: 412–13.

20. Barclay, "The Liberal Republican Movement," 37–43; Parrish, *Radical Rule*, 37–38.

21. Parrish, *Radical Rule*, 51–52.

22. In the 1870s Barton Bates took a leading role in the construction of the Eads Bridge. See Hyde and Conard, *Encyclopedia of the History of St. Louis*, 1: 118, 609.

23. On 4 July 1865 Governor Fletcher issued a proclamation declaring the new constitution to be in force. See Parrish, *Radical Rule,* 48.

24. Skinker, "Removal of the Judges," 244, 260–62. By fall 1865, Dryden and Bay accepted the reality of their removal and formally resigned. See Parrish, *Radical Rule,* 53–55.

25. Parrish, *Radical Rule,* 57.

26. Dorothy Garesché Holland, *The Garesché, De Bauduy, and Des Chapelles Families: History and Genealogy* (St. Louis: Schneider Printing Company, 1962), 169, 171, 174. See also Hyde and Conard, *Encyclopedia of the History of St. Louis,* 2: 867. The novelist Kate Chopin had a close childhood friendship with "Kitty" Garesché. This was Juliette, the daughter of Alexander J. P. Garesché. She is confused with Juliette McLane Garesché in *Kate Chopin, the Awakening: An Authoritative Text, Biographical and Historical Contexts, Criticism,* ed. Margo Cullen (New York: W. W. Norton and Company, 1976), 115.

27. Parrish, *Radical Rule,* 59–61.

28. Kenrick's letter is quoted in Beale, ed., *Diary of Edward Bates,* 495.

29. Following the death of his wife, Hawks remarried the daughter of Judge Abiel Leonard, a leading Whig and opponent of Claiborne Jackson. See Hyde and Conard, *Encyclopedia of the History of St. Louis,* 2: 1003, 1169.

30. Missouri's other senator, John B. Henderson, offered only a mild protest, declaring the test oath for the clergy "unwise." See Barclay, "The Test Oath," 361.

31. Ibid., 365; Galusha Anderson, "The Test Oath of Missouri," *Baptist Quarterly* 1 (July 1867): 287. Even in the *Cummings* case, offers of financial assistance would have procured the priest's immediate release if he had accepted them. See Barclay, "Liberal Republican Movement," 60n.

32. Quoted in Barclay, "The Test Oath," 351.

33. Harold C. Bradley, "In Defense of John Cummings," *Missouri Historical Review* 57 (October 1962): 1–15. When the issue of test oaths again became controversial in the 1940s and 1950s, U.S. Supreme Court Justice William O. Douglas noted that "legislatures, courts, and educational institutions in America forgot the lessons of the *Cummings* case." The Missouri test oath for clergy had been judged a bill of attainder, wrote Justice Douglas, because it deprived citizens of rights without judicial review. Similarly, the oath had been ex post facto, because there had been no law in Missouri making sympathy for the South illegal. So, too, the anticommunist loyalty oaths removed people "from government posts and from faculties of schools and colleges" because, in the past, they had been members of groups later deemed subversive. See William O. Douglas, *An Almanac of Liberty* (1954; reprint, New York: Greenwood Press, 1973), 205.

34. Barclay, "Liberal Republican Movement," 61; Parrish, *Radical Rule,* 64, 69.

35. Quoted in Barclay, "Liberal Republican Movement," 65.

36. Parrish, *Radical Rule,* 58–59.

37. Ibid., 60–61.

38. Barclay, "The Test Oath," 375–76.

39. Harold Melvin Hyman, *Era of the Oath: Northern Loyalty Tests During the Civil War and Reconstruction* (Philadelphia: University of Pennsylvania Press, 1954), 107–20.

40. Parrish, *Radical Rule,* 80.

41. The story of the murder and the subsequent failure to convict the well-known killer is told from memory in Huston Crittenden, "The Warrensburg Speech of Frank P. Blair," *Missouri Historical Review* 20 (October 1925): 101–4.

42. *Missouri Democrat*, 11 May 1866; Parrish, *Radical Rule*, 83–84.

43. Quoted in Peterson, *Freedom and Franchise*, 159–60.

44. Johnson rewarded Bogy's support with an appointment as commissioner of Indian Affairs in 1867. In 1872 Liberals and Democrats in the state legislature joined forces to elect Bogy to the U.S. Senate, where he supported the Greenback movement and opposed the Compromise of 1877 because it delivered the presidential election to the Republican candidate, Rutherford B. Hayes. Bogy died in St. Louis in 1877. See *DMB*, 93.

45. *Dictionary of American Biography*, 10: 597–98.

46. Galusha Anderson, *Memorial Sermon of Rev. J. Richard Anderson, Delivered April 9th, 1865, in the Second Colored Baptist Church of St. Louis* (Chicago: Church, Goodman and Donnelly, 1865); Kenneth C. Kaufman, *Dred Scott's Advocate: A Biography of Roswell Field* (Columbia: University of Missouri Press, 1996), 142.

47. Bruce's service in the Senate was limited to one term. Thereafter he made Washington, D.C., his home and held a series of federal patronage positions. He died in Washington in 1898. See *DMB*, 128.

48. Gary R. Kremer, *James Milton Turner and the Promise of America: The Public Life of a Post–Civil War Black Leader* (Columbia: University of Missouri Press, 1991), 19–20; William Clark Breckenridge to S. B. Laughlin, 15 April 1921, W. C. Breckenridge Papers, MHS.

49. Kremer, *James Milton Turner*, 19–20; William Cheek and Aimee Lee Cheek, *John Mercer Langston and the Fight for Black Freedom, 1829–1865* (Urbana: University of Illinois Press, 1989), 445–46; James Mercer Langston, *From the Virginia Plantation to the National Capitol*, Arno Press edition (New York, 1969), 240–44.

50. Eric Foner, *A Short History of Reconstruction, 1863–1877* (New York: Harper and Row, 1990), 117; Eric McKitrick, *Andrew Johnson and Reconstruction* (Chicago: University of Chicago Press, 1960), 422–27.

51. Parrish, *Radical Rule*, 92.

52. *Missouri Democrat*, 11 August 1866.

53. The split in Republican ranks in St. Louis in 1864 (between pro- and anti-Lincoln factions) had permitted Hogan's election; he lost his seat in the 1866 Republican sweep. He died in St. Louis in 1892. See McKitrick, *Johnson*, 428–38 (Johnson's St. Louis speech is quoted at 432 and 435–36), and *Biographical Directory of the American Congress*, 1225. See also Parrish, *Radical Rule*, 95–98, 235.

54. Peterson, *Freedom and Franchise*, 173–75, 214–15. The careers of Hume and Grosvenor later led to New York City, where Hume became a broker and Grosvenor, from 1875 until his death in 1900, became the economic editor of the *New York Tribune*. Also active in the Liberal Republican movement in St. Louis was Joseph Pulitzer. He served in the Union army with Schurz after arriving in the United States in 1864; by 1868 he was a reporter with the *Westliche Post*. See William Hyde, "Newspapers and

Newspaper People of Three Decades," *Missouri Historical Society Collections* 1 (1896): 10; David D. March, "Charles Daniel Drake of St. Louis," *Missouri Historical Society Bulletin* 9 (April 1953): 306n; *Dictionary of American Biography*, 8: 26–27 and 15: 260.

55. Beale, ed., *Diary of Edward Bates*, 537–38; Parrish, *Radical Rule*, 51, 229.

56. When Price arrived in St. Louis, Frank Blair offered to secure a presidential pardon for him from Andrew Johnson. Price responded: "I have no pardon to ask." See *DMB*, 625–27; Robert E. Shalhope, *Sterling Price: Portrait of a Southerner* (Columbia: University of Missouri Press, 1971), 288.

57. McKitrick, *Johnson*, 494, 498; Parrish, *Radical Rule*, 229.

58. The Republican victory was decisive but not overwhelming. Grant won with 72 percent of the electoral vote but only 53 percent of the popular vote.

59. Quoted in Parrish, *Frank Blair*, 254.

60. *Harper's Weekly*, 31 October 1868 and 7 November 1868.

61. Foner, *A Short History of Reconstruction*, illustrations following p. 144.

62. [Carl Schurz,] *The Reminiscences of Carl Schurz*, 3 vols. (New York: McClure Company, 1908), 3: 256, 293, 301.

63. Kremer, *James Milton Turner*, 22–23; Parrish, *Radical Rule*, 300–307.

64. The struggle for woman suffrage proved to be far longer than any of the women at the Mercantile Library meeting could have imagined. By 1913 twelve states (beginning with Wyoming in 1869) recognized the right of women to vote inside their borders. Women in St. Louis, however, were not allowed to vote until the ratification of the Nineteenth Amendment to the U.S. Constitution in 1920. Kenneth H. Winn, "It All Adds Up: Reform and the Erosion of Representative Government in Missouri, 1900–2000," in *Official Manual, State of Missouri, 1999–2000*, ed. Julius Johnson (Jefferson City: Office of the Secretary of State, 2000), 69; Monica Cook Morris, "The History of Woman Suffrage in Missouri, 1867–1901," *Missouri Historical Review* 25 (October 1930): 69; Susan Beattie, "The Suffrage Movement," in *In Her Place: A Guide to St. Louis Women's History*, ed. Katharine T. Corbett (St. Louis: Missouri Historical Society Press, 1999), 130–32; Necrology Collection, MHS.

65. Morris, "Woman Suffrage," 68.

66. Beattie, "Virginia Minor," in Corbett, ed., *In Her Place*, 132–34.

67. Ibid.

68. Ibid.

69. Justice Robert C. Grier had been incapacitated by paralysis and had been prevailed upon to resign effective 1 February 1870. See *Dictionary of American Biography*, 4: 612–13. See also Hyman, *Era of the Oath*, 117–18; John A. Garraty et al., eds., *American National Biography* (New York: Oxford University Press, 1999), 9: 123–24; and Parrish, *Radical Rule*, 280.

70. Parrish, *Radical Rule*, 281.

71. Drake's term did not end until March 1973. See *Biographical Directory of the American Congress*, 962; Earle Dudley Ross, *The Liberal Republican Movement* (Ithaca, N.Y.: Cornell University Press, 1910), 28–33; Parrish, *Radical Rule*, 269–71, 281–309.

72. Isidor Loeb, "Constitutions and Constitutional Conventions in Missouri," in *Journal [of the] Missouri Constitutional Convention of 1875* (Columbia: State Historical Society of Missouri, 1920), 7–71.

73. Section 3 of the Fourteenth Amendment barred from "any office, civil or military" in the United States or in any of the states, persons who joined or supported the rebellion after they had sworn "to support the Constitution of the United States." The amendment provided, however, that this disability could be removed by a two-thirds vote of the House and Senate. On the removal of these disabilities, see Foner, *Short History of Reconstruction*, 215.

74. Lloyd A. Hunter, "Missouri Confederate Leaders After the War," *Missouri Historical Review* 67 (April 1973): 381–85; *DMB*, 647–48, 691–92.

75. Hunter, "Confederate Leaders," 385–86; *DMB*, 519–20.

76. Hunter, "Confederate Leaders," 376; *DMB*, 264–65.

77. *DMB*, 9–10; *Dictionary of American Biography*, 1: 264–65.

78. *DMB*, 85–86; William C. Winter, *The Civil War in St. Louis* (St. Louis: Missouri Historical Society Press, 1994), 138; Kaufman, *Dred Scott's Advocate*, 238, 238n; John A. Bryan, "The Blow Family and Their Slave Dred Scott," *Missouri Historical Society Bulletin* 5 (October 1948): 22.

79. Necrology Collection, MHS.

80. *DMB*, 116–17; James Neal Primm, *Lion of the Valley: St. Louis, Missouri* (Boulder, Colo.: Pruett Publishing Company, 1981), 318–20.

81. George McCue, *Sculpture City: St. Louis* (New York: Hudson Hills Press, 1988), 33–39, 78.

82. Winter, *The Civil War in St. Louis*, 36–37.

83. Anderson, *Border City*, 181.

Bibliographic Essay

Several historians have ably demonstrated the value of viewing the Civil War era from a single locale. Willie Lee Rose, *Rehearsal for Reconstruction: The Port Royal Experiment* (Indianapolis: Bobbs-Merrill, 1964), brilliantly evoked the drama of emancipation in the Sea Islands region of South Carolina. W. McKee Evans, *Ballots and Fence Rails: Reconstruction on the Lower Cape Fear* (Chapel Hill: University of North Carolina Press, 1966), focused on a region held by the Confederacy until the close of the war. More recently J. Matthew Gallman, *Mastering Wartime: A Social History of Philadelphia During the Civil War* (New York: Cambridge University Press, 1990), and Iver Bernstein, *The New York City Draft Riots: Their Significance for American Society and Politics in the Age of the Civil War* (New York: Oxford University Press, 1990), examined wartime developments in the North's two largest cities. Ernest B. Furgurson, *Ashes of Glory: Richmond at War* (New York: A. A. Knopf, 1996), reexamined life in the Confederate capital. In two recent works, *Seasons of War: The Ordeal of a Confederate Community, 1861–1865* (New York: Free Press, 1995) and *Fredericksburg and Chancellorsville: The Dare Mark Campaign* (Lincoln: University of Nebraska Press, 1998), Daniel E. Sutherland examined the impact of war on two Virginia communities, rural Culpeper County and the town of Fredericksburg.

This attempt to examine the Civil War from the perspective of St. Louis could not have been completed without the work of previous generations of historians. James Neal Primm's *Lion of the Valley: St. Louis, Missouri* (Boulder, Colo.: Pruett Publishing Company, 1981) is an insightful and indispensable account of urban economic and political development over two centuries, and it is the only scholarly general history of St. Louis. Ernest Kirschten, *Catfish and Crystal* (Garden City, N.J.: Doubleday, 1960), offered a popular history of the city. Other general histories of St. Louis have been celebratory affairs. The first, Camille N. Dry and Richard J. Compton's *Pictorial St. Louis, The Great Metropolis of the Mississippi Valley: A Topographical Survey Drawn in Perspective* (St. Louis: Compton and Company, 1876) focused on the businesses of St. Louis and painstakingly portrayed the city, section by section, in hand-drawn bird's-eye view images. Equally celebratory but of more limited use to historians is L. U. Reavis's *St. Louis, the Future Great City of the World and Its Impending Triumph* (St. Louis: G. A. Pierrot, 1882). By the time Reavis launched his effort to relocate the nation's capital in St. Louis, several other late nineteenth-century compilations of the city's past were under way. J. Thomas Scharf's *History of St. Louis City and County*, 4 vols. (Philadelphia: Louis H. Everts and Company, 1883) led the way. It was followed fifteen years later by [John Devoy], *A History of the City of St. Louis and Vicinity* (St. Louis: John Devoy, 1898). William Hyde and Howard L. Conard's *Encyclopedia of the History of St. Louis: A Compendium of History and Biography for Ready Reference* (New York: Southern History Company, 1899) also belongs in the celebratory category although it remains an invaluable biographical source. The last of the celebratory histories, Walter B. Stevens's *St. Louis, History of the Fourth City, 1763–1909* (St. Louis: S. J. Clarke Publishing Company, 1909), provides additional biographical detail.

In recent years, the Missouri Historical Society Press in St. Louis has helped to revive historical interest in the city. It has republished Primm, *Lion of the Valley* (1998), and has issued other works important to an understanding of St. Louis in the nineteenth century. William C. Winter's *The Civil War in St. Louis: A Guided Tour* (1994) was written for the Civil War Roundtable of St. Louis and provides a wealth of detail, including an excellent bibliography of printed sources. Andrew Hurley, ed., *Common Fields: An Environmental History of St. Louis* (1997), offers important essays on the development of the early nineteenth-century urban infrastructure. Katharine T. Corbett, ed., *In Her Place: A Guide to St. Louis Women's History* (1999), includes detailed chapters on homefront efforts and on their relationship to the postwar fight for women's rights.

In the field of biography and autobiography, St. Louis is fairly well served. Lawrence O. Christensen et al., eds., *Dictionary of Missouri Biography* (Columbia: University of Missouri Press, 1999) provide a welcome new resource. Classic works include [Thomas Hart Benton], *Thirty Years' View; or a History of the Working of the American Government for Thirty Years from 1820 to 1850*, 2 vols. (1856), Greenwood Press edition, (New York, 1968); [Ulysses S. Grant], *Personal Memoirs of U. S. Grant* (New York: Charles L. Webster and Company, 1885); Allan Nevins, *Frémont: Pathmarker of the West* (1939), University of Nebraska Press edition (Lincoln, 1992); and William Nisbet Chambers, *Old Bullion Benton, Senator from the New West: Thomas Hart Benton, 1782–1856* (Boston: Little, Brown and Company, 1956).

William E. Smith's *The Francis Preston Blair Family in Politics,* originally published in 1933 and reprinted by Da Capo Press (New York, 1969), is a collective biography that includes extensive extracts from the Blair family papers. Elbert B. Smith, *Francis Preston Blair* (New York: Free Press, 1980), treats the life of the Blair family patriarch, and William E. Parrish, *Frank Blair: Lincoln's Conservative* (Columbia: University of Missouri Press, 1998), examines the life of the St. Louisan Francis P. Blair Jr. The sharp divisions in Unionist ranks in St. Louis become clear in Norma L. Peterson's *Freedom and Franchise: The Political Career of B. Gratz Brown* (Columbia: University of Missouri Press, 1965) and in Marvin R. Cain's *Lincoln's Attorney General: Edward Bates of Missouri* (Columbia: University of Missouri Press, 1965). Christopher Phillips, *Damned Yankee: The Life of Nathaniel Lyon* (Columbia: University of Missouri Press, 1990) takes a sharply critical view of the Union commander in St. Louis during the secession crisis. In his most recent work, *Missouri's Confederate: Claiborne Fox Jackson and the Creation of Southern Identity in the Border West* (Columbia: University of Missouri Press, 2000), Phillips explores the ideology and intentions of Missouri's governor in the secession crisis. Robert E. Shalhope, *Sterling Price: Portrait of a Southerner* (Columbia: University of Missouri Press, 1971), and Albert Castel, *General Sterling Price and the Civil War in the West* (Baton Rouge: Louisiana State University Press, 1968), examine Missouri's leading Confederate general.

[Basil W. Duke], *Reminiscences of General Basil W. Duke, C. S. A.* (New York: Doubleday, Page and Company, 1911), and Thomas L. Snead, *The Fight for Missouri: From the Election of Lincoln to the Death of Lyon* (New York: Charles Scribner's Sons, 1886), describe events in St. Louis during the secession crisis from the Confederate perspective. The Unionist point of view is presented in Henry Boernstein, *Memoirs of a Nobody: The Missouri Years of an Austrian Radical, 1849–1866,* translated by Steven Rowan (St. Louis: Missouri Historical Society Press, 1987); James O. Broadhead, "St. Louis During the War," in the Broadhead Papers, Missouri Historical Society; and William Tecumseh Sherman, *Memoirs of General W. T. Sherman,* Library of America edition, 2 vols. (New York, 1990).

Howard K. Beale, ed., *The Diary of Edward Bates, 1859–1866* (Washington, D.C.: U.S. Government Printing Office, 1933), reveals the perspective of a conservative and an ultimately disgruntled Unionist. By contrast, Galusha Anderson, *The Story of a Border City During the Civil War* (Boston: Little, Brown and Company, 1908), presents the radical Unionist view. Frank J. Lutz, ed., *The Autobiography and Reminiscences of S. Pollak, M.D., St. Louis, Mo.* (St. Louis.: St. Louis Medical Review, 1904), Peter Josyph, ed., *The Wounded River: The Civil War Letters of John Vance Lauderdale, M.D.* (East Lansing: Michigan State University Press, 1993), and [Emily Elizabeth Parsons], *Memoir of Emily Elizabeth Parsons* (Boston: Little, Brown and Company, 1880), describe the experiences of the men and women engaged in the care of the wounded and in related homefront activities.

A number of works help to re-create the political economy of St. Louis in the mid-nineteenth century. The evolution of western economic policy and development is treated in two classic studies: James Neal Primm, *Economic Policy in the Development of a Western State: Missouri, 1820–1860* (Cambridge: Harvard University Press, 1954), and Lewis Atherton, *The Frontier Merchant in Mid-America* (Columbia: University of Missouri Press, 1971). Charles G. Sellers, *The Market Revolution: Jacksonian America, 1815–1846* (New York: Oxford University Press, 1991), focuses on the social and political consequences of widening markets. The relationship between the Market Revolution and social reform, with clear implications for St. Louis, is the subject of Paul E. Johnson, *A Shopkeepers' Millennium: Society and Revival in Rochester, New York, 1815–1837* (New York: Hill and Wang, 1978). Jeffrey S. Adler, *Yankee Merchants and the Making of the Urban West: The Rise and Fall of Antebellum St. Louis* (New York: Cambridge University Press, 1991), argues, with selective evidence, that northeastern merchants diverted investment from St. Louis to Chicago to protest against Missouri border ruffian attacks against Free State settlers in Kansas.

The abolitionist interpretation of the killings of Francis McIntosh in St. Louis and Elijah Lovejoy in nearby Alton, Illinois, is provided in Timothy Dwight Weld, *American Slavery As It Is: Testimony of a Thousand Witnesses* (New York: Arno Press, 1969). Leonard L. Richards, *"Gentlemen of Property and Standing": Anti-Abolition Mobs in Jacksonian America* (New York: Oxford University Press, 1970), places these events in a wider context of social change. Paul A. Gilje, *Rioting in America* (Bloomington: Indiana University Press, 1996), and David Grimsted, *American Mobbing, 1828–1861: Toward Civil War* (New York: Oxford University Press, 1998), provide overviews of Jacksonian era mobs. The fullest accounts of mob activities in St. Louis and Alton in 1836 and 1837 are in Janet S. Hermann, "The McIntosh Affair," *Missouri Historical Society Bulletin* 26 (January 1970): 123–43, Merton L. Dillon, *Elijah P. Lovejoy, Abolitionist Editor* (Urbana: University of Illinois Press, 1961), and

Merton L. Dillon, *Benjamin Lundy and the Struggle for Negro Freedom* (Urbana: University of Illinois Press, 1966).

On the *Dred Scott* case, Walter Ehrlich, *They Have No Rights: Dred Scott's Struggle for Freedom* (Westport, Conn.: Greenwood Press, 1979), and Don E. Fehrenbacher, *Slavery, Law and Politics: The Dred Scott Case in Historical Perspective* (New York: Oxford University Press, 1981), offer detailed examinations. Kenneth C. Kaufman, *Dred Scott's Advocate: A Biography of Roswell M. Field* (Columbia: University of Missouri Press, 1996), examines the case from the perspective of Dred Scott's St. Louis lawyer.

The great fire of 1849 is described in Edward Edwards, *History of the Volunteer Fire Department of St. Louis* (St. Louis: Edward Edwards, 1906). On the cholera epidemic of 1849, see Charles E. Rosenberg, *The Cholera Years: The United States in 1832, 1849, and 1866* (Chicago: University of Chicago Press, 1962), who examines the emergence of public health policy in a number of cities, including St. Louis. Katharine T. Corbett, "Draining the Metropolis: The Politics of Sewers in Nineteenth-Century St. Louis," in *Common Fields: An Environmental History of St. Louis,* ed. Andrew Hurley (St. Louis: Missouri Historical Society Press, 1997), describes the problems posed by the city's sinkholes and contaminated groundwater.

On the politics of the 1850s in St. Louis, see John Vollmer Mering, *The Whig Party in Missouri* (Columbia: University of Missouri Press, 1967), and Steven Rowan, trans., ed., *Germans for a Free Missouri: Translations from the St. Louis Radical Press, 1857–1862* (Columbia: University of Missouri Press, 1983). William E. Parrish, *Turbulent Partnership: Missouri and the Union, 1861–1865* (Columbia: University of Missouri Press, 1963), presents a political history of Missouri during the Civil War. Important details are also available in Virginia Laas's *Wartime Washington: The Civil War Letters of Elizabeth Blair Lee* (Urbana: University of Illinois Press, 1991) and in Ray W. Irwin's, ed., "Missouri in Crisis: The Journal of Captain Albert Tracy, 1861," *Missouri Historical Review* 51 (October 1956): 8–21.

The problem of civilian disloyalty in St. Louis is treated broadly in Mark E. Neely Jr's. *The Fate of Liberty: Abraham Lincoln and Civil Liberties* (New York: Oxford University Press, 1991). One aspect of federal policy is examined in greater detail in W. Wayne Smith's "An Experiment in Counterinsurgency: The Assessment of Confederate Sympathizers in Missouri," *Journal of Southern History* 35 (August 1969): 361–80. William B. Hesseltine's "Military Prisons of St. Louis, 1861–1865," *Missouri Historical Review* 23 (April 1929): 380–99 remains useful. Useful as well is Michael Fellman's *Inside War: The Guerrilla Conflict in Missouri During the American Civil War* (New York: Oxford University Press, 1989), although it is flawed by the absence of regional distinctions. Allan Nevins's *Frémont: Pathmarker of the West,* University of Nebraska Press edition (Lincoln, 1992) should be supplemented with Pamela Herr's *Jessie Benton Frémont: A Biography* (New York: F. S. Watts, 1987) and Vernon L. Volpe's "The Frémonts and Emancipation in Missouri," *Historian* 56 (winter 1994): 339–54. Two studies by Frank L. Klement, *The Copperheads of the Middle West* (Chicago: University of Chicago Press, 1960) and *Dark Lanterns: Secret Political Societies, Conspiracies, and Treason Trials in the Civil War* (Baton Rouge: Louisiana State University Press, 1984), are less concerned with evidence of conspiratorial behavior in St. Louis than they are with what the author perceives to be federal paranoia and overreaction.

On the work of the Western Sanitary Commission, see William E. Parrish, "The Western Sanitary Commission," *Civil War History* 36 (March 1990): 17–35, and Robert Archibald, "Yeatman, Eliot Led Medical Effort During the Civil War," *St. Louis Business Journal,* 10–16 August 1992, 12. The topic is briefly treated in William Quentin Maxwell's *Lincoln's Fifth Wheel: The Political History of the United States Sanitary Commission* (New York: Longmans, Green, 1956). Jasper W. Cross, "The Mississippi Valley Sanitary Fair, St. Louis, 1864," *Missouri Historical Review* 46 (April 1952): 237–46, offers the standard treatment of this expansive philanthropic undertaking. Paula Coalier, "Beyond Sympathy: The St. Louis Ladies' Union Aid Society and the Civil War," *Gateway Heritage* (summer 1990), 38–51, explores connections between women's homefront activities and the postwar women's rights movement.

The best work on James B. Eads is Howard S. Miller's brief essay in Quinta Scott and Howard S. Miller, *The Eads Bridge* (Columbia: University of Missouri Press, 1979). Florence L. Dorsey's *Road to the Sea: The Story of James B. Eads and the Mississippi* (New York: Rinehart, 1947) is of limited use. Important details can be gleaned from William D. Huffstot, "The *Carondelet,*" *Civil War Times Illustrated* 6 (August 1967): 7–8; John D. Milligan, "The First American Ironclads: The Evolution of a Design," *Missouri Historical Society Bulletin* (October 1965): 3–13; James B. Eads, "Recollections," in *Battles and Leaders of the Civil War,* ed. Robert Underwood Johnson and Clarence Clough Buel, Castle Books edition (New York, 1956), 1: 340–41; Spencer C. Tucker, *Andrew Foote: Civil War Admiral on Western Waters* (Annapolis, Md.: Naval

Institute Press, 2000); and Dana Wegner, "Mr. Eads' Turret," *Civil War Times Illustrated* 12 (October 1973): 24–31.

Ira Berlin et al., eds., *Freedom: A Documentary History of Emancipation, 1861–1867,* particularly series 1, volume 1, *The Destruction of Slavery* (Cambridge: Cambridge University Press, 1985), series 1, volume 2, *The Wartime Genesis of Free Labor: The Upper South* (Cambridge: Cambridge University Press, 1993), and series 2, *The Black Military Experience* (Cambridge: Cambridge University Press, 1982), provide an immensely rich resource. The editors of *Freedom* have gathered together documents scattered through *The War of the Rebellion: A Compilation of the Official Records of the Union and Confederate Armies* (Washington, D.C., 1881) and have added previously unpublished records from the National Archives to reveal the complex story of slavery's demise. Useful as well is Joe M. Richardson's "The American Missionary Association and Black Education in Civil War Missouri," *Missouri Historical Review* 69 (July 1971): 433–48; John W. Blassingame's "The Recruitment of Negro Troops in Missouri During the Civil War," *Missouri Historical Review* 58 (April 1964): 326–38; and Michael Fellman's "Emancipation in Missouri," *Missouri Historical Review* 83 (October 1988): 36–56.

The political history of Reconstruction in Missouri is told in William E. Parrish's *Missouri Under Radical Rule* (Columbia: University of Missouri Press, 1965). Two essays by Thomas S. Barclay are indispensable: "The Test Oath for the Clergy in Missouri," *Missouri Historical Review* 18 (April 1924): 345–50, and "The Liberal Republican Movement in Missouri," *Missouri Historical Review* 20 (October 1925): 3–78. Indispensable as well is Isidor Loeb's "Constitutions and Constitutional Conventions in Missouri," in *Journal [of the] Missouri Constitutional Convention of 1875* (Columbia: State Historical Society of Missouri, 1920), 7–71. Earle Dudley Ross, *The Liberal Republican Movement* (Ithaca, N.Y.: Cornell University Press, 1910), and Harold Melvin Hyman, *Era of the Oath: Northern Loyalty Tests During the Civil War and Reconstruction* (Philadelphia: University of Pennsylvania Press, 1954), locate events in the national context.

Gary R. Kremer, *James Milton Turner and the Promise of America: The Public Life of a Post–Civil War Black Leader* (Columbia: University of Missouri Press, 1991), tells the story of the postemancipation struggle for black equality. By contrast, the ease with which most Missouri Confederate leaders regained social prominence in St. Louis is revealed in Lloyd A. Hunter's "Missouri Confederate Leaders After the War," *Missouri Historical Review* 67 (April 1973): 381–85.

Index

Note: Page numbers in *italics* refer to figures.